# Here's what reviewers are saying about *Zope: Web Application Development and Content Management*

"This resource would have saved me countless hours researching and finding sources on my own when I first started using Zope. This book is a must for anyone considering using Zope for the first time. Application architects will benefit from the overview of the components available that solve many standard development challenges."
—**Trevor Toenjes,** *President, Growth Labs*

"This book does a very good job of clearly showing the steps needed to use some of the available Zope applications and use these to build a powerful web site. The book anticipates well what an IT professional needs to know to use Zope effectively, but also shows how to complete more complex, but nonetheless very useful, tasks."
—**Adrian Blockley,** *Department of Environmental Protection, Western Australia*

"The information in this book is excellent and is presented (for once!) in context to give the reader a true feel for Zope. Aspects of Zope are presented with real world examples that build upon each other, which is one of the book's greatest strengths."
—**Larry Groebe,** *Vice President of New Media, Insider Marketing/Insider Creative*

"I wish I'd had this book when I started with Zope. The authors' in-depth knowledge of Zope is invaluable."
—**Mark Logan,** *CCS Systems Group, Northeastern University*

"This book provides a more interactive, thorough style than can be had from most of the existing Zope information. By explaining why things work the way they do, I think the enduser will get more out of it."
—**Matt Behrens,** *System Analyst III, Baker Furniture*

"This book provides a solid understanding of Zope as an answer for both compact systems and the enterprise application."
—**Michael Bernstein,** *Lead Web Developer, Inetz Media*

"This book would have been invaluable when I was first coming up to speed with Zope. When I read through it, I found a number of things that I could apply to current problems."
—**Frank McGeough,** *Architect, Data Synchronization, Synchrologic, Inc.*

Zope: Web Application
Development and Content
Management
Belongs to: Tom Weir
WEIR0506-29

Zope: Web Application
Development and Content
Management
Belongs to: Tom Weir
WEIR0506-29

# Zope

## Web Application Development and Content Management

## Contents At a Glance

# Zope

## Web Application Development and Content Management

Steve Spicklemire
Kevin Friedly
Jerry Spicklemire
Kim Brand

**www.newriders.com**
201 West 103rd Street, Indianapolis, Indiana 46290
An Imprint of Pearson Education
Boston • Indianapolis • London • Munich • New York • San Francisco

# Zope

## Web Application Development and Content Management



FIRST EDITION: December 2001



International Standard Book Number: 0-7357-1110-0

Library of Congress Catalog Card Number: *00-111669*

06 05 04 03 02 7 6 5 4 3 2 1

Interpretation of the printing code: The rightmost double-digit number is the year of the book's printing; the rightmost single-digit number is the number of the book's printing. For example, the printing code 02-1 shows that the first printing of the book occurred in 2002.

Printed in the United States of America

## Trademarks



## Warning and Disclaimer



**Publisher**
David Dwyer

**Associate Publisher**
Stephanie Wall

**Production Manager**
Gina Kanouse

**Managing Editor**
Kristy Knoop

**Development Editor**
Laura Loveall

**Product Marketing Manager**
Stephanie Layton

**Publicity Manager**
Susan Nixon

**Project Editor**
Suzanne Pettypiece

**Copy Editor**
Krista Hansing

**Indexer**
Chris Morris

**Manufacturing Coordinator**
Jim Conway

**Book Designer**
Louisa Klucznik

**Cover Designer**
Brainstorm Design, Inc.

**Cover Production**
Aren Howell

**Proofreader**
Katherine Shull

**Composition**
Ron Wise

# Table of Contents

## About the Authors

**Dr. Steve Spicklemire** holds a PhD. in Physics from California Institute of Technology. He teaches physics, astronomy, and Internet programming at the University of Indianapolis, where he uses Zope in both education and research. The Radio Astronomy Project at the University of Indianapolis (**http://www.radio.edu**) uses a Zope-based web interface to the data-collection software/hardware of a 5-meter radio telescope. Steve incorporates Zope into several courses, such as "Internet Programming" (**http://radio.uindy.edu/inetprog**), "Mathematical Methods of Physics" (**http://physics-earthsci.uindy.edu/ph280**), and "General Physics Labs" (**http://physics-earthsci.uindy.edu/ph155**).

Steve uses simulation to investigate physical systems that would either be too expensive, too impractical, or just too dangerous to study through direct experimentation.

**Kevin Friedly** earned his bachelor of science degree in physics from Purdue University. Kevin has been tinkering with technology since high school, when he successfully obtained a Kirlian image of the "phantom leaf effect." Kevin's professional life has included stints as a high school guest lecturer in physics, calculus, and advanced English, as well as a brief flirtation with teaching basic computer skills at the college level.

Kevin spent more than 10 years as a technical writer for a medical imaging company, Microsonics, and computer graphics innovator Truevision (creator of the TARGA system). Kevin's writing experience also includes several years as a technical ad writer for ITT and Howard Sams publishing. Kevin's current technical interests involve providing his clients with cost-effective web and e-commerce solutions.

Steve and Kevin are also the active partners of Silicon Prairie Ventures, Inc. (**http://www.spvi.com**), a high-tech consultancy specializing in Zope-based Internet/intranet software development. Silicon Prairie also provides web hosting and web application-development services with Zope, Python, and whatever else it takes to get the job done!

**Jerry Spicklemire** was quietly pursuing a vocation in luthiery and historic woodworking, but computer technology caught his interest when AutoCAD came along and "PCs learned how to draw." Jerry's IT career began as a CAD operator, where he also picked up database and programming skills. Desktop and LAN support roles soon followed, with temporary duty in triage during the great global GUI migration. When the web tidal wave began sweeping everything in its path toward the general direction of the Internet, Jerry got a firm grip on the gunnels of lifeboat

Linux and still won't let go. A Y2K survivor, Jerry now builds database-driven web applications with Zope and the open source programming language Python.

**Kim Brand** is a C/C++ programmer, systems consultant, and open source software entrepreneur—and he's insatiably curious about everything. (He ran for a seat in the Indiana House of Representatives as a Libertarian to learn how society worked.) His clients range from small Catholic grade schools to cemeteries to statewide Masonic organizations. (He is a 33rd degree Scottish Rite Mason.) Kim's writing credentials include authoring *Common C Functions*, which was published in 1986 by Que Corporation; several published articles on technology; and many papers delivered to groups at seminars and conventions. His current ventures include Server Partners', which plans to rent Linux-based servers to small businesses using local consultants for sales and support.

Kim's role as a consumer advocate on behalf of his clients is a valued "reality check," ensuring effectiveness and appropriateness of the practical examples presented in this manuscript.

## About the Technical Reviewers

These reviewers contributed their considerable hands-on expertise to the entire development process for *Zope: Web Application Development and Content Management*. As the book was being written, these dedicated professionals reviewed all the material for technical content, organization, and flow. Their feedback was critical to ensuring that *Zope: Web Application Development and Content Management* fits our reader's need for the highest-quality technical information.

**Evelyn Mitchell**, of tummy.com, ltd., has been working with computers since 1981, and she now leads an open source consulting company that specializes in Python and Linux. She started using Zope several years ago and is co-author of the *Zope Quick Reference* (**http://www.zope.org**). She has been involved in open source since she gave up her Macintosh for a much more powerful Linux box in 1994.

**Richard Waid** (richard@codestackers.com) holds a bachelor of science degree in computer science from the University of Canterbury (**http://www.canterbury.ac.nz**). He is a founding director of CodeStackers Ltd. (**http://codestackers.com**), a Linux software-development and system-integration company based in Christchurch, New Zealand. Richard wears way too many hats, a selection of which includes "Linux, Python, and Zope evangelist," "Software and Networking Engineer," and "Stupid Marketing Ideas Guy." His "Hardware Technician" hat was badly scorched in the Great Cable Fire of 2001 and is no longer worn.

# Acknowledgments

The authors would like to thank our savvy tech reviewers, Evelyn Mitchell and Richard Waid, who always knew just how to make this into a better book. As can be seen in the credits, a virtual platoon of New Riders staff, whom we've never met, also labored to get this book into the readers' hands. Above all, thanks to Laura, Stephanie, and Kristy for being patient and finding ways to adjust the schedule again and again, but always keeping the goal in front of us, even when we wished they wouldn't!

We'd also like to thank the folks at Zope Corporation, and all the Zope users who contribute code, documentation, and discussion that make Zope the powerful, flexible, evolving (and improving!) wonder that it is.

**Steve Spicklemire:** I'd like to thank my long-suffering wife, Tawn, for her apparently infinite patience and unconditional support; my neglected children, Zachary, Kami, and Clay, for their continual understanding; and my colleagues at the University of Indianapolis for their willingness to allow me to abdicate my responsibilities as I devoted all waking hours to the completion of this book. I'd like to thank my partners in crime, Kevin, Jerry, and Kim, for making this book happen.

**Kevin Friedly:** I'd like to thank my family for all their support and encouragement. To my wonderful daughter, Colleen, who gave up a lot of daddy-daughter nights for this book. Thanks for understanding when Dad had to work and couldn't do some things with you when we were on vacation. I'll try to be as understanding with you when you write your first book. To my loving wife, Lenore, for unfailing support during this project and for not complaining when I didn't help mow the lawn, tend our many gardens, and wash the dishes and such. Thanks for driving to all of our vacations so that I could write in the car, and thanks for understanding when I didn't eat dinner with the family. To my step-daughters, Jessica and Megan, for helping make the combining of our two families smooth and stress-free so that I had the right frame of mind for writing.

I also want to thank one of the best English teachers I ever knew, my late wife, Patricia Kuhn Friedly, for the many years that she encouraged my writing and supported my many attempts at being creative. Thanks for never complaining that I was wasting my time and not making money. I miss you.

To the best researcher/writer that I know, my dad, Robert Friedly. I've learned so much from you that I couldn't cover it all in this space. Thanks. Get that West Virginia book published. And to my mom, Celia Friedly, who has been there for all my projects and has supported me at every step. I love you both. I also want to thank my sister, Kim, and brother, Kirk, and their families for always being there when I need them.

Finally, to all my teachers who taught me to appreciate the fine art of sharing knowledge. To Jim Williams for teaching me to diagram sentences and create coherent and meaningful compositions in the seventh grade. To John Ervin for teaching me to appreciate the joy of language, and to the late Dick Hammond for appreciating and fueling my inquisitiveness.

Last but certainly not least, I would like to thank Steve, Jerry and Kim for making this book possible. Thanks for turning me on to Zope. You guys are the best.

**Jerry Spicklemire:** Thanks to Steve, the Zope Guru in residence, and Kevin, the relentless package-pounder and researcher. Also, thanks to Kim for having the chutzpah to figure out how to build a business supporting open source systems and helping us focus on real needs of real customers, and, of course, for the finishing touch. Thanks to my family for putting up with having to tell me, far too many times, "Everyone asked where you were."

**Kim Brand:** The open source movement is one of the great byproducts of the Internet. By providing cheap, nearly instantaneous communication, the Net has allowed far-flung volunteers to leverage small amounts of time into a development and support capacity that rivals the largest commercial companies. This has dramatically altered the landscape of software development and has become one of the most productive "unintended consequences" of the military/industrial complex that started the Net in the early 1960s. We have the visionaries of the early Internet community to thank for making all this possible.

The ability to deliver reliable systems for less money continues to make my work in technology fun. For that, I owe many thanks to the open source community. Every time I install a server, I silently thank Vinton Cerf and Robert Kahn (TCP/IP), Linus Torvalds (Linux), Eric Allman (Sendmail), the Samba team, the BIND project team, the Apache Group, and countless others for the ability to solve customer problems in clever ways[md]often getting the credit for what so many others have done. I hope to someday be able to make a contribution to the community in proportion to the benefits I've received.

Finally, I'd like to thank Rob Rash, principal of Our Lady of Lourdes Catholic School in Indianapolis, for giving my ideas a chance. His contributions to the lives of children produce a better world. And thanks to Little Flower Catholic School—in particular, Debbie Burks, the technology coordinator[md]for helping make this stuff work in a real school every day.

## Tell Us What You Think

As the reader of this book, you are the most important critic and commentator. We value your opinion and want to know what we're doing right, what we could do better, what areas you'd like to see us publish in, and any other words of wisdom you're willing to pass our way.

As the Associate Publisher for New Riders Publishing, I welcome your comments. You can fax, email, or write me directly to let me know what you did or didn't like about this book—as well as what we can do to make our books stronger.

*Please note that I cannot help you with technical problems related to the topic of this book, and that due to the high volume of mail I receive, I might not be able to reply to every message.*

When you write, please be sure to include this book's title and author as well as your name and phone or fax number. I will carefully review your comments and share them with the author and editors who worked on the book.

Fax: 317-581-4663
Email: stephanie.wall@newriders.com
Mail: Stephanie Wall
Associate Publisher
New Riders Publishing
201 West 103rd Street
Indianapolis, IN 46290 USA

# Introduction

Application development is generally described using words and images commonly associated with the building trades: foundation, architecture, framework, and so on. These concepts help convey the structural quality of programs. As the complexity of an application increases, its structure might come under stresses that reveal latent weaknesses in its design or implementation that can lead to failure. Unlike a building of steel and glass, most content-rich web sites are constantly changing to meet new requirements and are evolving to deliver more valuable information. This puts even more "pressure" on developers to start with a stable platform, enforce rigorous policies, and invest in technologies that give them the control they need to solve unforeseen problems. Today, the complexity of many web-development projects rivals the architectural sophistication of a 100-plus–story skyscraper. Zope provides solid underpinning for complex web sites.

Zope was created to address the challenges of high-performance web-site development and maintenance. The Zope development framework imposes control over the construction of objects to enforce consistency across an entire site. Zope implements a comprehensive system of permissions and roles to ensure that projects with multiple developers can work in harmony instead of chaos. The web-based Zope Management Interface (ZMI) provides a "Through the Web" (TTW) view of your site using any standard browser. Managing objects within the familiar hierarchy, reinforced with an innovative form of "inheritance," makes it easy to keep the big picture in perspective while you're wrestling with the details. The need for duplication of both content and effort is eliminated, resulting in simpler site design and lower maintenance cost. Best of all, Zope is Open Source, so if you need to extend your site with new features, you have total access to the system—including full source code.

In this book, you will be introduced to a new web-development paradigm that leverages the best object-oriented design/analysis practices and applies them to the most difficult problems you are likely to encounter on your most important projects, such as how to do the following:

- Create a consistent look across a web site, regardless of how many people are responsible for its content
- Take advantage of Zope's flexible Document Template Markup Language, DTML, and XML-compliant Page Templates (ZPT) to deliver dynamic content from local or remote sources
- Manage the security risks associated with delegation, collaboration, versioning, and scripting
- Exploit Zope's Content Management Framework to construct sites that empower users who contribute content to manage it themselves, online

- Add components from third parties (or from your own libraries!) to enhance your application, reduce your time to deliver, and integrate legacy systems
- Connect databases to your web site using independently testable and sharable SQL Query objects
- Use Zope's object-inheritance mechanisms, acquisition, and containment to reduce maintenance costs
- Protect your site from performance bottlenecks, accidental downtime, and catastrophic failure.

## What You Should Bring to the Zope Party

Developing a complex/content-rich web site requires talent and tools. We believe that Zope is the right tool for the job, and this book will add considerably to the talent that you bring to the task. You will benefit from having some background in web development, particularly a familiarity with HTML and any modern programming language. Some of the object-oriented programming concepts might seem strange if your only programming experience has been Pascal or C. We assume that you are familiar with (or can figure out) Internet jargon such as cookies, web servers, browsers, caching, and so on, along with the myriad acronyms associated with web technologies: FTP, SQL, SMTP, DOM, XML, CVS, CORBA, and so on. An understanding of basic database concepts such as relations, posting, transactions, roll-back, and indexes will be helpful. A glossary is included for your convenience (see Appendix A, "Glossary").

A recent book, *The Zope Book* (New Riders Publishing, 2001), by two of the developers of Zope, Amos Latteier and Michel Pelletier, offers an excellent study of basic Zope concepts. We hope that our book provides the logical next step in your progress toward *Zope Zen!*

## Who This Book Is Not For

Web sites come in all shapes and sizes. From personal pages to mammoth corporate e-commerce sites, the variety is endless. This book takes a look at how to use Zope to tame the content management, development, and maintenance complexities of larger sites. If you are well along on your journey to tackling these tougher web site issues, this book is for you. If you are just getting started, you may be better served by introductory books.

## How This Book Is Organized

As we designed this book, we determined that complex subjects should be laid out with concrete examples and numerous code snippets. We use Zope components to create mini-applications to bring clarity to the actual uses of Zope objects and demonstrate how they operate on the web. You will find a running theme throughout the book with reference to a hypothetical Zope user and the web master of a fictitious school district, which serves as a vehicle to expound on the range of Zope usage. We hope that bringing lots of working examples to the sometimes abstract nature of object-oriented web development will move you up the learning curve faster. All the examples from the book can be found at the companion web site: **http://webdev.zopeonarope.com** or **http://www.newriders.com**. Please see the inside back cover of this book for more information about the web site.

## Part I: What Makes Zope Different

In Part I, "What Makes Zope Different," our goal is to lay a foundation for later chapters and highlight the unique features of Zope's object-oriented development environment. In particular we introduce important Zope concepts such as object publishing, separation of content from business logic and presentation effects, object acquisition, and use of the Zope Management Interface (ZMI). Also, we discuss Python, the underlying object-oriented programming language of Zope.

In Chapter 1, "The Object of the Web—Optimizing Web Development," we present a big-picture view of the broadest Zope concepts, such as dynamic object publishing, interactive content management, acquisition, and delegation. These are described in the context of a series of examples intended to illustrate the ease with which web content can be created and presented efficiently without loss of flexibility. Finally, readers are directed toward the resources that they will need to install Zope, along with a few timely tips.

In Chapter 2, "Point and Click Web Building," we launch into hands-on exercises to put the concepts outlined in Chapter 1 into practice and to introduce the most basic of Zope's standard object types. Side trips touch on the usefulness of adding Python programming skills, by way of examples involving some of the more sophisticated Zope object types. A brief glimpse at the many optional Zope modules sets the stage for further explorations in Part II.

## Part II: Leveraging Zope Components

In Part II, "Leveraging Zope Components," our goal is to introduce you to the variety of plug-in Zope components available. You'll learn how Zope ZClasses provide an ideal platform for code reusability.

In Chapter 3, "Web Event Publishing," we put the parts together to create working applications. Several common Zope objects, available for free, are examined and used in a web application for a mythical school system. We also introduce you to several Python products that can be used with minor modification to produce highly useful results.

In Chapter 4, "Zope Discussion Tools," we look at five different drop-in products for Zope that facilitate the "two-way web." These products help support the process of allowing end users to become an active part in providing content to your web sites. We also take an introductory look at Zope's built-in, multitiered security features and how to use them to create areas of your web site that are accessible only by a trusted community of users.

In Chapter 5, "Web Mail," we look at the various uses of email both as a tool for "pushing" information out to users and as a means of getting information into the system. We look at the `sendmail` tag that enables you to produce email messages dynamically. We also look at Zope's support for POP and IMAP mail servers.

In Chapter 6, "News, Polls, and Web Tools," we look at a number of different products that can be dropped into your existing web sites to provide useful or fancy features with relatively little effort. We look at ways to access constantly changing content from other web sites for incorporation into your own site. In particular, we discuss the RDF/RSS protocol, which is used to syndicate information among web sites, and we examine how the Zope RDFSummary product makes data integration of this type easy. We also look at creating online polls using the Zope Poll product. Finally, we look at two products that provide basic web form creation and fancy graphics.

## Part III: Site and Content Management

In Part III, "Site and Content Management," our goal is to acquaint you with Zope's powerful security model that provides for authentication of users and the assignment of roles and permissions on a discreet object level. We also discuss connections to high-performance SQL databases, catalogs, and site-hosting issues.

In Chapter 7, "Delegation, Databases, and Users," we introduce Zope systems for delegation of content management. This means that topic experts—not web masters—can be in charge of their part of the web site. Next, we apply Zope SQL Objects (ZSQL Objects) to add dynamic data access to your web site using popular relational databases. These parallel lines converge at the point where Zope connects to external directory systems for cooperative user validation.

In Chapter 8, "Getting Content Under Control," we continue to develop solutions for large-scale content management with a tour of Zope modules aimed directly at bringing growing web sites under control. Highlights include the recently introduced Zope Content Management Framework (CMF) and Zope Page Templates (ZPT). The ZPT is a next-generation web page model designed to work seamlessly with popular web design tools and HTML editors.

In Chapter 9, "Time Management and ZCatalogs," we look at a powerful way to deal with time objects in Zope. We look at the ZCatalog product and how it can be used to help manage dynamic content from various sources. We also show how Zope can be used to integrate content from other web sites into your site.

In Chapter 10, "Survival Gear for Web Masters," we discuss how to integrate Zope into an existing web server environment. We examine how to serve multiple domains from a single Zope instance using the incredibly flexible "Virtual Host Monster." We demonstrate how to set up a Zope server that is connected to Apache's modssl module so that you can take advantage of SSL encryption. Finally, we present strategies to get detailed diagnostic information about the information being exchanged between Zope and your browser.

## Part IV: Web Application Development

In Part IV, "Web Application Development," our goal is give you a practical example of how using a particular Zope tool: ZPatterns can help make you a more productive programmer. We candidly show why this is hard to do but important to achieve. We also discuss how Zope supports larger projects that involve multiple developers, and how Zope provides connections to external systems.

In Chapter 11, "Design for Integration the ZPatterns Way," we describe the use of a sophisticated object-oriented feature of Zope, known as ZPatterns. The goal of ZPatterns is to allow for object reuse by providing the tools needed to assign arbitrary data storage for objects and connections between components. We examine how this can be done effectively with a variety of off-the-shelf Zope objects.

In Chapter 12, "Integrating Separate Modules with ZPatterns," we examine many of the powerful application-integration features of ZPatterns. We show how one application can be embedded in another after the first is "finished." We also show how object models can be merged, and we offer several different strategies for making what were originally separate applications cooperate using shared resources.

In Chapter 13, "User Management: Interfacing with External Systems," we study the details of Zope's security model at the Python product level. From this perspective, it's easy to demonstrate how the Python Security Model influences everything that Zope does.

In Chapter 14, "Multi-Developer Projects: Testing and Version Control," we introduce issues related to multideveloper projects. We discuss version control, unit testing, staging, and deployment. We admit that tools are no substitute for communication and clear areas of responsibility. However, understanding and using the tools that are available will make what would otherwise be an extremely difficult job manageable.

# Part V: Mission-Critical Web Publishing

Finally, in Part V, "Mission-Critical Web Publishing," our goal is to teach you about strategies to implement when your web site becomes wildly successful—and steps to take to avoid disaster!

In Chapter 15, "Scaling Up," we discuss the many facets of testing and Zope server performance enhancements. We include a description of tools that allow developers to analyze performance and present strategies for improving performance.

In Chapter 16, "Backup, Disaster Recovery, and Distributed Processing," we discuss how to export and backup Zope applications. These skills become important if (or should we say *when*) disaster strikes. We provide concrete examples of backup scripts that we have used in our production environments to ensure that our Zope instances are backed up nightly. We also present information about other Zope storage mechanisms, including mounted storages and the newly released "Berkeley Storage." Finally, we explain some of the distributed processing technologies available to Zope, including XMLRPC and Client.py.

## Part VI: Appendix

In Appendix A, "Glossary," we have provided definitions to all the terms that we suspect might be unfamiliar to average readers, or that have peculiar uses in the context of Zope or Zope-based web site development.

# Conventions

This book follows a few conventions:

- **Italic text**—A new term is set in *italics* the first time it is introduced.
- **Code text**—Program text, functions, variables, and other "computer language" are set in a fixed-pitch font—for example, `gunzip Calendar-1.0.6.tar.gz`.
- **Code listings**—Code listings are provided with both listing numbers (for example, Listing 1.1) and line-by-line numbering. Of course, the line-by-line numbering is not part of the code itself. It is there simply for cross-referencing purposes. The same code without the line-by-line numbering is available on the companion web site.
- **Code continuation characters**—Code continuation characters (➥) appear where the line would not ordinarily break but had to be broken to fit on the printed page.
- **Zope version**—The code in this book was developed and tested with Zope 2.3.3. Although we know that much of the code works with Version 2.4.0, at the time of this writing, some of the products described in this book are known to have problems running under Zope 2.4.0. By the time the book is available in stores, Zope will probably be at 2.5 or 2.6! We will do our best to make available versions of the Zope products described in this book that work with whatever version of Zope is released at the time the book is available. We will make pointers or actual copies of these products available on our companion web site (**`http://webdev.zopeonarope.com`**).
- **Zope root**—When you install Zope, there is a zope root directory on the filesystem of the computer itself. When we need to refer to this folder (or directory), we will call it "$ZOPEROOT" in the text.

# I

# What Makes Zope Different

# 1

# The Object of the Web—Optimizing Web Development

THIS CHAPTER PRESENTS AN OVERVIEW of the concepts of "object publishing" and provides examples of how to create dynamically published web pages with Zope.

## Zope—an Object Publishing Environment

Even though you know that Zope stands for *Z Object Publishing Environment*, you might be wondering exactly what that peculiar mix of buzzwords means. Zope is all about objects, but that doesn't mean that you have to be a veteran object-oriented (OO) programmer to use Zope. Actually, you can do quite a bit of Zope web development without thinking much about objects at all. In fact, many web content providers aren't even aware that the web site they work on every day is really a Zope site. Still, it's best for you to have a solid understanding of the many ways that OO features can be helpful providing power and flexibility that would be difficult to achieve any other way. You will learn the fine points of building sophisticated web applications in Part IV, "Web Application Development," but, for now, a general overview is in order, starting with three points that you can think of as "the facts of Zope:"

- Every page flows from a process, known as *object publishing*.
- Each page is composed of *separate elements*.
- Page composition is *automatic*.

To keep things familiar, let's first look at typical "hit" on a conventional web site and compare that to the *object-publishing process*. As you know, a simple web page is nothing more than a computer file, an ordinary text document stored in a directory on a hard disk. For example, you might want to browse a web page called **`http://www.PlainOldWebSite.com/home.html`**.

When you make this selection, your browser sends a "request" to the `PlainOldWebSite` domain, where the local web server promptly finds a file named `home.html`, opens it, and reads its contents. Then a stream of bits is pointed back toward your side of the planet, where it is reconstituted into a faithful copy of the original and is displayed for your web-surfing pleasure. The recognition that the web began as an alternative means of copying files does not diminish the experience of instant global communication.

## Publishing Is a Process

Now let's contrast the conventional web with the *object-publishing process*, which is fundamentally different. Consider the simplest case in Zope: When your browser requests **`http://www.ObjectOfTheWeb.com/MyHome.html`**, the Zope Object Publisher (ZPublisher) at the `ObjectOfTheWeb` site responds by executing the `render` *method* of the `MyHome.html` object. In OO parlance, a method is a way to *do something*. In this case, the something that gets done is the composition of a page, according to the "definition" of the page *content*, which will most likely incorporate additional objects and their methods. When the process is complete, the finished page is sent back to your browser much the same as in a conventional system.

The finished page doesn't look different from any other simple example; it's still just a web page, right down to the HTML "source." That should come as no surprise because that's about all a browser can display anyhow.

Even so, that personal portal page might be largely unique to you, based on selections made at some earlier time, when you registered your preferences. It could also include frequently updated items, such as late-breaking headlines or topics of new messages from your email account. That might not sound too unusual either, especially because such features are now considered standard fare on popular portal sites. If this kind of dynamic page creation is exactly what you've been wanting to incorporate into your web site, then you're reading the right book. If you've been procrastinating because of concerns that such features can be complex, then it's time for the "good news" part of the answer: Making complexity manageable is one of the great strengths of Zope.

## The Dynamic Web

The important point for you to catch is that hitting **`http://www.ObjectOfTheWeb.com`** doesn't just retrieve a copy of a file on a disk; rather, it retrieves the finished output from a process. When you browse `MyHome.html`, your request causes the `MyHome.html` object to "do" its `render` method—that is, to *render* an HTML representation of itself. Object publishing is *the process of composing and distributing* a web page. That's why requests to `/MyHome.html` can result in two entirely different pages when two individuals request the URL.

#### Pages Are Composed "On the Fly"

Comparing a static file page and the object-publishing process is like comparing an off-the-rack garment to a custom-tailored suit. Because each page is published "fresh" at request time, the system has the luxury of composing different pages for you than for someone else. When you grasp that single point, it becomes obvious why dynamic, interactive features are so natural in an object-publishing environment. When every page is *composed on demand*, tossing any bit of unique or frequently updated information into the mix is just adding one more item to a page made up of nothing but such items. This book uses the generic term *element* for any dynamically published term.

## How to Build a Web Site

The next fact, which is even more important in a practical sense, is that object publishing generates pages made up of discrete objects, or elements. That means that each element can be created and updated individually, by one or more persons responsible for the *presentation* and *content* of the site. For example, you often see a standard banner and navigation menu on all pages of a site. In a Zope environment, page elements are maintained separately and "inserted" during the object publishing process.

### A Built-In GUI for Content Management

The usual way of providing a user interface to the content providers of a Zope site is a web form–based web application. The browser itself is the graphical user interface (GUI) of a Zope site, not only for visitors, but also for those who create and update site content.

This brings up another distinctive feature of Zope: the built-in administration and content-creation tools, known as the *Zope Management Interface* (*ZMI*), are themselves web based, an example of Zope's pervasive *Through the Web* (*TTW*) paradigm. TTW is an example of the power and flexibility that results from using the web directly in its own maintenance and management processes.

When a web site is built this way, content providers are able to make updates to any element, at any time, with no other software than a web browser. That's *interactive content management*.

Then, as the very next request arrives, the web surfer at the other end sees the updated version of that element, on any page where it appears, without requiring changes to any other elements. That's *dynamic object publishing*.

As convenient as TTW is for web surfers and content providers, it is just one of several interfaces available to Zope developers. You will find out more about using FTP to interact with Zope in Chapter 2, "Point and Click Web Building," where you'll also learn about the emerging WebDAV standard.

## Elements Are Like SSI—Done Right

Because each page element is individually updated and dynamically published, Zope is similar in some ways to a web-development technique called *Server Side Includes* (*SSI*). SSI makes it easy to provide standard elements for use throughout a web site. However, Zope is not limited by certain restrictions that hamper SSI. For example, it is ideal to have exactly one active copy of each element that is part of our web site so that only current elements are published. SSI helps with this goal but requires each element to be specifically referenced on every page where the element is included. Changing the element that is to be inserted often requires making updates to every reference as well. Zope provides the means to eliminate such tedium and adds the power of dynamic element selection into the bargain. Consistently referring to up-to-date elements is a basic tenet of *best practices* in both database management and computer programming. Object publishing leverages the dynamic power of the web to extend the SSI concept far beyond the practical possibilities of common usage, bringing best practices within reach of every web developer.

To understand how object publishing can be applied in a common setting, think about a commercial site. Consider how simple it would be for the banner artist to swap in the snazzy new look that the marketing folks have been asking for once it is "broken out" as a separate element, independent of the pages it appears on. Likewise, the navigation guru can update every menu, on every page, without any downtime for the web site. This dynamic, interactive way of working is the ultimate in content management, and it reaches its full potential in an object-publishing environment.

### Acquisition Rules

Let's look closer at those standard elements discussed in this chapter. For instance, a site banner is often supplemented by subbanners that identify sections of a site. Object publishing lets you build entire sections of your site that always display the correct subbanner, without specifying which subbanner belongs to each page. The mere reference to a subbanner object in a page definition causes the correct subbanner to be selected during the object-publishing process. Further element references can be made, right down to a page specific sub-sub-subbanner, regardless of how "deep" the final element actually is in the site hierarchy. The same principle can be applied just as easily to any type of content, including graphics, scripts, sound, video, and so on.

#### Intelligent Element Selection

You might have guessed that this talent for "doing the right thing" is really a result of that third fact that you've been wondering about, *automatic page composition*. The object-publishing process follows strict rules that make it possible to intelligently select all the right elements to make up any given page. The term for this is *acquisition*, and it is possible only within a *process*, as opposed to a static file-based system. ZPublisher is a constantly running engine that recognizes the nature of every element so that each page and everything that it depends upon is promptly tended to behind the scenes. This process can be compared to the service provided by a good waiter who notices when your cup needs refilling, along with any number of other details, and quietly takes care of everything. Continuing the analogy, the notion that an empty cup is a cup that needs refilling is *implied*, or *implicit*, so it isn't necessary to state the fact "out loud," or *explicitly*. Relations between elements and the pages where they appear are as obvious to ZPublisher as an empty cup is to a waiter.

As you might imagine, there is a complex mechanism at work here, but, in practice, the behavior is very simple and predictable. When an object appears within a page definition, ZPublisher tries to find that object. First, it searches the same Zope folder object where the page definition is found. A Zope folder is very much like a filesystem directory because it is a container used to group related objects in an organized way. If the object that ZPublisher is attempting to locate isn't found in the same folder as a page definition that refers to that object, ZPublisher continues searching. Next, ZPublisher looks "up" to the "parent" folder, the one that contains the folder where the search began. ZPublisher keeps looking "up" this way until the object is found. This simple but powerful search is the reason it is so easy to build sites with minimal duplication of resources. Any page definition that refers to an object will be published with the first object of that name found by ZPublisher. Changing any object will result in the update being displayed the next time any page is published that refers to that object.

An image that might help to clarify acquisition is to think of Zope pages as *acquiring* their elements from the environment, as effortlessly as a chameleon changing colors to blend with its surroundings. Although it might seem mysterious at first, ZPublisher is just responding appropriately by automatically publishing pages with all the correct elements. You'll come to take this surprising ability for granted as you gain experience.

### Acquisition Is Like OO Inheritance

There are striking similarities between acquisition and the OO concept of "inheritance," but acquisition is very much a built-in feature, so you won't have to tend to the details of classes and such to make good use of it. Like the site banner example, acquisition also can be applied to enhance the navigation menu with supplemental selections related to the section of a site currently being browsed. This sort of complexity is never mandatory, but it is hard to resist using it once you know how to make it work for you!

You will learn more of the inner workings of acquisition in Chapter 9, "Time Management and ZCatalogs." If you're curious about the general concept and other possible uses of acquisition, the link **http://www.ccs.neu.edu/home/lorenz/papers/oopsla96/** points to a whitepaper about where it all began, by Joseph Gil and David H. Lorenz.

### Objects Have Properties and Behavior

This kind of *behavior* might sound almost like a computer application, which is to be expected because Zope is, in fact, a web application server, a readymade framework for system development. The nice side effect of using Zope to build web sites that incorporate application-style functionality is that the finished products have their own GUI-driven content-management system built in. The universality of the web has led many experienced software developers to the conclusion that the future of desktop applications is evolving in the direction of "webtop" applications. Anyone who has had to keep a large number of network-connected desktop computers operating can instantly understand the advantage of running applications within a standard browser interface that is accessible from anywhere on the planet!

### Grouping Related Elements

Before moving on, consider one final point about the SSI concept. You can define page elements, such as a banner or menu, which can themselves be made up of other elements. Furthermore, because each page will likely have a corresponding banner object, along with any number of other elements, it is convenient to aggregate many standard items within a sort of "macro element" or wrapper, that, in turn, contains all the rest. We'll refer to these kinds of objects and the facility that they provide by "wrapping up" many elements within a single package simply as *wrappers* and *wrapping*. You will learn how to apply wrappers, acquisition, objects, and methods to easily and quickly build complex web sites, and complete web applications.

#### Wrapping Is Like SSI with OO Encapsulation

The notion of a wrapper parallels well-known principles of OO programming, such as the practice of *encapsulating* basic information in the form of a *superclass*. Even though the concept is simple, in a typical SSI scenario, anything beyond the most rudimentary wrapping quickly becomes impossibly complicated and unmanageable. Fortunately, object publishing and acquisition makes all of this truly easy, as you will see when you master the techniques and start to see the productivity benefits of wrapping.

## Unique Combinations

In an environment where reusing elements is easy and straightforward, you can have any number of pages that are unique combinations of elements, even though everything on the page already exists. In fact, that is often a typical case, especially for a Portal site, where users can choose from a set of options to determine which elements show up on their very own personal pages.

## The Web Factor—Acquisition Alchemy

Even though looking at a web site as a collection of elements doesn't sound distinctly different from the viewer's perception of a web page, as seen in a browser screen, it is a far cry from the way an HTML editor displays the "source" of a static HTML file. Imagine how much simpler it will be to manage and update separate elements, with perfect assurance that each element will find its proper place on every finished page. Although you might not have thought of a web site "decomposed" into elements before, and although the mind-set that you are starting to use might be a new way of looking at the web for you, the OO world knows it as *factoring*. Factoring means that once you begin treating the many elements that make up a web site as discrete entities, you had better consider carefully where each element "belongs."

### Zooming In

Moving beyond the web surfer's view of each icon and link on a page, also consider all the *factors* that make up a section and then the "big picture" of an entire site. From the topmost view, at the entire site level, you notice a site banner element, which appears to be a single *factor*. Because nearly every page of the site displays this banner, it follows that it should be included, or *factored into*, a wrapper that defines elements at the highest level.

Section-level factors should be located within a section wrapper, and so on. By continuing this process, you will start to get a sense for the point in a site hierarchy where each item should be positioned so that the definition of each page can be expressed in the simplest possible terms. Refinement of the site's factoring will pay huge dividends in better manageability and greatly reduced maintenance. Tales of seemingly immense web sites being built in record time are common among Zope experts. Effective site design results in ease of use, for visitors and maintainers alike. The value of current information made available by ongoing interactive updates can be verified by high "hit rates" and repeat visits. The easier your site is to manage, the more current, useful, and valuable it will be.

### Review Time—What and Why

Several key concepts have been covered so far that might be absolutely new to you. So, this is a quick review of the most important parts.

You have now been introduced to the basic *Facts of Zope*:

- Every page flows from the *object-publishing process.*
- Each page is composed of *discrete elements* that are *interactively updated.*
- Page composition is *dynamic*, with *implicit element inclusion*, thanks to *acquisition.*

You also have a basic understanding of how these facts both require and support one another. Certainly, no static file based system could possibly stay current with constantly changing information, such as news headlines or email topics. A *process* is necessary to automatically *acquire* the appropriate elements of a page and ensure that all are up-to-date. Only an *interactive* content-management approach could adequately support such a *dynamic* system. With this foundation, you are ready to see some simple working examples, learn where you can see these ideas in action, and learn how to put them to work in your own web site.

## Wrappers—from the Inside

We won't be dwelling on the details of Hypertext Markup Language (HTML) in this book, but there will be many examples written in HTML for the purpose of illustrating Zope concepts. The first example will show you how a very simple web page might be composed in HTML and then show you how to publish the same result from Zope. Assuming that the `PlainOldWebSite` domain has a standard text banner, which appears on every page, you would expect to see something like the following when browsing the site (see Figure 1.1).

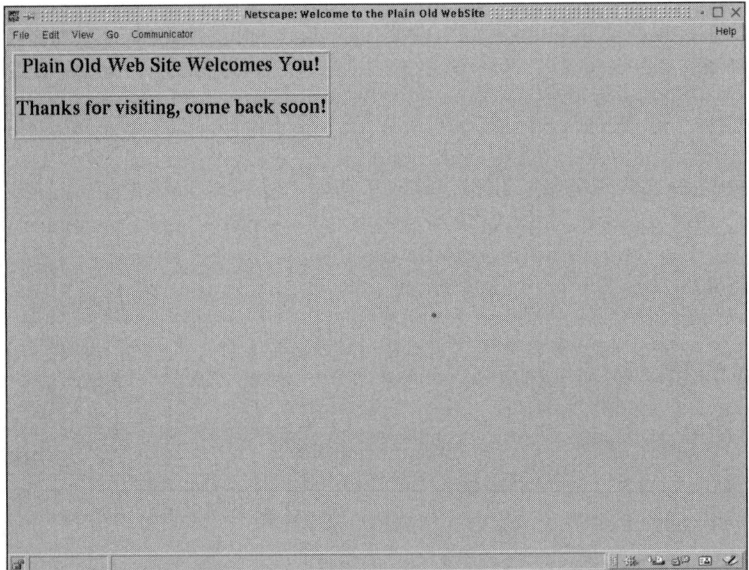


**Figure 1.1** Example of a very simple web page.

Examining the HTML source of the same "home page," you might see this:

```
<HTML>
<HEAD>
<TITLE>Welcome to the Plain Old Web Site</TITLE>
```

```
</HEAD>
<BODY>
<table border='1'><tr><td align='center'><H1>Plain Old Web Site Welcomes
You!</H1></td></tr>
<tr><td align='center'><H2>Thanks for visiting, come back
soon!</H2></td></tr></table>
</BODY>
</HTML>
```

This source is just an exact copy of a file named `home.html` that resides on the web server at `PlainOldWebSite.com`. Examining the HTML output (source) of `MyHome.html` from `ObjectOfTheWeb.com`, as displayed in a browser, would reveal little new insight. Instead, let's look at the original elements as they exist in the form of Zope objects. The pages from `ObjectOfTheWeb` are nearly all wrapped by an object named `standard_dtml_wrapper`. Listing 1.1 shows one version, which will de developed further in Chapter 2.

Listing 1.1 **A DTML Method Example—ID: standard_dtml_wrapper**

```
<HTML>
<HEAD>
  <TITLE><dtml-var title></TITLE>
 </HEAD>
 <BODY>
  <dtml-var banner>
  <dtml-var expr="_[page_body]" fmt=structured-text>
 </BODY>
</HTML>
```

This is, of course, a simplified example, but it is useful and effective for getting the basic points across at this introductory stage. The first thing you should notice is that there are several items that look something like HTML "tags" but that start with `<dtml-`. They seem to show up where you'd expect to see normal HTML, along with text that should display in the browser. These are references to page elements. An explanation of what each reference means is presented in detail next.

The Zope object `standard_dtml_wrapper` is one type of object known as a *DTML Method*. Remember, a method is a *way to do something*, so you will be studying an example of "how things get done" in Zope.

This unfamiliar bit of almost-HTML doesn't look very much like a process, does it? That's because the actual process of object publishing is carried out by the ZPublisher "engine," which "interprets" the contents of each object and carries out the specified *action*. Even though you can count on Zope to "interpret" for you, it is important to learn a bit of the lingo yourself. DTML stands for "Document Template Markup Language," and, as you can see, it is similar to HTML, with tags that start with < and end with >. When Zope interprets the meaning of `standard_dtml_wrapper` and carries out the instructions that it contains, the object-publishing process is underway.

## Code Concepts 101—Assigning Variables

Look at the `<dtml-var` reference inside the `title` tag in Listing 1.1. You would expect to see a page title in the form of some simple text, such as, "Behold the Object of the Web!" Instead you see this:

```
<dtml-var title>
```

This is a reference to a *DTML variable* named `title`. Zope *variables* are really just the same as variables in computer code, or a mathematical equation. That is, the *value* can vary, depending on certain conditions. In this case, the title of the page being wrapped is the value that `<dtml-var title>` represents. The main thing that you will use DTML for is to insert such references into pages—that is, to place the names of objects (page elements) at the point where the content of each element should appear. This is exactly like placing a hyperlink (`href`) or a graphic image (`img`) on a normal HTML page.

You are probably wondering where the `title` variable came from because each page must require its own unique title. The answer has to do with another object type, known as a DTML Document. Recall that the actual URL requested in the original example was for a page (DTML Document) named `MyHome.html`. The DTML Document with that name also has a `title` property, which is swapped for the `<dtml-var title>` reference during the object-publishing process. That's because when a DMTL Document *calls* (has a reference to) a DTML Method, the *properties* of the DTML Document are acquired by the DTML Method. The content of a very simple DTML Document might look like Listing 1.2.

Listing 1.2 **DTML Document MyHome.html**

```
<dtml-let page_body="'MyHome.stx'">
 <dtml-var standard_dtml_wrapper>
</dtml-let>
```

Not very impressive, is it? By now you recognize the second line as a reference to the wrapper (DTML Method) `standard_dtml_wrapper` that we've been reviewing. The first line assigns the value of another variable (`page_body`) to the name of yet another Zope DTML Document (`MyHome.stx`), where any unique page elements are "factored in." At this point, it is understandable for you to be wondering why it should take three elements to make one simple page and to question whether it is faster just to type the HTML and be done with it. If all the pages you would ever need to create and maintain were as simple as the example, such concerns would be perfectly valid.

Keep in mind the wrapper is reused for every page, so there are really only two new elements. It also might help to think about the easy way that existing elements can be "included" in a new page, by including objects in the wrapper itself. Some elements already mentioned are a standard banner and menu. Also, even though this is a very simple example, the power of acquisition is already being put to use.

Let's run through that again because this is your first glimpse of acquisition at work. Although it may seem anticlimactic, the point is that adding *one more page* to your site requires just about this much effort:

1. Create a new DTML Document.
2. Give it two DTML tags.
3. Add *only the unique content* in a separate DTML Document (as in `MyHome.stx`).

All the common page elements, such as the standard banner, are provided by the readymade wrapper. Now ask yourself, when was the last time adding a page was that easy? If you're thinking, "Never!", welcome to Zope!

## Initial Page Setup—Identifying Elements

It might appear as if `MyHome.html` is a kind of a wrapper, too, but that's not quite correct. In fact, `MyHome.html` exists just to "set up," or *initialize*, some useful variables, such as the page title and the value of the variable `page_body`, so that the real wrapper will *acquire* them. Notice that the wrapper itself doesn't change and that it can wrap any number of pages using this same technique. When `MyHome.html` sets the values that tell the wrapper which title to use when `MyHome.stx` is the `page_body` element, all related elements are also found and included during the object-publishing step.

Absolutely nothing is duplicated. There are common page elements and unique page elements, but only one of each. When any element is updated, the very next time a page is requested that includes that element, the updated version will be returned to the requestor.

To cover in detail exactly how this sort of thing is done with more complete "real-world" examples, you will need a running Zope installed so that you can begin to get the full "hands-on" experience.

## Where and How to "Get Zope!"

It is best to start with the current version, so browse to **`http://www.zope.org/`** and click on the Download link in the top bar of the page. There is another link near the top of the next page that leads to a selection of packaged Zope "distributions." Keep in mind that these instructions are based on the way the Zope.org site was set up at the time this book was written. Such things can change, so you might need to look around a bit if you don't find the links as described.

If you have a slow web connection, you definitely won't want to do this often, but the Zope packages are less than 6 MB, so an occasional complete update isn't out of the question. Zope is big in features and flexibility, but the actual size is amazingly tiny compared to many web application server downloads. Start the download, go about your business, and it will be over before you know it. You will also notice that Zope can run on several operating systems. Be sure to carefully pick the one that matches your needs because there are often upgrade, or "patch," versions listed for folks who just want to update an existing Zope installation without undertaking a complete overhaul.

### Where to Find More Help

Most newbies don't have any trouble getting Zope up and running easily, but just in case you hit a snag, there are some great resources that you can use to find help quickly. The first place to look is Zope.org itself, where there are "How-To" pages for initial setup and many other subjects, from beginning to advanced, as well as powerful search features. Another favorite site is the searchable email archives hosted by New Information Paradigms (NIP), at **`http://zope.nipltd.com/public/lists.html`**.

You can search for single key words, and you can sort by date, author, and topic. If you don't find anything there that helps with your particular problem, you can also send an email request for advice to `:zope@zope.org`.

You can do that for any question you have, not just when you're starting out, but it's best to search thoroughly first. You'll most likely be searching for answers to questions that have already been answered, so you might as well make the most of what's already there. The Zope community is a marvel of support, and soon you'll be able to answer newbie questions with the best of them.

There are just a few details that you need to know about ahead of time so that you won't have to go searching for them. When you install Zope, you will be presented with, or asked to enter, an admin password, depending on your platform and installation type.

That's no problem—just be sure to make a note so that you don't forget it!

As with any download, you should carefully study the `read_me` file that comes with the system files. Then run the Zope `start` command. Depending on the speed of your system, it might take a little extra time to get started the very first time you run Zope.

### Default URL:8080

It might come as a surprise that Zope has an internal web server, or you might have assumed that from the start. Either way, the default address where Zope is accessed seems a little unusual to most folks. You need to add `:8080` after the IP address of your host system. The `:8080` tells the host system that the browser means to connect at a specific "port" instead of the standard HTTP port (:80). Zope assumes that you might already have another web server using port `80` and, to prevent conflicts, chooses a different port by default.

Most systems have an internal "loopback" address, which allows applications running on that system to communicate with a server running on the same unit, whether or not a physical network is actually in place. This means that your browser can "see" your Zope web server at the loopback address, even if your computer isn't on a LAN. The default IP address for a loopback is `127.0.0.1`, and the alias is `localhost`. If you are accessing your Zope by using the internal loopback IP address, you will most likely use one of these URLs to see the Zope welcome screen: **`http://localhost:8080`** or **`http://127.0.0.1:8080`**. To sign on to the TTW administrative screen, add `manage` to the URL, like so: **`http://127.0.0.1:8080/manage`**.

On some desktop systems, you might need to activate a form of network services for Zope to start successfully. For example, connect to your ISP via modem and then start Zope. You can disconnect from your ISP once Zope is started; you don't have to stay online.

When you sign on to Zope for the first time, you need to create your own user account by clicking Add; on the next screen, enter your name and a password (twice, to make sure it's correct). Then select "Manager," and click Add to save your changes. You will see a folder icon labeled `acl_users`. Select the `acl_users` folder to create your user account. Then shut down your browser completely, restart the browser, and sign back in as yourself rather than as admin. The Zope administrator is not allowed to create Zope objects, but a user with proper rights can. After your user account has been created, you sign on under that name. It's a security thing.

If this much has gone smoothly, then your experience has been the same as many thousands of curious Zope newbies, and you are ready to Zope.

## Zope's Through the Web (TTW) Management Interface—at the Controls

When you see the *Zope Management Interface* (*ZMI*) of a new Zope installation, some of the most obvious items are the navigation view on the left side, the tabs at the top of the page, and the control "buttons" (see Figure 1.2).

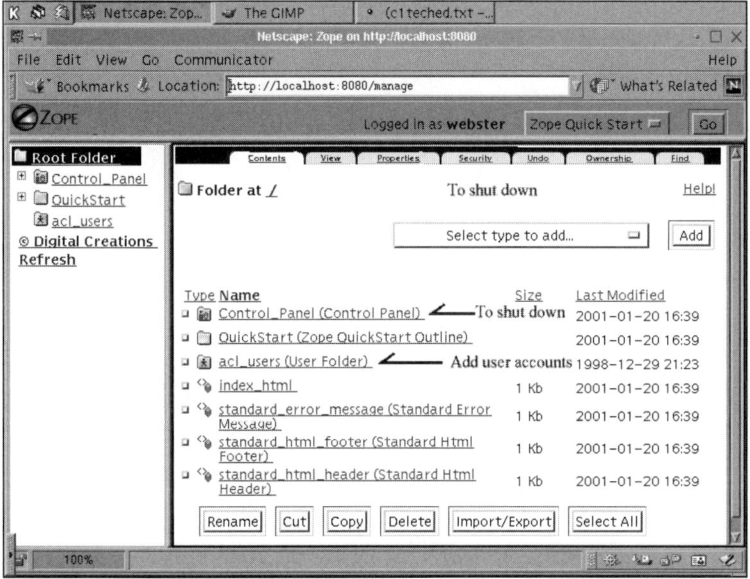


**Figure 1.2** Zope TTW Management Interface.

Notice the Delete button. You might be wondering, "What if I delete the wrong object accidentally?" If not, it's just a matter of time. Either way, Zope has an answer. Click the tab at the top of the page labeled Undo. If you have executed any "undoable" changes, a list will be displayed with the most recent change at the top. To undo the most recent change, click the check box next to the top item so that it is marked, and then click the Undo button. If you need to restore a version of an object that was changed before other changes, you must undo all the changes until you reach the item that you need to restore. Keeping track of such things can be difficult. Therefore, it's always best to test thoroughly as you go so that you can undo at the earliest point.

Another thing that you probably want to know about any new system is how to turn it off. Click `Control_Panel`, just under `RootFolder` in the navigation view. The button labeled Shutdown does just that. Before you turn off your host unit, you should shut down Zope to make sure that the internal data is properly saved. In case of an unexpected system shutdown, such as a power outage, Zope has the capability to recover, but the next time you run the Zope `start` process, it will take a little longer than normal.

## Summary

That's all for your first look at Zope and the high-level explanation of object publishing. You've also had a very brief glimpse of Zope objects in action and a look at making acquisition work for you in the form of a reusable wrapper. Then you downloaded and installed Zope so that you can begin experimenting. In Chapter 2, you can try your hand at some more complex examples, using Zope features to publish dynamically composed pages and to solidify your understanding of the basics.

# 2

# Point and Click Web Building

THIS CHAPTER PRESENTS THE BASIC FEATURES OF ZOPE in hands-on exercises. You will build more complete examples of web pages, using several new object types and powerful dynamic publishing techniques.

To bring a "real-world" flavor to the examples and exercises, you are about to be cast in the role of an information systems administrator for the school district of the charming village of New Millennium. Now that the millennium has dawned, no matter how you count it, your superiors have decided that the school system should take steps to live up to its namesake. You, dear reader, have been assigned the task of linking New Millennium Schools to the web.

Being an experienced techie, you realize that there is inadequate funding and little training for users. Choosing a toolkit that supports an efficient development and maintenance cycle is critical to your success. You need a web environment that minimizes effort up front and day to day. Hopefully, finding one with many "off-the-shelf" modules that can be plugged in as needed won't be too much to ask. Searching for a platform favorable to your needs has led you to Zope, and you are beginning your first "proof of concept" project.

# Through the Web

Zope's Through the Web (TTW) interface is one of its most appealing aspects, especially to less technically inclined users. Nearly any page element can be created, updated, and managed using a generic web browser.

## Managing Web Pages and Elements

Let's look at the details of the typical elements found in any HTML document. By "decomposing" web pages into component parts, you have begun to develop a new way of thinking that is the first step on the road to effective site management. Even though there is no tag for it, the reason for a page to exist is the information it displays. This is often referred to as content, and it includes unique elements as well as common elements.

A brief list of the essential tagged elements of any web page must include the following:

- **html**—A tag that wraps the entire document and identifies it as a web page
- **head**—The tag between html and body where page information is stored
- **title**—The name of the page, an example of an head section element
- **body**—The section that is displayed in the browser screen

You could extend the list with specific types of content, such as text, forms, images, tables, and so on, but set those aside for the moment to keep things simple. In the Wrapper example from Chapter 1, "The Object of the Web—Optimizing Web Development," recall that two DTML documents were created to publish a single web page. The first included some simple DTML to initialize variables, such as an identifier for the second DTML document. The second document contained the unique page body content.

A third object, a DTML Method, was called a "wrapper." It "wrapped" all the pages on the site in a standard template. Those examples were about as primitive as possible while still producing a valid HTML document. At this point you are ready to create some more fully developed pages, step by step, using Zope's power to optimize your efforts.

# A New Zope Object Type—the Folder, a "Container" Object

Because these are your first Zope documents, you must first create some Zope folder objects to keep the storage and retrieval of your documents organized. Folders are also called *containers* because they hold objects, including other folders. Use the Zope's TTW interface, also known as the Zope Management Interface (ZMI).

In your browser location bar, enter the URL for your ZMI—for example, **`http://127.0.0.1:8080/manage`**, which may also be available as **`http://localhost:8080/manage`**.

You might want to create a bookmark to make it easy to find your way back. After you sign on with your user ID and password, you will see a screen like Figure 2.1.

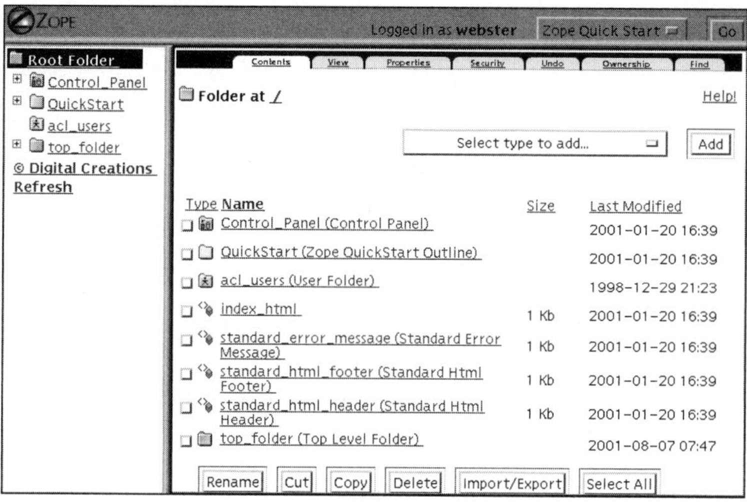


**Figure 2.1** First look at the ZMI.

Looking ahead to the needs of a systemwide web site, you realize that it will be easiest to understand a hierarchy that models a known structure, such as the divisions that already exist within the school district organization. Set that aside for now, and focus on learning the implications of a Zope site structure. That will help solidify your understanding and improve your solution in the end.

To add a folder, select Folder from the drop-down list labeled Select Type to Add. Some browsers take you to the next screen immediately, but, if not, click Add. Experience has shown that it's best to have a folder hierarchy with at least one level between the Root folder and storage folders where you will keep site objects. So, fill in the next screen as in Figure 2.2, giving your new folder and ID of top_folder and a title of Top Level Folder. Be sure to check the box labeled Create User Folder.

The ZMI has a "tree" interface on the left, with a Refresh link at the bottom. Click Refresh any time you want to update the current view of the tree. You will notice that in the tree, only the ID of the folder is displayed, while in the TTW form area, an icon, the ID, and the object name are all visible. The difference is really just to keep the tree area narrow, to leave more space for the form area. You also will notice the boxes with + and – next to folder IDs. This has become a familiar way to indicate that a folder can be expanded or collapsed. Try clicking on them to see how they work.

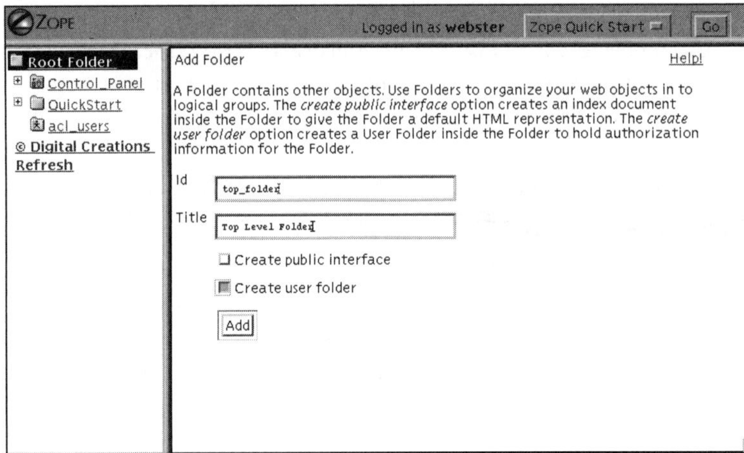


**Figure 2.2** Creating a top-level folder.

Select your new folder when it appears, by clicking on top_folder. Now you're ready to create a folder to store all the elements that are related only to the new site that you will be building. Click the Select Type to Add drop-down list again, but pause for a moment to scan the range of standard Zope object types. What you see before you is a well-stocked tool chest. There are also many optional Zope modules to choose from, which you can add as you see fit. You have a lot to look forward to! Now, go ahead and select Folder, and create the next folder.

This time, also check the box labeled Create Public Interface, and give your folder an ID (site_folder) and a title (Site Level Folder), as in Figure 2.3.

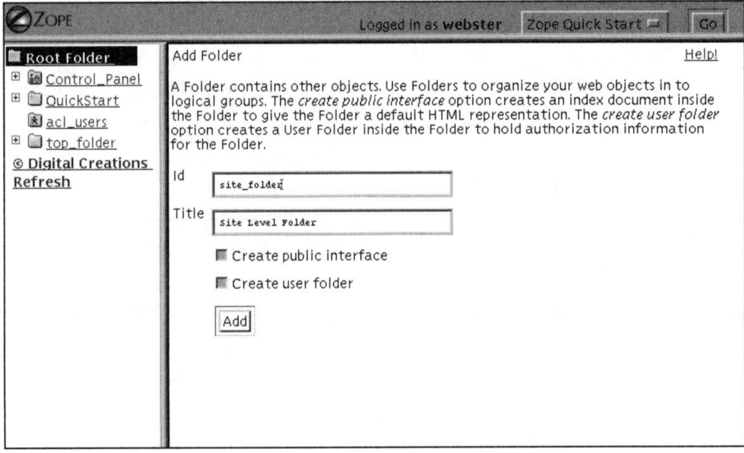


**Figure 2.3** Creating a site folder.

Now click on site_folder, and this time add a DTML document, instead of a folder. Give your new DTML document an ID of MyHome.html and a title of Object of the Web. Click Add and Edit to see the default DTML document object. The text area has some template text in place, but you won't be needing that. Click the text area, delete the template text, and replace it with the text shown in Listing 2.1.

Listing 2.1 **DTML Document MyHome.html**

```
<dtml-let page_body="'MyHome.stx'">
 <dtml-var standard_dtml_wrapper>
</dtml-let>
```

At this point, the example in Listing 2.1 is identical to the example in Chapter 1, Listing 1.1. Click Save Changes to save your edited DTML document. Because you are catching on as you go along, the instructions for each step will get simpler, and some of the details will be left out, such as Save Changes.

Select Site Level Folder again, and create the second DTML document. This time, the ID is MyHome.stx and the title is My Home Page. Use the content shown in Listing 2.2.

Listing 2.2 **A DTML Document with Content**

```
The Object of the web- *Optimizing* Web Development

 This chapter presents an overview of the concepts of
 "Object Publishing", with examples of how to create
 dynamically published web pages with Zope.

   - What is an "object publishing environment"?
```

The text in Listing 2.2 is in an easy to use format called *Structured Text*, which uses indentation as its primary document formatting markup. Notice that the sentence is indented one space more than the single line of text above it, which is automatically interpreted as a title line. The asterisks around the word `optimizing` are the markup for emphasis. Zope has a filter that converts Structured Text to HTML.

This handy feature can greatly ease the burden of content providers, who often struggle to keep up with a full workload and then are expected to master HTML as well.

Structured Text format might look too basic to be useful, but, in fact, entire books have been written in `structured-text`.

For an overview of Structure Text markup, see **http://www.zope.org/Members/millejoh/structuredText**.

Next, create a DTML method object with an ID of `standard_dtml_wrapper` and a title of Site Wrapper Method. As before, the text is identical to the original example in Chapter 1, and it is shown again in Listing 2.3.

Listing 2.3 **A "Wrapper" DTML Method**

```
01 <HTML>
02  <HEAD>
03   <TITLE><dtml-var title></TITLE>
04  </HEAD>
05  <BODY>
06   <dtml-var banner>
07   <dtml-var expr="_[page_body]" fmt=structured-text>
08  </BODY>
09 </HTML>
```

Notice line 07, which says `fmt=structured-text`. That is the notation that activates the filter to convert from Structured Text to HTML.

You will refine the wrapper as the exercise progresses. At this point, your wrapper is identical to the example from Chapter 1, but an element is missing. The fourth line from the bottom references a banner object, which doesn't exist yet. So, that's next.

## More Object Types—Images and Files

The banner is usually a means of establishing the identity of a site with a logo and possibly a custom font. If you have a small image that you would like to use, you can upload it into Zope as an image file. You will probably want to choose an image no more than about 80 pixels tall and 120 pixels wide. Anything will work, but that's a typical range. Image formats such as .jpg and .gif are compatible with nearly all browsers. If you prefer .png files, you will need a more up-to-date browser. Create an Image object, and give it an ID of `banner_logo` and a title of Site Logo. This time, use the File option by clicking the Browse button to find the image file that you want to use on your local filesystem. When you have the path to the image file displayed in the text box, click Add. Uploading a text file into Zope is just as easy when you select File from the Select Type to Add drop-down list.

The treatment of the banner logo represents an example of applied acquisition that should be particularly easy to understand. When you develop your site hierarchy further, you might want to have a district-level folder that, in turn, has a folder for each school. You could include a different image in each folder but then give each one the same ID. When ZPublisher starts looking for the `banner_logo` object, acquisition causes the appropriate image to be selected and published on each page.

You won't see a reference to the logo image in the wrapper because it is really "part of" the banner. Create your banner object as a DTML method, with the ID of banner and the title Site Banner. This time, replace the default text with this line:

```
<dtml-var banner_logo><h1><dtml-var title></h1>
```

You might be surprised that the reference to `banner_logo` doesn't specify the image size—or even the fact that the element is an image. Zope handles all of that for you because you created the object as an image type. In some cases, you might need to specify a width and height if you want to scale the image differently from its original dimensions. Notice that the banner text is simply the title of the MyHome.html object, which has been rendered as a heading.

You are now ready to test the page. Open another browser window, and "hit" the URL for the page **http://127.0.0.1:8080/top_level_folder/site_folder/MyHome.html**.

Watch all the pieces just fall into place! You might find it helpful to view the HTML source of the page to see how elements that aren't stored as native HTML are transformed in the publishing process so that the image file and the body text are rendered with all the appropriate tags and qualifiers.

### Options for Serving Static Files

If you work on sites with lots of images, you will probably want to consider some of the alternate ways of serving images within the Zope environment. Especially if you have a fast server where most of the images that you need are already in place, it might be simplest to call them with the same URLs that you are already using. It's not quite as cool as the Zope Image Object type, but it is quite effective for serving static files.

For tips and a peek at other intriguing possibilities for handling images, see these links:

**http://www.zope.org/Members/kslee/pseudo_image**

**http://www.zope.org/Members/penny/smart_images**

You will most likely want to master more of the basics of Zope before tackling the advanced topics covered in these links. It can be inspiring, though, just to get a preview of the cool stuff that lies in store at Zope.org—from the excellent pointers and "How-to" pages, to the many modules contributed by Zope fans from around the globe.

Another very popular option is to create a LocalFS object, using the Zope Module contributed by Jonathan Farr. LocalFS provides the means to directly access the filesystem of the Zope host. Among other things, this means that you can allow users to upload images that can be stored and referenced as static files, but still be managed from within Zope.

For details of how to install and use LocalFS, see these links:

**http://www.zope.org/Members/jfarr/Products/LocalFS**

**http://www.zope.org/Members/jfarr/Products/LocalFS/installing**

**http://www.zope.org/Members/jfarr/HowTo/DTML_with_LocalFS**

Because you are now looking at add-on packages for Zope, numerous and useful as they are, this is a good point to mention a few other tools that you might not be familiar with. The common zip format isn't universal, and you might need the gnu zip utility program as well. You can find it at **http://www.gzip.org/**.

The most common form for distribution of Zope modules is a .tgz file, and the usual command to extract files is as follows:

```
gzip -d filename
```

Just replace the word `filename` with the actual file name that you need to unzip, for example,

`gzip -d localfs.tgz`

At this point you will have an unzipped Tape Archive (".tar") file. To complete the process, you can use the venerable `tar` utility with the command: `tar -xvf filename`.

Recent versions of `tar` have `gzip` functionality built-in, so you can do this all in one step using the following command: `tar -zxvf filename`.

If you don't already have a version of `tar`, you can most likely find a `tar` that will work on your system at one of these links:

**http://helpdesk.uvic.ca/how-to/support/msdos/tar.html**

**http://www.strout.net/macsoft/mactar/**

Typical installation instructions are to copy the downloaded file to the Zope directory and run the extraction command, as shown previously. That isn't the only way to install an add-on module; it's just the most common. Always take the time to carefully read the installation instructions for each module.

The `tar` format is also used to package small sets of files for distribution when they aren't large enough to benefit from data compression.

## More Interfaces—FTP and WebDAV

You probably already have a toolkit for web development, stuffed with all of your personal favorites. Did you know that in addition to serving HTTP, like a conventional web server, Zope also provides FTP access? Although many Zope fans find the TTW interface ideal, others are quite relieved to learn that they can still use a favorite editor to create Zope objects and just FTP your work to the Zope host, as if it were a filesystem. Any of the text Zope object examples that you've seen so far could have been created and updated just this way.

The default FTP port for a Zope server is 8021. If you haven't changed the standard Zope startup, your host system is probably serving FTP right now. For more details on connecting to Zope over the FTP interface, here are some links:

**http://www.zope.org/Members/mblewett/ZopeFTP**

**http://www.zope.org/Members/dparker/alternativeeditors**

**http://www.zope.org/Members/nemeth/usingEmacsWithZope**

**http://www.zope.org/Members/cybertad/how_to/homesite**

There are some limitations because FTP has no notion of certain Zope features. For instance, the Zope object ID is the same as a filename when using the FTP interface, but FTP has no inherent means of recognizing a Zope object's title property. The simplest way to compensate is to use FTP just for moving files that you've been editing elsewhere and to use the ZMI for everything else, such as property assignment.

Zope has yet another option for browser interface fans with first-generation WebDAV features. *WebDAV* stands for Web Distributed Authoring and Versioning, and it is a relatively new set of HTTP extensions to allow editing of web documents "in place." Just from the name and brief description, you could get the idea that it fits very neatly into Zope's dynamic, interactive content-management paradigm. The eye opener is that you can update a web page directly, without having to switch to ZMI or to FTP files. While you're viewing at a page in a WebDAV-capable browser, edit it in place! You might already be using a web tool that supports WebDAV and not even know it.

Don't dwell on this enticing possibility just now, even though it is difficult not to picture a system in which every user—such as each administrator and teacher throughout the school district—can update their own web pages directly. WebDAV holds much promise for the future, but it is still in the very early stages of development and standardization.

> **For More Information**
>
> WebDAV is covered in more depth in Chapter 8, "Getting Content Under Control," along with other content-management topics, but you can find out more today at these links:
>
> **`http://www.webdav.org/`**
>
> **`http://www.webdav.org/other/faq.html`**

### More Point and Click—Copy, Paste, and Delete

You will be happy to learn that you can copy/paste any object, even an entire folder and everything in it, in a couple of steps. To make a copy of your wrapper, click the check box next to the `standard_dtml_wrapper` object. Now click Copy. Did you notice that a Paste button suddenly appeared? Select the RootFolder; when it appears in the ZMI form area, click Paste. Because you really don't want that object there, click the check box next to the new copy, and click Delete.

## Code Concepts 101

If you happen to be a newcomer to programming, a very brief guide to the fundamentals of logic as applied to dynamic publishing is included here just for you.

### More DTML Options—Process Flow Control

As was demonstrated in Listings 2.1, and 2.3, a value stored as a variable can be created at one point in a process and referred to at some later point. This is truly the most basic aspect of computer programming, but it might be new to some readers who have been working primarily with conventional HTML and graphics. Things really get interesting when the process itself relies on the stored value to determine which one of a set of possible actions to carry out. This is a type of automation being put to work in the creation of dynamic web pages.

### Branching—a Fork in the Decision Tree

Consider the variable page_body, which serves to identify the unique page content of this example. The standard_dtml_wrapper is written so that it assumes that this variable has been assigned. The example is simple and easy to understand, which suited your needs, but it is not comprehensive. What would happen if a call were made to the wrapper method, but the variable didn't yet exist? You will see the Zope error screen often enough, so start applying a bit of prevention right now. Select standard_dtml_wrapper from the site_folder.

You need to add a logical "branch," a decision point where Zope can check to see if the variable has been set. That way, the process can continue normally when all goes well, but it can carry out default behavior in case of an omission.

The new DTML syntax that you will use is called <dtml-if>, and can be inserted into the existing dtml method object standard_dtml_wrapper, as seen in Listing 2.4:

Listing 2.4 **Adding a Branch to the Wrapper**

```
01 <html>
02  <head>
03   <title><dtml-var title_or_id></title>
04  <head>
05  <body>
06   <dtml-var banner>
07   <dtml-if page_body>
08    <dtml-var "_[page_body]" fmt=structured-text>
09   <dtml-else>
10    <dtml-var default_page>
11   </dtml-if>
12  </body>
13 </html>
```

The tag at line 07, <dtml-if page_body>, simply checks to see that a variable with the name page_body exists. The <dtml-if> asks ZPublisher to confirm whether calling an object named page_body results in a nonempty value, which, in code lingo, is interpreted as "true." If so, the next line carries on as before, but the <dtml-else> line allows for the possibility that the result was "false," such as in a case where the variable does not exist. If that happens, the line after <dtml-else> will be carried out.

Of course, now you have to create a default_page object that will always be available for such contingencies. In this case, the new object could be a document that displays a line of text saying something like, "The page you requested is not available at this time." At least that would be more polite and considerate than an alarming "ERROR!" message. Go ahead and create a DTML document with an ID of default_page and a title of Default Error Massage, and replace the template text with the message of your choice. You can improve it as you gain expertise, but at least it will work well enough for now.

### Looping—Doing It Until It's Done

Another basic flow-control construct is known as a *loop*. Loops enable iteration over a set of elements so that each one is processed in turn. For example, the cases that were allowed for in the previous code allow only two possible objects for insertion into a page after the banner. Another approach might be to create a list of possible object names and test for each one from the most common to the least. While cumbersome, this idea could come in handy when you have a set of possible conditions that is neither too short nor too long in number. If you need a name to help you remember this sort of judgment call, which arises frequently in the programming field, you could call it the "Goldilocks Principle" (as in "too hot, too cold, just right"). The choices that programmers make are less often the consistent application of clear-cut "laws" as much as "guesstimates" that are arrived at through experience and personal preference.

The most-used loop construct in DTML is <dtml-in sequence_name>, which applies a template or process to each item that is "in" a set if items. You will be using <dtml-in> loops frequently, especially when working with databases and queries.

### Nested Branches

You might be thinking of any number of other ways to handle this. So, take a look at one more variation of this method—this time with two branches, one "nested" inside another—with the text in Listing 2.5.

Listing 2.5 **Choosing One of Three Options**

```
01 <html>
02  <head>
03   <title><dtml-var title_or_id></title>
04  <head>
05  <body>
06   <dtml-var banner>
07    <dtml-if page_body>
08     <dtml-if "page_body[-4:]=='.stx'">
09      <dtml-var "_[page_body]" fmt=structured-text>
10      <dtml-else>
11      <dtml-var "_[page_body]">
12     </dtml-if>
13    <dtml-else>
14     <dtml-var default_page>
15    </dtml-if>
16   </body>
17  </html>
```

The new case you are handling in Listing 2.5 covers the possibility that the page_body variable names an object that isn't formatted as structured_text. An example of this case is an existing HTML page that has been adapted so that it can be wrapped and used on this new site. Line 08 in this version, <dtml-if "page_body[-4:]==.stx'">, tests whether the value stored as page_body has the string ".stx" as the last four characters. The brackets, -4, and colon are an example of the "slice syntax" used in Python.

The number and colon in this example mean, "All the characters in this string, from the fourth from the last, to the end."

> **Knowing Python Helps You Understand Zope**
>
> Many articles about Zope, beginners tutorials, and helpful Zope users will assure you that mastery of Python isn't required to use Zope effectively. However, plenty of enthusiastic Python coders got their first glimpse of Python when they tried Zope. No one will dispute the fact that the more Python you know, the easier it will be to get the most out of Zope.
>
> So, don't let the fact that you can indeed use Zope without really understanding Python keep you from adding this powerful and popular language to your toolkit. Especially if you are new to programming, look no further than Python. Python is famous for both its approachability and its practical usefulness.
>
> To start your Python explorations, see any of the excellent tutorials listed at these links:
>
> **http://www.python.org/doc/Intros.html**
>
> **http://www.ibiblio.org/obp/thinkCSpy/**
>
> **http://www.honors.montana.edu/~jjc/easytut/easytut/**
>
> Zope is nearly all Python code—and not by accident. When the Zope folks chose Python, they did so because they knew that the benefits of a language steeped in object-oriented concepts with unmatched clarity and ease of use would empower Zope to support challenging and sophisticated web development projects. Python's capability to run on a wide range of hardware and software platforms is another essential ingredient. The web is only beginning to demonstrate the need to accommodate diverse and unanticipated uses, from cell phones and handhelds to smart cars and global satellite systems. Even if your projects don't demand absolute state-of-the-art technology, it can be very comforting to know that "it's in there."

A bit of explanation is in order regarding the specifics of the references to the variable `page_body` at different points in the `standard_dtml_wrapper` in Listing 2.5. Sometimes it's in quotes, and sometimes not. Sometimes it's in brackets but not quoted. Looking back at the original instance, recall that the variable is assigned with the name of the object enclosed in single quotes and then double-quoted as well. This all looks mysterious, and it certainly takes some of getting used to, but hang in there. We'll go through each case—and then show you how to totally bypass the worst of it altogether with a wonderful new feature called Python Scripts that appeared in Zope as of Version 2.3.

## DTML expressions

The most important DTML concept to get your hands around right away is the difference between a name and an expression. The simplest way to refer to a Zope object is by name (ID). The example in Listing 2.5 includes several instances in which an object is simply referred to by name and the syntax is crystal clear—for example, look at line 07: `<dtml-if page_body>`.

As mentioned earlier, this `<dtml-if>` tag asks a question, "Is there a variable, at this time, with the name `page_body`?" However, the simplicity is misleading because this is actually a shorthand version, which is allowed for ease of use. The complete syntax is `<dtml-if name="page_body">`.

This syntax is still pretty clear and not too difficult. Now look at the next line, the second `<''dtml-if>`, on line 08:

```
<dtml-if "page_body[-4:]=='.stx'">
```

Like I said, a bit of explanation is in order.

### From Names to Expressions

The previous line of DTML asks a much more complicated question, with specific details about character order and placement within a text string. This sort of question cannot be expressed by referring to the name of an object. It is an example of an "expression," a programming term for a construct that must be interpreted to be understood. If you call out someone's name and that person hears you, she will probably respond, and you've accomplished your goal. If you have to go about inquiring after an individual by description, things get more complicated. That's why the entire expression is contained in double quotes. They tell ZPublisher, "This is complex, so put on your interpreting hat."

You've already looked at the "slice" syntax. So, move on to the `==` part. This is the equality comparison operator. There are two equals signs to distinguish this from the action of assigning a value to a variable. For that, you use a single `=`, which is the variable assignment operator. The comparison to be made in this case is to determine whether the value stored in the `page_body` variable is an exact match in its last four characters for the character string ".stx".

So, you've seen that DTML expressions must always be enclosed in double quotes. Fortunately, single quotes are just as effective for designating character strings, or this would have been even more confusing. The single quoted string is "nested" within the double-quoted expression to eliminate confusion about where each type of quotation starts and ends. Look around for other instances of single quotes within double quotes. Whenever you see this configuration, it is a case of a character string "nested" within an expression.

Things get even more complicated when you realize that in the example shown in Listing 2.5 the value stored in the variable, `page_body` is just a text string, which happens to be the name of another object. That's why you are able to compare the last four characters to another string (".stx"). However, when you want to insert the object that the `page_body` variable refers to, you don't want to have that object's name accidentally appear on the web page where you expected to see the object that the name "means." After all, having your name on a place marker at a meeting isn't quite the same as actually being there yourself. To avoid rendering an object's name on a web page when you want to display the object itself, you need a way to express *an object with a name that is the same as the string stored in this object.* That's where the `_[page_body]` bit comes in.

The special variable _ indicates that ZPublisher should search the current "name space" for whatever is between the brackets. You have likely guessed that _ is called the *name space variable*. The item between the brackets is a variable, `page_body`. When a variable is presented this way, as `_[variable_name]`, ZPublisher "knows" that it must look for an object with the name that is stored in that variable. It is a subtle point, but once you have this clear in your mind, many details become considerably easier to grasp.

Now, what is a "name space"? Think of the name space as the collection of all the names of all the objects that are available at the present moment. The `<dtml-let>` tag is a good example of the importance of the "present moment" part. From the start of the `<dtml-let>` to its close, any variables assigned by it are available in the name space. Afterward, those variables are gone and can't be found. Searching for them after they cease to exist in the name space will result in an "empty" value (`false`), which will generate an error.

As you are no doubt coming to realize, there is much more to this than can be covered in a paragraph. Still, a basic understanding will serve for the majority of cases. For a precise explanation of the name space, see **http://www.zope.org/Members/michel/HowTos/NameSpaceHow-To**.

Zope's talent for finding objects is also seen in the concept of acquisition, which was discussed briefly in Chapter 1. There is a web "slide show" on that topic at **http://www.zope.org/Members/jim/Info/IPC8/AcquisitionAlgebra/index.html**.

### How to Use DTML and When Not To

The previous listings are adequate to demonstrate that DTML is potentially a very powerful programming tool. Now that you know that, try not to use it that way. You've seen enough in this brief exposition to realize that it can only get more difficult to understand as the tasks that you need to accomplish become more complex. DTML is a fine tool for building page templates with wonderful features for meeting your web presentation needs. Understanding that DTML was never meant to serve as a complete programming system is the most important part of learning when to use DTML and when to reach for another tool.

## Keeping Code Simple

Instead of trying to make DTML do things that it can only do poorly, in this section you will get a look at doing things in a different way, using Python scripts. The most obvious difference is that when you use Python scripts, the need for nested quotes to designate expressions just goes away. That would be enough to make Python Scripts worth using, but it's truly much better than that.

We've already mentioned that much of the syntax in the previous examples is really just Python syntax with DTML peculiarities tacked on. Python scripts are Python syntax with web security and safety built in. DTML has similar security restrictions, but for many development tasks, Python Scripts are the best choice.

### A Python Script Version

Analysis of the DTML example shows that everything between the sixth line, `<dtml-var banner>`, and the second-to-last line, `</body>` is there just to choose among three possible options for inserting an element. Because DTML is intended to allow dynamic page element insertion, this seems reasonable. What isn't so reasonable is the need to treat every line as if it will result in HTML that will show up on the rendered page, by adding `<dtml->` tags. Wouldn't it be better to create a Python script, give it a representative name, such as `choose_page_body`, and then call it once? Nine lines of DTML are reduced to one. This is seen as line 07 in Listing 2.6.

Listing 2.6 **Simpler DTML, Thanks to Python Script**

```
01 <html>
02  <head>
03   <title><dtml-var title_or_id></title>
04  <head>
05  <body>
06   <dtml-var banner>
07   <dtml-call choose_page_body>
08  </body>
09 </html>
```

Of course, now you need to create that `choose_page_body` object, which, of course, is a Python script. Select the Site Level Folder, and create a Python script object with an ID of `choose_page_body` and the Title Choose Page Body. Enter the text from Listing 2.7.

Listing 2.7 **Python Scripts Are Easier to Read**

```
##bind namespace=_
from Products.PythonScripts.standard import special_formats

if page_body :
  if page_body[-4:] == ".stx" :
    return special_formats['structured-text'](_[page_body])
  else :
    return _[page_body]
else :
  return default_page
```

As you can see, converting to a simple Python script might not greatly reduce the number of lines needed to carry out a task, but it will certainly reduce the difficulty of understanding what those lines mean, compared to the DTML version. Pay special attention to the colons (:) at the end of `if` and `else` lines (branch statement). Leaving them out will cause an error. Also note that the indentation is not optional. Though many programming languages allow and encourage indentation as an aid to clarity, Python enforces clarity by treating indentation as a syntax feature.

The next time you update this Python script, you might be surprised to see that the first line is missing from the text. The ZMI has incorporated the `##bind namespace=_`

directive into the object's internal properties. Look above the edit box, and you will see a list of `bind` variables, such as `context` and `container`. Notice that _ is now part of that list.

You will continue to use Python scripts frequently throughout the rest of the book, so, you will have plenty of examples to learn from. For more details, search at **http://zope.org** for "Python scripts."

As mentioned earlier, Zope uses a "filter" to convert documents in Structured Text format to HTML. When you use DTML to insert documents directly, the option to use the parameter `fmt=structured_text` is built in. When you need to do the same thing within a Python script, the "filter" functionality must be explicitly included. The second line in Listing 2.6 takes care of making sure that the filter is available. The name of the library that contains the structured text filter is `special_formats`. Then, when the `page_body` element is returned to be inserted into the page, at publishing time it is "filtered" when the next line is executed:

```
return special_formats['structured-text'](page_body)
```

This statement is nearly as complicated as the one that it replaces in the DTML version, but at least it doesn't have the distracting quotes, brackets, and `<dtml->` surrounding each line. The ability to easily use added features by "importing" them is one of the significant advantages of Python scripts and Python in general, which leads directly to the next topic.

### Python Libraries—Batteries Included

One potent feature of Python that can save you countless hours of research and coding is the wealth of ready-to-use modules and function libraries that are available. All the standard Python libraries can be used from within Zope, but some perform insecure operations that also can be used, such as writing data directly to a disk on the server. For this reason, Python scripts are not allowed to call certain libraries and functions. If you are faced with a task that you suspect will require a good deal of research and effort, spending some time early on searching through the existing libraries can often save many hours of toil. See the Standard Python Library at **http://www.python.org/** and the Vaults of Parnassus, a popular collection of additional modules, at **http://www.vex.net/parnassus**.

You might already be thinking of many technical housekeeping chores that the Python standard library can help you with. Even more compelling might be the possibility of web enabling the many duties of a school district web master within the Zope environment. You can even delegate certain routine chores through a web interface with built-in security, such as creating user and email accounts for newly hired staff.

### External Methods

If you need to use a Python library that performs insecure processes, one way is to call it as an *External Method*. This is a type of Zope object is essentially a separate Python program, stored as a disk file. You cannot upload an External Method through the ZMI. You must have direct access to the server filesystem, via FTP or some other means. The assumption is that if you have write access to the filesystem, you are already authorized at a security level that implies a high degree of trust. In other words, if you can personally write directly to the disk, which, by definition, is an "insecure" operation, then you can also enable a program to carry out the same operation. Alternative approaches to file system access restrictions are explored in Chapter 10, "Survival Gear for Web Masters," along with other site administration topics.

Another reason to resort to an External Method is to leverage an existing library of functions with minimal effort. Although it might be possible to create a Python script that uses the library or a more advanced Zope object, such as a Zope Product, your immediate need might be simply to implement something quickly. In that case, write a Python program that uses the library you need, and copy your program to the "Extensions" directory under the Zope directory on the server. If there is no directory named "Extensions", go ahead and create it.

Calling an External Method is very much like placing any other call to a DTML function, such as the way the Python script version was called in Listing 2.7. One difference is that any parameters required by the function you are calling must be passed explicitly. As a fictitious example, if you use an external method named `folder_max` to compare an arbitrary maximum value to the number of non-folder objects currently stored in any folder, you would need to pass the current count along with the DTML call. After assigning the number of objects to a variable named `current_count`, you could call the function as shown here:

```
<dtml-call "folder_max(current_count)">
```

You can clearly see how a value is passed to a function.

**For More Information**

This link has a more complete explanation of how to create and use external methods:

**http://www.zope.org/Documentation/How-To/ExternalMethods**

Although Zope is written in Python, there are several ways to call functions from other languages and even from completely separate systems. To learn more about Perl scripts (formerly known as "Perl methods"), start here:

**http://www.zope.org/Members/andym/wiki/FrontPage**

Find out about other extra-Zope function calling options, such as Zope's well-known support for XML-RPC, plus experiments and explorations of other distributed object models such as CORBA and SOAP, at these links:

**http://www.zope.org/Members/Amos/XML-RPC**

**http://www.zope.org/Members/jheintz/ZODB_CORBA_Connection**

**http://www2.linuxjournal.com/articles/briefs/038.html**

# Putting Your Site to Work

As you work through these initial exercises, you can start to see that, in Zope, you have a powerful resource at hand. A few more examples in this section will expand on that theme and prepare you for more advanced projects with practical usefulness.

## Generating HTML

Your wrapper, combined with Structured Text, has proven quite effective at presenting perfectly respectable web pages. Still, with WYSIWYG HTML editors readily available, that might not seem particularly significant. An attractive site should be "a given," no matter how the content was created. The more challenging goal, and one that has a greater long-term benefit, is producing a well-organized site that makes management and maintenance of current information easier.

Your previous experience with web development might not have prepared you for a comprehensive approach to content management. Regardless of the means you have used up to now for creating web pages, viewing HTML source reveals a redundant, tedious text format that is ineffective to create and maintain by manual editing. Serving web pages by generating HTML dynamically is one option that many web developers will be unfamiliar with, but it represents an essential ingredient in any complete content-management solution. Two ways to output a simple table by combining DTML and Python scripts are compared here.

The table that you will be generating is an alternative keypad, such as those used for the touch-screen display of palm computers. This version is a 5-by-6 grid arranged in alphabetical order with all the vowels clustered around the center of the grid.

Start by creating a new folder, and give it the title `sand_box` because this is where you'll be "playing" with DTML and Python scripts. Select `sand_box`, and add the DTML document named setup with the content in Listing 2.8.

Listing 2.8 **Setting Up for a New Keypad Layout**

```
<dtml-let page_body="'key_pad'">
 <dtml-var standard_dtml_wrapper>
</dtml-let>
```

The title of `key_pad` is given to a DTML document that has the content from Listing 2.9.

Listing 2.9 **DTML for a Generated Table Showing New Keypad Layout**

```
<table border='1' cellpadding='3' cellspacing='3'>
 <dtml-in key_pad_sequence>
  <tr align='center'>
   <dtml-let key_row=sequence-item>
    <dtml-in key_row>
     <dtml-let char_key=sequence-item>
      <td><dtml-var char_key></td>
     </dtml-let>
```

```
      </dtml-in>
    </dtml-let>
  </tr>
</dtml-in>
</table>
```

You can see several lines in Listing 2.9 that are simple HTML, but most are DTML, including two `<dtml-in>` loops—one nesting within the other. Also notice the keyword `sequence-item`, which occurs twice. In each pass through a `<dtml-in>` loop, the item being processed in the current loop can be referred to as `sequence-item`. In both loops, the `sequence-item` is relabeled by a `<dtml-let>` assignment, for clarity.

The final component is a Python script, titled `key_pad_sequence` with the contents shown in Listing 2.10.

Listing 2.10 **A Sequence of Sequences**

```
a_b = '  ','!','"','A','B'
c_g = 'C','D','E','F','G'
h_l = 'H','I','J','K','L'
m_q = 'M','N','O','P','Q'
r_v = 'R','S','T','U','V'
x_z = 'X','Y','Z',',','.'

return = a_b, c_g, h_l, m_q, r_v, x_z
```

The Python sequence objects created in the first six lines of Listing 2.10 are combined as another sequence in the last line. The first `<dtml-in>` loop refers to the return sequence, which contains all the others. The second `<dtml-in>` loop treats each of the packaged sequences of letters and punctuation in turn.

A little imagination might suggest the possibility of using a slight variation of this idea to generate web-based monthly calendars for the school district. That very thought is developed and implemented in Chapter 3, "Web Event Publishing," with impressive results.

There are several advantages to this approach to creating and maintaining a web site using dynamic HTML generation. One is the assurance of consistency and correctness that results from simple but reliable programmed components. Another is the flexibility of updating. For example, an entirely different key layout could be created by changing the `key_pad_sequence` component without changing the other elements. This is an example of separation of content from presentation. The actual letters that are displayed are separate from the HTML table tags that define the way that the letters appear. The sequences could have been incorporated in the `key_pad` DTML document, but there would be no advantage, and the DTML would have been somewhat more cumbersome than the very simple Python script in Listing 2.10.

Likewise, the HTML tags could have been incorporated within the `key_pad_sequence` Python script, but, again, there would have been little to gain. To illustrate the point, this idea has been implemented in Listing 2.11, as a Python script with an ID of `key_pad_in_table`.

Listing 2.11 **Generating HTML in a Python Script**

```
import string

a_b='  ','!','"','A','B'
c_g='C','D','E','F','G'
h_l='H','I','J','K','L'
m_q='M','N','O','P','Q'
r_v='R','S','T','U','V'
x_z='X','Y','Z',',','.'

rows = a_b,c_g,h_l,m_q,r_v,x_z

key_list = []
key_list.append("<table border='1' cellpadding='3'  cellspacing='3'>\n")

for row in rows:
 key_list.append(" <tr align='center'>\n")
 for key in row:
  key_list.append("  <td>" +  key + "</td>\n")
 key_list.append(" </tr>\n")
key_list.append("</table>")

return string.join(key_list,'')
```

To see the Listing 2.11 version, replace the first line in Listing 2.9 with this:

```
<dtml-let page_body="'key_pad_in_table'">
```

Just as DTML is awkward for complex programming, Python scripts have limitations when used to generate HTML. Notice how easy it is to grasp the simple "`for` loop" structure. Even so, the added overhead of building up HTML tags from text strings suggests that DTML still has a place in simple HTML Templates. Recognizing the trade-off that must occur when moving from one tool to the other will help you decide when to choose each for a particular task.

## Summary

You have gotten a feel for the possibilities that Zope offers, and you've tried a few of the fundamental object creation and updating processes, all within your familiar browser. In Part II, "Leveraging Zope Components," you will get to try out several readymade Zope modules that can help you provide for the needs of your web audience.

# II

# Leveraging Zope Components

# 3

# Web Event Publishing

In this chapter and the remaining chapters in Part II, "Leveraging Zope Components," we are going to show you how existing Zope objects and products can be used with little or no modification to solve real-world problems. In the context of your imaginary role as the Information Systems Administrator for the New Millennium school system, which we presented in the first three paragraphs of Chapter 2, "Point-and-Click Web Building," you will see how common Zope objects can be utilized to perform very useful tasks.

Having been given the unenviable task of moving the entire school district into the Internet/intranet age quickly, and being given the traditional budget of a public school system to work with, you are understandably nervous. When we introduced our mythical school system to you, we promised to show you how Zope was going to be an ideal way for you to deploy powerful web applications very quickly without a huge investment of time or money. Now it's time for us to make good on that promise.

Most of the issues that you'll face are not unique to this school system, nor to school systems in general. They are issues faced daily by thousands of IS managers all around the world at many different kinds of businesses. What this means is that, in many cases, others have already found solutions to these problems. And, more importantly, other Zope developers have probably solved these problems with Zope objects that you can download and incorporate into your own web applications. Because of the ease with which Zope products can be modified (customized), they are perfect for rapid web development.

## Identifying the Needs of the User

The proper way to begin this project is for you to spend some time with the potential users of your systems. Rather than making guesses about what you "think" they need and how you "suspect" they might perform their work, you should spend some time with your user base and listen to their needs and desires. There are a number of ways to approach this, including the methods used by Extreme programmers (see the "Extreme Programming" sidebar). Many programming design systems highlight the need for programmers and designers to "listen" to the users and respond to their needs, as opposed to "imposing" their own beliefs on the users.

### Extreme Programming

A thorough discussion of extreme programming can be found at **http://www.extremeprogramming.org** and **http://www.xprogramming.com**. In short, extreme programming, or XP, is a new paradigm for programming that revolves around the concepts of simplicity and communication. It was designed for small teams of programmers who need to produce products quickly where the specifications are constantly changing. Sound familiar? The idea is that, by keeping things simple and by maintaining constant communications among the programmers on the team and between the programming team and the customer, a more satisfying product will be produced in a much shorter time more economically.

One of the truly novel aspects of XP is that XP teams begin by writing tests that will exercise all the facets of the final product *before* the product is created. Then a product is produced that will pass all the tests. As bugs are discovered, new tests are added to watch for these bugs, and the code is modified to fix the bugs. Tests are written before, during, and after the product is created. In this way, the product is being tested throughout the entire development process. In other words, when the final product is created, it has already been tested by design.

XP focuses on the idea of a team. The team includes the managers, the customers, and the programmers. The team concept keeps all parties involved in the development process at every step. In many traditional programming processes, the customer delivers a request for a product, and the programmers go off to create this product. When the product is delivered to the customer and he sees it in action, the customer then might be inspired by the working product to think of things that he should have asked for in the beginning but didn't think of. In the XP process, the customer is involved in the development every step of the way and can be driven to think of additions and changes to the design *while* the design is being implemented. In this way, the changes to the design can occur much more organically.

XP lists 12 practices that provide the structure for an XP project. Directly quoted from the **http://www.xprogramming.com** site[1], the practices and descriptions are:

1. **The Planning Process, sometimes called the Planning Game**—The XP planning process allows the XP "customer" to define the business value of desired features, and uses cost estimates provided

1. Jeffries, Ron. "What is eXtreme Programming?" XProgramming.com (July 2001). Available from the Internet: **http://www.xprogramming.com/what_is_xp.htm**.

by the programmers to choose what needs to be done and what needs to be deferred. The effect of XP's planning process is that it is easy to steer the project to success.

2. **Small Releases**—XP teams put a simple system into production early and update it frequently on a very short cycle.

3. **Metaphor**—XP teams use a common "system of names" and a common system description that guides development and communication.

4. **Simple Design**—A program built with XP should be the simplest program that meets the current requirements. There is not much building "for the future." Instead, the focus is on providing business value. Of course, it is necessary to ensure that you have a good design, and in XP this is brought about through "refactoring," discussed shortly.

5. **Testing**—XP teams focus on validation of the software at all times. Programmers develop software by writing tests first and then software that fulfills the requirements reflected in the tests. Customers provide acceptance tests that enable them to be certain that the features they need are provided.

6. **Refactoring**—XP teams improve the design of the system throughout the entire development. This is done by keeping the software clean: without duplication, with high communication, simple, yet complete.

7. **Pair Programming**—XP programmers write all production code in pairs, two programmers working together at one machine. Pair programming has been shown by many experiments to produce better software at similar or lower cost than programmers working alone.

8. **Collective Ownership**—All the code belongs to all the programmers. This lets the team go at full speed because, when something needs changing, it can be changed without delay.

9. **Continuous Integration**—XP teams integrate and build the software system multiple times per day. This keeps all the programmers on the same page and enables very rapid progress. Perhaps surprisingly, integrating more frequently tends to eliminate integration problems that plague teams who integrate less often.

10. **40-Hour Week**—Tired programmers make more mistakes. XP teams do not work excessive overtime, keeping themselves fresh, healthy, and effective.

11. **Onsite Customer**—An XP project is steered by a dedicated individual who is empowered to determine requirements, set priorities, and answer questions as the programmers have them. The effect of being there is that communication improves, with less hard-copy documentation—often one of the most expensive parts of a software project.

12. **Coding Standard**—For a team to work effectively in pairs and to share ownership of all the code, all the programmers need to write the code in the same way, with rules that make sure the code communicates clearly.

Let's suppose that after some discussions with the teachers and administrators of the New Millennium school system, you identify four basic areas of need:

- A calendar of activities and events that is easily available to everyone
- A way for teachers, administrators, parents, and students to share ideas (online discussions)
- A way to improve remote access to email without compromising security
- A way to track and organize feedback from teachers, administrators, parents, and students about various topics

### Public Announcements, the "One-Way" Web

In this chapter, we'll show you some ways to tackle the first issue just raised, that of an accessible calendar of events and activities. This type of system is "one-way." In other words, information is flowing in one direction, from the keepers of the calendar to the rest of the school community. Someone or some group will be responsible for adding events to the calendar that others can view. There is no flow of information back from the end user. Systems for two-way flow are discussed in the remaining chapters of Part II.

## Calendar Tag

The first need that we have identified is for an online calendar of events. Many companies have a need for just such a product, and, for that reason, you can assume that someone has probably already addressed this issue using Zope. In fact, this is true. Part of this problem can be solved using a powerful Zope product called, appropriately enough, the Calendar tag. We will be using version 1.0.6 for the following examples.

### A New DTML Tag Defined

The Calendar product can be obtained from the **`www.zope.org`** site. Its location is **`http://www.zope.org/Members/jdavid/Calendar`**. The installation instructions contained on the web page do not explain how to install this new tag. The instructions simply explain that before version 0.9.7, the package was installed from the Zope root directory and that now the package should be installed from the Products directory. Use the following instructions to install the Calendar product:

1. Download the zipped file to your Zope server.
2. Copy this file to $ZOPEROOT/lib/python/Products.
3. Unzip the Calendar-1.0.6.tar.gz file. On UNIX-flavored machines, you can type `gunzip Calendar-1.0.6.tar.gz`.
4. Next untar the resulting Calendar-1.0.6.tar file. On UNIX machines, type `tar -xvf Calendar-1.0.6.tar`. This produces a folder within the Products folder called Calendar.

5. Restart Zope from the Control Panel.
6. Now go into the Product Management folder within the Control Panel, and make sure that the Calendar product installed correctly. If the icon associated with the Calendar product is a small closed box, then everything is installed properly. If the product did not install properly, a message will indicate that the product is broken. In this case, you will need to try to download and install it again. If it still doesn't work, then you will need to consult one of the online discussion groups to see if anyone else has encountered similar problems and whether any solutions are presented. One very good resource for this kind of information is provided at **`http://zope.nipltd.com/public/lists.html`** (New Information Paradigms, Ltd.). The site maintains several discussion groups related to Zope and Zope development.

After downloading and installing the Calendar tag product and then restarting Zope, you will find that you have a new DTML tag to work with, `<dtml-calendar>`. To begin using this new tag, you will need to create a DTML object from which you can invoke this new tag. Start by creating a DTML method and giving it the ID `ViewableCalendar`. Actually, you can create either a DTML Method or a DTML Document because both allow you to write DTML code from which you can invoke the Calendar tag. A thorough discussion of the differences between a DTML Document and a DTML method is included in *The Zope Book*[2] and the "DTML Method Versus DTML Document" sidebar. After you have created the DTML method object, you need to edit its content to contain the code listed in Listing 3.1.

> **DTML Method Versus DTML Document**
>
> The differences between a DTML document and a DTML method are subtle but important. The main difference is that a DTML document is a complete object in and of itself, while a DTML method is a component of its container. What this means is that the concept of "self" for a DTML method is actually its container. For instance, the line `<dtml-var title>` in a DTML document would produce the expected title, whereas, in a DTML method, the line would produce the somewhat less expected title of the object that contains the method. The names give a clue to their usage. A DTML document is generally meant to contain content, whereas a DTML method is generally used to manipulate or display the content of another object.

A very simple example of the Calendar tag is shown in Listing 3.1.

Listing 3.1 **A Simple Use of the Calendar Tag**

```
<HTML>
<HEAD>
  <TITLE>New Millennium Event Calendar</TITLE>
```

*continues*

2. Latteier, Amos, and Michel Pellatier. *The Zope Book*. Indianapolis, IN: New Riders Publishing, 2001.

Listing 3.1 **Continued**

```
</HEAD>
<BODY>
  <CENTER>
  <dtml-calendar>
  </dtml-calendar>
  </CENTER>
</BODY>
</HTML>
```

As you can see, `<dtml-calendar>`, like most DTML tags, has both an opening and a closing tag. In this simple example, nothing is placed between the opening and closing tags. When the code in Listing 3.1 is viewed, the result is shown in Figure 3.1.

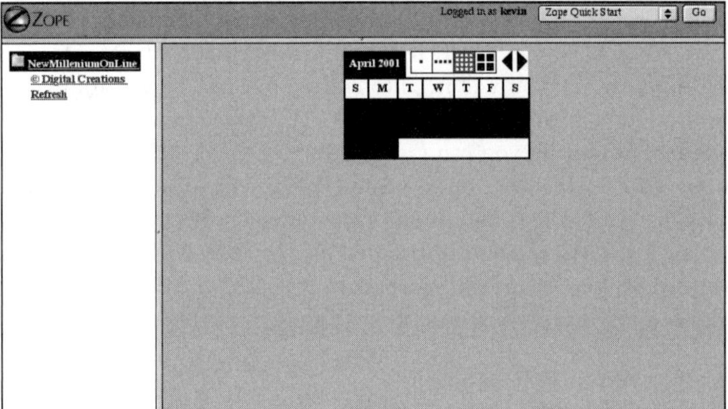


**Figure 3.1** Default display of calendar object.

This, by itself, is not very impressive, but it does have the basic look of what you might normally think of as a calendar, and all with only two extra lines of DTML. By its design, the Calendar tag is purely a display mechanism. It creates an HTML table with cells whose contents can be connected easily to date-specific information. As you can see from the previous example, the simplest use of the Calendar tag creates a table with a header that contains the month and year, plus several buttons that are used to control the layout of the calendar. Clicking the box with the single dot in it displays the current day. The next box with the single row of dots creates a display of the current week, followed by a box with a square array of dots for display of the current month. The final box containing the four large squares displays the entire year.

## Between the Tags

Although the calendar looks like a calendar, it will not be very useful unless you can attach useful information to the display. To do that, you need to know a little bit more about how the Calendar tag works. What goes on between the opening and closing tags?

The Calendar tag works like an iteration loop. The code enclosed by the beginning and ending tags is evaluated once for each of the days displayed by the calendar.

Place a simple text string in between the two Calendar tags, and see what the result is (see Listing 3.2).

Listing 3.2 **An Example of Simple Iteration Using the Calendar Tag**

```
<HTML>
<HEAD>
  <TITLE>New Millennium Event Calendar</TITLE>
</HEAD>
<BODY>
  <CENTER>
  <dtml-calendar>
    Have a good day!
  </dtml-calendar>
</CENTER>
</BODY>
</HTML>
```

When this code is rendered, Figure 3.2 is the result.

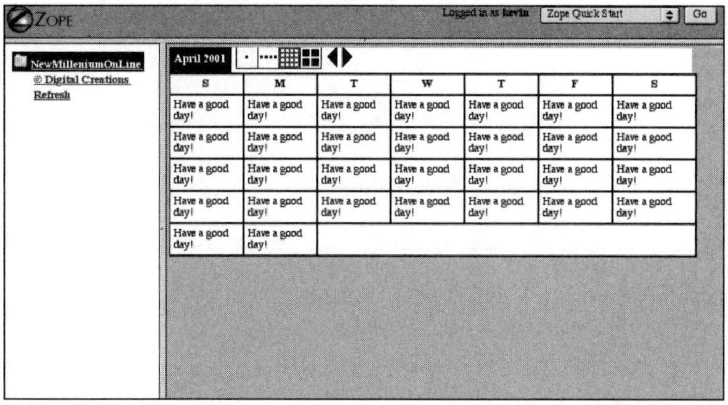

**Figure 3.2** Output of calendar with simple text string in all cells.

As you can see from Figure 3.2, the text enclosed by the Calendar tag is applied to each cell of the resulting table. Although this is interesting, it is not very useful because all of the information is the same. Let's do something that shows some variation from day to day.

During each pass through the Calendar tag loop, a date object is made available in the namespace that represents the day currently being rendered. This variable is named, appropriately, date. Replace the static text that you used in the previous example with some code that makes use of the dynamic date object. Listing 3.3 demonstrates the use of that date object.

Listing 3.3 **Use of the *date* Object Within the Calendar Tag**

```
<HTML>
<HEAD>
  <TITLE>New Millennium Event Calendar</TITLE>
</HEAD>
<BODY>
  <CENTER>
  <dtml-calendar>
    <dtml-var date>
  </dtml-calendar>
</CENTER>
</BODY>
</HTML>
```

When Listing 3.3 is rendered, the result is Figure 3.3.

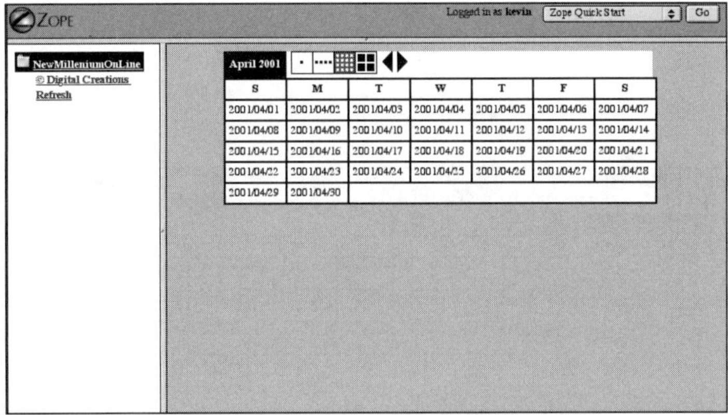


**Figure 3.3** Rendered calendar with date applied to each cell.

## Simple Event Objects

Notice now that the contents of each cell are different. In fact, the contents of each cell are connected, in a rather obvious way, with the actual date being displayed. In other words, with some logic and with data that is in some way associated with a particular date, your calendar actually becomes useful. The next thing to do is to find a way to store text information and then associate it with a particular date so that it can be quickly retrieved and inserted into your calendar. There are a number of ways to do this, from creating objects that are maintained in ZODB to retrieving information from an external database. We'll take a look at a very simple method here and then see other ways to enhance and improve on this in Chapter 7, "Delegations, Databases, and Users," and Chapter 11, "Design for Integration the ZPatterns Way." Keep in mind that one of our goals in this section is to help you get up and running as quickly as possible and to show you how to utilize existing objects and products. After you are up and functioning and satisfying the needs of your clients, you can go back and make improvements and enhancements with more customized objects.

One of the simplest ways to store textual information (content) in ZODB is to use a DTML document. The documents can contain whatever text you want to display in the cells of your calendar. Then, to associate each document with a particular date, you can give each document an ID that matches the desired date.

The default string representation of the date object contains forward slashes and, as such, is unacceptable for the ID of an object that will appear in a URL because slashes have special meaning in a URL. Therefore, you'll need to use the format yyyy-mm-dd as your DTML document ID.

You can begin by instantiating a DTML document through your web browser and then providing whatever text data you want to appear in the calendar as the content of the DTML document. When creating each document, remember to use the desired date (in the yyyy-mm-dd format) as the ID of the newly created document.

Next, to read the information into the appropriate cells, you will need a bit of DTML code between the opening and closing Calendar tags. Take a look at Listing 3.4.

Listing 3.4 **Use of the *date* Object Within the Calendar Tag**

```
01 <HTML>
02 <HEAD>
03   <TITLE>New Millennium Event Calendar</TITLE>
04 </HEAD>
05 <BODY>
06   <CENTER>
07   <dtml-calendar>
08     <dtml-let year="date.year()"
09       month="date.month()"
10       day="date.day()"
11       key="'%.2d-%.2d-%.2d' % (year,month,day)">
12       <dtml-var day><br>
13       <dtml-if "_.has_key(key)">
14         <dtml-var "_.getitem(key)">
15       </dtml-if>
16     </dtml-let>
17   </dtml-calendar>
18   </CENTER>
19 </BODY>
20 </HTML>
```

The DTML code includes a <dtml-let> in line 08, wherein you define a couple of variables that will be used within the loop. The first three assignments use the provided date object and call its `year()`, `month()`, and `day()` functions to obtain the associated values. The fourth assignment creates the date string that you will use as your ID for the DTML documents. For every pass through the loop, a string representing the ordinal value for each day is printed (<dtml-var date>).

> **Go to the Source**
>
> In Listing 3.4, three methods of the `date` object (`year()`, `month()`, and `day()`) were called. How do you find other methods that are available to the `date` object? Unfortunately, it is sometimes difficult to locate information about Zope components and products and how they are to be used. Often the best way to learn about a Zope object is to "go to the source." The source for the `date` object is found in the $ZOPEROOT/lib/python directory in a product folder called DateTime. The `date` object is actually an instantiation of a `DateTime` object. In the DateTime folder, you'll find several files. In particular, notice the file named DateTime.py. This is the main file that defines the `DateTime` object.
>
> Inside you'll find all kinds of treasures related to the `DateTime` object. You'll find definitions for methods such as `lessThan()` and `greaterThan()`, which can be used to compare two `DateTime` objects. You'll also find methods such as `earliestTime()` and `latestTime()`, which return new date objects that represent the earliest and latest times, respectively, that still fall within the day of the calling `DateTime` object. There are also a number of methods that help in formatting your output. As an example, notice the methods `month()`, `Month()`, and `aMonth()`. Each returns the month of the calling `DateTime` object, but the first returns the numeric, ordinal value of the month (for example, a day in March would return `3`). The second method returns the full month name as a string. The final method also returns a string but uses the abbreviated version of the month (for example, `Mar` instead of `March`). The `date` object is a very powerful object, and a thorough understanding of its inner-workings can bring great rewards in your future Zope developments.
>
> This capability to examine the source code of the inner workings of Zope is one of the things that makes it such a malleable tool. When you have questions about how to use an object, the source code should be one of the first places you go for help.

Next, the code determines whether an object with the associated ID exists. The underscore character represents the current namespace, and the `has_key()` method is one of the methods available within that namespace. The `has_key()` method checks in the current namespace to see whether an object exists with the associated ID. If it does exist, its contents are rendered by the `<dtml-var>` tag. If not, then nothing but the day string is printed.

To test this, create a DTML document in the current folder with the ID of `2001-04-15`. For contents, type the `string "Tax Day!"`. When the calendar is rendered, the contents of the document that you just created are displayed in the appropriate place in the calendar (see Figure 3.4).

## Avoiding Clutter by Isolating Events

You can continue to add DTML documents to the current folder as new events arise; however, the folder can get rather cluttered as the number of events rises. One way to avoid this is to create an Events folder in which to place all the DTML documents that contain event information. To do this, you will have to modify your DTML code within the Calendar tag to adjust your context to the Events folder. Listing 3.5 shows this modification.

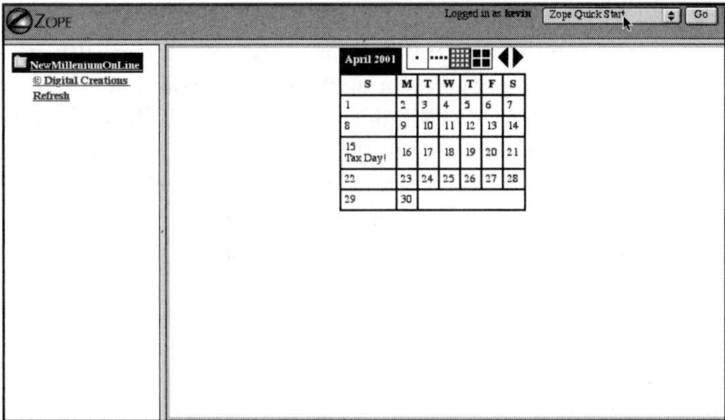


**Figure 3.4** Rendered calendar with simple text message on specific date.

Listing 3.5 **Use of a Separate Folder for Events**

```
01 <HTML>
02 <HEAD>
03   <TITLE>New Millennium Event Calendar</TITLE>
04 </HEAD>
05 <BODY>
06   <CENTER>
07     <dtml-calendar>
08       <dtml-let year="date.year()"
09         month="date.month()"
10         day="date.day()"
11         key="'%.2d-%.2d-%.2d' % (year,month,day)">
12       <dtml-var day><br>
13       <dtml-with Events>
14         <dtml-if "_.has_key(key)">
15           <dtml-var "_.getitem(key)">
16         </dtml-if>
17       </dtml-with>
18       </dtml-let>
19     </dtml-calendar>
20   </CENTER>
21 </BODY>
22 </HTML>
```

Notice how the `<dtml-with>` tag in line 13 of Listing 3.5 sets the current context to the Events folder. Other than the `<dtml-with>` tag, the code in Listing 3.5 is the same as that in Listing 3.4. Now when the `has_key()` method checks for the existence of a particular document (line 14), it is looking in the Events folder, not the local folder. As long as the document 2001-04-15 is located in the Events folder, the output will be the same as that shown in Figure 3.4.

Now you have a basic calendar system to which you can add, edit, and delete events all through the web using the standard Zope management interface. When someone in the school system asks you to put an event on the calendar, you simply go to the Events folder and determine whether a DTML document exists with the desired date as its ID. If so, you simply add the new event to the existing text contained in the document; otherwise, you create a new DTML document with the ID reflecting the desired date using the yyyy-mm-dd format, and add the event description to its content. The next time that the calendar is rendered, the new event description will appear on the desired day.

## User Control of the Calendar

This will work for a while. However, as more people ask you to add and remove things from the calendar, you will begin to wish that you could shift this responsibility to others in the administration. While the Zope web interface is very intuitive and easy to learn, it would be better if you could give your clients an easier way to add and edit events.

One way to accomplish this is by linking the date indicator at the top of each cell to another object that analyzes the selected date to determine whether an event document already exists for it. If it does, the user is taken directly to the `manage_editForm` for that document. If not, the object creates a new DTML document with the proper ID and then calls the `manage_editForm` for this new document. You can see from the code in Listing 3.6 that the date display is now linked to an object called `editEvent`. In addition, the object passes the date string that it created to the `editEvent` object as a parameter:

Listing 3.6 **Link to Object for Controlling Event Editing**

```
<HTML>
<HEAD>
  <TITLE>New Millennium Event Calendar</TITLE>
</HEAD>
<BODY>
  <CENTER>
    <dtml-calendar>
      <dtml-let year="date.year()"
        month="date.month()"
        day="date.day()"
        key="'%.2d-%.2d-%.2d' % (year,month,day)">
        <a href=editEvent?date=<dtml-var key>><dtml-var day></a><br>
        <dtml-with Events>
          <dtml-if "_.has_key(key)">
            <dtml-var "_.getitem(key)">
          </dtml-if>
        </dtml-with>
      </dtml-let>
```

```
    </dtml-calendar>
  </CENTER>
</BODY>
</HTML>
```

Next you need to create a DTML method object called `editEvent` that will make the determination about whether a document already exists for the selected day. Listing 3.7 is code for the `editEvent` object.

Listing 3.7 **DTML Code for Editing Event Objects**

```
01 <dtml-with Events>
02   <dtml-if "_.has_key(date)">
03     <dtml-call "RESPONSE.redirect(URL1 + '/Events/' + date
       ➥+ '/manage_editForm')">
04   <dtml-else>
05     <dtml-call "manage_addDTMLDocument(id=_['date'], title='',file='')">
06     <dtml-var editEvent>
07   </dtml-if>
08 </dtml-with>
```

Once again you establish the context to be the Events folder using the `<dtml-with Events>` tag in line 01. Next, check to see if a DTML document already exists with the desired date ID using the `has_key()` method of the current namespace (line 02). If one does, then call the `manage_editForm` method to allow the user to edit the text contained in the document. If the desired document does not exist, you create it with a call to `manage_addDTMLDocument` at line 05, and then you call `editEvent` again. The `manage_addDTMLDocument` method takes three arguments: `id`, `title`, and `file`. The `id` and `title` parameters map directly to the ID and title of the new document. The `file` parameter, if not empty, specifies a file whose contents are to be read in as the contents of the newly created DTML document. This time, the document will be found and the edit form for the document will be called.

The only problem that this presents is that now anyone can add and edit events associated with the calendar. This is probably not what your clients intended. In general, it would be better if everyone could view the calendar, while only a select few could edit it.

That can easily be accomplished with Zope's built-in security features. One way of doing it is to create a "view-only" calendar and an "editable" calendar. The view-only calendar can be made available to all users, while the editable calendar can be restricted to users with a specific role. The view-only calendar can be the same as the one shown previously, with the exception that the `<a href>` anchor is removed. That way, the `editEvent` method won't be accessible to the general public. The view-only calendar could then be linked from the public web site, while the editable calendar could remain in a private, manager's area of the web site. In addition, for further protection, the security access to the editable calendar could be set using the Security tab of the editable calendar object itself.

# TinyTablePlus

Although the calendar you've created so far satisfies the goal of getting something up and running quickly, it doesn't accomplish the goal of making it easily extensible.

Suppose, for example, that you now wish that you could include the starting time and ending time to your events. Of course, you could simply add that information as text to the existing description; however, there would be no easy way to extract the starting or ending time of an event or to search on that data. Another thing you could do is to add the starting and ending times as properties of each DTML document. This would make it easier for you to request either time from the document or to search for all the DTML documents that share a particular start time. However, as the number of events begins to get large, the searching process will begin to slow down. You need a better way to store these events so that they can be searched and categorized more easily.

An alternate way of creating event objects is to use another popular Zope object that is available from the zope.org site called a *TinyTablePlus*.

## A Mini Spreadsheet

TinyTablePlus can be downloaded from the zope.org site, but, at this writing, it is difficult to locate. For some reason, when you type TinyTablePlus into the search engine at **`www.zope.org`**, nothing particularly useful is returned. With some more poking around, you can locate the TinyTablePlus product at **`http://www.zope.org/Members/hathawsh/TinyTablePlus`**. TinyTablePlus is installed a bit differently than the Calendar tag:

1. Download the .tgz file to your Zope server.
2. Copy this file to $ZOPEROOT (*not* the Products folder, like you did for the Calendar tag).
3. Unzip the TinyTablePlus-0.9.tgz file. Type `gunzip TinyTablePlus-0.9.tgz`.
4. Next untar the resulting TinyTablePlus-0.9.tar file. Type `tar -xvf TinyTablePlus-0.9.tar`. This produces a folder way down in the /lib/python/Products folder called TinyTablePlus.
5. Restart Zope from the Control Panel.
6. Now go into the Product Management folder within the Control Panel, and make sure that the TinyTablePlus product installed correctly. Remember to check the user groups, if any problems occur.

Once the TinyTablePlus is installed, it will appear in the pop-up list of available objects.

Add a TinyTablePlus to the root of your current project, and give it the ID `eventTable`.

You'll notice that, in addition to a place for an ID and a title, there is a place for specifying column names. A TinyTablePlus is, like its name implies, a small table of data, and it can be used to simulate a small spreadsheet or database. In the new object creation step, you can specify how many columns the table will have and provide a name for each one.

For this project, create a TinyTablePlus with an ID of `eventTable` and with columns titled `eventDate`, `description`, `startTime`, and `endTime`. The names of the columns are separated by spaces, not by commas. This can be confusing because the data is separated by commas when entered. Like a standard spreadsheet, each row can be thought of as an individual record, with each column representing a different field of data.

Information for the table is provided as a list of comma-separated values, with rows being separated by a newline character. Strings are enclosed in single or double quotes, while numbers are entered in standard Python format.

In the `Data` field of the TinyTablePlus management screen, you can enter the information needed for each event, as shown in Figure 3.5.

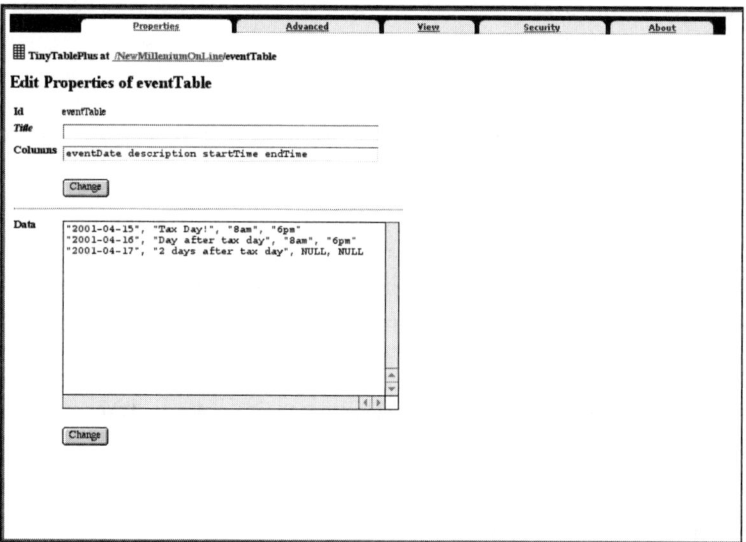


**Figure 3.5** Instantiation of a TinyTablePlus.

Once again, you will use the same date format that you used earlier for the ID as the first column data. Because it is a string, it should be enclosed in single or double quotes.

## Accessing Data in a TinyTablePlus

You can access data from a TinyTablePlus in three ways: using a full query, an index query, and a filter query. The query is specified using a `<dtml-in>` tag. A full query uses the name of the table in the tag:

```
<dtml-in eventTable>
    do something
</dtml-in>
```

In a *full query*, the entire table is iterated through row by row. During each iteration, the row data will be available in the namespace as variables, with the given column name as the key.

An *index query* makes use of the fact that the first column of data is unique. An automatic index is created on the first column data, which helps makes index queries fast. To implement an index query, a single value is passed to the table. The name of the data column to match is implicit, as follows:

```
<dtml-in "eventTable('2001-04-15')">
    do something
</dtml-in>
```

This would return the row of data where the first column is equal to `2001-04-15`, if it exists. In the case of an index query, no column name is specified. The first column is used by default.

The third query method is a filter query. A filter query is similar to an index query, except that the name of the column or columns to match is included in the `<dtml-in>` tag:

```
<dtml-in "eventTable(eventDate='2001-04-15',startTime='8am')">
    do something
</dtml-in>
```

For your project, you can make use of TinyTablePlus to store the information for each event so that you can easily query the table individually for each piece of data (`description`, `startTime`, `endTime`, and `eventDate`). See Listing 3.8.

Listing 3.8 **Calendar Object Calling TinyTablePlus for Event Data**

```
<HTML>
<HEAD>
  <TITLE>New Millennium Event Calendar</TITLE>
</HEAD>
<BODY>
  <CENTER>
    <dtml-calendar>
      <dtml-let year="date.year()"
        month="date.month()"
        day="date.day()"
        key="'%.2d-%.2d-%.2d' % (year,month,day)">
        <a href="eventTable/manage"><dtml-var day></a><br>
        <dtml-in "eventTable(eventDate=key)">
            <dtml-var startTime> - <dtml-var endTime><br>
```

```
              <dtml-var description>
            <br>
        </dtml-in>
      </dtml-let>
    </dtml-calendar>
  </CENTER>
</BODY>
</HTML>
```

Notice how the `<dtml-with>` and `<dtml-if>` tags from Listing 3.6 are replaced by a single `<dtml-in>` tag. Both the context setting and the conditional check are provided by the TinyTablePlus index query. If the requested key is located in the first column of TinyTablePlus, then the values of that row's `startTime`, `endTime`, and `description` field are printed; otherwise, nothing is printed.

Notice also the `<a href>` tag. It points to the manage screen of the `eventTable`. As before, you should include the `<a href>` tag in the editable calendar and leave it out for the view-only calendar.

TinyTablePlus also includes several methods for modifying the data in a TinyTablePlus from DTML or Python or Perl. The four methods are: `setRow`, `delRow`, `delAllRows`, and `getRows`.

The `setRow()`, `delRows()`, and `getRows()` methods all take a list of column names and values as parameters (for example, `setRow(columnName=value, columnName2=`value2,...)). The `delAllRows()` method takes no parameters. An example of `setRow()` follows:

```
<dtml-call "eventTable.setRow(eventDate='2001-4-17',
description='2 days after tax day')">
```

After the previous code is executed, the following entry will appear in the `eventTable`:

```
"2001-04-17", "2 days after tax day", NULL, NULL
```

Notice that for the columns that were not specified in the `setRow` call, the value `NULL` is inserted.

Now if the same code is executed again, another entry with exactly the same values will appear in the `eventTable`. In many cases, this may be the behavior you want; however, if you were attempting to replace the previous entry, you're going to have to make some changes to the table. For your project with the Calendar tag, the default behavior is perfect. It will allow you to add multiple events associated with the same day. When the code in Listing 3.8 is executed, entries in the table with the same `eventDate` value will be printed together in the appropriate spot on the calendar.

In the default case, no columns have any special significance over any others except the first column. Remember, however, that the first column is automatically used to produce an index that can be used for rapid searches. If you use an index query on a table in which you have more than one row with the same first-column value, the search will return only the last row containing that first column value. To return *all* the rows with the selected first-column data, you'll need to use a filter query with the name of the first column explicitly included. The line `<dtml-in "eventTable('2001-`

`04-15')">` produces only the last row in `eventTable` that has `2001-04-15` as its `eventDate` value, whereas `<dtml-in "eventTable(eventDate=key)">` produces all the desired rows of data.

Now suppose that instead of adding another row to the eventTable with the `eventDate` of `2001-04-15`, you want to edit the values in the existing row. To do this, you'll need to designate the first column of data as an index column. In an index column, the value for an entry must be unique to that column of the table. In other words, at most one row can contain a particular value in that column. You know that it was mentioned previously that the first column was already special in that an index is created on the data in that column. Unfortunately, the fact that this is so does not prevent `setRow` from adding new rows with the same value, thus resulting in the strange behavior described for an index query. To force an edit instead of an addition, you must further indicate to the TinyTablePlus that you want the column to contain only unique data. That way, when you call `setRow` with a first-column value that already exists, `setRow` will know to edit the existing row rather than adding a new row. In fact, when you attempt to use `setRow` to modify your TinyTablePlus, the `setRow` method will first determine whether any of the specified columns are index columns. If so, `setRow` then attempts to determine whether the table already contains a row with that exact data in the indexed column. If it finds a match, then the operation is an edit of that row; if not, it performs an addition to the table.

The way to designate that you want a column or columns to contain unique data is to include an asterisk (*) after the name of the column or columns, as shown in Figure 3.6.

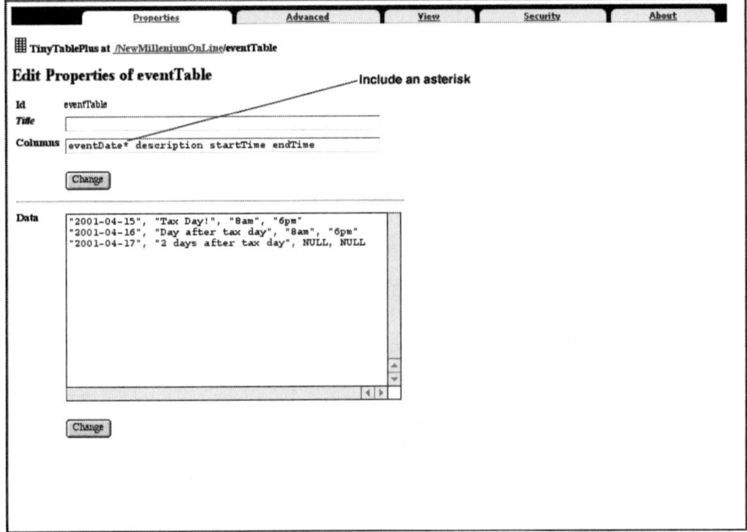


**Figure 3.6** Specifying a TinyTablePlus column as an index column.

Now using the `setRow`, `getRows`, `delRows`, and `delAllRows` methods, you can create an alternate interface for entering events into `eventTable` that might be more intuitive for your users than the standard management interface associated with the TinyTablePlus.

# ZCatalog

One of the main problems we had with maintaining event data in separate DTML documents was the issue of quick searches based on various properties of the event (for example, date, start time, end times, and so on). We introduced the TinyTablePlus as one means of handling the indexing issue. Another, much more powerful and flexible way is to use another Zope product called a *ZCatalog*. We will take a look at some of the basics of ZCatalogs, but a more thorough discussion can be found at **`http://www.zope.org`** and in *The Zope Book*.

## A Powerful Search Engine for Zope

A ZCatalog is a Zope object that is used to index objects and perform rapid searches on those indexed objects. When instantiated, a ZCatalog looks very much like a standard folder object. In fact, many of the tabs along the top are the very same tabs shared by folder objects. Like a folder, a ZCatalog can contain other objects. But in addition to containing other objects, a ZCatalog can catalog other objects. It is important to understand the difference between an object that is *contained* and one that is *catalogued*. Objects that are contained by the ZCatalog actually reside within the hierarchy of the ZCatalog. Objects that are catalogued by the ZCatalog may actually exist somewhere else, even other web sites.

When an object is catalogued, certain properties of the object are included in an index, plus the actual location of the object being catalogued is stored within the ZCatalog. In addition, some specially selected properties of the object called *metadata* are also stored in the database of the ZCatalog to facilitate rapid retrieval and use.

## Indexing, the Tough Part

The first thing you need to do is create a ZCatalog within your web site into which you will catalog your event documents. A ZCatalog can be instantiated at any level of your site by selecting it from the pull-down menu labeled Select Type to Add. After you select a ZCatalog as the type of object that you want to add, you will be asked to provide an ID for the new ZCatalog. Give it an ID of `EventCatalog`. You will also see a pop-up asking for the type of vocabulary to include with the new ZCatalog. Accept the default vocabulary.

Before you attempt to get objects into this new catalog, you need to specify what properties of the event objects you will be indexing. In other words, what properties of the object do you want to be able to search on? From our earlier discussions, it seems that you would want to index the ID of the objects because the calendar object needs to retrieve data based on this ID. Also, you might want to consider indexing the `startTime`. This would allow you to do things such as ask the ZCatalog to give you a list of all events that start before noon between two dates, or ask the ZCatalog to show you a list of events that occur after regular school hours. Any property upon which you want to search must be indexed.

To create an index, you click the ZCatalog that you created and then click its Indexes tab. This brings up a screen that describes the type of indexes available and the indexes that are already created by default (see Figure 3.7).

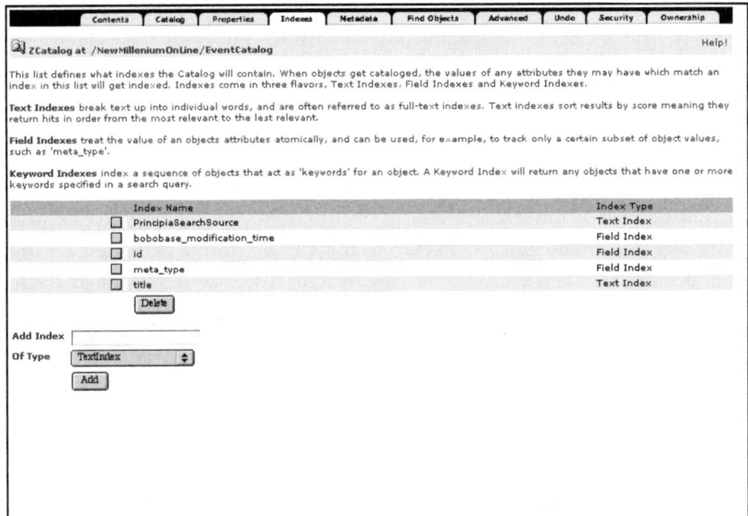


**Figure 3.7** Creating an index in a ZCatalog.

The use of ID as an index has already been included as one of the defaults. However, you'll need to add the `startTime` as an index. Before you can add this index, however, you'll need to decide what kind of index it is going to be.

You can see on the Indexes screen that there are three types of indexes defined: Text Indexes, Field Indexes, and Keyword Indexes.

*Text Indexes* break the contents of the property being indexed into individual words and index each separate word. What defines a word is specified in the Vocabulary object that was added to your ZCatalog when you instantiated it. The default vocabulary defines words as space-separated text. Other Vocabulary objects in the future might define "word" in a different way. Searches performed on a `Text Indexed` property function like a full-text search.

*Field Indexes* do not break the property contents into individual words, but rather analyze the contents of the property as a single unit for indexing purposes. To match using a Field Index, the entire contents of the object's property must match the specified search string. Field Indexes are especially useful when a property can have any of a number of predefined values.

How about the case where a property can contain multiple values at the same time? In these cases, a Keyword Index is best. *Keyword Indexes* will return a list of those cataloged objects where one or more of the keywords is contained in the associated property.

In this particular example of event objects, the `description` property might best be indexed using a Text Index. In other words, you might want to be able to search on any word contained in the description. A person might want a list of all the events where the word "PTA" is included in the description. For the `location` property, a Field Index would work best. Some possible values for the `location` are: `boiler room`, `gymnasium`, `lecture hall 1`, `lecture hall 2`, and `lecture hall 3`. A Text Index would not work well here. For instance, if someone attempted to search for all events being held in lecture hall 2 and the `location` property was indexed as a Text Index, the result list would include any event whose `location` property contained any of the words "lecture" *or* "hall" *or* "2." For that reason, events in any of the lecture halls and any events in the study hall would show up. However, if you make the `location` index a Field Index, then the search will look only for the complete permutation of the words "lecture hall 2."

As an example of the use of the Keyword Index, add a property to your event object called `invitees`. This property will be a "list" type property because you want it to contain multiple values. Imagine a list of possible values for this field that includes "teachers," "students," "parents," "administrators," "smart people," "happy people," and "all." Each of these entities can be thought of as a "keyword." The value for the `invitees` property can contain more than one of these "keywords." If a particular event were available to `teachers` and `happy people` only, then its `invitees` property would contain both values. If a search were made for events where "happy people" were invited, the returned list would be highly dependant upon what type of index was created on the `invitees` property. If the index is a Field Index, then the search will return those events to which *only* "happy people" are invited. Events to which "happy people" and "teachers" are both invited will not be returned because the Field Index looks at the *entire* contents of the property. It works like a logical AND filter. If the index is a Text Index, it still doesn't work as you expect. The returned list will include events that might be only for "smart people" because the Text Index indexes each word separately (that is, "happy" AND "people"). A Keyword Index is exactly what you need for this property. Remember the Keyword Index returns any object where *one or more* of the keywords is contained in the property. The event to which "happy people" and "teachers" are invited will be properly returned because the keyword "happy people" is *one* of the values in the `invitees` property of the event. See how it works?

Specifying the indexes is only half of the job. Indexes indicate what properties are important on the input or search side of things. On the output or report side of things, you need to tell the ZCatalog what properties you want it to include in its database for reporting purposes. This is accomplished by using the Metadata tab of the ZCatalog. Any fields of data that you think you might like to display when reporting back results from a search should be included in the metadata table. Keep in mind that *all* the data for a particular object is available if the object is accessed directly. For the results of a search, it would be time-consuming to access every object and extract its properties just to produce a search report. The report should probably show only enough data to help the end user make a choice on which object he is really looking for. When that determination is made, the user can select the actual object and extract its data directly. Only those properties that would be useful in a report should be included in the metadata table.

In the case of DTML documents, the *content* contained in the document has a property name of `PrincipiaSearchSource`. This name is historical (as well as hysterical) in nature. Zope was a combination of two different projects called Bobo and Principia. If you want to include the contents of the DTML documents in your reports, you'll need to include `PrincipiaSearchSource` as one of the metadata table elements.

Now that you have created the desired indexes for your catalog and have selected the metadata that you want to be available quickly for reporting, you need to get the objects that you want to catalog actually *into* the catalog. There are two methods for accomplishing this:

- Use the Find Objects feature of the catalog.
- Have the objects themselves automatically communicate changes to the catalog when they are created, edited, or deleted.

We'll save this second method for Chapter 11, when we talk about ZClasses, and then further when we discuss DataSkins and SkinScripts.

For now, we'll look at using the Find Objects feature of the catalog to incorporate objects into the catalog. Go back to the Events folder that you created earlier in this chapter. Add three events with IDs of `2001-04-15`, `2001-04-16`, `2001-04-17`; put the event descriptions "Tax Day!", "day after tax day", and "2 days after tax day" into their respective content areas. Also go into the properties area for each of these documents and give each a `startTime`, `endTime`, `location`, and `invitees` property.

Next, click the Find Objects tab of the EventCatalog object and select DTML Document as the type of object to find. You'll notice that there are several other ways to limit the scope of the objects that will be "found" to the catalog. For your events project, simply choose to find DTML documents. The catalog will then search the catalog's container and all its subcontainers for DTML document objects. It will find the DTML documents that you have created in the Events folder and acquire the required information about them. It will create the selected indexes for these objects and incorporate the actual location of each of these objects into its database.

## Search Forms

When the objects are in the ZCatalog's database, you need to create ways to search on the indexed properties and return selected data to a user.

A quick and simple way to create a page for querying a ZCatalog and for reporting results back is to use another Zope object called a *Z Search Interface* object. A Z Search Interface works with any searchable Zope database object (such as a Z SQL method object). When you instantiate a Z Search Interface object, it enables you to specify which of the available searchable Zope databases to use (in this case, the EventCatalog), plus it gives you the capability to choose between Tabular and Records as output for the resulting report. You can also specify an ID for both the input form and the output report. The input form ID is optional. If you choose not to create an input form, then the resulting output report simply produces a basic accounting of all the objects in the database. If an input form ID is included, then a default search form is created, including all the properties that were indexed. Both forms are intended to be edited because they both exhibit simplistic behavior.

For the calendar project, you need to perform the searches programmatically with no user input. To search the ZCatalog from DTML, you use a similar syntax to your call to the TinyTablePlus (see Listing 3.9).

Listing 3.9 **Calendar Object Using EventCatalog for Event Data**

```
01 <HTML>
02 <HEAD>
03   <TITLE>New Millennium Event Calendar</TITLE>
04 </HEAD>
05 <BODY>
06   <CENTER>
07     <dtml-calendar>
08       <dtml-let year="date.year()"
09         month="date.month()"
10         day="date.day()"
11         key="'%.2d-%.2d-%.2d' % (year,month,day)">
12         <dtml-var day><br>
13         <dtml-in "EventCatalog({'id':key})">
14             <dtml-var startTime> - <dtml-var endTime><br>
15               <dtml-var PrincipiaSearchSource>
16             <br>
17         </dtml-in>
18       </dtml-let>
19     </dtml-calendar>
20   </CENTER>
21 </BODY>
22 </HTML>
```

Notice that the <dtml-in> line has changed slightly (line 13). It makes a call to the EventCatalog, but instead of passing in a simple equation like you did in Listing 3.8 for TinyTablePlus, the parameter to the EventCatalog is an object known as a dictionary.

A dictionary is enclosed in braces and includes at least one key/value pair. The key and its value are separated by a colon. Additional key/value pairs, if they are used, are separated from others by a comma. The key or keys used are indexed column names, and the value is the value to search on. The code in Listing 3.9 asks the ZCatalog to return the event whose ID is the key value, if that event exists. If there is an object in its database that matches the selected search criteria, it makes available within the `<dtml-in>` loop the metadata associated with object. Because one of the metadata values is the PrincipiaSearchSource data, you can use that in the loop. If the ZCatalog doesn't find a match, then nothing is printed.

This works fine, but you still have a major problem. Remember, you used the date of the event as the ID for the DTML document. Because the IDs of objects within a container must be unique, this leaves you with the dilemma that you can have only one event object per day. But also remember the reason that you originally chose to use the date as the ID. It was to facilitate easy location of the object. With the ZCatalog, you now have a better method of doing the same thing. So give up the notion of making the ID relate to the date of the event, and add a property to the DTML documents that is the date of the event. Call it `eventDate`, like you did with the TinyTablePlus example. Now you can make the ID anything you like.

To make this work, you simply go back and add the `eventDate` as a property to each DTML document and place the current ID string in as data. Then add `eventDate` as an index to the EventCatalog (make it a Field Index), and add `eventDate` as an entry in the metadata table so that you can use it for output. Finally, change the code shown in Listing 3.9 to Listing 3.10.

Listing 3.10 **Modified Calendar Object Using EventCatalog for Event Data**

```
<HTML>
<HEAD>
  <TITLE>New Millennium Event Calendar</TITLE>
</HEAD>
<BODY>
  <CENTER>
    <dtml-calendar>
      <dtml-let year="date.year()"
       month="date.month()"
       day="date.day()"
       key="'%.2d-%.2d-%.2d' % (year,month,day)">
        <dtml-var day><br>
        <dtml-in "EventCatalog({'eventDate':key})">
            <dtml-var startTime>- <dtml-var endTime><br>
              <dtml-var PrincipiaSearchSource>
            <br>
        </dtml-in>
      </dtml-let>
    </dtml-calendar>
  </CENTER>
</BODY>
</HTML>
```

Notice that the key name passed into the EventCatalog in line 13 of Listing 3.10 is now `eventDate`, the name of the new property you've added. Now that you've removed the dependence of the ID on the date of the event, you can have multiple event objects for the same day. Each event exists as a separate DTML document that can be independently edited and searched. Now you're getting close to a usable model for managing events that you can tie back to your calendar object.

## ZClasses

Although this method of using DTML documents to store your event information and then using a ZCatalog to index those documents works fairly well, it suffers from a serious drawback. Suppose that you create several hundred events as DTML documents and then decide that you need to add another property, such as `MeetingCoordinator`. At this point, you would have to go back to each one of those event documents and add a property to them for `MeetingCoordinator`. Although this method works for now, it is not very flexible and doesn't allow for easy upgradeability. You need a better way. The solution is customized Zope products.

One of the powers of Zope is that it can be easily customized and enhanced. You can extend Zope's capabilities by creating your own objects. Extensions to Zope are contained in *Products*. Products can be written in the Python programming language, or they can be created through the web interface to Zope. Products created through the web are composed of *ZClasses*. ZClasses are the secret to solving your extensibility issue.

When you add a new property to your DTML documents representing events, those properties are applied only to the individual instance being edited. What you'd like is a way of adding a property that immediately gets added to *all* the instances of the object, even after they have been instantiated. In other words, you need to be able to add properties at the object description level as opposed to the object instance level.

To add a ZClass to Zope, you go to the Control Panel at the root of your Zope installation. Go into the Product Management section, and there you will see the Products that are currently appended to your Zope installation. Click the Add Product button, and you will be asked to give an ID to your new product. Call it CalendarEvent.

When the product is created, you will see a small box icon named CalendarEvent. Click the icon to open your new product. Within the product are all the objects that you can instantiate in other parts of your Zope site. In the list, you will see an entry for ZClass. Choose to add a ZClass to your product.

### Creating a ZClass

Follow these steps to create a new ZClass:

1. To create a new ZClass, you are required to provide an ID for the class and a metatype. Both are required. The metatype is the name that will be used to define the object type for instances of this new class. For this project, give the new ZClass an ID of `CalendarEvent` and the same for its metatype.

2. Leave the Create Constructor Objects? and Include Standard Zope Persistent Object Base Classes? boxes checked. Now you will need to select the base classes for your new ZClass. Base classes are existing classes that have behavior that you need in your new class. You can *inherit* behavior and properties from existing classes, thus saving you time in development. You don't have to "reinvent the wheel" every time.
3. DTML documents have inherent behavior that you've already found useful for your earlier event objects. For this reason, select DTML document as one of your base classes for this new ZClass. Now click the Add button to create this ZClass definition.
4. Click the CalendarEvent itself so that you can finish defining it. The first screen that you will see is the Methods screen. This new object is a container object and, as such, can contain other objects. It currently contains no objects, but you can add methods and other objects to it just like you can a folder (see Figure 3.8).

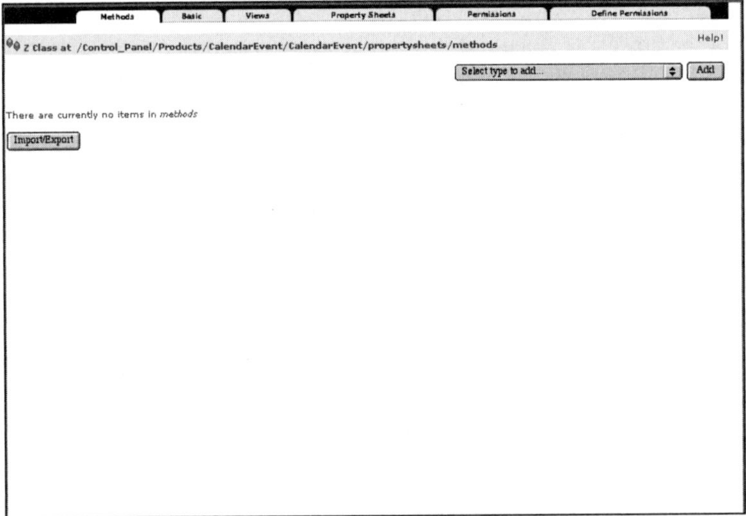


**Figure 3.8** Management screens for defining a new ZClass.

For now, we'll skip over the next two tabs: the Basic tab and the Views tab. The Basic tab contains the basic descriptions of the object, such as the base classes and the metatype for this new ZClass. The Basic screen is also where you can specify an icon to represent your new ZClass. You can enter a path for the icon image, or you can use the Browse button to locate the image that you want to use for your new ZClass. For the moment, we'll skip the Views tab and go directly to the next tab.

The most important tab for your purposes is the Property Sheets tab. Property sheets are lists of the properties that all instances of your ZClass share. Click the button to Add Common Instance Property Sheet. You will be asked to supply an ID for the new property sheet. For this project, call the new property sheet Fundamental.

Now open the Fundamental property sheet and add some properties to it. You add the properties the same way you did for each DTML document. Add properties as shown in Figure 3.9.

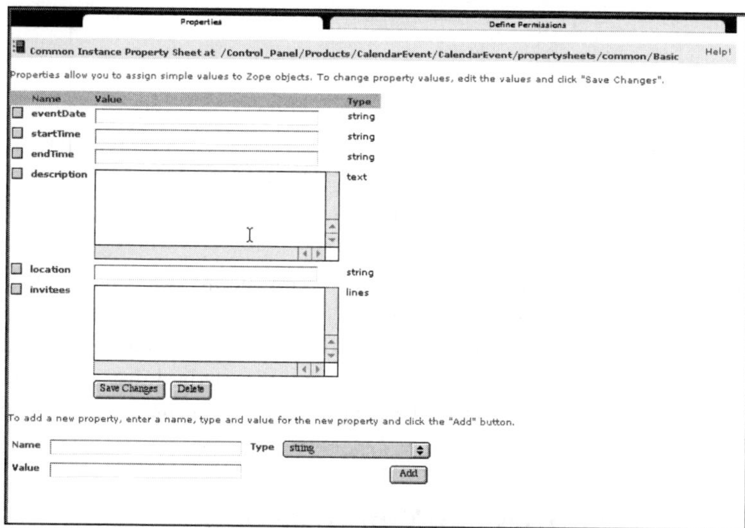


**Figure 3.9** CalendarEvent Fundamental property sheet.

Now for the Views tab. Views are associated with the management of objects. You can create rendering methods or editing screens for your ZClasses and then associate views with these methods or screens. The names of the views appear at the top of the main management screen for the class. Several views are standard when you create a new ZClass, but you can create whatever custom views you need. You also can associate the various views with a number of different methods, including custom-designed methods. The first view in the list is the default view that is presented when an object is referenced. In this case, the default view is the Edit view.

The default method for the Edit view is the standard management screen for a DTML document (remember that you based your new class on the DTML document class). What you'd really like when you edit an instance of a CalendarEvent is to have the edit screen for the Fundamental property sheet show up. You can do that by selecting the Views tab (see Figure 3.10).

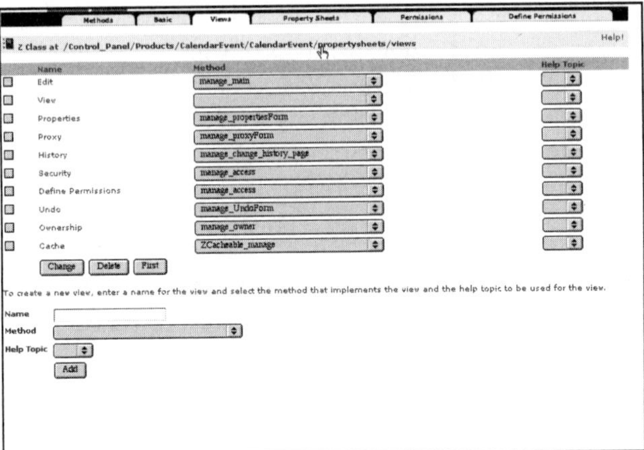


**Figure 3.10** Creating an index in a ZCatalog.

Notice that the Edit view is currently associated with the method `manage_main`. This is not the method that you want if you want to give access to the new properties that you just created. Click the pop-up menu, and you'll see that there is an entry in the list for `propertysheets/Fundamental/manage`. This is the method that you really want to associate with the Edit view. Select the `propertysheets/Fundamental/manage` method and click Change.

## Incorporating ZClasses into Your System

Now when you return to the development area of the web site, you will find that the `CalendarEvent` shows up in the pop-up menu of available objects to add. Go into the Events folder and create an instance of a `CalendarEvent`. You can give it any ID you'd like because you no longer have the dependence of linking the ID to the date of the event. To keep things simple, choose an ID of `1`. The object will show up in the Events folder. When you click the newly created object, the default (Edit) view will appear. Values can be provided to all the properties that you defined earlier when you created the CalendarEvent class.

Create several `CalendarEvent` objects and then fill in the Fundamental property sheet for each. Next, return to the `EventCatalog` and remove the DTML documents currently stored there. Go to the Indexes area, and create an index on the `eventDate` property. Next edit the metadata table elements. Make sure that you include the `description` property. Remember that previously the description was contained in the content area of the DTML document and was referenced by the `PrincipiaSearchSource` property. To use the description of the event now, you need to include the `description` property in the table of metadata. Finally, edit the `ViewOnlyCalendar` method, as shown in Listing 3.11.

Listing 3.11 **ViewOnlyCalendar Using CalendarEvent ZClass Objects**

```
<HTML>
<HEAD>
  <TITLE>New Millennium Event Calendar</TITLE>
</HEAD>
<BODY>
  <CENTER>
    <dtml-calendar>
      <dtml-let year="date.year()"
       month="date.month()"
       day="date.day()"
       key="'%.2d-%.2d-%.2d' % (year,month,day)">
        <dtml-var day><br>
        <dtml-in "EventCatalog({'eventDate':key})">
            <dtml-var startTime>- <dtml-var endTime><br>
              <dtml-var description>
            <br>
        </dtml-in>
      </dtml-let>
    </dtml-calendar>
  </CENTER>
</BODY>
</HTML>
```

For the EditableCalendar, you can use the code in Listing 3.12.

Listing 3.12 **EditableCalendar Using CalendarEvent ZClass Objects**

```
<HTML>
<HEAD>
  <TITLE>New Millennium Event Calendar</TITLE>
</HEAD>
<BODY>
  <CENTER>
    <dtml-calendar>
      <dtml-let year="date.year()"
       month="date.month()"
       day="date.day()"
       key="'%.2d-%.2d-%.2d' % (year,month,day)">
        <dtml-var day><br>
        <dtml-in "EventCatalog({'eventDate':key})">
            <a href=<dtml-var absolute_url>><dtml-var startTime>-
            <dtml-var endTime></a><br>
              <dtml-var description>
            <br>
        </dtml-in>
      </dtml-let>
    </dtml-calendar>
  </CENTER>
</BODY>
</HTML>
```

Listing 3.12 produces a calendar display where the event can be clicked to bring up the edit screen for the chosen event.

Now you're getting somewhere! You have a custom-designed event class with which you can store event information. Plus, you can have more than one event on a specified day without conflict. Also, you have a mechanism for indexing and searching these events, and a display mechanism for presenting these events in a familiar calendar format.

# Python Scripts

There's another powerful tool in Zope that was introduced in Chapter 2, and it comes into play more heavily here. It's *Python*, the programming language upon which Zope is based. Although DTML is a useful language and is pretty powerful, it is really designed for display issues, just as HTML is. When you start making calculations and logical decisions, you need to move out of the realm of DTML and into the domain of Python. Throughout most of this chapter, you have seen how DTML can incorporate some basic logic and perform calculations, but, in most of those cases, the work is being done inside of double quotes. The stuff inside those double quotes is really Python code. Although it appears in the context of a DTML statement, it is really working at the Python level.

Another, cleaner way of getting to Python is through the use of another Zope object called a *Script (Python)* object. Python Scripts are Zope objects that enable you to work in Python and to have access to most of the libraries and modules available to Python programmers (with a few exceptions made for security) and, in addition, to have available the namespace of the calling Zope object. This means that you can make use of all the objects and variables that you could in a DTML method, without the cumbersome structure of DTML.

## A First Look

Take the `ViewOnlyCalendar` code from Listing 3.11, and add a link to a method called `displayEventDescription` around `startTime` and `endTime`. Pass the key to this script as the `eventDate` (see Listing 3.13).

Listing 3.13 **ViewOnlyCalendar Using link to Python Script**

```
<HTML>
<HEAD>
  <TITLE>New Millennium Event Calendar</TITLE>
</HEAD>
<BODY>
  <CENTER>
    <dtml-calendar>
      <dtml-let year="date.year()"
        month="date.month()"
        day="date.day()"
        key="'%.2d-%.2d-%.2d' % (year,month,day)">
```

```
            <dtml-var day><br>
             <dtml-in "EventCatalog({'eventDate':key})">
                   <a href="displayEventDescription?eventDate=<dtml-var
                   ➥startTime> - <dtml-var endTime></a><br>
                     <dtml-var description>
                   <br>
          </dtml-in>
        </dtml-let>
      </dtml-calendar>
    </CENTER>
  </BODY>
</HTML>
```

Create a Python script with an ID of `displayEventDescription` and enter the code from Listing 3.14.

Listing 3.14 **Python Script to Display CalendarEvents Description**

```
01 the Event = container.EventCatalog({'id':context.REQUEST['key']})
02 print theEvent.description
03 return printed
```

Let's briefly analyze this code. Line 01 references a "container" object and a "context" object. Where do they come from? When a Python Script is called, it is automatically bound to the object that contains the script. The default name for this object is `container`. In addition, the script is bound to the object on which the script is called. Sometimes this is the container, but it might be different depending on the URL used to access the script. This object is called `context`.

Go to the Bindings tab of the Python Script to see what other things are automatically bound to the script when it is called. When you click the Bindings tab, you'll see a list of five different things: Context, Container, Script, Namespace, and Subpath. Here are the definitions as they appear on the Bindings page associated with the script:

- **Context**—This represents the object through which this script is being called. In the URL **`http://www.domain.com/container1/container2/container3/myObject/myMethod`**, `myMethod` is being called in the "context" of `myObject`. In other words, even if `myMethod` is up at the root of your Zope installation and `myObject` is several levels down in some containers, the way `myMethod` views things is the way it would view things if it were in the same neighborhood as `myObject`. Now the context for `myMethod` can change even if the location of `myMethod` doesn't. If another object higher up in the hierarchy calls `myMethod`, **`http://www.domain.com/container1/anotherObject/myMethod`**, `myMethod`'s view will now be the same as `anotherObject`.
- **Container**—This represents, very simply, the object in which this script is contained, its immediate parent.
- **Script**—This represents the actual script itself. Once again, this is a fairly straightforward concept.

- **Namespace**—When the script is called from DTML, this is the caller's DTML namespace; otherwise, it is an empty namespace. It gives the script access to all the variables and objects that were available to its calling object.
- **Subpath**—When this script is invoked from a URL, this represents the portion of the string *after* the name of the script. In other words, if this script is named myScript, it is invoked using the URL **`http://www.domain.com/myScript/folder1/object1`**. Subpath = folder1/object1.

Now when the event `startTime/endTime` is clicked in the `ViewOnlyCalendar`, the description of the selected event is displayed. Line 01 retrieves the selected event from the EventCatalog. Line 02 prints the `description` property of theEvent object. Every print statement in a Python script is buffered up until the end of the script. If the Python script is to actually print anything, it must end with the line `return printed` (line 03). This allows the print buffer to be emptied back to the web browser.

Now for a more complex example. Take the EditableCalendar code from Listing 3.12 and add a link to a method called `createNewEvent` around the day of the week (see Listing 3.15).

Listing 3.15 **EditableCalendar Using Link to Python Script**

```
<HTML>
<HEAD>
<TITLE>New Millennium Event Calendar</TITLE>
<HEAD>
<BODY>
  <CENTER>
    <dtml-calendar>
      <dtml-let year="date.year()"
       month="date.month()"
       day="date.day()"
       key="'%.2d-%.2d-%.2d' % (year,month,day)">
            <a href=createNewEvent?eventDate=<dtml-var key><dtml-var
            ➥day><</a><br>
             <dtml-in "EventCatalog({'eventDate':key})">
                <a href=<dtml-var absolute_url>><dtml-var startTime>-
                <dtml-var endTime></a><br>
                  <dtml-var description>
                <br>
             </dtml-in>
          </dtml-let>
        </dtml-calendar>
     </CENTER>
   </BODY>
   </HTML>
```

Notice that the added link around the day of the week calls a method named `createNewEvent` and passes it the key string in the parameter `eventDate`. Instantiate a Script (Python) object and give it the ID `createNewEvent`. The new Python script should include the following code in Listing 3.16.

Listing 3.16 **Python Script to Create New CalendarEvents**

```
01 newob = container.Events.manage_addProduct['CalendarEvent'].CalendarEvent.
   ➥createInObjectManager(`context.ZopeTime().timeTime()`,context.REQUEST)
02 newob.propertysheets.Basic.manage_changeProperties(context.REQUEST)
03 context.REQUEST.RESPONSE.redirect(newob.absolute_url() +
   ➥'/propertysheets/Basic/manage')
```

This Python code in Listing 3.16 takes the `eventDate` that was passed in to the script and creates a new CalendarEvent with the `eventDate` already set.

In Listing 3.16, we make use of the container object that is bound to the script. Line 01 calls the `manage_addProduct` method of the Events folder, which is a subobject of your container. The `manage_addProduct` method take a metatype as its argument. It continues by passing an ID and the REQUEST object to the ObjectManager. In this case, the code uses the method `timeTime()` of the ZopeTime object to create a unique ID. The reverse quotes are used to convert the resulting floating-point number to its string representation. The REQUEST object contains the parameter `eventDate`, which the code then passes to the Basic property sheet of the new object to automatically set the `eventDate`. Finally, the code redirects to the manage screen for the Basic property sheet, where you will see that the `eventDate` has already been filled in. At this point, you (or, ultimately, the person managing the calendar) can add the other properties for the event.

When the Save Changes button is clicked, the new event will be ready and available in the Events folder. However, the new event will not yet appear in the calendar because it is not yet in the EventCatalog. It is necessary to get the new event into the catalog. To do this, you should create another Python script; call it `catalogAllEvents`. This script will remove all the items currently in the catalog and perform the Find to Catalog function that you used earlier in this chapter. The code for `catalogAllEvents` is shown in Listing 3.17.

Listing 3.17 **Python Script to Place CalendarEvents into the EventCatalog**

```
import string
container.EventCatalog.manage_catalogClear()
for theObject in container.Events.objectValues('CalendarEvent'):
                container.EventCatalog.catalog_object(theObject, string.
                      join(theObject.getPhysicalPath(),'/'))
return "The catalog has been re-populated."
```

Now, the process to add an event to your calendar involves clicking on the day in the EditableCalendar and then filling in the properties for the event. When you have entered all the pertinent data for the new event, click the Save Changes button at the bottom of the screen, and the event will be created in the Events folder. While the event object now exists, it must somehow be incorporated into the catalog. To do this, execute the `catalogAllEvents` method. In fact, an easier procedure might be to enter several new events before running the `catalogAllEvents` method. Still, this is a bit cumbersome, and it would be nice if you could automate this in some way. In fact, there are several ways that you can automate this process that we will discuss in future chapters. In Chapter 4, "Zope Discussion Tools," we will be looking further at ZClasses and, in particular, at the base class, CatalogAware. This base class makes adding an object to a catalog much easier. In Chapter 5, "Web Mail," we will work with XRON, an object for scheduling periodic tasks. This task could be connected with XRON to make it easier for the calendar manager to use. Finally, in Chapter 11, you will be introduced to the very powerful concept of ZPatterns and will see an even easier way to manage the automatic cataloging of objects.

## EventFolder

Another nifty Zope product that is available for download is called EventFolder, written by Jeff Sasmor. This product has a lot of the features we've been creating here in Chapter 3. If this is true, you might be wondering, why didn't we skip all this previous work and introduce you to EventFolder right away? There are three main reasons:

- After seeing all the pieces involved and the development of those pieces, you can more clearly appreciate what a drop-in product, such as EventFolder, does for you and all the time it saves.
- You might be better prepared to modify it if you find a bug or it doesn't do everything you need.
- We hope, through this book, to help you further develop your skills for writing your own Zope products, and the best way to do this is to have you develop your own code. EventFolder can be downloaded from **`http://www.zope.org/Members/jeffsasmor/EventFolder`**. The latest version at the time of this writing is version 1.31. You can see a demonstration of this product at Jeff's site, **`http://www.netkook.com`**.

## Summary

In this chapter, we introduced you to several Python products that can be used with minor modification to produce highly useful results. These objects will be visited again in Chapter 5, where we will help you refine the work you did in this chapter to make things cleaner, faster, and more easily extensible.

# 4

# Zope Discussion Tools

THIS CHAPTER COVERS SOME MORE of the drop-in Zope products that can help make web site development quick and painless. In particular, it covers products that help facilitate two-way communication through the web. Chapter 3, "Web Event Publishing," looked at the one-way web and how information could be presented or published to end users via the web. This chapter looks at several ways to allow those users to deliver information back to you through the web. Specifically, five popular Zope products are covered that are designed for collaborative work on the web. When you begin to talk about information coming into your web site from the outside, it is time to start thinking about security. This chapter begins with a discussion of security as it applies to Zope.

## Zope Security Issues

One of the most powerful aspects of Zope is its built-in security system. To understand and use the security features of Zope, you'll need to clearly understand the terms *role*, *permission*, and *user* and what they mean in the context of Zope.

A *permission* is the right to perform some action within Zope. One of the most basic permissions is the permission to view objects. If the view permission is not given, then objects cannot be viewed through the browser. When Zope is installed, a long list of permissions is created as a default set. These permissions relate to the basic operation of Zope itself and the default objects that are included with Zope. As new products are added, additional permissions may be defined and added to the list automatically.

A *role* is the term given to a specific configuration of permission settings. A role is given a name, and then each of the listed permissions is either granted or denied for that role.

The concept of a *user* is the way Zope assigns roles and, consequently, permissions to individuals. When a person browses a Zope site, he is assigned, by default, a generic user status of anonymous. Until that user authenticates with a username and password, he maintains the status of anonymous. An anonymous *user* is assigned the *role* of anonymous with whatever *permissions* are granted to the anonymous role.

Roles and permissions are accessed through the Security tab, as shown in Figure 4.1. Roles and permissions can be defined at all levels of a Zope installation. When a role or permission is defined at the root level, then it is available to all objects within the Zope installation. If a role or permission is defined down in the hierarchy of a Zope installation, then acquisition rules apply and the role or permission is available only to those objects that acquire it.

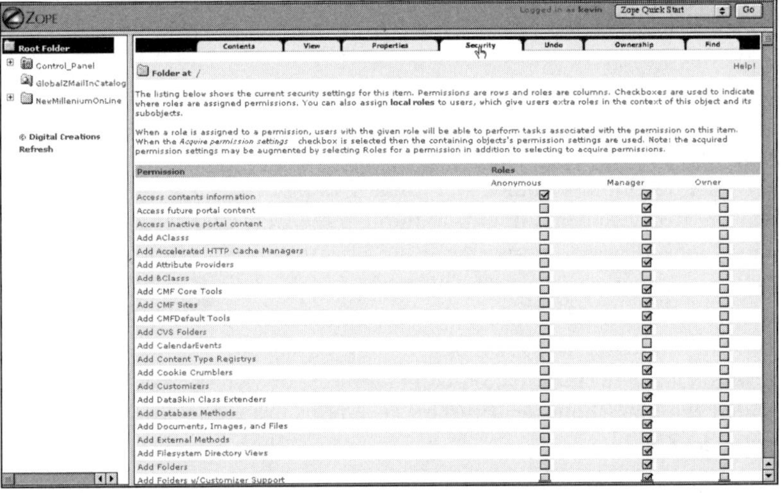


**Figure 4.1** Zope Security tab.

When Zope is installed, three roles are created automatically: *anonymous*, *manager*, and *owner*.

Anonymous is the role assigned to anyone who comes to the Zope site via the web, unless that user is asked to authenticate as a particular user. In general, you should be very careful what permissions you grant to an anonymous user. If you change the default permissions for the role anonymous, think carefully about the reasons for the change. Make sure that it is really necessary. If a permission grants too much power to an anonymous user, maybe it is time to think about creating a specific login for certain users and granting that permission only to those authenticated users.

When Zope is first installed, it grants only the view permission to the anonymous role. As other products are added, they may assign other permissions to the anonymous role that they determine are necessary for any user to be able to perform.

The manager role, by default, is granted most of the permissions that exist. You might decide, however, that for your particular installation, you want your manager role members to have fewer permissions. You can establish this easily by going to the Security tab at the root of your installation and unchecking some of the permissions given to the manager role.

The final default role is called owner. As a default, Zope gives the owner role no permissions except that of "taking ownership." Zope leaves it pretty much up to you what you want the owner of a site to be able to do.

Starting with Zope 2.4 (this book was written using 2.3.3), a new default role has been added called *authenticated*. The *authenticated* role cannot be "assigned" to users; it is simply attributed to a user who has authenticated in any way. In other words, if a user is not anonymous, he is considered to have the authenticated role by default. This role has just been added at the writing of this book, so for more up-to-date information about this role, see the **`http://www.zope.org`** site and our site, **`http://webdev.zopeonarope.com`**.

To change the permissions granted or denied a particular role, simply go to the Security tab and check or uncheck the permission box listed under each role. Then click the Save Changes button at the bottom of the screen.

## Applying What You've Learned

Now you need to apply what you've learned about users, roles, and permissions to your project with the New Millennium school system.

Start by creating a folder at the root of your Zope site called TeacherArea by using the pop-up list of objects. A screen appears that asks you to provide an ID for the new folder. In addition, you will see two check boxes labeled Create Public Interface and Create User Folder. For now, leave those boxes unchecked. Within the new TeacherArea folder, create a default index_html file that you can use to control the display of the contents of the folder. When the URL of a folder is given, Zope first looks for an object within the folder with an ID of `index_html`. If it finds one, then it renders that object. If it doesn't find an index_html object within the specified folder, then it begins to look up the acquisition list for an index_html object. Zope renders the first one that it locates. So, to make things sane, provide the new folder with its own index_html file. Within the new folder, select DTML method from the pop-up list of objects. Give it an ID of `index_html`. Click the Add and Edit button. When the management screen of the `index_html` method comes up, change the contents of the method to what is shown in Listing 4.1.

Listing 4.1 **Default index_html for TeacherArea Folder**

```
<dtml-var standard_html_header>
    <h2>Welcome to the New Millennium Teacher's Area</h2>
<dtml-var standard_html_footer>
```

From the root of your web site, click the Security tab at the top of the screen. This brings you to a screen where the various existing roles are defined, along with their permissions. At the bottom of the screen, you will notice a button labeled Add Role next to an empty text field. Type `Teacher` into the text field, and click the Add Role button. You've added the teacher role at the root of your web site because you might want the role of teacher available in other parts of the web site as well. If you create the role within the TeacherArea folder, then that role would be available only from the TeacherArea folder.

When the screen is refreshed, you will see that a column has been added for the new teacher role. Decide what permissions you want users who are assigned the teacher role to have. You'll want the teacher role to minimally include the view permission.

Next you'll need to add some users to whom you can assign the teacher role. Go to the root of your web site and see if there is an existing folder called *acl_users*. If there isn't, then you need to create one. The letters "acl" stand for *access control list*. This is a fancy way of saying "the list of users, roles, and permissions." Select User Folder from the pop-up list of objects. Now open the acl_users folder. Inside the acl_users folder is a button labeled Add. Click the Add button and create an account. For this example, use the username hammond and the password physics. You'll also notice a list of roles that can be assigned to this new user account. Choose the teacher role. Notice that multiple roles can be selected for a particular user. In the case of the school system, you might imagine an additional role called parent. The parent role might have certain permissions that the teacher role doesn't, and vice versa. You could also imagine creating a user account for the principal and giving him both the role of a teacher and a parent. In this case, you would select both roles from the list.

Now a person who logs in using the username hammond and the password physics will be granted the permissions that have been assigned to the role teacher.

Now you need to have a way to require users to authenticate when they attempt to view the TeacherArea folder. In this way, you can remove them from the ranks of the anonymous. Right now, anonymous users have the permission to view all of the files and folders in your web site, including TeacherArea. Go to the TeacherArea folder and click its Security tab. Within the Security area, you'll see the four roles that have been defined. Also notice that the far left column is titled Acquire Permission Settings?. Because all of the boxes are checked right now, it means that each of the roles will have the same permissions in this folder as it does in every other area of the site. Remember that the one permission granted to the anonymous role (and, hence, an unauthorized viewer) is the capability to view objects. For this folder, you'll want to remove that permission from the anonymous role. In other words, when an anonymous user attempts to view this folder, you want to force that user to authenticate as a user who has a role that includes the permission to view.

Uncheck the view permission in the Acquire Permission Settings column. Now you must explicitly check or uncheck the view permission for each of the defined roles; they will no longer automatically acquire this permission setting from the higher definition of the role. In essence, you are re-creating these roles within this folder and selectively overriding certain permissions.

For the manage and owner roles, check or uncheck the view permission as you would like it to be for this folder. For the anonymous role, uncheck the view permission so that anonymous users (who are automatically assigned the anonymous role) are not able to view this folder. Make sure, however, that you check the view permission for the teacher role because it won't automatically acquire that setting from the higher-level definition of the teacher role. Click the Save Changes button to set these new role definitions within the TeacherArea folder.

## Testing Your Work

Now you need to test to make sure that you are seeing the behavior that you expect. You are probably already logged in as a specific user with a manager or better role to make the edits that you have been making to your web site. In the upper frame of your management screen, you'll see a pop-up that currently says, Zope QuickStart. Click that pop-up and select Logout. Next you will be asked to authenticate. Click Cancel, and you will be logged out. Now you are considered an anonymous user again, and you can properly test whether your security for the TeacherArea folder is working. Type the URL of anything else in your web site, and make sure that you can view it. Anonymous users should still be able to get to all of the unprotected areas. When you are certain that is working, then type the URL of the TeacherArea folder. If everything is working okay, you should be asked to authenticate. Type `hammond` as the username and `physics` as the password; you should see the result of the index_html file located in the TeacherArea folder. If not, go back and review the previous paragraphs to make sure that you didn't miss anything.

This same security policy can be applied to other folders or even to individual objects. As an example, click on the EditableCalendar that you created in the latter part of Chapter 3. Like the TeacherArea folder, it has a Security tab. Click that tab, and perform the same role editing that you did previously for the TeacherArea folder. When you are finished, the EditableCalendar should require a visitor to authenticate before viewing it.

Now you can imagine extending the work you've just done with the teacher role to add further security to your school system web site. Create a folder called ParentArea and one called StudentArea. Now go back and create roles for both parent and student. Within the TeacherArea folder, make sure that the parent and student roles do not have view permissions. For the other two folders, make sure that only the proper role has view capability for the folder.

Although you unchecked only the Acquire Permission Settings box for the view permission, it is probably safer to uncheck the Acquire box for *all* of the permissions and grant or deny each permission separately for each role. This takes longer, but it's probably a good practice to force you to think about the permissions that you are granting to each role.

Remember, people visiting your site are associated with users; users can have roles, and roles are simply lists of permissions.

## User Input—the "Two-Way Web"

In Chapter 3, you took web pages from the static realm into the world of dynamic page design. The content of pages was dependent upon information that was being continually updated by a content manager (your calendar manager). Although your end users were able to participate in the process as passive viewers, sometimes you might want to allow your end users to provide some of that content themselves. You want to move from the one-way web that we analyzed in Chapter 3 to the two-way web. One of the main problems with the two-way web is the issue of control. When you open up the content of your web sites to the outside world, you set yourself up for attacks by vandals. The concept of the two-way web is based on the idea of trust. You must have a minimal amount of trust in your users for the two-way web concept to work.

Zope is a perfect environment for two-way web design because you can take advantage of its built-in security features to limit access to the systems that you want to make two-way.

## ZUBB

One of the first systems that we'll look at in this chapter is called *Zope Ultimate Bulletin Board* (*ZUBB*). For this book, we are using version 0.6.0.

### ZUBB—a Zope Implementation of a BBS

ZUBB is a Zope implementation of the BBS concept (see the sidebar "Definition and History of Electronic Bulletin Boards" for more information about BUSSs). It makes use of a ZCatalog (see Chapter 3) to facilitate quick searches based on authorship, subject, or content. It also can take advantage of the flexible, built-in security features of Zope to help control who has access to the bulletin board.

**Definition and History of Electronic Bulletin Boards**

According to Christos J. P. Moschovitis, Hilary Poole, Tami Schuyler, and Theresa M. Senft in their book, *History of the Internet,*[1] the first computerized bulletin board was created in 1978 by Ward Christensen and Randy Suess. It was called Computerized Bulletin Board System (CBBS), and it functioned as a virtual thumb-tack bulletin board. The system was made available to the public in 1979. This bulletin board system represented the first civilian (ARPANet was restricted to defense-funded institutions) attempt to create an interactive, online community.

CBBS was the start of a revolution. Keep in mind that this was well before the advent of the World Wide Web. After CBBS was launched, numerous other similar systems began popping up. They were all given the generic term *bulletin board system* (BBS). In those early days, BBSs were often run out of individuals' homes, with a limited number of phone lines and modems connected to the server. To access a BBS, a user was required to dial into the hosting server via a modem. The number of people who could be connected at any one time, therefore, was limited by the number of modems and phone lines that the hosting server could afford. Later, multiple servers were connected in mini-networks to provide greater access. In the early 1990s, things began to change as BBSs began to connect to the Internet, thus providing wider accessibility. By the mid-1990s, the use of BBSs began to decrease as the World Wide Web took over with its use of graphics and other media.

The concept of an electronic bulletin board still has its place and can be very useful as a central location for discussions to take place about a subject or area of interest.

## Installing ZUBB

To install ZUBB, complete the following steps:

1. Download the ZDiscussions-0.6.0.tar.gz file to your Zope server from **`http://www.zope.org/Members/BwanaZulia/ZUBB`**.
2. Copy this file to the $ZOPEROOT directory.
3. Unzip the ZDiscussions-0.6.0.tar.gz file. Type `gunzip ZDiscussions-0.6.0.tar.gz`.
4. Next untar the resulting ZDiscussions-0.6.0.tar file. Type `tar -xvf ZDiscussions-0.6.0.tar`. This produces a directory called ZDBase in the $ZOPEROOT/lib/python/Products folder, and also creates a ZDiscussions.zexp file in the $ZOPEROOT/import directory.
5. Restart Zope from the Control Panel.
6. Although the ZDBase product installs automatically when Zope is restarted, the ZDiscussions product must be imported into the Control_Panel/Products directory. While in the Control_Panel/Products folder, click the Import/Export button.

1. Moschovitis, Christos J.P., Hilary Poole, Tami Schuyler, and Theresa M. Senft. *History of the Internet: A Chronology, 1843 to the Present.* Santa Barbara, CA: Abc-Clio, 1999. (ISBN 1-57607-118-9)

7. Type `ZDiscussions.zexp` into the Import Filename field, and click Import. The ZDiscussions product should now appear in the Products folder. Make sure that the message indicates that the product was installed successfully.
8. Check to make sure that both ZDBase and ZDiscussions are installed and don't show icons that are broken.
9. Remember to check the user-support mailing lists on **http://www.zope.org** if any problems occur.

## Setting Up and Using ZUBB

To set up a ZUBB, you need to go to a location in your Zope site where you want the ZUBB to be. For now, create one at the root of your school system project. Select ZDiscussion Topic from the list of objects that can be instantiated. You will be asked to provide both an ID and a `title`. Make sure that you give it a `title`, as well as an ID, because the `title` will be used as the subject for the postings. Unfortunately, you won't be able to change this later. For this example, give your new ZUBB an ID of `SchoolMascot` and a `title` of School Mascot. Make sure that you leave the Add Default Interface box checked for now.

When you have created the ZDiscussion topic, click its Regenerate Methods tab in the upper-right corner (see Figure 4.2). Click the Regenerate button to recreate the basic methods that you will need for this ZDiscussion topic. That's it. Your new ZUBB is in place and ready to use.

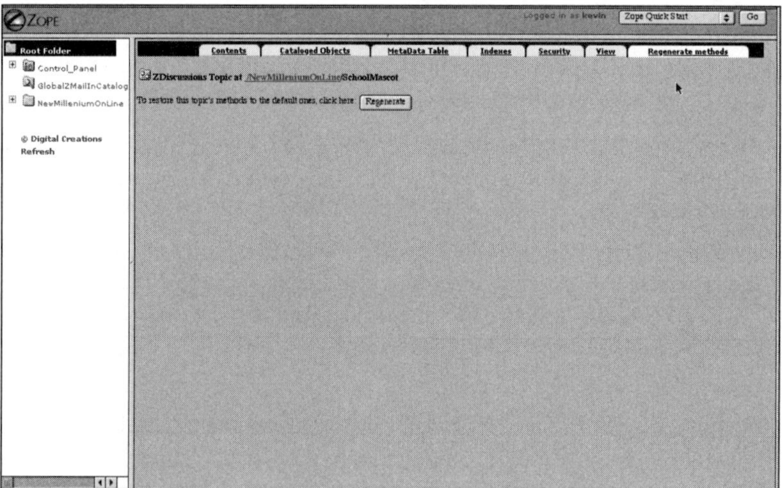


Figure 4.2 Regenerate methods for a new ZUBB.

Now you can click the View tab, and you will see what an end user would see when coming to the new ZUBB (see Figure 4.3). You also can get a look at the user's view of things by typing the URL of the method into your web browser (such as **`http://www.yoursitename:8080/SchoolMascot`**). Along the top is the name of the ZUBB. Below that is a set of four links: *Post*, *Search*, *Instructions*, and *New*.

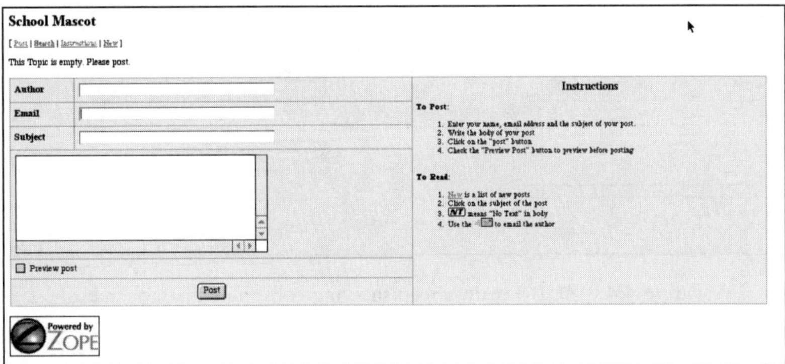


**Figure 4.3** ZUBB main screen.

Submitting a message is the basic operation performed with a ZUBB. Each message is either the start of a new discussion or the response to an existing message. A new discussion, sometimes known as a *thread*, is started by clicking the *Post* link at the top of the screen. This brings up a screen that allows a user to create a new message. Each message has an author, an email, a subject, and the contents of the message. A message that is posted to start a new discussion is included in the list of subjects on the ZUBB main screen.

When a thread has been started, other users can *reply* to the original message. In fact, users can reply not only to the original message, but even to the replies. The thread can become nested very quickly. ZUBB handles the display of the nesting of messages very well by using a collapsible tree feature (see Figure 4.4). If a reply has a small plus sign icon next to it, it means that it contains other messages that are replies to it. Click the plus sign icon, and the message tree will open up, allowing you to see the other messages involved. The plus sign icon will change to a minus sign icon. To close the tree again, click the minus sign.

To reply to a message, you simply click the link associated with the message and then fill in the fields for a new message. You'll notice that the button at the bottom of the screen says Reply instead of Post. That way, you know whether you are properly replying to someone else's post or are starting a whole new discussion.

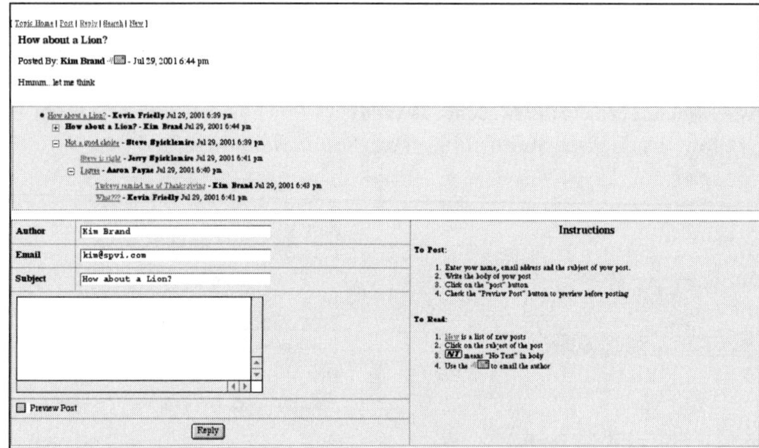


**Figure 4.4** ZUBB main screen showing collapsible message trees.

You can see, therefore, that each message submitted to the ZUBB is either the start of a new discussion (POST) or a response to someone else's post (REPLY).

In the early stages of a ZUBB, there will be very little need for the search function. However, as more postings occur, it will become harder to find a previous discussion. The search function allows a user to search for existing messages by a particular author, or those containing certain key words in the subject line or the body of the message. Click the *Search* link at the top of the page, and you will see the basic search screen shown in Figure 4.5.

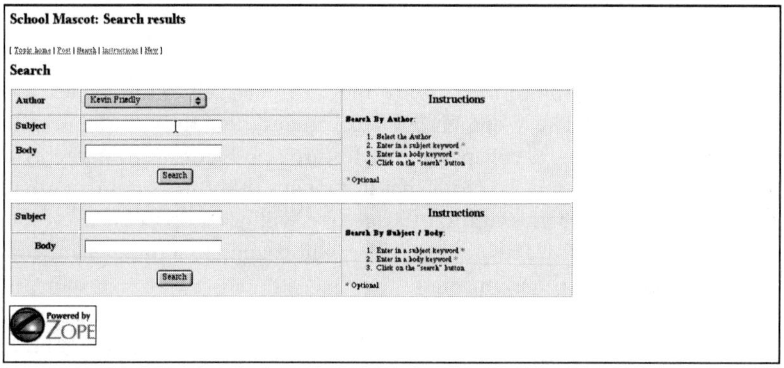

**Figure 4.5** ZUBB search screen.

To search for postings by a particular author, simply select the author's name from the pop-up box and then click the associated Search button. If you have some knowledge about the subject or the content of the message you are searching for, you can further focus your search by providing optional keywords for the subject or body content.

To search for postings without regard for who the author is, use the search function at the bottom of the screen. Here you can enter keywords for the subject, body content, or both.

The New feature allows you to list the newest postings to the ZUBB. The postings are listed from latest to earliest, without regard for which thread they belong to. It is simply a time-ordered list of posts.

The real art to using ZUBB (and other BBS) systems is determining when a new ZUBB is needed. Because a person can start a discussion about anything within a ZUBB, you can imagine a situation in which so many discussions are going on that it is hard to locate the subjects you are interested in. In general, you should make the topic of your ZUBB broad enough that it covers several issues but narrow enough that people aren't tempted to include issues about everything.

A good resource for the design issues presented herein is a book by Jon Udell called *Practical Internet Groupware* (published by O'Reilly). Unfortunately, the book is out of print, but some of the information is included on John's web site, **http://udell.roninhouse.com**.

# Zwiki—a Shared Whiteboard

The previous section discussed a mechanism for allowing users to post content to a web page in the form of a threaded discussion. Once information was included on the web page, though, it became static and was no longer capable of being edited. One could, of course, append more content that contradicted or suggested changes to a previous post, but the previous post would remain unchanged. In this next section, you will explore a Zope product that allows content to be modified multiple times by multiple users.

## Wiki—the Predecessor

A very popular system for implementing the two-way web is called a *Wiki*. A Wiki is a web page whose contents can be edited directly by a user through his web browser. Wikis can be instantly edited by anyone. That capability is its greatest asset but, at the same time, also its greatest drawback. On the positive side, a Wiki facilitates collaborative, interactive design. On the negative side, a Wiki provides web vandals with an easy avenue to mayhem. The Wiki concept was developed by a man named Ward Cunningham.

## A Zope Implementation of a Wiki

Combining the best aspects of a Wiki and the powerful, extensible features of Zope is the purpose of a Zope product called a *ZWiki*.

The ZWiki product can be found at **`http://zope.org/Members/simon/ZWiki`**; for this book, we are using version 0.9.4. Another valuable resource for information on ZWiki is the ZWiki home page, located at **`http://www.zwiki.org`**.

To install ZWiki, complete the following steps:

1. Download the .tgz file to your Zope server.
2. Copy this file to the $ZOPEROOT/lib/python/Products directory.
3. Unzip the ZWiki-0.9.3.tgz file. Type `gunzip ZWiki-0.9.3.tgz`.
4. Next, untar the resulting ZWiki-0.9.3.tar file. Type `tar -xvf ZWiki-0.9.3.tar`. This produces a directory called ZWiki.
5. Inside the ZWiki directory is a file called ZWikiWebs.zexp. Copy this file into the $ZOPEROOT/import directory.
6. Restart Zope from the Control Panel.
7. Now go into the Product Management folder within the Control Panel, and make sure that the ZWiki product is installed correctly.
8. Although the ZWiki product installs automatically when Zope is restarted, the ZWikiWebs product must be imported into the Control_Panel/Products directory. While in the Control_Panel/Products folder, click the Import/Export button.
9. Type **`ZWikiWebs.zexp`** into the into the Input Filename field, and click Import. The ZWikiWebs product should now appear in the Products folder. Make sure that the message indicates that the product was installed successfully.
10. Remember to check the user-support mailing lists on zope.org if any problems occur.

After the ZWiki and ZWikiWebs objects are correctly installed, you can instantiate a ZWiki anywhere in your Zope installation. For this example, go to the root of your Zope installation. Choose a ZWikiWeb object from the pop-up list of objects. You will see a screen like the one shown in Figure 4.6.

To create a new ZWiki web, you will need to first provide an ID and an optional `title`. Give this ZWiki an ID of `MyZWiki`.

Next, you need to decide what kind of ZWiki to create. There are three choices listed: basic, classic, and zwikidotorg. For now, choose the default Zwiki, which is a basic ZWiki.

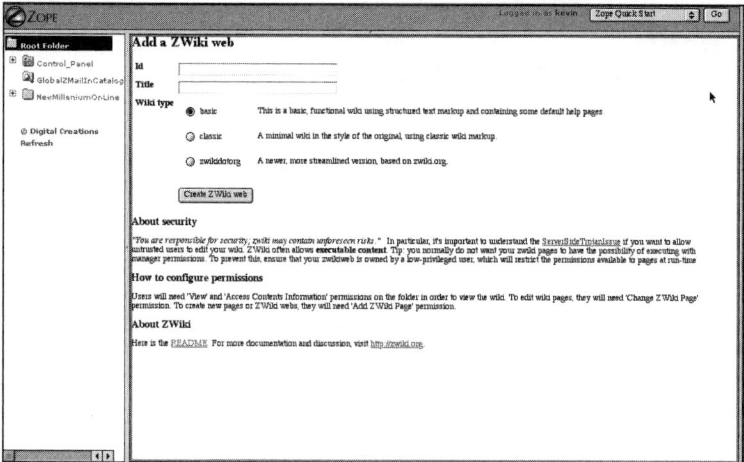


Figure 4.6 Instantiating a new ZWiki web object.

Before proceeding, notice the messages found on the main screen concerning security. Because the concept of a Wiki (and, consequently, a ZWiki) is to allow anyone the capability to edit as well as read the contents of the Wiki, it is important that you understand exactly what permissions are given to various users. In general, it is best to have the ZWiki "owned" by a low-security user so that it executes with limited capabilities. You probably don't want the ZWiki to have manager permissions. To simply view a ZWiki's contents, a user will need to have View and Access Information Contents permissions on the ZWiki folder. To edit contents of a ZWiki, users will also need Change ZWiki Page permissions. Finally, to create new pages or ZWiki web objects, users will further need Add ZWiki Page permissions. Think carefully about what capabilities you want your users to have before granting them. Give your users only as many permissions as are absolutely necessary to prevent security breaches.

When a ZWiki is created, it looks and functions very much like a folder. The icon for a ZWiki is a folder. Inside the folder representing your new ZWiki, you'll find numerous default ZWiki page objects and DTML methods already created for you.

The default index_html file is fairly simple. It redirects the browser to the ZWiki page called FrontPage. The contents of the FrontPage ZWiki object are shown in Listing 4.2.

Listing 4.2 **Default Contents of the FrontPage ZWiki Object**

```
**Welcome!**
This is ZWiki's "basic" wiki template.
HelpPage - RecentChanges - SearchPage - ZWiki
```

When viewed, the FrontPage ZWiki object produces the output shown in Figure 4.7.

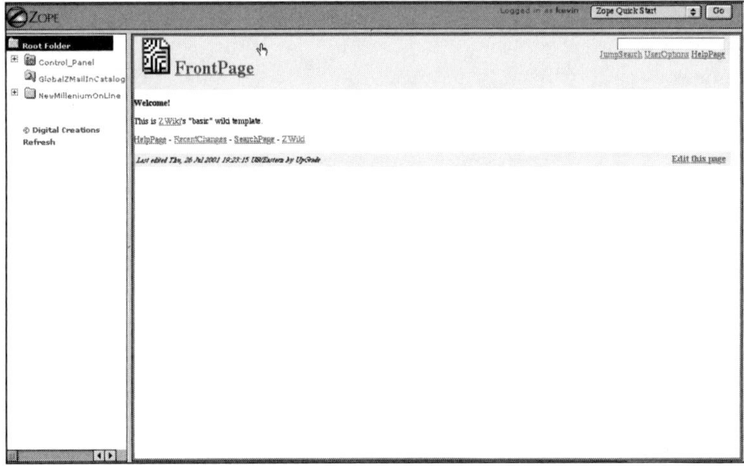


Figure 4.7 View of the default FrontPage ZWiki object.

Looking at the contents of Listing 4.2 and the view shown in Figure 4.7, you might be wondering how the two are related. Clearly, there is not enough information contained in the default content of FrontPage to produce the output that you see in Figure 4.7. Although the contents of the FrontPage object don't contain any DTML or HTML, the rendered object certainly appears to be composed of standard HTML. There must be some magic going on somewhere. In fact, the magic is contained within the ZWiki web object itself. Let's explore that machinery a bit.

Within the MyZWiki folder, select ZWiki page from the pop-up list of objects. Give the new object an ID of `TestPage`. To begin, put nothing in the content area. Now click the View tab of the new object. The result is shown in Figure 4.8.

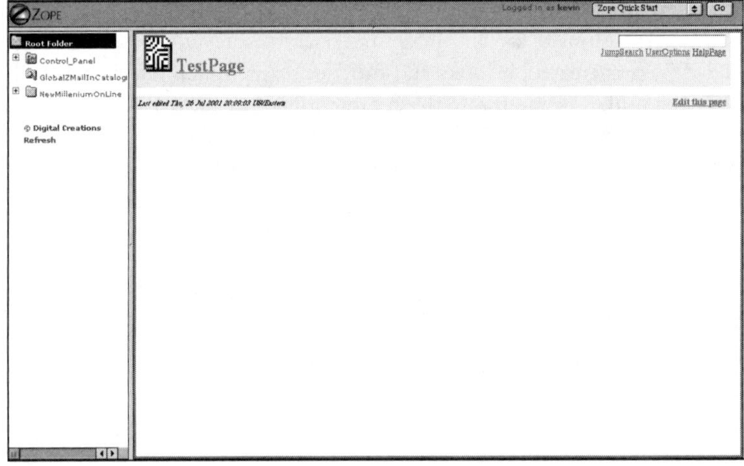


Figure 4.8 View of a blank ZWiki object.

That's a heck of a lot of display for an empty object. In the upper-left corner of the screen, you will see the icon representing a Zwiki, plus the name of your ZWiki page TestPage. Below this, you'll see a line indicating the time when this page was most recently edited.

In the upper-right corner of the screen, you will see three default links: *JumpSearch*, *UserOptions*, and *HelpPage*. These three links jump to three other ZWiki pages that are contained in the MyZWiki folder. Below this is a link titled Edit the Page. Clicking this link brings up a page for adding content to the ZWiki. We'll take a look at that in a moment.

Click the Back button on your browser, and go back to the page which shows the content of your TestPage ZWiki. Type `This is my ZWiki page` into the content area, and press Save Changes. Now press the View tab again. The result is shown in Figure 4.9.

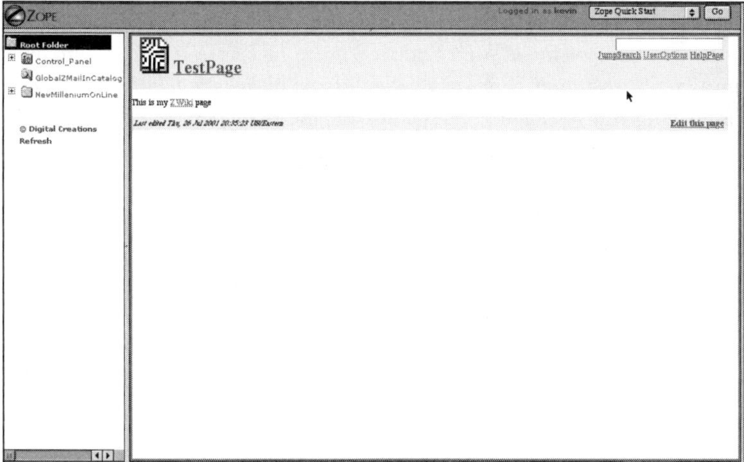


**Figure 4.9** View of a basic ZWiki object.

Notice that the text that you typed into the content area appears in the ZWiki. However, notice that the word *ZWiki* appears as a hyperlink. Now go back and edit the content again, and add the line: `Another ZWiki page I have is called FrontPage.`

Now when the page is rendered, you will notice that not only is the word *ZWiki* linked (in both instances), but the word *FrontPage* is linked as well. Use your browser to locate your MyZWiki folder, and open it. Inside you will see a list of the objects that it contains. Notice that in addition to the FrontPage ZWiki page, there is a ZWiki page called ZWiki. It almost looks like the ZWiki machinery "knows" what ZWiki pages are contained within the ZWiki web object and automatically links to them when their names are listed in the contents of a ZWiki page. To test this, pick another ZWiki page from the ZWiki web folder and use its name in the contents of your TestPage ZWiki. For example, use the name of the StructuredTextRules ZWiki and see what happens. You will find that, once again, the name of the ZWiki page is linked automatically to the actual page.

Although it appears that the existing ZWikis are automatically linked when they are mentioned in a page, the truth is actually a little more involved. ZWiki names must conform to a special rule. All ZWiki names must be a single word (no spaces) containing at least two capital letters. In general, ZWiki names are created by using two or more descriptive words run together to form a single megaword. Examples of proper ZWiki names include ZWiki, MyZWiki, BigZWiki, and SeveralWordsRunTogetherZWiki. In fact, whenever a word in the content area of a ZWiki contains two or more capital letters, the ZWiki web machinery considers it special. If the word matches the name of an existing ZWiki page, then the word is automatically linked to the associated ZWiki page. If not, then a linked question mark is appended to the end of the word. If the question mark is clicked, then a ZWiki with the specified name is automatically created. In other words, the ZWiki machinery assumes that if you use a word that follows the ZWiki naming convention, you intend to refer to a ZWiki.

This is the mechanism by which nonmanagers can create new ZWiki objects. They can include the name of the ZWiki that they want to create in their contribution to an existing Zwiki, and then click on the resulting link to actually create a new ZWiki.

While viewing the TestPage ZWiki, click on the name of the current page, which is located in the upper left of the screen. This is linked to a DTML method called backlinks. Backlinks produces a page containing a list of any other ZWiki pages that refer to this page. In other words, if the name of TestPage appears in any other ZWiki page contained within the current ZWiki web object, its linked name will appear on this page. You can begin to see how the ZWiki machinery automatically links the separate pages together. This is a very powerful feature of ZWiki.

The previous description gives a view of the ZWiki from a manager's standpoint. How does this thing work from the viewpoint of a user? Create a basic ZWiki and then look at how it works for an end user. For the case of the fictitious school project that we introduced in the beginning of Chapter 2, "Point and Click Web Building," imagine that you've been asked to provide a system for allowing multiple teachers to work collaboratively on developing a curriculum for a new science course. Having just studied ZWikis, you realize that this is a great place to start.

Go into your MyZWiki folder and create a ZWiki page using the pop-up list of objects. Call the new ZWiki "Science101." For its contents, type the text in Listing 4.3.

Listing 4.3 **Contents for Science101 ZWiki Object**

```
Welcome to the Science 101 development area.

Click on the "Edit this page" button to add your comments and suggestions after this message.
```

Now you need to edit the default text of the index_html file. Remember that, by default, it redirects the browser to the FrontPage ZWiki page. One way that you might want to edit the index_html file is shown in Listing 4.4.

Listing 4.4 **Modified Contents of index_html**

```
01 <dtml-var standard_html_header>
02   <center>
03   <table>
04         <tr>
05               <td>
06               <h3>Welcome to the New Millennium Curriculum
07                     Development Area</h3>
08               </td>
09         </tr>
10         <tr>
11               <td>
12                     <B>Class areas</B>
13               </td>
14         </tr>
15         <tr>
16               <td>
17                     <a href=Science101>Science 101</a>
18               </td>
19         </tr>
20   </table>
21   </center>
22 <dtml-var standard_html_footer>
```

Line 17 in Listing 4.4 links to the new Science101 ZWiki object. As other ZWikis are added, more links could be included. View this modified index_html object. Next, click on the link for Science101; you'll see the text that you entered from Listing 4.3.

The message that you included instructs the user to click the Edit This Page link to contribute to this ZWiki. To see how this works, click the link and you'll see the screen shown in Figure 4.10.

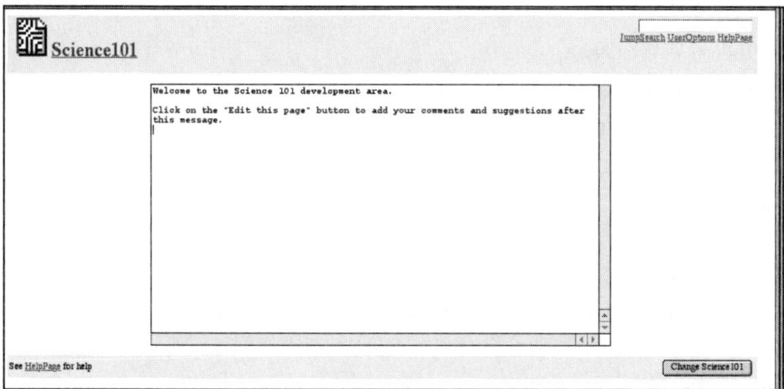


**Figure 4.10** View of a basic ZWiki object.

Notice that the message you started with appears in an editable text box. You can add to the bottom, or you can completely remove the text that is there. Even your original "instructions" can be modified or even removed completely. This is one of the potential weaknesses of a ZWiki. You must be able to trust the community members who are using your ZWiki. Otherwise, the results can be highly disappointing. The complete contents of the ZWiki can be modified at will by all those who have access to it. You can certainly imagine multiple teachers using this "whiteboard" as a means of collaboratively developing a new course curriculum.

To avoid having people who are not involved in the project accidentally (or intentionally) damage the content of the ZWiki, you might want to take advantage of Zope's built-in security features discussed at the beginning of this chapter to limit access to the ZWiki to only those users with a certain level of security.

Move the Science101 ZWiki object into the TeacherArea folder that you created at the beginning of this chapter. Go to the root of your web site, and check the box next to the Science101 object; click the Cut button at the bottom of the screen. Next, open the TeacherArea folder and click the Paste button. This will move the Science101 ZWiki to the TeacherArea folder.

When we discussed permissions in the section "Zope Security Issues" at the beginning of this chapter, we stated that when new products are added, additional permissions may be defined and added to the list automatically. For instance, when ZWiki was installed, several new permissions were added to the permissions list. These additional permissions are defined in the installation files for ZWiki found in $ZOPEROOT/lib/python/Products/ZWiki/ZWikiPage.py. The new permissions that have been added to the list are as follows:

- Add ZWiki Pages
- Append to ZWiki Pages
- Change ZWiki Page Types
- Change ZWiki Pages
- Change ZWiki Regulations
- Reparent ZWiki Pages
- Send ZWiki Pages to Recycle Bin

## Using the ZWiki

Now you have your Science101 ZWiki contained in a secure folder that gives access only to users who have been assigned the teacher role. If you log out as an administrator of your Zope installation and type in the URL of the TeacherArea folder, you should be asked to authenticate. Authenticate as the user hammond with a password of physics. Now you should see the index_html object that you created in Listing 4.1. Click the link to the Science101 development area, and you should see the FrontPage of the Science101 ZWiki. Voilá! It's ready to use.

Users who reach this point will now see the message that you provided, instructing them to click the Edit This Page link to add or modify the ZWiki. It's that easy. The ZWiki can now act as a shared whiteboard for collaborative development. The group using the ZWiki is a select group and, therefore, a fairly trusted group. Thus, the built-in security of Zope is being used to take the idea of a Wiki one step further.

# Squishdot

One of the most popular features of dynamic web sites today is that of a news area. In this day of "latest and greatest," news areas provide us with absolutely the most up-to-date information. Up until the 1980s, television news programs were seen nightly. At most, the news was 24 hours old. As cable television took over in the 1980s, shows such as "CNN Headline News" were developed that brought news every half hour. The success of this show and shows like it attest to our desire for the most up-to-date information. Like cable television, the web must provide timely news to keep our interest.

Combining the ideas of a web news service and a discussion group is the purpose of a *weblog*. A weblog acts somewhat like an interactive newspaper. News items can be posted, and then readers have the capability to comment on those news items and participate in a discussion related to them. This is similar to the ZUBB that you created at the beginning of this chapter, except that the "subject" of each discussion is an entire news item as opposed to a simple sentence.

A prototypical example of a weblog is a web site called *SlashDot*. SlashDot was started as a technical news and discussion group to support the open source community. SlashDot can be accessed at **`http://www.slashdot.org`**.

## Squishdot—a Weblog for Zope

Squishdot is a Zope product that was inspired by SlashDot. The authors make it clear that it in no way is it associated with SlashDot. Squishdot makes use of the ZCatalog and built-in security features of Zope to implement the features of a full-fledged weblog.

## Installing Squishdot

The Squishdot product can be found at **`http://www.zope.org/Members/chrisw/Squishdot`** or at **`http://squishdot.org/Download/Squishdot`**. For this book, we are using Version 1-2-1. To install a Squishdot, use the following steps:

1. Download the Squishdot-1-2-1.tar.gz file to your Zope server.
2. Copy this file to the $ZOPEROOT/lib/python/Products directory.
3. Unzip the Squishdot-1-2-1.tar.gz file. Type `gunzip Squishdot-1-2-1.tar.gz`.
4. Next, untar the resulting Squishdot-1-2-1.tar file. Type `tar -xvf Squishdot-1-2-1.tar`. This produces a directory called Squishdot.

5. Restart Zope from the Control Panel.
6. Now go into the Product Management folder within the Control Panel, and make sure that the Squishdot product is installed correctly.
7. Remember to check the user-support mailing lists on zope.org if any problems occur. You also can visit **`http://www.squishdot.org`** for more help.

## Using Squishdot

At this point, you can go to any point in your Zope installation and instantiate a Squishdot site object from the pop-up list of objects (see Figure 4.11).

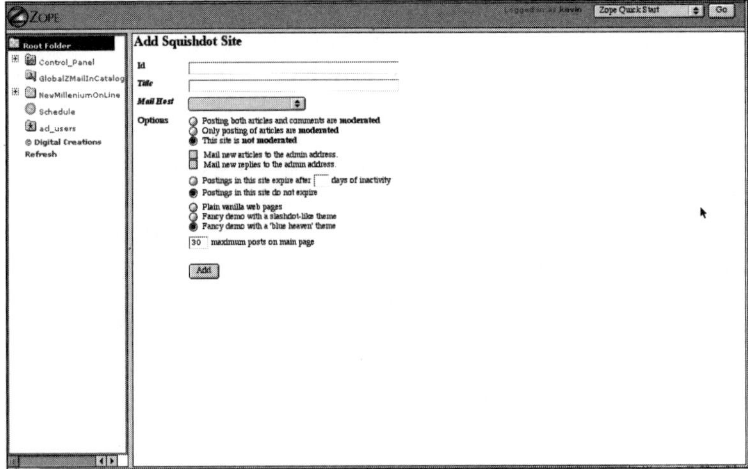


**Figure 4.11** Adding a Squishdot site.

Like all Zope objects, Squishdot requires that an ID be entered when creating a new one. Next is the ubiquitous optional `title`. Enter one, if you'd like. The next piece of information is the MailHost that this Squishdot will use to send email. For now, leave it blank. You'll need to add a MailHost object to connect this Squishdot to.

The next set of radio buttons is used to specify the level of moderation that the site maintains. Depending on the trust level of the community using this Squishdot, you might want to require that all news items and comments be sent through a moderator before becoming visible on the site. Or, you might require only that the news items themselves be moderated. In the case of a highly trusted user base, you might choose to have neither the news items nor the comments moderated. For now, set the site to unmoderated for both news items and comments.

The next two boxes indicate whether you want the administrator to receive email copies of the news items and comments that are posted. Because this site is fully moderated, you don't need to check either box; the administrator has to get a copy of each anyway. Those options are for the case where the site is only partially moderated or completely unmoderated. Even if you don't moderate the items, you still might want to receive email notification when new items are posted. For now, leave them unchecked.

The next set of radio buttons specifies whether news items that are posted ever expire, and, if so, when. For this example, leave the default of no expiration time.

The last set of radio buttons allows you to choose among three styles for the site. You can explore this further on your own. For now, just leave the default.

Click the Add button, and your new Squishdot site will be created. View the new Squishdot, and you'll already see some news items posted, as in Figure 4.12. These items are related to your new Squishdot and provide further information about setting up your Squishdot. In particular, notice the news article titled "Feature: Installation Instructions." This item indicates that you have 90% of the installation complete. Click the Read More button to see what else you have to do to clean up your installation and prepare it to be used.

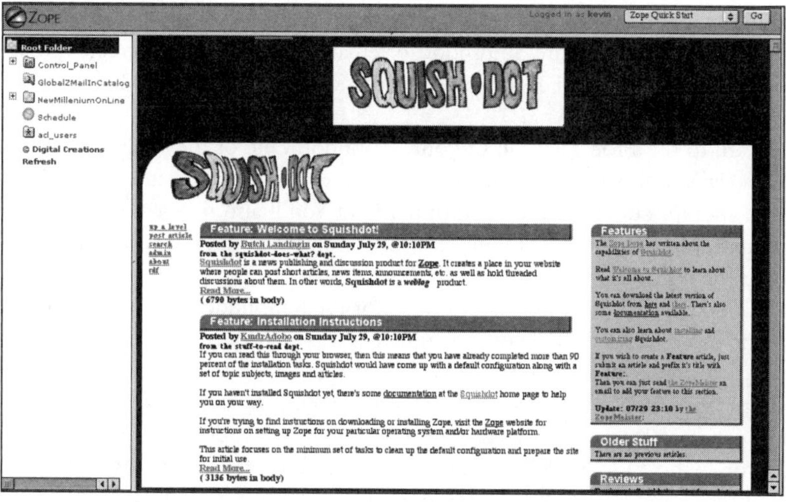


Figure 4.12 View of the default Squishdot site.

First you need to remove the default postings that were included with your Squishdot installation. In the management interface of your Zope site, go to the new Squishdot that you just created. Click on the Postings tab. Place a check in the box to the left of each of the existing postings. Finally, click the Delete button to remove these postings. Now if you view your Squishdot, you'll see that it has no postings.

Next, you need to set up the list of possible "subjects" to which the news items can relate. Basically, this list is created to help your users categorize their news items. Like the ZUBB that you explored at the beginning of this chapter, a Squishdot can be made too narrow or too broad in its scope. The real art is determining how many subjects to include before deciding to create another Squishdot.

To change the subjects list, click on the Subjects tab in the management interface of your Squishdot. The current list of subjects will appear. Put a check in the box next to any subjects that you want to remove, and click the Delete button. Now on the bottom of the page, you'll see a field titled Subject and one below it titled Image URL. Type the name of a subject that you'd like to include and an optional URL for the image that you'd like. Then click the Add/Edit button, and the new subject will become part of the Squishdot.

### Setting Up Email on Squishdot

Another very important part of making your Squishdot work is to set up the email portion. Squishdot uses email in several ways, so the email portions must be configured properly for Squishdot to be capable of performing as advertised. Squishdot uses email if you choose to have news items or comments emailed to the Squishdot administrator, or if a user submitting a post asks to be informed when others respond to his post. First, to configure Squishdot for email, you will have to create a *MailHost* for your Squishdot to use. For a detailed discussion on setting up a MailHost, see Chapter 5, "Web Mail."

Next, go to the Properties tab of your Squishdot. One of the properties is called `admin_address`. This should be the email address of the administrator of this Squishdot. Type the appropriate email address into the field. You'll also notice a property called `admin_name`. Enter the name of your Squishdot administrator. Click the Save Changes button at the bottom of the screen.

You'll also need to go to the Options tab for the Squishdot. You'll see a screen similar to the one that you saw when you first instantiated your Squishdot (see Figure 4.11). Now you should see that your MailHost has been included in the pop-up list of possible mail hosts. Choose your new MailHost object, and click Change.

Now for a totally unmoderated Squishdot, things are basically set up and ready to run. Anyone who can get to the Squishdot can read its articles and either post new ones or post comments about existing ones. To see how this works, click the View tab of the Squishdot, and you'll see what an end user will see when he comes to the Squishdot. Notice the Post Article link along the left side of the screen. Click this link, and you will see the screen for submitting a new article. Only four items are required: a name, a title, a subject, and a lead summary. One of the properties at the bottom of the screen is one for Encoding. In general, users probably will want to select Plain Text. However, those who know some HTML can select that option. Another option is Structured Text. Fill out the form with a test posting, and click the Add button at the bottom of the screen.

Now when you view the Squishdot, you'll see the test item that you submitted. It appears on the Squishdot immediately because you have chosen to have this Squishdot totally unmoderated.

Things are a bit different for a partially or fully moderated Squishdot. To make your Squishdot fully moderated, click on its Options tab again. Choose the first radio button option to require that both articles and comments be moderated. What this means is that before an article or comment appears on the Squishdot for everyone to see, the administrator has to review the posting and approve it. Periodically, the administrator should go to the Moderation tab of the Squishdot. If there have been any articles or comments posted, they will show up under the Moderation tab. The administrator can then review the posting and either approve it or delete it. If approved, the posting will go immediately to the public portion of the Squishdot. If deleted, then it will be removed and will never become viewable by the general public.

There are numerous ways to customize your Squishdot, but this gives you the basics to get it up and running. Feel free to explore the other settings and refer to the mail lists and the **http://www.zope.org** site for more information on Squishdot.

# CMF

*Content Management Framework* (*CMF*) is a product for creating content-management systems and portals. As such, CMF is not a product, but, rather, it is a backbone onto which products can be added to create powerful, dynamic, and easily manageable web sites. While by design CMF is not a product, it does come with an example application that can be used as an out-of-the-box example portal that you can use as is or modify to your own needs.

CMF is a very large work and, as such, is beyond the scope of one chapter (or even one book). We will give a brief introduction to CMF in this chapter and then visit CMF again in a bit more detail in Chapter 8, "Getting Content Under Control."

CMF is the heir to a previous product called the Portal Toolkit (PTK). Both the PTK and CMF were created by Digital Creations (the developers of Zope).

## Portals Defined

We just described CMF as a portal toolkit. While some of you might have an idea of what you think a portal is, others might not, so it might be instructive for us to discuss portals before we proceed with a discussion of CMF.

As more information has been made available on the web, the process of filtering that information down to useful content has become more important. The concept of an individualized or specialized view into the plethora of data on the web is encompassed in the idea of a *portal*. There is no solid definition of a portal, but some of the common components of most definitions include the ideas of a user-centered or member-based, customizable view of a site, plus a readily searchable content. In addition, the capability to share information with other users is present in most definitions.

Many portals allow users to customize not only what information is being included in their view of the portal, but also where that information is coming from. Many portals now allow content to be provided by outside sources via content channels. Using a portal content language such as RSS (an XML format), content from diverse sites can be syndicated and brought together in one location as directed by the web user.

> **For More Information**
>
> Here are some web sites where you can go to read about the RSS standard and its usage:
>
> **`http://my.netscape.com/publish/formats/rss-spec-0.91.html`**
>
> **`http://www.oasis-open.org/cover/rss.html`**
>
> **`http://www.xml.com/pub/a/2000/07/17/syndication/rss.html`**

Although most portals that you think of serve large audiences on the Internet, another use of portals is on an intranet serving large corporations. A company knowledge base of corporate policies, procedures, and research data can be viewed as a kind of portal.

## A Description of CMF

CMF takes advantage of many of the built-in features of Zope to deploy portals quickly and efficiently. In particular, though, CMF implements a more intuitive interface for end users than the standard Zope management interface. Missing are the tabs seen along the top of most Zope management screens. Instead, CMF gives access to its objects and features through a list of links found along the left side of the screen. Also, addition of objects is limited to only those object types that are generally needed in a portal.

One of the beauties of CMF is that it allows members to participate in the process of providing content. This takes a great burden off the web administrator. Members can create content objects and then submit them for inclusion in the site. The administrator(s) can review the submitted material and then simply accept the work, and it will immediately become available on the site in the public areas.

## Installing CMF

The latest version of CMF can be found at **`http://cmf.zope.org/download`**. For this book, we are using Version 1.1. To install CMF, complete the following steps:

1. Download the .tar.gz file to your Zope server.
2. Copy this file to the $ZOPEROOT/lib/python/Products directory.
3. Unzip the CMF-1.1.tar.gz file. Type `gunzip CMF-1.1.tar.gz`.
4. Next, untar the resulting CMF-1.1.tar file. Type `tar -xvf CMF-1.1.tar`. This produces a directory called CMF-1.1.

5. The CMF-1.1 directory contains four subdirectories: CMFCore, CMFTopic, CMFCalendar, and CMFDefault. Move these four directories out of the CMF-1.1 directory and into the $ZOPEROOT/lib/python/Products directory.
6. Restart Zope from the Control Panel.
7. Now go into the Product Management folder within the Control Panel, and make sure that the CMF products are installed correctly.You should see four products: CMFCore, CMFCalendar, CMFDefault, and CMFTopic. Remember to check the user-support mailing lists on zope.org if any problems occur.

## Using CMF

Now go to any location on your Zope site where you want to instantiate a new CMF site. In the pop-up list of objects that can be added, you'll see several new objects: `CMF Core Content`, `CMF Core Tool`, `CMF Event`, `CMF Site`, `CMF Topic Objects`, `CMFDefault Content`, and `CMFDefault Tool`.

Start by instantiating a `CMF Site` object. Give it `MyPortal` as an ID and a `title`, as in Figure 4.13. For now, choose the default for Membership source. A new acl_users folder will then be created for you in the new portal.

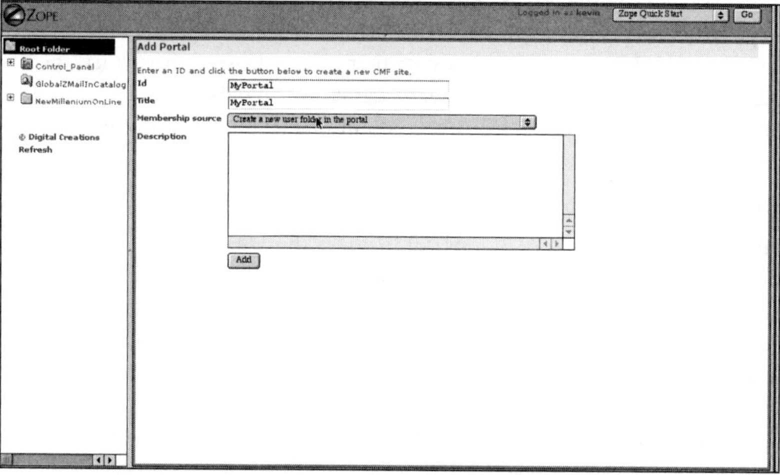


**Figure 4.13** Instantiating a new CMF Site object.

After you create your CMF Site object, the default user screen will be displayed as shown in Figure 4.14.

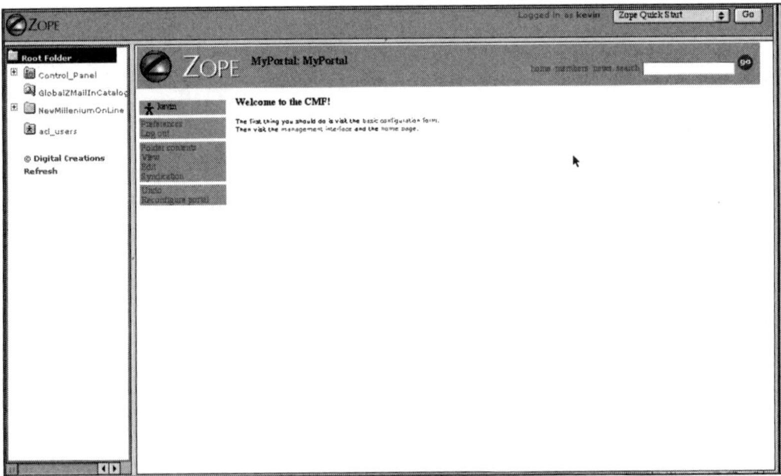


Figure 4.14 Default CMF screen.

The first thing you'll want to do is go to the acl_users folder within your new portal and open it. You should create a new user account for the person who is going to act as administrator of this portal. An administrator is needed to review and approve items that are posted by members to the portal. There are also other basic jobs that your administrator needs to be able to perform. Create a user, and make sure that he has the manager role selected. You can create as many user accounts as you'd like with the manager role. This will allow those users to perform the administrative functions of the portal.

## Becoming a Member

Remember that the definition of a portal includes the idea of a *user*-centered view of the content of a web site. In other words, the concept of a user is central to the idea of a portal. Consequently, becoming a member of the portal is the first thing a visitor to the site might want to do. While many of the features of a CMF portal are generally available to guests, its real power is its capability to allow members to actively participate in providing content to the site.

When you view the new portal that you just created, a screen shows up and indicates that you are already logged in. The reason for this is that you previously logged in to manage your Zope installation. To simulate what users see, you will need to log out. In the upper-right corner of the Zope management screen, you will see a pop-up box currently set to Zope Quick Start. Select Logout from this box. You will see a message indicating that your authorization failed. Click the Cancel button, and you will be logged out. Then type the URL for your new portal, and you will see a screen similar to that shown in Figure 4.15.

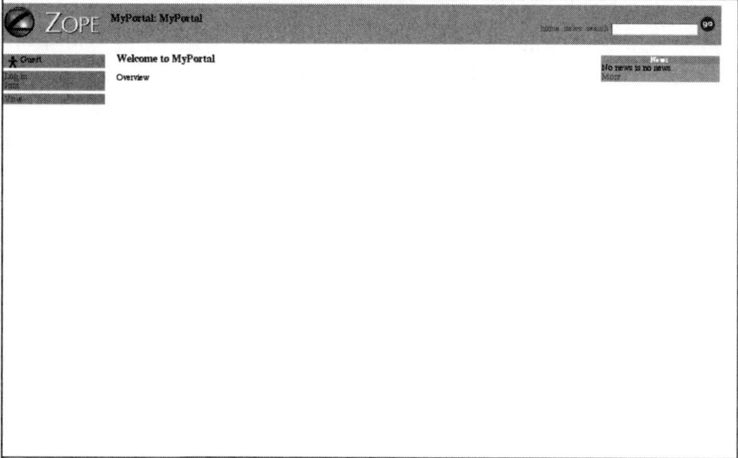


**Figure 4.15** User login screen for CMF.

This is the screen that a web viewer would see when he first comes to your portal. Notice that the user is currently logged into the portal as a guest. A guest has the capability to view news items and search for content on the site. However, a member has the additional capability to customize his view of the site and submit items or comments to the site. In other words, to a guest, the site is a standard web page, whereas, to a member, the web site has the full features of a portal (customizability and participation). A new user probably would want to *join* this portal. Notice the join option listed along the left side of the screen.

When a visitor clicks the Join link located along the left side of the main portal screen, he will see the main membership screen shown in Figure 4.16.

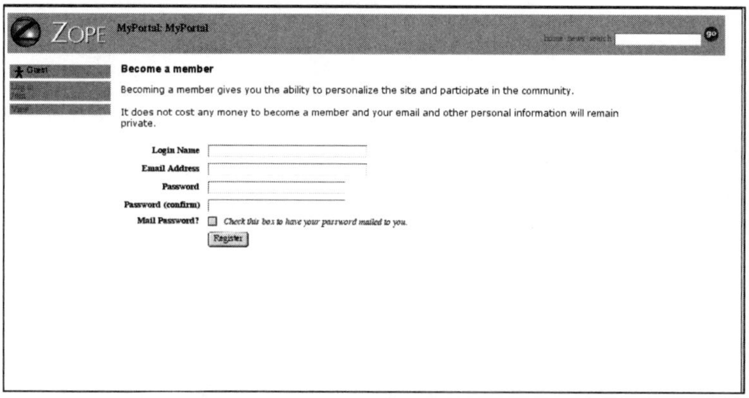

**Figure 4.16** Main membership screen for CMF.

To become a member of the portal, you need to provide a login name, an email address, and a password. You also can indicate to the portal that you want to have your password emailed to you as a safety. When you have provided all of the necessary information, click the Register button. You will be informed that you have successfully registered as a member of the portal, and you will be given a link to click to log in. Click the link to log into the portal.

At this point, there is no content in the portal. So, searching and looking around the portal will be a bit frustrating.

## Providing Content to the Portal

Click the navigation link to the left of the screen titled My Stuff to take you to your area of the portal. Click the New button to create a new object. The screen shown in Figure 4.17 will now appear.

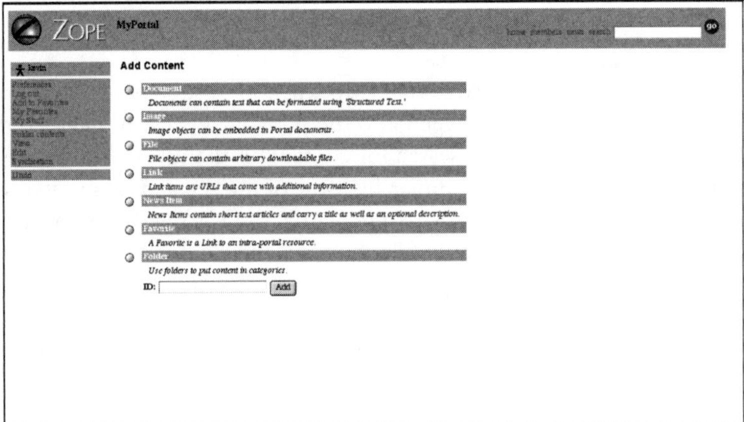


**Figure 4.17** Add CMF content.

The types of objects that you can add are:

- Document
- Image
- File
- Link
- News item
- Favorite
- Folder

Most of the objects that you can add are obvious, but the two most important and the two we are going to take a quick look at are a document and a news item. In Chapter 8 section, "Adding Your Own Content Type," we will look at how you can design completely new content type objects that can be instantiated by members and incorporated into the CMF site.

Begin with the news item object. Click the radio button next to News Item, give a unique ID, and then click Add. A title will appear asking you to supply a `title`, `description`, and `subject`. Enter the requested data and click Change. The item is now included in your personal folder. However, the item is visible only to you. To make the item available to other folks, you need to submit the item for review by the portal manager. To do this, click MyStuff and then click open the news item from the list. Now you will see a navigational link along the left side of the screen called Submit Item. Click this link, and you will be given the opportunity to submit this item. You can enter a comment about your submission and then click the Submit button below it. The news item will now be added to the items to be reviewed by the manager.

How does this item get reviewed? Log into the portal as one of the users you designated as an administrator (if you are not already logged in as such). You will immediately see that there are two control links along the left side of the screen that are for administrators only. They are Reconfigure Portal and Pending Review. Because you just submitted a news item for review, the number 1 should be in parentheses after the words Pending Review. Click this link, and you will see a list of all items that are awaiting your review (in this case, only one). Click the item that you want to review. Now you will be able to view the item under review. In addition you will see several new links along the left side of the screen: Publish, Retract, Reject, and Status History. Click the Publish link. This brings up a screen that allows you to make a comment before making the item available to the general viewing audience. Type any comment that you'd like to make, and then click the Publish This Item button. Now other members of the portal who perform a search where this item matches the criteria will find this news item and can click on it and read it.

If at some later time you decide that the item should not be viewable anymore (because it is incorrect or out-of-date, for example,), you can return to this screen by clicking the item and then clicking the Retract link. This removes the item from availability to anyone but the submitter and the administrative staff.

The Status History link allows you to see the various states (submitted, published, retracted, and so on) that this item has been in. It also shows who changed the state and when the state was changed, plus the comments that were included.

Earlier we discussed that one of the most important aspects of a portal is its capability to allow the user (member) to customize his site. One of the easy ways that is accomplished is by allowing users to "bookmark" or "tag" items that they find in the portal as important to them. This is done using the Favorites folder. When a user is looking at an item of interest that he wants to return to often, that user can click the Add to Favorites link in the left control panel. A link to the current item is then placed in the Favorites folder so that the user can quickly return at a later time.

This is a very basic introduction to CMF. A thorough discussion of CMF, its design goals, and its implementation would require an entire book of its own. Make sure to visit the **http://www.zope.org** site and **http://webdev.zopeonarope.com** for the latest on this developing technology. As we mentioned in the beginning of this section, CMF is actually more of a framework for creating portal products. What we have just looked at is a specific implementation of CMF used as a demonstration. It is a functional portal, but the real beauty of CMF is that it allows developers to create additional modules that conform to the CMF spec and that can be used to provide even greater functionality. We will look at CMF in more depth in Chapter 8.

# Tracker

One of the things that almost every organization needs to run smoothly is a way to track problems or issues. When people in the organization report problems, there needs to be a way to document whether the problem was resolved and, if so, how it was resolved and when. A very nice Zope product exists that can be dropped in and used with an existing site very easily. The product is called *Tracker*.

## Installing Tracker

Tracker is composed of some ZClasses, External Methods, and a Python product. It is available via read-only public *CVS* from cvs.zope.org. Concurrent Version Control (CVS) is an open-source, network-transparent version-control system. Most of the products that you have downloaded so far in Chapter 3 and that you will download and use in the remainder of this chapter and in Chapters 5 and 6 were obtained via the web browser and were contained in a .tar or .tgz file. Tracker is different. It is stored as source in a CVS repository at zope.org. We will discuss CVS in more depth in Chapter 14, "Multi-Developer Projects: Testing and Version Control," but for further reference, visit **http://www.cvshome.org**. To install Tracker, complete the following steps:

1. Log into the cvs.zope.org server by typing `cvs -d :pserver:anonymous@cvs.zope.org:/cvs-repository login`, followed by a Return.
2. Go to the $ZOPEROOT/lib/python/Products directory of your Zope installation.
3. Type `cvs -d :pserver:anonymous@cvs.zope.org:/cvs-repository co Products/TrackerBase`, followed by a Return.
4. You'll now have a TrackerBase directory in your Products folder.
5. Create a symlink in your $ZOPEROOT/Extensions directory to the $ZOPEROOT/lib/python/Products/TrackerBase/TrackerMethods.py file. (You could also copy the TrackerMethods.py file to the $ZOPEROOT/Extensions directory.)
6. Move the Tracker.zexp file to $ZOPEROOT/import. (Create one, if it doesn't exist.)

7. Restart Zope.
8. Go to the Product Management folder within the Control Panel, and click the Import/Export button. Type `Tracker.zexp` into the import field, and click the Import button. This will import the Tracker ZClass product.
9. Now make sure that the TrackerBase and Tracker products are installed correctly. Remember to check the user-support mailing lists on zope.org if any problems occur.

## Configuring Tracker

The basic object that Tracker works with is an *issue* object. The Tracker allows issues to be submitted and then tracks correspondence about those issue objects as they progress. An issue is submitted to the Tracker by a person who is designated the *requester.* Every issue is then assigned to a person or persons who are in charge of handling the issue. Individuals assigned to handle an issue are called *supporters.* Issues can have attributes or properties, called *traits*, which help define the nature of the issue.

Issues exist in one of many stages or states. The various states of an issue are as follows:

- **Pending**—This is the state of an issue when it is first submitted, before a supporter has accepted the issue for review.
- **Accepted**—The issue is under review by one or more supporters who have accepted responsibility for the issue.
- **Resolved**—A supporter has marked this issue as resolved.
- **Rejected**—The issue is considered completed, but without any resolution.
- **Deferred**—The issue has been put aside until a later time.
- **Diverted**—The issue has been grouped with another issue.

The Tracker can operate in either of two modes: *Open* or *Dedicated.* In open mode, a Tracker can be used by anyone who is capable of accessing it. In other words, use of the Tracker in open mode is controlled by the built-in security of Zope (users, roles, and permissions). If the Tracker is located in an area that is accessible to an anonymous user, then anyone will be able to look at the issues posted to the Tracker and post new issues to it.

A further level of security is provided by the dedicated mode of the Tracker. In dedicated mode, the Tracker uses its own user-management system to control access to its features.

To learn more about Tracker, install one in your school system web site that you can work with. As a practical example, create a Tracker to track issues relating to maintenance of building and grounds. At the root of your web site, select Tracker from the pop-up list of objects. The Tracker installation screen will appear requiring you to supply an ID for the new Tracker object (see Figure 4.18). Give it an ID of `MaintenanceProblems`, and click Add. Next there are two configuration screens that lead you through the process of setting up the Tracker.

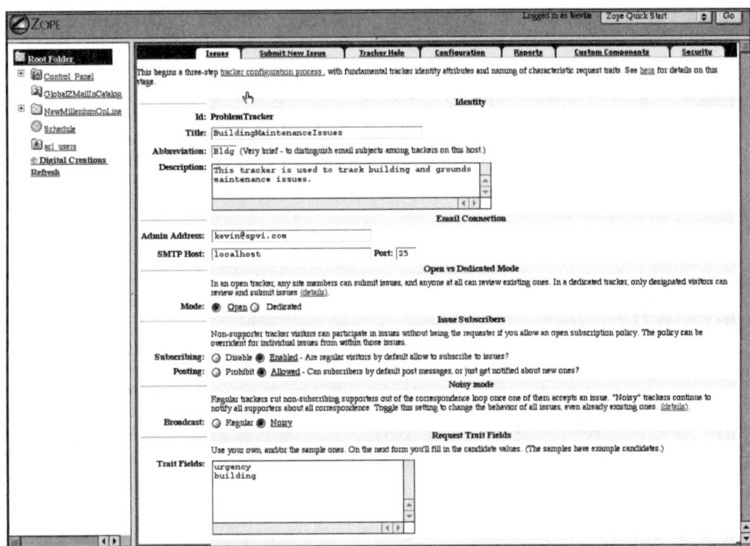


Figure 4.18 Tracker basic configuration.

The first configuration screen allows you to provide an optional `title` for the Tracker. The next piece of information is an *abbreviation*. The abbreviation is especially important on a web site where more than one Tracker is being used. The abbreviation is included on any emails sent out by the Tracker and will help to differentiate among the various Trackers. The abbreviation should be very short, with just enough information to communicate its source. Next, a *description* field is provided to allow you to enter a short description of the Tracker and its purpose. This description will appear at the top of the main page of the Tracker to help clarify its use for visitors.

Next, you need to supply the email address of the person who is the administrator for this Tracker. After this field is the domain name and port number of the SMTP host that will be used for outgoing email. Next are two radio buttons for specifying whether this Tracker will be running in open or dedicated mode, as discussed a few paragraphs back.

Trackers can limit participation in an issue to just the supporters and the requester of the issue, or they can be open to anyone. The next two sets of radio buttons relate to this issue. The first set enables you to specify whether the Tracker allows others to subscribe to an issue and, thus, be informed via email when there are changes to its status. This represents passive participation in an issue. The second set of buttons allows you to specify whether others can actively participate with the issue by being able to post messages related to the issue.

In the default case, once an issue has been accepted by a supporter, the rest of the supporters are shielded from further postings related to the issue. However, in some cases you might want to have all supporters continue to monitor the progress and discussion on an issue even after one of them accepts the issue for resolution. In this latter case, you would click the radio button flagging this Tracker as a *noisy* tracker.

The last field on this configuration page lists the traits associated with the issues in this Tracker. You can accept the default list or add and delete to create your own list. For your "buildings and grounds" Tracker, make things simple and delete all of the traits except for the "urgency" trait. Now add the trait "building" to the list. You'll use this trait to specify which building the issue involves. In the case of a school system, you will probably be in charge of several different schools and administration buildings—hence, the need for a "building" trait. When you have finished with the issue traits, click the Submit button at the bottom of the screen.

This brings you to the second configuration screen of your new Tracker, shown in Figure 4.19. This configuration screen is used to configure the supporters and the traits for your Tracker.

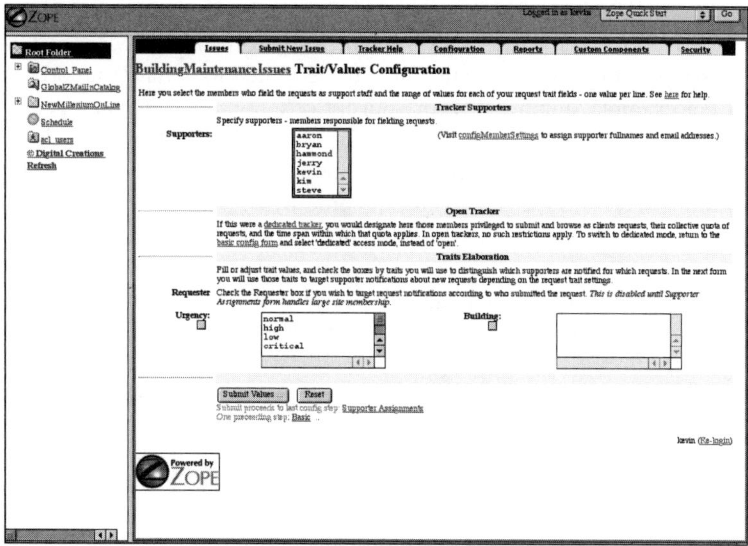


**Figure 4.19** Tracker traits and supporters configuration.

A supporter list is automatically created for you. The Tracker looks through the acl_users folders that are in its acquisition path. Any users that it finds are included in this list. In most cases, you will want to remove users from this list. You will probably have a couple of people who are designated as supporters. In the case of your school system, you'll certainly not want most of your teachers, parents, or students on the list of folks who could be assigned to resolve issues relating to the building and grounds. This list simply gives you a starting place. In addition to the names that are included, you might need to add users who currently don't have user accounts defined in your Zope installation. Simply add their names to the list and delete those that you don't want to be on the list of issue supporters.

Below the list of supporters is an area for defining the possible values for each of the issue traits that you specified in the previous configuration page. Notice that the "building" trait that you created in the previous configuration screen shows up here, but with no values specified. You will need to list the possible values for this trait here. In addition, you can add or delete any values for the other traits on this screen. The values for these traits will make it easier for users to delineate the nature of an issue. For your school system example, add the values "school 2" and "admin building" to the list of possible values for the "building" trait. Click Submit Values.

Now you have a list of possible supporters, plus you have a list of the traits of an issue and their possible values. The way that the Tracker is configured right now, email will come to the Tracker administrator only when a new issue is posted. It would then be the administrator's job to contact one or more of the supporters and assign them to the issue. At that point, the supporter would go to the Tracker and mark the issue as being "Accepted." In many cases, this is the best way to handle new issues. However, in some cases you might want certain issues to be routed to certain supporters automatically. For example, suppose that for your list of supporters, you want issues with "building 2" to go to Steve and Jerry. How do you tell the Tracker about this?

Click the Configuration tab at the top of the screen. This is the main configuration screen of the Tracker and the place you can come whenever you want to alter the way the Tracker is set up. Click the link for Traits and Supporters. You saw this configuration screen just a moment ago when you first set up the Tracker. Put a check in the check box next to the trait "Building." This indicates that you want to route email based upon the value in this.

Now you are finished configuring your Tracker; it is ready to be used. Configured this way, when an issue is submitted to the tracker, the person whom you designated as the administrator will receive notice of the issue posting.

## Using Tracker

One of the best things about the Tracker product is that it has loads of help screens and support documentation that are linked to from many of the management and user screens. Take advantage of this, and read them. They are extremely helpful and instructive.

Once again, the issue of authenticated users comes up. Like you did for the Science101 ZWiki earlier in this chapter, you might want to restrict use of the Tracker to users with certain roles. You can put the Tracker in a secure folder like you did for the Science101 Zwiki, or you can adjust the security of the Tracker itself, like you did for the ViewOnlyCalendar (also earlier in this chapter). If the Tracker is located in an area that is accessible to anonymous users and no special security is included, then anyone can post an issue to it. Although an anonymous user can post an issue to the tracker, numerous restrictions exist that make it less than ideal for the requester. Because there is no way for the Tracker administrator to verify the identity of the requester, the anonymous requester is not allowed to post any follow-ups to the issue.

In addition, the anonymous requester cannot include attachments of any kind to the issue submission, nor can he make the issue confidential. While anonymous access to a Tracker is allowed, it is generally not considered a good idea. Like the ZWiki discussed previously, a Tracker is better utilized within a controlled and trusted community of users.

To explore how to use the MaintenanceProblems Tracker, type its URL into your browser. The main screen of the Tracker will appear.

Notice that the description that you gave for the MaintenanceProblems Tracker shows up on the main screen under the heading Purpose. This helps potential users of this Tracker understand its intended purpose. Keep that in mind when you create your Tracker descriptions. The Tracker main page also instructs potential users about how to post an issue. Click the tab at the top of the screen labeled Submit New Issue. You will now see the screen shown in Figure 4.20.

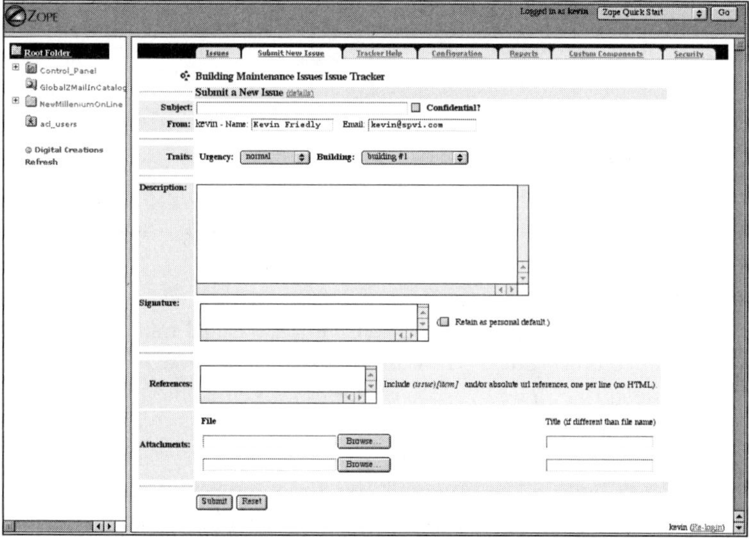


Figure 4.20 New tracker issue entry screen.

The first thing that you need to provide to submit an issue is a subject. Like email subject lines, you should make the subject short but informative. Next, you need to specify who the requester is. If you are an authenticated user, then this information might already be filled in for you. If not, then enter your name and email address. You email address is important if you want to be alerted via email when changes or additions to your issue occur. Next, you will see the traits listed with pop-ups containing the possible values. Set these pop-ups to the values that best reflect the nature of your issue.

Next, provide a description of the issue. The final three fields are optional, providing requesters with a way to add attachments to an issue, reference information, and a signature.

After you have filled in the relevant fields and clicked Submit, you will be returned to the main screen, and the issue that you created will appear (see Figure 4.21).

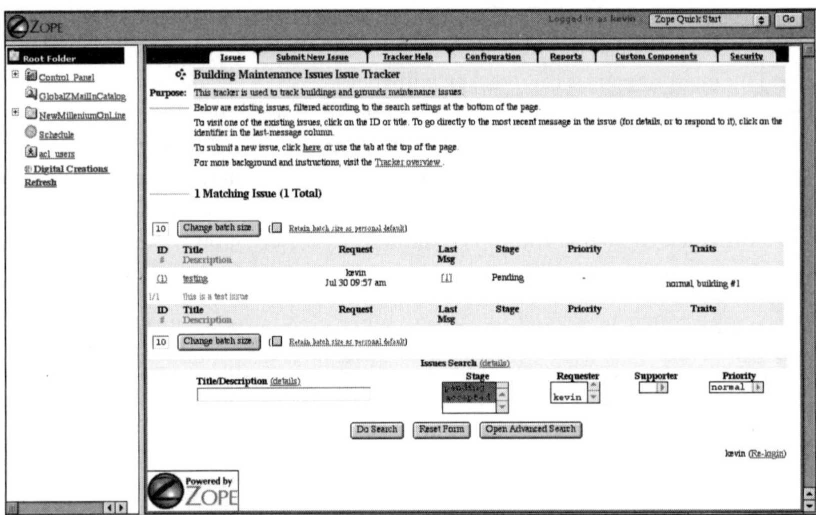

Figure 4.21 Main tracker screen with existing issue.

Click on the linked title of the issue. If you are currently logged in as one of the users who was listed as being a supporter, then you will a tab called Edit State at the top of the screen. Click the Edit State tab, and this brings you to a new screen (see Figure 4.22) that allows you to change the state of the issue. Remember that when an issue is first submitted, it acquires a state of "pending." A supporter then needs to review the issue and either accept, resolve, reject, defer, or divert it. Set the desired state, and click the Submit Changes button. The issue will now show the new state.

Finally, click the Reports tab at the top of the screen. This reports the status of all issues and shows the number of issues assigned to each supporter.

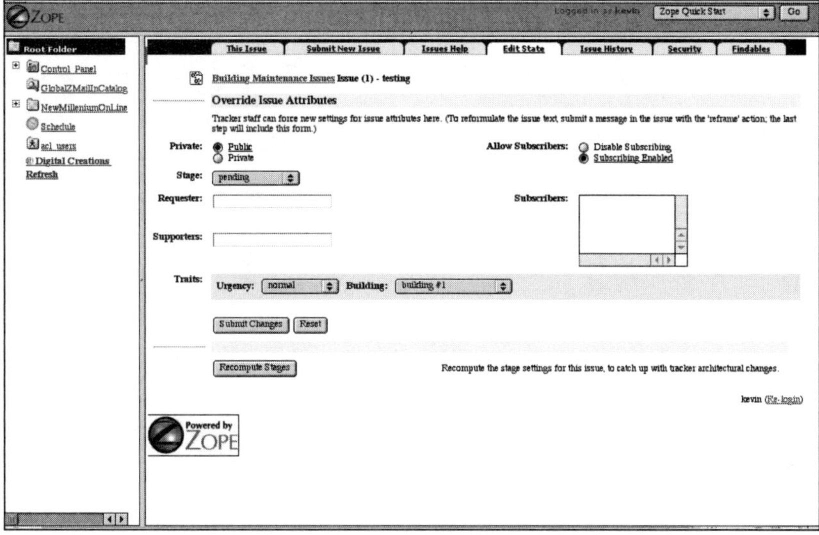


Figure 4.22 Changing the state of an issue.

# Summary

This chapter covered five different drop-in products for Zope that facilitate the two-way web. These products help support the process of allowing end users to become an active part in providing content to your web sites.

We also took an introductory look at Zope's built-in, multitiered security features and how to use them to create areas of your web site that are accessible only by a trusted community of users.

# 5 Web Mail

THIS CHAPTER RETURNS TO THE WORK started in Chapter 3, "Web Event Publishing," with the calendar and event tracking. In particular, this chapter covers how email can be integrated into this system. Email will be used to facilitate communications both *to* and *from* the user. And because many corporate systems today exist behind a firewall of some sort, this chapter looks at how to make email available to your users outside a firewall without compromising security.

This chapter looks at ways to use Zope to work with both POP and IMAP mail servers. Finally, it looks at a way to schedule periodic tasks in Zope and then how to use this feature to integrate email with the calendar project.

## Messaging Directly to Individuals

In Chapter 3, you created a mechanism for logging events and for displaying them on a web calendar. While the calendar is a great way to present event information to users, this is a passive mechanism. In other words, the calendar "sits and waits" until someone comes to it to view the events. Sometimes relying on the participants to remember to come to the calendar on a regular basis to be reminded of a meeting or event is not a wise thing. It would be better to provide a means of "actively" reminding your users of particular events.

Email is an active way of communicating information to users. You can use email to "push" information out to people. However, proper *netiquette* suggests that you obtain permission from users before sending them email; otherwise, it can be viewed as *spam*. For this reason, you should create a mechanism for allowing users to choose for themselves whether they want to receive email about a particular event. What you're going to create next is a way for users to *subscribe* to a particular event. After a user has subscribed to an event, you can email him about the event without fear of irritating him.

First return to the event Z Class that you created in Chapter 3. Remember that you edit Z Classes in the Product Management folder of the Control Panel. Your CalendarEvent Z Class has a property sheet called Fundamental, shown in Figure 5.1. To this property sheet, add a lines property and call it emails.

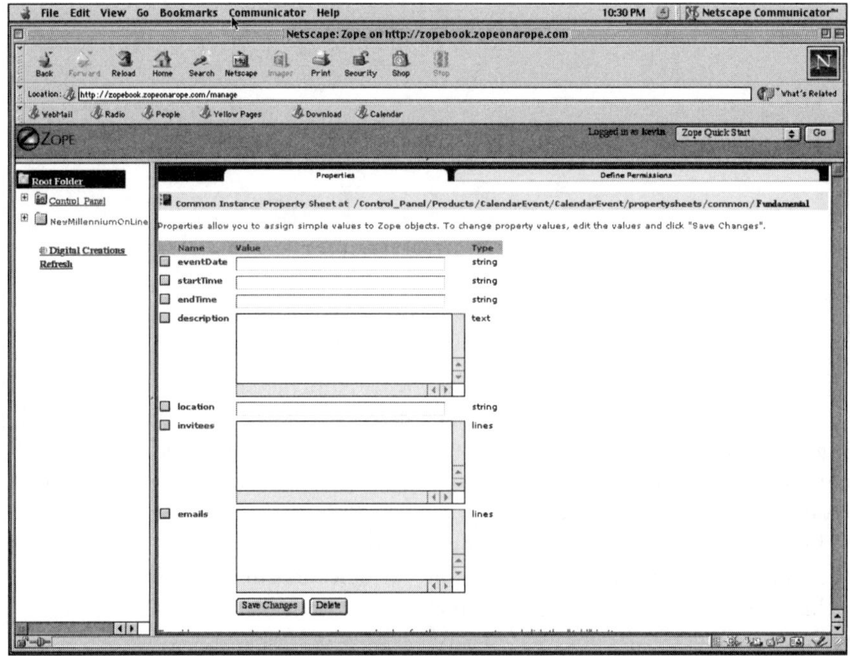


**Figure 5.1** Adding an email property to the CalendarEvent Z Class.

You will use this new property to store the email addresses of those who want to be reminded of this particular event. A lines property is especially useful for this kind of thing because it is stored as a Python *list* and can be iterated through easily with a `<dtml-in>` tag.

Because you want to give anyone the capability to add his name to a particular event, you will want to make it available on the ViewOnlyCalendar instead of the EditableCalendar, which is accessible only to a select group of people. Link each of the events displayed on the calendar to a method that will prompt for the user's email and then add it to the emails property of the selected event.

The code for the ViewOnlyCalendar from Listing 3.11 has been modified only slightly to make individual events clickable (see Listing 5.1).

Listing 5.1 **ViewOnlyCalendar Modified to Link Events to *addEmailToEvent* Method**

```
<HTML>
<HEAD>
  <TITLE>New Millennium Event Calendar</TITLE>
</HEAD>
<BODY>
  <CENTER>
      <dtml-calendar>
        <dtml-let year="date.year()"
        month="date.month()"
        day="date.day()"
        key="'%i-%i-%i' % (year,month,day)">
            <dtml-var day><br>
            <dtml-in "EventCatalog({'eventDate':key})">
                  <a href=addEmailToEvent?key=<dtml-var id>>
                  <dtml-var startTime> - <dtml-var endTime>
                  </a><br>
                      <dtml-var description>
                  <br>
            </dtml-in>
        </dtml-let>
      </dtml-calendar>
  </CENTER>
</BODY>
</HTML>
```

Now when an event is clicked in the ViewOnlyCalendar, a method `addEmailToEvent` will be called with the variable `key` set to the ID of the event. The `addEmailToEvent` method will use that ID to modify the selected event. Next you need to create the `addEmailToEvent` method. As you discovered in Chapter 3, a Python script is preferred over a DTML method when logic is involved, but a DTML method is easier when display is the purpose. Because the `addEmailToEvent` method will need to display a screen inviting users to provide their emails, you should use a DTML method. After the email is collected, the DTML method can then call a Python script to add the provided email to the selected event object. A sample DTML method is given in Listing 5.2.

Listing 5.2 **DTML Method *addEmailToEvent***

```
<HTML>
<BODY>
    <H2>Enter you email address below if you wish to be reminded
        about the event show below.<br><br></H2>
    <dtml-with "getAnEvent(REQUEST['key'])">
        <H2>
        <dtml-var description><br>
        <dtml-var eventDate><br>
        <dtml-var startTime> - <dtml-var endTime>
        </H2>

        <form action="addEmailToEvent_Feedback" method="post">
            <input type="hidden" name="key" value="<dtml-var key>">
            <input type="text" name="email">
            <input type="submit">
        </form>
    </dtml-with>
</BODY>
</HTML>
```

This method presents a simple form asking for the user to provide his email address. It also creates a hidden variable called `key` to maintain and pass on the ID of the event that is involved. The `addEmailToEvent` method calls another method, `getAnEvent`, to get the information about the desired event. Because this method provides calculations only and not output, you should use a Python script. The `getAnEvent` script should be configured to accept a single parameter called `anID` (see Listing 5.3).

Listing 5.3 ***getAnEvent* Python Script to Return a Particular Event from the Events Folder**

```
try:
    theEvent = container.Events[anID]
    return theEvent
except:
    return ''
```

While the code in Listing 5.3 is very simple and could have been performed just as easily using DTML in Listing 5.2, it is included as a separate method because, depending on how events might be stored in the future, the process of retrieving an event might be a little more involved. The best plan is to separate that process now and not have to make large adjustments later.

The action of the `addEmailToEvent` method is to invoke another method called `addEmailToEvent_Feedback`. This second method will provide the output to the user acknowledging that the email was properly added to the event or informing the user that an error occurred. Because this method is used to provide display to the end user, you should again use a DTML method (see Listing 5.4).

Listing 5.4 ***addEmailToEvent_Feedback*** **DTML Method Providing Result of Attempt to Add Email Address**

```
<HTML>
<BODY>
    <dtml-let returnVal="addEmailToEvent_Property()">
    <dtml-if returnVal>
        <h2>Thank you for your interest in this event.
        You will be reminded of this event at the email address
            listed below:
        <br><br>
        <dtml-var returnVal></h2>
    <dtml-else>
        <h2>Sorry.  An error has occurred.  Please try again.</h2>
    </dtml-if>
    </dtml-let>
    <br><br>
    <a href="ViewOnlyCalendar">Return to the Calendar</a>
</BODY>
</HTML>
```

The `addEmailToEvent_Feedback` method calls another method to do the actual work of adding the provided email to the property sheet of the selected event. Listing 5.5 is some sample code, `addEmailToEvent_Property`, which is used to perform that function.

Listing 5.5 ***addEmailToEvent_Property*** **Python Script to Add Email Address to a CalendarEvent Object**

```
try:
    theEvent = container.Events[context.REQUEST['key']]

    theEmails = theEvent.emails
    if theEmails:
        theEmails = theEmails + [context.REQUEST['email']]
    else:
        theEmails = [context.REQUEST['email']]

    theEvent.propertysheets.Basic. \
        manage_changeProperties({'emails':theEmails})
    return context.REQUEST['email']
except:
    return ''
```

This script makes use of the fact that the REQUEST object is available in the current context and that earlier you made the ID of the desired event object available in the namespace by attaching it to the REQUEST object. The email address is also available in the REQUEST object because it was entered into an HTML form before the call.

The `addEmailToEvent_Property` method first obtains the current setting of the emails property, which was set as a *lines* type property. A lines property is treated as a Python list. If there is something already in the emails property of the event, the new email is added to the list. Notice that the email is surrounded by square brackets ([]). This indicates that it is a list element and should be appended to the end of the existing list. If there is no current emails property, then a single-item list is created containing the new email address.

Next the `manage_changeProperties` method of the Fundamental property sheet is called with the new emails property passed in through a Python dictionary. At this point, the added email address is returned as a confirmation that the add process was successful. Notice that this process is enclosed in a try/except clause. If anything fails during the add process, then an exception is thrown and the script returns a string indicating a problem. This allows the `addEmailToEvent_Feedback` method to check for the existence of a non-null return value. If it finds a value, then it knows that the email was added correctly, and it informs the user of that fact. If it gets back a null value, then it knows that an error occurred, and it can appropriately inform the user.

## Creating Emails Programmatically Using the *sendmail* Tag

Now your calendar has the capability to display events and also to allow users to "subscribe" to events with the anticipation of being reminded, via email, of the selected event. Next you need to create a mechanism for retrieving the emails from the events and sending a message to those in the list reminding them of the event.

Start by creating a DTML method called `ReminderCalendar`. This method will be similar to the code in Listing 5.1. The only change will be the specific link. Instead of linking to the `addEmailToEvent` method, you will need to link the event to a method called `sendEmails`.

Listing 5.6 **DTML Method for ReminderCalendar**

```
<HTML>
<HEAD>
<TITLE>New Millennium Event Calendar</TITLE>
</HEAD>
<BODY>
   <CENTER>
       <dtml-calendar>
         <dtml-let year="date.year()" month="date.month()"  \
             day="date.day()" key="'%i-%i-%i' % \
             (year,month,day)">
             <dtml-var day><br>
             <dtml-in "EventCatalog({'eventDate':key})">
                   <a href="sendEmails?key=<dtml-var id>">
                   <dtml-var startTime>- <dtml-var endTime>  \
                       </a><br>
                     <dtml-var description>
                   <br>
```

```
                </dtml-in>
            </dtml-let>
        </dtml-calendar>
    </CENTER>
</BODY>
</HTML>
```

Notice that when an event is clicked the ReminderCalendar, it links to the `sendEmails` method and passes it the event ID through the variable `key`. The code for the `sendEmails` method is given in Listing 5.7.

Listing 5.7 **DTML Method for Sending Emails Using *sendmail* Tag**

```
<dtml-try>
     <dtml-with "getAnEvent(REQUEST['key'])">
           <dtml-in emails>
             <dtml-sendmail mailhost="calendarMailHost">
                 To: "<dtml-var sequence-item>" <<dtml-var sequence-item>>
                 From: <NewMilleniumnSchoolDistrict@spvi.com>
                 Subject: Event Reminder from NewMillenium School District

                 This is your reminder email for the following event:

                 Event: <dtml-var description>
                 Date: <dtml-var eventDate>
                 Start time: <dtml-var startTime>
                 End time: <dtml-var endTime>
                 Location: <dtml-var location>
             </dtml-sendmail>
           </dtml-in>
     </dtml-with>
<dtml-except>
</dtml-try>
```

## The Mail Host Object

The `sendEmails` method makes use of a built-in tag, `<dtml-sendmail>`, which you can use in a DTML method or document. As with most tags, there is an opening tag and a closing tag, `<dtml-sendmail>` and `</dtml-sendmail>`. The `<dtml-sendmail>` tag has six different possible parameters that can be used with it. The first is required. Either a mailhost or an smtphost parameter must be specified. To send email, a *Simple Mail Transfer Protocol (SMTP)* mail host must be specified. You can specify the desired smtp mail server as one of the parameters of the `<dtml-sendmail>` tag (as in `<dtml-sendmail smtphost="mail.spvi.com">`). However, there is another way that is much easier to manage when you have a large number of methods using the `<dtml-var sendmail>` tag.

Imagine, for instance, that you have 20 or 30 sites on your Zope installation all using the `sendmail` tag. What happens when your ISP changes? You have to go through all of your code looking for places where you have used the `sendmail` tag to make the change. What a headache! The Mail Host object is an object that can be instantiated to act as a sort of mailserver proxy (see Figure 5.2). The metatype for this object is MailHost. Instead of specifying a specific smtphost as a parameter to the `sendmail` tag, you can include the Mail Host object in the tag (as in `<dtml-sendmail mailhost="calendarMailHost">`). The actual domain name of the real smtp mail host is listed in the properties of the Mail Host object. When your mail host changes, you need only change it in one spot, and all of the sendmail calls will be adjusted.

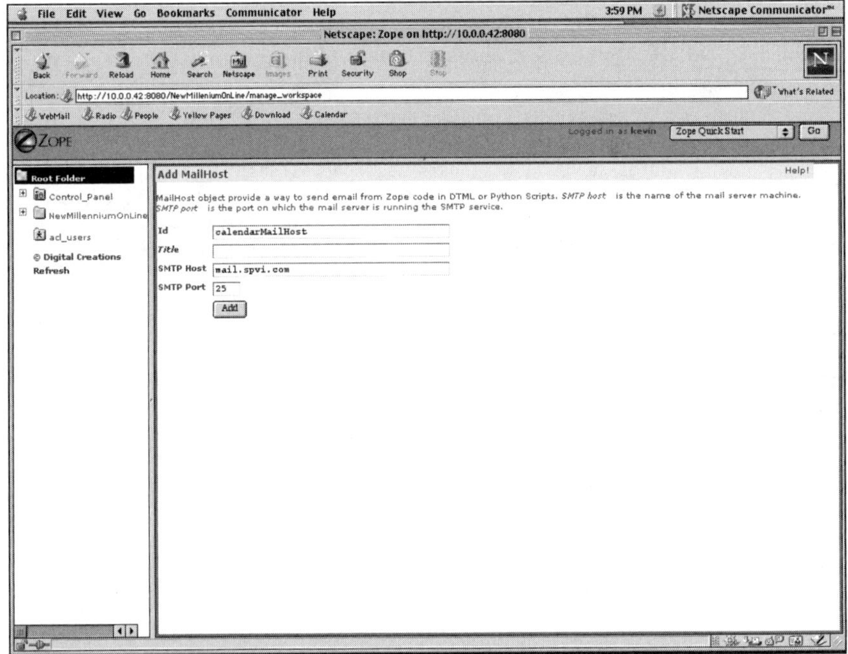


**Figure 5.2** Adding a Mail Host object.

Notice there are three required fields (ID, SMTP Host, and SMTP Port) and one optional field (title) for the Mail Host object. The default port for an smtp mail server is 25. This is the value that is included automatically when you instantiate a Mail Host object. The SMTP Host will probably be one of your own servers or will be one specified by your ISP. In the old days of the Internet, it was possible to specify almost any known smtp server for relaying your mail, but with the rise in commercial usage and with the inevitable increase in misuse and abuse of email, the use of smtp servers is becoming very controlled and you will need to make sure that the server that you associate with your Mail Host object is one that your Zope server has permission to use.

If neither of the keywords `smtphost` or `mailhost` is used but a value is found inside the `sendmail` tag (such as `<dtml-var sendmail calendarMailHost>`), then it is "assumed" to be the name of a Mail Host object. If neither is specified and there is *no* other value found within the `sendmail` tag, then an exception is thrown indicating that no Mail Host was specified.

## Optional Mail Host Parameters

Four other parameters can be included within the sendmail tag. They are `mailto`, `mailfrom`, `subject`, and `encode`:

- The `mailto` parameter specifies, as its name implies, the address for the recipient or recipients of the email. The `mailto` parameter is a comma-separated list of valid email addresses.
- `mailfrom` specifies the address to which replies will come. When a user receives this email and hits Reply, the mailfrom address is automatically inserted.
- The `subject` parameter is also obvious. The subject line should contain something that lets the recipient know what the email concerns. In this case, it is a reminder of a particular event.
- The fourth parameter, `encode`, is used to specify alternate encodings to be used for the email message. Possible values for this parameter are `base64`, `quoted-printable`, and `uuencode`.

This final parameter is optional, but the first three are required. They *must* appear either within the `sendmail` tag or in separate lines between the opening and closing tags.

Between the opening and closing `sendmail` tags, you place the contents of your email. The email is separated logically into a *header* and a *body*. It is in the header where you can specify the `mailto`, `mailfrom`, and `subject` if they are not included within the sendmail tag itself. If the `mailto`, `mailfrom`, and `subject` information is included in the header, the words *mailto* and *mailfrom* are replaced by the words *to* and *from*, as shown in Listing 5.7. A very important thing to remember is that there needs to be at least one blank line between any header information and the body of the email.

In Listing 5.7, the `<dtml-sendmail>` is contained within the body of a `<dtml-in>` loop. The values in the email property of the selected event individually are evaluated and inserted into the *to* line of the header using the `<dtml-var sequence-item>` tag. In other words, the `sendmail` method is called for each member of the emails property.

The body of the email can contain anything that you would normally put in the body of an email message, and then the message is terminated with the `</dtml-sendmail>` tag.

You're making progress. You've given the end user the capability to include himself on an email reminder list for each event. The good thing about this is that it can be accomplished without your intervention or the time and energy of the person in charge of the calendar. The user doesn't have to bother either of you to be added to an event's notification list. However, one of you still has to get involved for every event by clicking the event when a reminder needs to be sent out. While it's not difficult, it is still irritating that you have to remember to do this on a periodic basis. Wouldn't it be nice if this process could be automated in some way? It would be great if each event could "know" on its own that it needed to send out a reminder and then do it without even bothering you or your calendar manager.

# XRON, Automating Periodic Tasks

Well, you've probably guessed that we wouldn't have brought up the issue of automating the reminder process unless we had a solution to suggest. Again, the solution comes from a downloadable Zope product that can be instantiated and configured very easily. The product is called *XRON* (pronounced kron). XRON provides Zope with features similar to the familiar *cron* process found on UNIX systems.

## Installing XRON

For this book, we are using version 0.0.9 of XRON. To install XRON, complete the following steps:

1. Download the Xron-0-0-9.tgz file to your Zope server from **`http://www.zope.org/Members/lstaffor/Xron/Xron-0-0-9.tgz`**.
2. Copy this file to the $ZOPEROOT directory.
3. Unzip the Xron-0-0-9.tgz file. Type `gunzip Xron-0-0-9.tgz`.
4. Next untar the resulting Xron-0-0-9.tar file. Type `tar -xvf Xron-0-0-9.tar`. This produces a directory called Xron in the $ZOPEROOT/lib/python/Products folder.
5. Restart Zope from the Control Panel.
6. Check to make sure that XRON is installed properly and doesn't show a broken product icon.
7. Remember to check the user-support mailing lists on zope.org if any problems occur.

The XRON product installs a new object into the pop-up list of available objects. The object is called a Xron DTML method. As its name implies, it's essentially nothing more than a standard DTML method. However, this method also has a couple of additional properties associated with it that are related to time. You can include anything in an Xron method that you would in any other DTML method. When you instantiate a new Xron method, however, you are given the capability to associate a specific date and time with it. The date and time are provided in the form of a Zope date/time object. You are also given the opportunity to specify a retrigger period for the event called a *reschedule interval*. This interval is specified as a floating-point number and represents the number of days until the event is re-executed. A value of 1.0, for instance, means the same time every day. A value of 0.5 means to execute the method every 12 hours. Every hour would require the value of approximately 0.0417 (4.17E-2). Every minute would be 6.944E-4.

Create a Xron method, call it `sendEmailsAuto`, and then give it an execution time of 06:00:00 and a date that is some time after the current day. Now give it a reschedule time of one day. Be careful not to schedule it for a time and date that have already passed. Even if you set the reschedule interval to be every day, the method will never execute if the original time is in the past because the reschedule interval is applied only when the event method actually executes. In other words, when the method runs, it then looks at its own setting for the reschedule interval and queues itself to run again at the specified interval from the current time. If the method doesn't execute the first time, then it never gets the opportunity to reschedule itself; it sits and waits forever for its initial date/time to occur. Now your screen should look like what is shown in Figure 5.3.

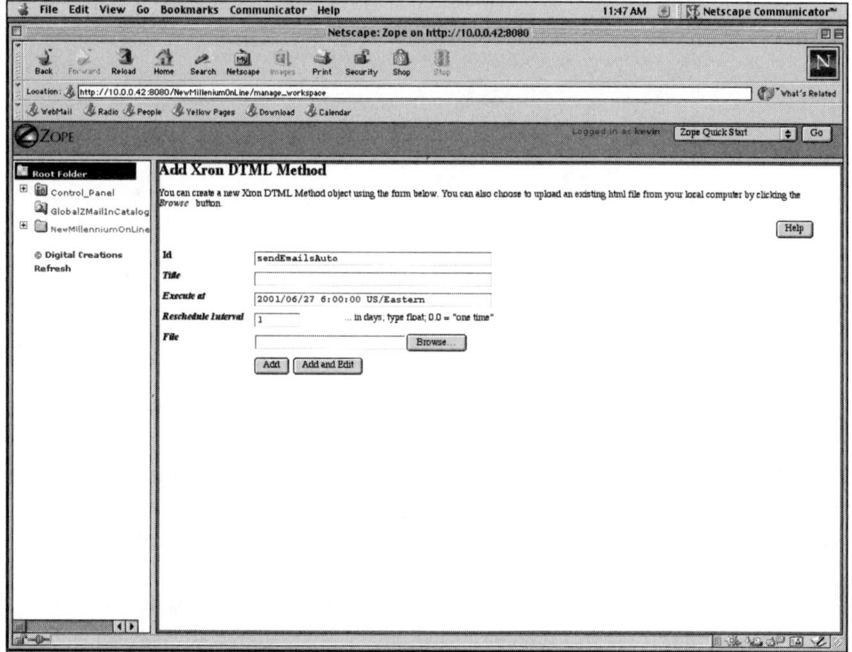


Figure 5.3 Adding a Xron method.

When you instantiate a Xron object, XRON looks at the root of your Zope installation for a ZCatalog named *Schedule*. If this ZCatalog object already exists, then the Xron object that you just created is added to this catalog. If the Schedule catalog does not exist, then Xron creates it and logs the current event in it. The Schedule ZCatalog is automatically configured to catalog objects of the metatype XronDTMLMethod.

Now you have a method that will execute every morning at 6 AM. Before you start work on the code to automate the process of sending emails for events scheduled for the current day, take a brief look at the Schedule ZCatalog that exists at the root of your Zope installation (see Figure 5.4).

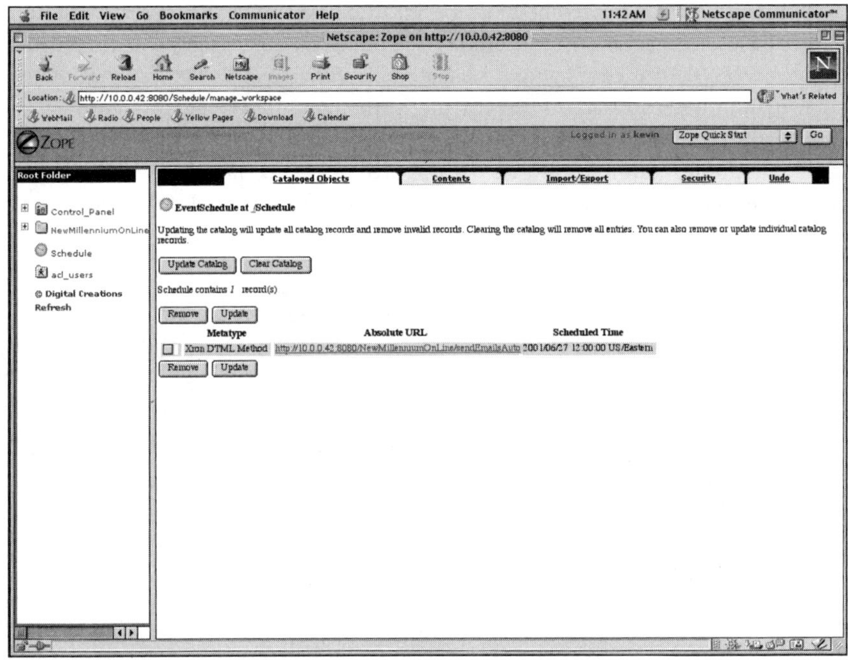

**Figure 5.4** Schedule ZCatalog of XronDTMLMethod objects.

Notice that the catalog contains a reference to your Xron object. Although this Schedule object is a ZCatalog, it does not include many of the tabs that you are accustomed to with a standard ZCatalog. There is no way to "find" objects into the catalog or to specify properties, indexes, or metadata for the catalog. This stuff is done automatically for you when the Schedule catalog is created. Some of the operations normally accessed through the Advanced tab in a standard catalog (Update Catalog and Clear Catalog) are available on the primary screen for the Schedule catalog. When an XronDTMLMethod executes, it updates its own entry in the catalog automatically; however, if you makes changes to its date/time or reschedule time, you will have to update the catalog to reflect those changes. Chapter 11, "Design for Integration the ZPatterns Way," covers ZPatterns and how this kind of updating can be made to happen automatically.

## A Specific XRON Task

Now return to the XronDTMLMethod object that you just created and add some code to it to send out the emails. When you open the new XronDTMLMethod, you'll see that a single line has been placed in the content area by default. The line is Content-type: text/plain. This line is included to facilitate output to the web. This text is required if your XronDTMLMethod is required to produce output. If it produces output, then the web server must be informed that the type of output is text. Otherwise, it will attempt to "download" the output to your local machine. You must include at least one blank line between the content-type line and whatever output you intend. A XronDTMLMethod does not have to produce any output, but any output that it does produce is sent to the Zope log file. For this method, you can remove the default text and replace it with the following code in Listing 5.8.

Listing 5.8 ***sendEmailsAuto* DTML Method for Sending Emails Automatically**

```
<dtml-let today="ZopeTime()"
    year="today.year()"
    month="today.month()"
    day="today.day()"
    key="'%i-%i-%i' % (year,month,day)">

        <dtml-in "EventCatalog({'eventDate':key})">
            <dtml-call "REQUEST.set('key',id)">09
            <dtml-var sendEmails>
        </dtml-in>
</dtml-let>
```

Listing 5.8 begins by getting the day, month, and year strings from ZopeTime(). These represent the day, month, and year for today's date. In the same way in which you combined those strings to create your eventDate string for each event, sendEmailsAuto combines the strings representing today's date into a string that will be used as a search parameter for the EventCatalog. The <dtml-in> tag uses today's date key and returns a list of the objects whose eventDate property are the same. For each item in the returned list, a value called *key* is set in the REQUEST object and a call is made to the sendEmails method, which you created earlier in Listing 5.7. The *key* value is the actual ID of the calendarEvent object whose email property you want to access. Just as it did for the "manual" reminder system that you designed earlier, sendEmails uses the *key* to retrieve the calendarEvent object and then sends an email to any addresses listed in the emails property of that object.

One further modification that you might want to make is to remind folks *before* the actual day of the event. For instance, you could modify the system to send reminders every day starting three days before the actual event (see Listing 5.9).

Listing 5.9 ***sendEmailsAuto*** **DTML Method for Sending Emails Automatically Starting Three Days Beforehand**

```
<dtml-in "_.range(4)">
     <dtml-let today="ZopeTime()+_['sequence-item']"
          year="today.year()"
          month="today.month()"
          day="today.day()"
          key="'%i-%i-%i' % (year,month,day)">

          <dtml-in "EventCatalog({'eventDate':key})">
               <dtml-call "REQUEST.set('key',id)">
               <dtml-var sendEmails>
          </dtml-in>
     </dtml-let>
</dtml-in>
```

The code listed in Listing 5.9 is essentially the same as that shown in Listing 5.8, except that it is enclosed in a <dtml-in> loop that increments through the list [0,1,2,3] produced by the Python *range* function. That index is then added to the ZopeTime object representing the current date. Adding an integer to a date/time object is equivalent to adding a day. This is one of the big advantages of using date/time objects instead of managing the day, month, and year by yourself. When you need to specify a date in the past or future, you don't have to hassle with incrementing or decrementing the month or year appropriately. That is all handled internally by the date/time object. So, you are now checking for events that are to occur today and for the next three days—just what you wanted. You can imagine modifying this even further to allow each event to have its own "schedule" for reminder emails. Some events could be scheduled to send reminders every week starting a month in advance, while others could have a schedule that calls for reminders to be sent every day for a week before the event. Others might require only a single reminder sent on the morning of the actual event.

At this point, you have a fairly sophisticated system for managing calendar events. A person designated as the calendar manager can use the EditableCalendar to add new events to the calendar or edit existing ones. Those events then show up on the ViewOnlyCalendar that users can peruse. In addition, users can click an event of special interest and "subscribe" to the event to be reminded of the event via email. Your system has a method that is set to execute at 6 AM every day. The method searches the EventCatalog for events that are scheduled any time in the next three days. If it finds any events matching that criterion, it passes the IDs of those events to the method `sendEmails`, which loops through any email addresses for the selected events and sends a reminder message to the included addresses. Because you made it easy to add new events and edit existing ones, and because you made it possible for users to add their emails to an event by themselves, you have relieved yourself of a lot of responsibility, giving you the time and freedom to continue making your online school system even more productive.

# POPMail

One of the problems encountered by many businesses and organizations is the need to provide access to resources such as email from outside the organization while maintaining a reasonable level of security. Many corporate systems exist behind a firewall. In cases like this, email might be available to employees when they are at the office but might not be accessible from outside the office. Even if the mail server is not behind a firewall, as such, it might be configured to allow POP access only from certain domains or IP ranges for added security. One way around this that when an employee is out of the office, business email can be forwarded to the employee's personal account, which can be accessed from home or from the road. Again, however, maintenance becomes an issue. As people come and go, you will need to turn forwarding off and on and try to keep track of where everyone is at all times to make sure that email is directed to the correct location.

You now have a way for folks in your organization to be reminded via email of certain events on your school calendar. However, this is not much good if you have a person who is out of the office for several days or maybe for the whole summer and can't check email from home because of a firewall. You don't want to breach your security to allow this kind of access, but it would be nice if you could provide a means for remote email access.

Again, Zope comes to the rescue with another drop-in product that you can add that gives *Post Office Protocol (POP)* mail access to users through the web. The product is called *POPMail*. It comprises two separate pieces. One is a Python product called *POPMailBase* and is installed in the ControlPanel/Products folder.

The other piece is a Z Class product called POPMail, which contains a Z Class object called a *POPMailAccountFolder*. This product makes use of the POPMailBase product to accomplish its tasks. Within the POPMailAccountFolder product, another product is defined called a *POPMailAccount*.

## Installing POPMail

This product comprises two parts, POPMailBase, a Python-based product, and POPMail, a Z Class–based product. For this book, you are using versions 0.5 for both. To install POPMail, complete the following steps:

1. Download the POPMailBase-0.5.tgz file to your Zope server from **`http://www.zope.org/Members/dshaw/POPMailProduct/POPMailBase-0.5.tgz`**.
2. Copy this file to the $ZOPEROOT/lib/python/Products directory.
3. Unzip the POPMailBase-0.5.tgz file. Type `gunzip POPMailBase-0.5.tgz`.
4. Next, untar the resulting POPMailBase-0.5.tar file. Type `tar -xvf POPMailBase-0.5.tar`. This produces a directory called POPMailBase in the $ZOPEROOT/lib/python/Products folder.
5. Restart Zope from the Control Panel.

6. Check to make sure that XRON is installed properly and doesn't show a broken product icon.
7. Remember to check the user-support mailing lists on zope.org if any problems occur.
8. Next download the POPMail-0.5.zexp file to your Zope server from **`http://www.zope.org/Members/dshaw/POPMailProduct/POPMail-0.5.zexp`**.
9. Copy this file to the $ZOPEROOT/import directory.
10. Go to the Control_Panel/Products folder of your Zope installation and click the Import/Export button. Type `POPMail-0.5.zexp` into the box labeled Import File Name. Click Import, and the product will be imported into your Zope installation.
11. If you have any trouble importing this file, check the user-support mailing lists on zope.org.

## Using POPMail

To use the POPMail product, you create a POPMailAccountFolder in your Zope installation. Select POPMailAccountFolder from the pop-up list of products, and call it myPopMailAccounts. A POPMailAccountsFolder is used to hold instances of POPMailAccount objects. You can create an instance for each of your email accounts by clicking the AddPOPMailAccount button. Each POPMailAccount object requires four parameters: `Unique Account Identifier`, `User name`, `Password`, and `Server name`. The account identifier is used like an ID. The username and password are the ones associated with the particular email account that you are setting up, and the server name is the fully qualified name of the domain server that controls your POP3 mail account. Fill in the fields with the appropriate information and click Add Account. You can add a POPMailAccount for each of your email accounts. To retrieve your mail from an account, click the account object and press the View tab. The headers for your mail will be retrieved and displayed as shown in Figure 5.5.

If you want to read the contents of an email message, you simply click the subject line and the entire contents of the message will be retrieved and displayed. It's that simple.

In your actual production site, you might want to create folders for each user who needs access to email from outside the office. In this way, you can give password protection for each user's folder adding to the security of the system. Within each user's folder, you can place a POPMailAccount folder and a POPMailAccount object connected to the user's email account.

## POPLib Python Library

The POPMail product makes extensive use of a Python library called POPLib. It might be useful for you to know some of the features of this library so that you can create your own POPMail related products and services, if needed. Or to allow you to modify the existing POPMail product.

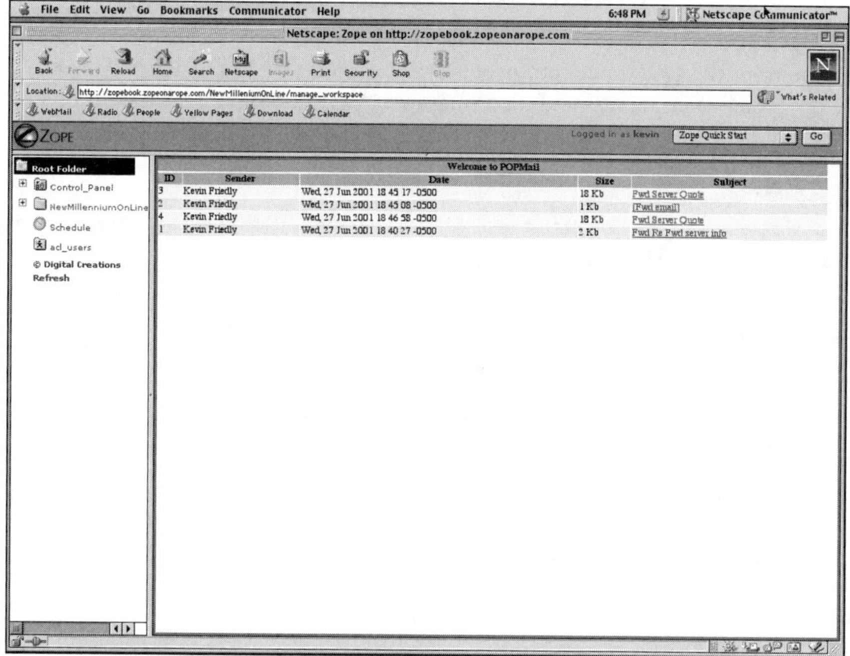


**Figure 5.5** Retrieval of POP3 Mail Using POPMailAccount Product.

The library defines a class POP3 that "wraps" a connection to a POP3 server. All of the standard POP3 commands are available as methods of the class and have the same name as the corresponding command (all lowercase).

> **For More Information**
>
> Detailed information about POPLib can be found at **`http://www.python.org/doc/current/lib/module-poplib.html`**.

When you instantiate a POP3 object, you pass in a hostname for your pop server. Optionally, you can pass in a port number if it is anything other than the default pop port 110. The instantiation phase sets a few of the properties of the POP3 object and then attempts to make a connection to the selected host and port. When a connection is established, the standard POP3 calls can be made. You first need to call the `user` method and pass in your username. Next you must make a call to the `pass_` method and provide your email password. At that point, you can call `list` and receive a list of the current emails. When you have finished all of your processing, you need to make a call to `quit`, which closes the file and socket connection that were created when the POP3 object was instantiated. This quick look at POPLib should help you understand how the POPMail product works and how to modify it if you need or want to.

# IMapClient

In addition to the POP3 mail protocol, there is the *Internet Message Access Protocol (IMAP)*, which is in popular and increasing use. IMAP is a more recent creation and is better designed for use with mail that must be retrieved from multiple locations.

> **For More Information**
>
> A good discussion of the differences between IMAP and POP3 can be found at **`http://www.imap.org/imap.vs.pop.brief.html`**.

The main advantage to IMAP is that a user's mail remains on the server instead of being downloaded to a local machine. This helps a user stay "in sync" even if he has multiple machines with which to read mail. Emails don't become distributed over multiple systems. Several products for Zope support IMAP, and more are coming. The most popular products are ZopeGUM (Grand Unified Messenger); its successor, ZopeGUD (Grand Unified Desktop); and a product called IMapClient. Most of these products are beyond the scope of this book. However, if your system uses IMAP, you should download these products from **`http://www.zope.org`** and experiment with how they might fit into your Zope installation. A short discussion of IMapClient, though, is appropriate because it can be incorporated quickly into your system.

## Installing IMapClient

For this book, you are using version 0.1.2 of ImapClient. To install ImapClient, perform the following steps.

1. Download the ImapClient-0.1.2.tar.gz file to your Zope server from **`http://www.zope.org/Members/jack-e/ImapClient/ImapClient-0.1.2.tar.gz`**.
2. Copy this file to the $ZOPEROOT.
3. Unzip the ImapClient-0.1.2.tar.gz file. Type `gunzip ImapClient-0.1.2.tar.gz`.
4. Next untar the resulting ImapClient-0.1.2.tar file. Type `tar -xvf ImapClient-0.1.2.tar`. This produces a directory called ImapClient in the $ZOPEROOT/lib/python/Products folder.
5. Restart Zope from the Control Panel.
6. Check to make sure that ImapClient is installed properly and doesn't show a broken product icon.
7. Remember to check the user-support mailing lists on zope.org if any problems occur.

When IMapClient is installed, there are two objects that you can instantiate, an *ImapClient* and an *ImapMailbox*. The main work is done in the ImapMailbox object. It appears that the expected way of using ImapClient is to instantiate an ImapClient folder and then add ImapMailbox objects to it. While this appears to be the designed way of using it, there appears to be no reason why ImapMailboxes can't be instantiated outside of ImapClients. Both instances appear to retrieve IMAP email the same way.

Clearly, ImapClient is a product that is still in flux, but even at this stage of development, the product can be added to your Zope installation to provide almost instant functionality with IMAP. There are a couple of problems with the current version (0.1.2) of ImapClient, but considering the smallness of its version number, this is to be expected. By the time you are reading this book, the problems might be fixed—but, if not, the source code provides a great starting point for further development. The most obvious problems at this point have to do with the ImapMailbox object. The pop-up box listing the kinds of objects that can be added to an ImapMailbox comprises two objects, a Folder and a Message. At this writing, the Message object does not appear to work. However, when you add a Folder object to the ImapMailbox, it appears to correctly add the named folder to your actual mail folder located on the file system of your IMAP mail server.

In addition to the problem with the Message object not appearing to be fully implemented, there is an unnerving situation when creating a new ImapMailbox. One of the properties that you are asked to provide to the ImapMailbox is the password of your mail account. Instead of using a standard password type input line, the default form for creating a new ImapMailbox uses a standard text input field. The result is that rather than appearing as a series of dots, your private password is shown in its entirety on the screen. The reason for this is that the form used to add a new ImapMailbox simply defines the input box for the password as a standard text input box. An HTML form can define an input line of the type password and, when a user types anything into it, only dots appear. This gives a bit of security and certainly makes the user more comfortable.

While the idea of concealing a password from prying eyes is a comfort, you should be aware that the POP mail protocol sends passwords, by default, in an unencrypted way. The following paragraphs describe how to modify the code to hide your password when you type it in, but don't allow yourself to become complacent and assume that this means that your password is safe. It isn't necessarily! Although it might not be seen by eyes over your shoulder, it can still be viewed by a skilled hacker who is monitoring your network traffic. Real security involves much more than hiding passwords on the screen.

There is an easy fix for this problem. It involves going into the Python source code for the ImapClient product and making an edit to the input form for the ImapMailbox object. Use the trick shown in Listing 5.10 when you edit the form.

Listing 5.10 **HTML Code for Hiding Password Input**

```
<form action="doSomething">
    <input type="password" name="thePassword">
    <input type="submit">
</form>
```

The source code for the ImapClient product is found in the $ZOPEROOT/lib/python/Products folder. There you will find an ImapClient folder with the source code for the ImapClient product. In the __init__.py file, you will find the following lines in Listing 5.11.

Listing 5.11 **Partial Source for __init__.py for the ImapClient Product**

```
# Product meta-data:

# Names of objects added by this product:
meta_types=(
            {'name':'ImapClient','action':'manage_addImapClientForm'},
            {'name':'ImapMailbox','action':'manage_addImapMailboxForm'},
            )

# Attributes (usually "methods") to be added to folders to support
# creating objects:
methods={
            'manage_addImapClientForm': ImapClient.addImapClientForm,
            'manage_addImapClient': ImapClient.addImapClient,
            'manage_addImapMailboxForm': ImapClient.addImapMailboxForm,
            'manage_addImapMailbox': ImapClient.addImapMailbox
            }
```

The __init__.py is the starting place for a Python product. When you start digging into the code for a product, this is generally the first place to go. This particular __init__.py uses a deprecated technique to register the ImapClient objects with Zope, but it is still supported. You'll get a chance to try out the new registration procedure in Chapter 12, "Integrating Applications with ZPatterns," when you create your own TotallySimpleProduct for Zope. Notice in this code that the metatypes that can be used are listed as ImapClient and ImapMailbox. The "action" associated with the ImapMailbox is `manage_addImapMailboxForm`.

Following the metatypes dictionary definition, you'll see the definition for another Python dictionary called *methods*. In this dictionary definition, you can see that the manage_addImapMailboxForm is associated with the ImapClient object.

Next, look in the ImapClient.py file for information about the addImapMailboxForm. You'll see this line:

```
addImapMailboxForm=HTMLFile('manage/addMailbox',globals())
```

This indicates that the addImapMailboxForm is an HTML file named addMailbox and that its location is in a directory called *manage*. Locate the manage folder within the ImapClient folder; inside you'll find a file called addMailbox.dtml. The file is actually a DTML file, not an HTML file, but to a browser they are equivalent. Inside this file you will find the lines shown in Listing 5.12.

Listing 5.12 **Partial Source for addMailbox.dtml File**

```
<tr>
    <th align="LEFT" valign="MIDDLE"><em>Password</em></th>
    <td align="LEFT" valign="MIDDLE"><input type="text"
      name="password" size="50"></td>
</tr>
```

Notice that the input type for the password field is set as text. Change that to be type password, and browser magic will happen. For this fix to take effect, you will need to restart Zope. When this is done, you will find that when you instantiate a new mailbox and type in your password, it will show up as dots in the predicted manner.

The only problem remaining with regard to the password is that if you attempt to edit the properties of the ImapMailbox, the standard property sheet will show up and the password will once again be visible. To remedy that, you will need to supply a property sheet edit screen to override the default one because property sheets don't have the concept of password fields.

Let's look in the ImapMailbox.py file for information about where the screen is that controls management of properties. In this file, you will find the line shown in Listing 5.13.

Listing 5.13 **Partial Source for ImapMailbox.py File**

```
manage_options=(    {'label':'Contents','icon':icon,'action':'manage_main',
➥'target':'manage_main'},     {'label':'ACL','icon':icon,'action':
➥'manage_editACLForm','target':'manage_main'},     {'label':'Sieve','icon':icon,
➥'action':'manage_sieve','target':'manage_main'},     {'label':'Properties',
➥'icon':icon,'action':'manage_propertiesForm',      'target':'manage_main'},
➥{'label':'Security','icon':icon,'action':'manage_access','target':
➥'manage_main'},     )
```

Notice that the Properties tab is associated with an action controlled by `manage_propertiesForm`. This is the default screen that is invoked when properties are to be edited. Use the same format as was used previously for locating the addMailbox dtml file, and create a line in the ImapMailbox.py file that associates a new file with `manage_propertiesForm`. In other words, you are going to specify a file that will override the default behavior of `manage_propertiesForm`. Call the file editMailboxProperties.dtml, and place it in the manage folder. Insert the following line into the ImapMailbox.py file:

```
manage_PropertiesForm = HTMLFile('manage/editMailboxProperties',globals())
```

Now you need to create the source for the editMailboxProperties file. As a starting point, use the source from the addMailbox.dtml file. You'll need to change the action method of the form to `manage_edit`, which is the method that was called by the default form for editing properties (you could discover that by looking at the HTML source for the page on which properties are edited). If you look at the source for `manage_edit`, you'll see that it simply changes the values of the properties based on the values in the REQUEST object and then puts up a message box that acknowledges the edits. That dialog box has `manage_main` as its action, which returns the user to the default screen for the ImapMailbox, which is just the contents.

Listing 5.14 **Source for *manage_edit* Method in the ImapMailbox.py File**

```
def manage_edit(self,title='Mailbox',username='',password='',host='localhost',
    userfolder='INBOX.',REQUEST=None):
        """edit ImapMailbox"""
        self.title=title
        self.username=username
        self.password=password
        self.host=host
        self.Folder = userfolder
        if REQUEST is not None:
            return MessageDialog(
                title='Edited',
                message='<strong>%s</strong>has been edited.' % self.id,
                action = './manage_main'
                )
```

In addition to changing the form's action method, you will need to add default values in each of the fields that come from the ImapMailbox's property sheet. That is accomplished with <dtml-var> statements. Also, for aesthetic reasons you will want to change the title from Add to Edit, and change also the value of the Submit button from Add to Edit (see Listing 5.15).

Listing 5.15 **Source for *manage_edit* Method in the ImapMailbox.py File**

```
<html>
<head>
<title>Edit ImapMailbox</title>
</head>
<body bgcolor="#FFFFFF">
<h2>Edit ImapMailbox</h2>
<form action="manage_edit" method="POST">
<table cellspacing="2">
    <tr>
        <th align="LEFT" valign="MIDDLE">Id</th>
        <td align="LEFT" valign="MIDDLE"><input type="TEXT" name="id"
            size="50" value="<dtml-var id>"></td>
    </tr>
    <tr>
        <th align="LEFT" valign="MIDDLE"><em>Title</em></th>
        <td align="LEFT" valign="MIDDLE"><input type="TEXT" name="title"
            size="50" value="<dtml-var title>"></td>
    </tr>
    <tr>
```

```
        <th align="LEFT" valign="MIDDLE"><em>Username</em></th>
        <td align="LEFT" valign="MIDDLE"><input type="TEXT"
            name="username" size="50" value="<dtml-var username>"></td>
    </tr>
    <tr>
        <th align="LEFT" valign="MIDDLE"><em>Password</em></th>
        <td align="LEFT" valign="MIDDLE"><input type="password"
            name="password" size="50" value="<dtml-var password>"></td>
    </tr>
    <tr>
        <th align="LEFT" valign="MIDDLE"><em>Host</em></th>
        <td align="LEFT" valign="MIDDLE"><input type="TEXT"
            name="host" value="localhost" size="50" value="<dtml-var
            ➥host>"></td>
    </tr>
    <tr>
        <th align="LEFT" valign="MIDDLE"><em>Userfolder</em></th>
        <td align="LEFT" valign="MIDDLE"><input type="TEXT"
            name="userfolder" value="INBOX." size="50"></td>
    </tr>
    <tr>
        <td></td>
        <td><br><input type="SUBMIT" value="Edit"></td>
    </tr>
</table>
</form>
</body>
</html>
```

Now restart Zope, and the new add and edit files will be available. When you add a new ImapMailbox, your password will be hidden in the standard way. Plus, it will remain hidden when you attempt to edit the properties of your ImapMailbox.

# ZmailIn

In the beginning of this chapter, you looked at ways that email can be used to communicate information to users from your system and how to facilitate those users' access to their email even outside a firewall. Next you're going to look at how email can be used to communicate "in" to your system. In other words, you're going to look at how Zope can read your email and do intelligent things with what it reads.

The product available at **http://www.zope.org** that makes this task much easier is called *ZMailIn*.

## Installing ZMailIn

For this book, you are using version 1.0 of ZMailIn. To install ZmailIn, complete the following steps:

1. Download the ZMailIn-1-0-0.tgz file to your Zope server from **`http://www.zope.org/Members/NIP/ZMailIn/ZMailIn-1-0-0.tgz`**.
2. Copy this file to the $ZOPEROOT.
3. Unzip the ZMailIn-1-0-0.tgz file. Type `gunzip ZMailIn-1-0-0.tgz`.
4. Next untar the resulting ZMailIn-1-0-0.tar file. Type `tar -xvf ZMailIn-1-0-0.tar`. This produces a directory called ZMailIn in the $ZOPEROOT/lib/python/Products folder.
5. Restart Zope from the Control Panel.
6. Check to make sure that ZMailIn is installed properly and doesn't show a broken product icon.
7. Remember to check the user-support mailing lists on zope.org if any problems occur.

## Configuring ZMailIn

A new object is now available for use called ZMailIn Client. When you instantiate an instance of ZMailIn Client, you will be asked to provide four pieces of information. You will need a unique ID, as with all Zope instances, a title, an email, and a method. The ID and title are obvious. The email property is the email address that you want to connect to Zope. This will be the "to:" field for any message destined for this ZMailIn client. You'll need to supply an email address for a domain over which you have some control because you will be required to do some configuring of your mail transfer agent (MTA). The method property should contain the name of a Zope object that will handle the incoming message. The ZMailIn client essentially provides an association between an incoming email address and an object that handles the email. The actual work is done in the method object itself.

When ZMailIn is installed, a *GlobalZMailInCatalog* is installed at the root of your Zope installation. The catalog keeps track of all the ZMailIn clients that are installed on your system. When an email comes into your MTA, it must be directed by the MTA to a program rather than a user. Most MTAs can be configured to deliver mail to a process. Each system is different, so you will need to research your particular system to determine how to configure your MTA.

**Procmail**

Vectoring email to a process instead of a user using an MTA requires you to have root access to your system. Sometimes this is not possible or convenient. Another means of accomplishing the same thing without the need for root access is to use a program called Procmail, which can be installed on your system by your system administrator. The Procmail program passes all emails that are directed to your email address through a filter that determines the final destination of each message. One way to make use of procmail is to specify that every message sent to you with the subject line "Send to Zope" should be routed to the zopeMailIn.py program.

In our work, we are using FreeBSD and the `sendmail` program provided with it. To configure `sendmail` to redirect email to a process, you need to add the following line to the /etc/mail/aliases file:

```
newmillennium: "| /usr/local/etc/Zope2b/lib/python/Products/ZMailIn/zopeMailIn.py"
```

The word before the colon (:) is the email address without the domain name. After the colon is the path to the process preceded by a UNIX pipe character, all enclosed in parentheses. The pipe tells sendmail that the mail is to be redirected to a process, not a user. The process to which you want to direct these emails is the *zopeMailIn.py* program found in the /lib/python/Products/ZMailIn product folder of your Zope installation.

This Python program parses the incoming email for the destination address. Keep in mind that if you have several ZMailIn clients established for a particular Zope installation, you might have several different emails being routed to Zope through this same program. Therefore, it must first determine which incoming email address is involved and then determine the final destination object for this email. The destination is determined by querying the GlobalZMailInCatalog for the associated ZMailIn client and then retrieving the method property from the selected client. This provides the final destination object for the email. The program zopeMailIn.py then calls the method object specified for this client and passes it a single parameter, *theMail*, which is a Python dictionary containing the parts of the email message. The parts of the message are: *headers*, *localpart*, *body*, and *attachments*.

- The headers element contains another Python dictionary whose elements are the various components of the header: `mime-version`, `content-type`, `message-id`, `to`, `date`, `from`, `subject`, and `received`.
- The localpart element contains the name of the local receiver of the email, minus the `@domainname.com` portion.
- The body element contains a single string that represents the contents of the email message.
- The attachments part is another Python dictionary containing the paths to the attached files.

## Using ZMailIn

Let's take a look at a practical use for this ZMailIn product. Suppose that you want to keep a record of emails sent to you asking for help. You could set up an email address—say, `help@newmillenniumonline.com`—and publicize its use for help-related issues. In your aliases file, you could create an alias, help, and point it to your own email address plus the zopeMailIn.py program. That way, you would receive a copy of the mail to read (and hopefully act on), plus Zope would receive a copy of the mail to process. What do you want Zope to do with the email? You might want to log each help email into a database that can be searched and organized. In addition, you might want Zope to reply to each request for help and indicate that the sender's request has been received. This makes the person on the other end a little more comfortable knowing that the email made it to a "real" destination. Let's create a mail handler that does these two things.

After you have created your help email alias and pointed it to your own email address and the zopeMailIn.py program, you are ready to create the mail handler. For this example, you'll need to instantiate an object programmatically and add it to a ZCatalog. Because this work will not involve much display, you should probably make your mail handler a Python script instead of a DTML method or DTML document. Before you can create your mail handler, though, you'll need to create an object to hold the various components of each email. In Chapter 3, you created a Z Class object to hold your calendar events. You should do the same thing for the email events.

Although there are other components of the email, these seem to be the properties that are the most useful. You can add any of the other components listed previously if you see a use for them. Notice that in Figure 5.6, the property for date has been chosen to be a Zope date/time object. Remember this when you start creating your mail handler to create an EmailObject.

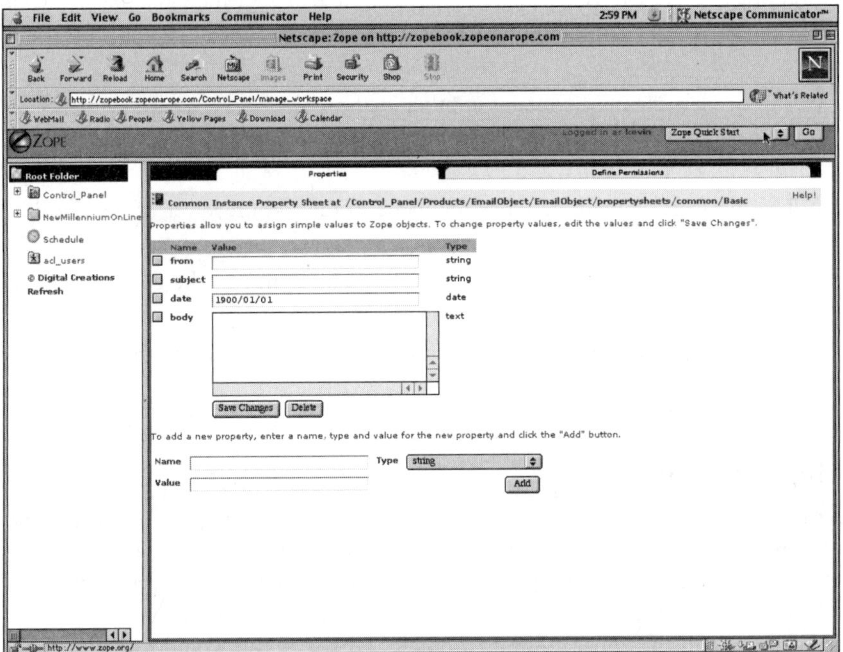


Figure 5.6 Property sheet for EmailObject Z Class.

Next you should create a folder in which to store the actual email objects and a ZCatalog in which to catalog the emails. Configure your ZCatalog to index the `from`, `subject`, `date`, and `body` fields so that they are all searchable. Now you're ready to create your mail handler to extract the email components, create a new instance of an EmailObject, and fill its properties with the values from the email. Finally, the mail handler should add the newly created MailObject to the MailCatalog.

Remember that in Chapter 3, you wrote a Python script for creating new CalendarEvents and then another one for adding new events to the catalog. In Listing 5.16, you create a Python script that creates a new instance of an EmailObject and also adds it to the EventCatalog at the same time. For this example, call the Python script `helpMailLogger`.

Listing 5.16 ***helpMailLogger* Python Script to Create and Catalog an Instance of EmailObject**

```
01 import string
02
03 newob = container.MailObjects.manage_addProduct['EmailObject'].
04 EmailObject.createInObjectManager(`context.ZopeTime().timeTime()`,
05       context.REQUEST)
06
07 newob.propertysheets.Basic.manage_changeProperties
08 ({'from':theMail['headers']['from'],
09       'subject':theMail['headers']['subject'],
10       'date':context.ZopeTime(),
11       'body':theMail['body']})
12
13 thePath = string.join(newob.getPhysicalPath(),'/')
14 container.MailCatalog.catalog_object(newob, thePath)
```

This script starts by importing the Python string module that will be needed to create a path to the newly created EmailObject. Line 03 is the line that actually creates the new object. It is similar to the line that you used in Chapter 3 to create the new CalendarEvent, except that the metatype of the created object is replaced with EmailObject. Notice again the use of `ZopeTime()` to create a unique ID for the object. The next line accesses the Basic property sheet of the new object and passes it the desired values (in a Python dictionary) of the properties. Remember that you elected to make the `date` property an actual Zope date/time object, so you won't be able to use the date property directly from the email. You could use the information from the email to create an actual date/time object, but, in this case, it is easier to simply use the date/time object returned by `ZopeTime()`.

Now you have a method of capturing emails sent to a particular address. This kind of capability will be highly useful in a number of different situations related to your school system. Because the emails are cataloged in a ZCatalog, they can be searched for content or by sender or date very easily.

More detailed information on the standard format of email messages can be obtained by reading the "Standard for the Format OF ARPA Internet Text Messages"[1] document, which can be found at **`http://www.ietf.org/rfc/rfc0822.txt`**.

## Summary

This chapter looked at the various uses of email both as a tool for "pushing" information out to users and as a means of getting information into the system. It covered the `sendmail` tag that allows you to produce email messages dynamically. It also covered Zope's support for both POP and IMAP mail servers. Finally, you learned about automated task controlled by the XRON product. With these added features, the Event Calendar has now turned into a pretty sophisticated tool.

1. "Standard for the Format OF ARPA Internet Text Messages," Revised by David H. Crocker, August 13, 1982, The Internet Engineering Task Force.

# 6

# News, Polls, and Web Tools

THE PREVIOUS THREE CHAPTERS of Part II, "Leveraging Zope Components," looked at a number of drop-in products for Zope that can be modified slightly to become very powerful tools in a company's IS department. Section II started with tools to help "publish" information, dynamically to the web (the one-way web). Chapter 4, "Zope Discussion Tools," looked at products that facilitate communication back from the end user (the two-way web). Chapter 5, "Web Mail," continued with two-way web products, with a particular focus on how email can be brought into play. This chapter continues the work on drop-in products, emphasizing products that reach out to information sources beyond your immediate control and also on products that collect and store information for quick retrieval and use. The chapter finishes with a couple of products that help make web development faster and easier.

## Local Access to External Resources

One of the most important aspects of web sites today is their ability to keep us connected to the latest information and news. In the early days of the web, a quality web site was one that included its own company's important information, plus lots of links to other quality web sites where its users could go for more of the "latest and greatest." In other words, a good web site in those days was one that gave its visitors quick access to other sites with important information.

The feeling is different today. People don't want to come to your web site and then have to follow the myriad of links you've listed to get the information that you think is important. They want you to get that information for them and present it right on your web site—"one-stop shopping," so to speak. It would be nice and convenient if these other web sites that you've deemed so important could ship their most up-to-date information to you in a timely way so that you could incorporate it right into your web site. In this way, you could collect information from many different sites and present it all together on your site. Your visitors could get the benefit of numerous web sites all at one web location.

There are certainly easy ways to go out to a web site, read in the pages of that web site, and lay them down in a table element of your own web page. One of the problems with this is that, when you do it this way, all the layout (HTML) from the other organization's web site comes with it. You need to either time-consumingly remove this HTML and filter the content for the things that you want or just drop the whole thing into your page. You can well imagine that if your page contains "drop-in" web sites from several different sources, each using its own colors and layout, your web site might have a truly horrible look. It would be better if you could get the content from these web sites without all the HTML and then decide how to dress up the content yourself so that it integrates cleanly with your own web site. In addition, it might be nice for the content pieces to be accessible singularly as individual packets with a description of the content so that you could decide on a chunk-by-chunk basis whether the particular content is something you want to display.

Folks have been thinking about this for some time. Several mechanisms have been devised and currently are being used that allow web sites to share or *syndicate* information to others. You can tap into this syndicated information and incorporate it right into your web site. Your visitors won't even have to leave your web site to get the latest in news, stock quotes, sports stories, and weather. Sources of syndicated content are called *channels*.

Most of these syndication methods are coded using the *Extensible Markup Language* (*XML*). A specification called the *Resource Description Framework* (*RDF*) was developed by the World Wide Web Consortium (**http://www.w3.org**) to codify and support information interchange on the web. More information on RDF can be found at **http://www.w3.org/RDF**. One of the first syndication methods based on the RDF specification was devised by Netscape for use in its My Netscape Network service. Users could customize their personal web pages at Netscape and incorporate news from different sources as long as they used Netscape's format. That format was called *RDF Site Summary* (*RSS*). Later the name was modified (by some) to be *Rich Site Summary*.

The first five chapters of this book discussed the use of Zope in the context of your invented role as an IT manager of a fictitious school system called New Millennium. This chapter continues in that vein. Outside news sources can be a vital resource for both teachers and students. Providing a location or locations on your web site where they can go to get up-to-date information from diverse web locations can be a valuable service.

A number of Zope products support the RDF and RSS formats. Let's take a look at some of those and how to incorporate them into your web sites. There is no way that a book of this breadth can go into the kind of detail that is really necessary for a complete working knowledge of RDF, RSS, and XML; those topics are best left for another book. However, many of these products still can be successfully utilized without a deep knowledge of these ideas. This book will be capable of only skimming the surface of these products and will have to leave the bulk of the research to you.

**For More Information**

Hjelm, Johan. *Creating the Semantic Web with RDF: Professional Developer's Guide.* New York: John Wiley & Sons, 2001.

Brickley, Dan, et. al. *RDF Specifications: Containing Resource Description Framework RDF Schema Resource Description Framework RDF Model and Syntax Specification.* World Wide Web Consortium. iUniverse.com, 2000.

## RDFSummary

*RDFSummary* is a Zope product that can be dropped into a web site quickly to provide access to other sites that provide free, RDF-formatted content. For this book, version 1.4 is being used. The developer of this product is listed as the European Environment Agency (EEA). Of note is an acknowledgement included at the bottom of the "Release Information" page that the authors make to the work of Edd Dumbill in his product *SiteSummary* (**`http://www.zope.org/Members/EIONET/RDFSummary/RDFSummary-1.4.tgz/README.html`**).

The authors state that the RDFSummary product would "probably never have seen the daylight" if they hadn't been able "to build on top of Edd Dumbill's SiteSummary product." This is the battle cry of the open source movement (of which Zope is a part). Open source development allows authors to take great works done by others and modify, enhance, augment, and improve on them. The result is that *everyone* in the community benefits. You will see acknowledgements included with many products, and you should feel completely free to make your own enhancements or bug fixes to products that you use. When you do, inform the original author and the rest of the Zope community; and be sure to acknowledge the previous work and its author.

## Installing RDFSummary

To install RDFSummary, complete the following steps:

1. Download the RDFSummary-1.4.tgz file, which can be found at **`http://www.zope.org/Members/EIONET/RDFSummary`**, to your Zope server.
2. Copy this file to the $ZOPEROOT directory.
3. Unzip the RDFSummary-1.4.tgz file. Type `gunzip RDFSummary-1.4.tgz`.
4. Now untar the resulting RDFSummary-1.4.tar file. Type `tar -xvf RDFSummary-1.4.tar`. This produces a directory down in $ZOPEROOT/lib/python/Products called RDFSummary.
5. Restart Zope from the Control Panel.
6. Make sure that RDFSummary is installed correctly and doesn't show a broken product icon.
7. Remember to check the user-support mailing lists on zope.org if any problems occur.

## Making an RDFSummary and Incorporating It into a Site

To make an RDFSummary and incorporate it into your site, go to the root of your school system project and check the pop-up list of objects that can be added. You will see a product there called RDFSummary. Select this product and, when asked, provide it with an ID of `SquishdotRDFSummary`. In the URL of RSS File line, type **`http://www.squishdot.org/rdf`** to point to an RDF encapsulation of the popular Squishdot site mentioned in Chapter 4. Leave the Optional Proxy Server field blank.

When you click the Add button an RDFSummary object will be created. Click the new object and take a look at its management interface. You'll notice a View tab along the top of the screen and will certainly be tempted to click it to see what happens. If you do, to your great disappointment, you'll find that nothing very useful is displayed. That's because the new RDFSummary object needs to be populated first with new information. This is accomplished using the Update tab at the top of the screen. When you click this, you will see a message that the contents of the RDFSummary object have been successfully updated. Now you can click the View button to see what you have. You will see something similar to what is shown in Figure 6.1.

You'll notice that there are four separate sections of data designated: *Properties*, *Channel Information*, *Image information*, and *Items*. Channel Information and Image Information are implemented as Python dictionaries. The Items section is implemented as a Python list of Python dictionaries.

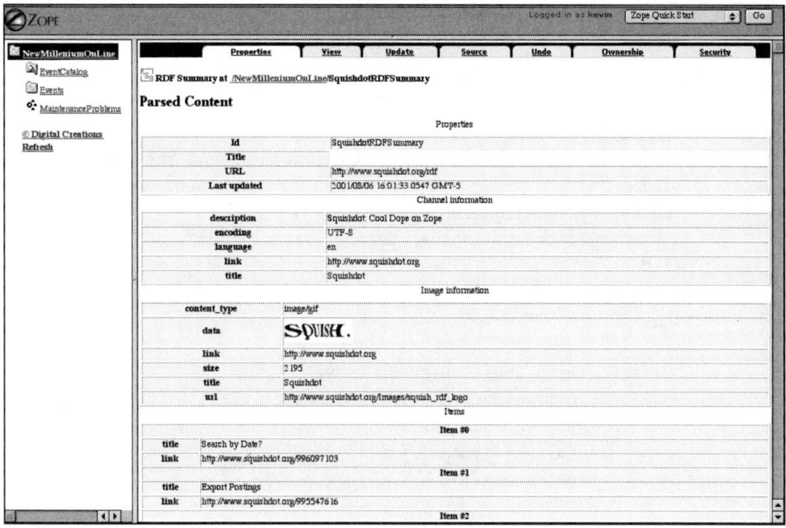


Figure 6.1 RDFSummary object contents.

Properties simply lists the descriptive properties of this RDFSummary object. The channel information gives basic information about the source of the RDF information that is included. This information is provided by the remote source. It gives things such as the title, a description, and the type of encoding that is being used.

The next piece is called the Image Information area. Most RDF sources provide a signature image with their data that they hope you will use in some way on your site to acknowledge the use of their content. This section describes the included image and contains the actual data.

The final section is where the real meat is. This section is called the Items section. It includes the individual pieces of content that the RDF site provides. Each item has a title and a link to the actual content. You can use both the title and link information to provide access to the data in your web site.

After you have created an RDFSummary object, a channel, you will need to incorporate its data into your actual web site. Start by creating a DTML method with an ID of `TestRDFSummary`. Place the code from Listing 6.1 into it.

Listing 6.1 **TestRDFSummary DTML Method Accessing RDFSummary Data**

```
<dtml-var standard_html_header>
<center>
<table border=5>
    <tr>
        <td colspan=4 align=center>
            <h2>New Millennium School District Banner</h2>
```

*continues*

Listing 6.1 **Continued**

```
        </td>
    </tr>
    <tr>
        <td align=center>
            Up-to-the-minute Information<br>from around the web
        </td>
        <td colspan=3 align=center>
            <h3>Welcome to another year at school</h3>
        </td>
    </tr>
    <tr>
        <td>
            <dtml-with SquishdotRDFSummary>
                <center><B><dtml-var "channel['title']"></B></center><br>
                <dtml-var picture>
                <dtml-var "image['title']">
                <font size=-1>
                <UL>
                <dtml-in items mapping>
                    <LI><a href="<dtml-var link>">
                    <dtml-var title></a><br>
                    <dtml-if "_.has_key('description')">
                        <dtml-var description>
                    </dtml-if>
                </dtml-in>
                </UL>
                </font>
            </dtml-with>
        </td>
        <td colspan=3 rowspan=4>
            This is an area where you can place pertinent news for the \
            ➥school district
        </td>
    </tr>
    <tr>
        <td>
            Another RDF source
        </td>
    </tr>
    <tr>
        <td>
            A third RDF source
        </td>
    </tr>
    <tr>
        <td>
            A fourth RDF source
        </td>
    </tr>
    </table>
<dtml-var standard_html_footer>
```

When the code from Listing 6.1 is rendered, you will see a display similar to the one shown in Figure 6.2.

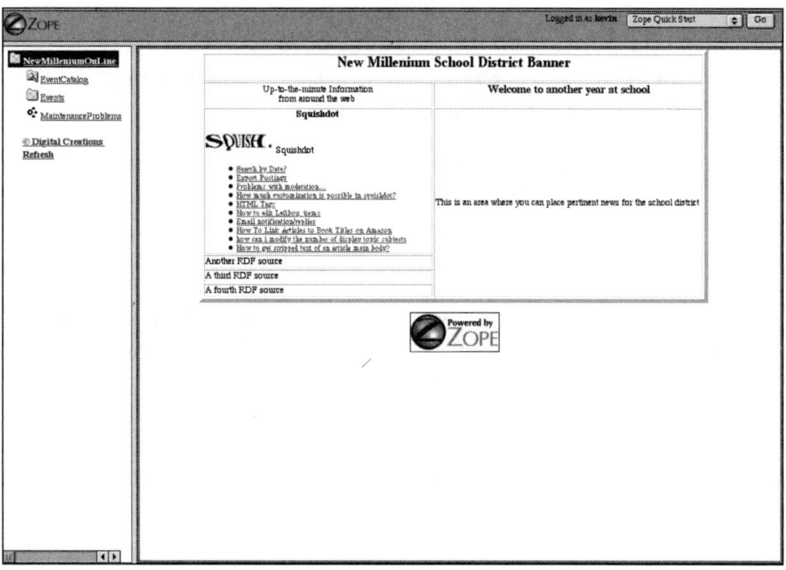


**Figure 6.2** RDFSummary object contents.

Take a look at how DTML was used to gain access to some of the elements of the `SquishdotRDFSummary` object. The magic occurs between lines 19 and 34. In line 19, the context is set to the `SquishdotRDFSummary` object. Next, in line 20, the variable channel is referenced. Its elements can be accessed like a Python dictionary. Line 20 accesses the `title` element. Line 21 references a method called "picture," which renders the image object of the RDFSummary.

Next, create a `<dtml-in>` loop to step through the various item objects in the RDFSummary object. This `<dtml-in>` loop uses a parameter "mapping" that tells it that the items in the returned list may be objects and that some attributes might not be available by simply referencing them by name; they need to be looked up. This is the case for the RDFSummary product. Now when you refer to `link`, `title`, and `description`, they will be available.

It should be obvious from the code in Listing 6.1 and the display from Figure 6.2 that multiple RDFSummary objects can be created and their results can be dropped into the remaining parts of the HTML table.

One last thing that you need to do is to create a way to update an RDFSummary automatically so that you don't have to go to each one's Update tab every hour. To cause an RDFSummary object to update itself, you simply call its `update` method.

That method is called when you add `/update` to the end of the URL for the RDFSummary, or it can be called using Python syntax, as shown in the code in Listing 6.2. Create a DTML method called `UpdateRDFSummaries`, and use the code shown in Listing 6.2.

Listing 6.2 **Updating All RDFSummary Objects Programmatically**

```
<dtml-var standard_html_header>
<dtml-in "objectValues('RDF Summary')">
    <dtml-with sequence-item>
        <dtml-call "update()">
    </dtml-with>
</dtml-in>
<dtml-var standard_html_footer>
```

Now the code in Listing 6.2 enables you to update all the RDFSummary objects that are in the acquisition path of this object, but you still have to remember to execute it on a periodic basis. It would be nice if you could automate this task in some manner. Go back to Chapter 5 and make use of the XRON product discussed there.

In general, remember to make sure that you have permission to use the RDF information from a source before you start grabbing it. Also, it is not considered good "netiquette" to access RDF information more often than about once an hour. Remember, there are others who are probably downloading copies themselves.

# Polls

So often in community situations someone needs to take a poll about an issue. Every day on the cable and network news stations, you hear about a national poll being taken concerning some issue. Polls are useful devices for collecting people's opinions about issues. You can certainly imagine that a school district would have multiple uses for polls.

## Poll Product

In the case of online polls, Zope again comes to the rescue with a nice product called, appropriately enough, *Poll.* The current Poll product that we are using in this book is a modification of the original Poll product by Amos Latteier, one of the co-authors of *The Zope Book*[1].

One of the nice little extra features of this product is its capability to take the poll results and build nice graphical pie charts of the results. This feature, however, requires you to install the *Python Imaging Library* (*PIL*). You can use the Poll product without PIL being installed, but the fancy little pie charts will not be available.

1. Latteier, Amos, and Michel Pelletier. *The Zope Book.* Indianapolis, IN: New Riders Publishing, 2001.

PIL is available from **http://www.pythonware.com/downloads/index.htm**. Installation instructions also can be found at this location. We will not go into details on installing this library because the Poll product will work without it.

## Installing the Poll Product

Version 0.7.1 is being used for this book. To install the Poll product, complete the following steps:

1. Download the Poll product from **http://www.zope.org/Members/mega/poll** to your Zope server.
2. Copy this file to the $ZOPEROOT directory.
3. Unzip the poll-0.7.1.tgz file. Type `gunzip poll-0.7.1.tgz`.
4. Now untar the resulting poll-0.7.1.tar file. Type `tar -xvf poll-0.7.1.tar`. This produces a directory down in $ZOPEROOT/lib/python/Products called Poll.
5. Restart Zope from the Control Panel.
6. Make sure that the Poll product is installed correctly and doesn't show a broken product icon.
7. Remember to check the user-support mailing lists on zope.org if any problems occur.

## Creating an Online Poll

When you have the Poll product successfully installed, go to the root of your school district web site and use the pop-up object list to add a Poll object. Give this new Poll an ID of `LunchMenu` and a `title` of "Recent Changes to the Lunch Menu."

Click the new LunchMenu Poll and take a look at its management interface (shown in Figure 6.3). The first two boxes that you will see after the ID and `title` are labeled Open and Anonymous. An open poll is one that is available to any who can access it. In other words, if the poll object is placed in a public place on your web site that is not restricted by Zope's built-in security and the `Open` property is set, then anyone is permitted to participate. The `Anonymous` property is used to specify whether a participant can respond to the poll without identifying himself. If the `Anonymous` box is checked, then respondents can participate without identifying themselves. For now, leave both boxed checked.

Put a question like, "What do you think about the addition of burger buddy casserole to Friday's menu?" in the `Question` field. Now provide several answers to the question (one question per line) in the `Poll Answers` property. Then click the Add button.

You will be returned to the management screen, where you will see the question that you just entered and another area to enter another question. You can keep adding questions until your poll is complete.

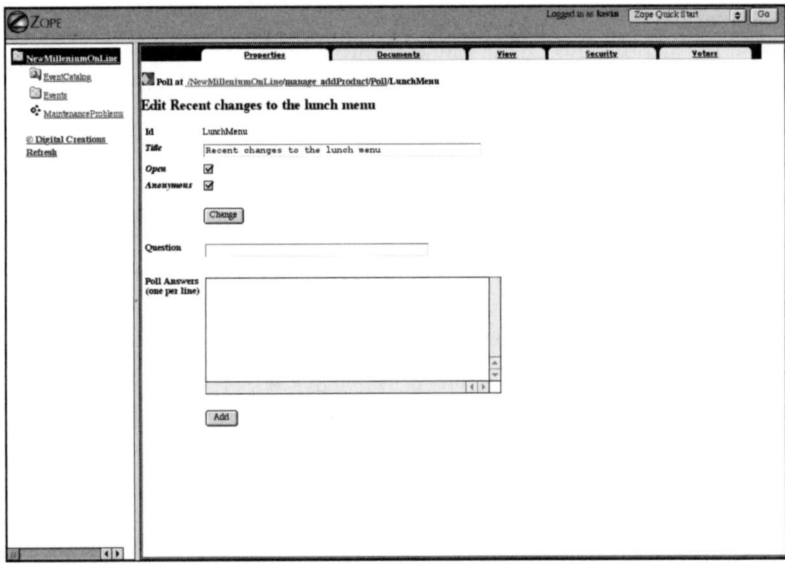

Figure 6.3 Poll object-management screen.

To view this poll, simply type in its URL directly or reference it from another object (for example, `<dtml-var LunchMenu>`). Figure 6.4 shows a sample poll with two questions.

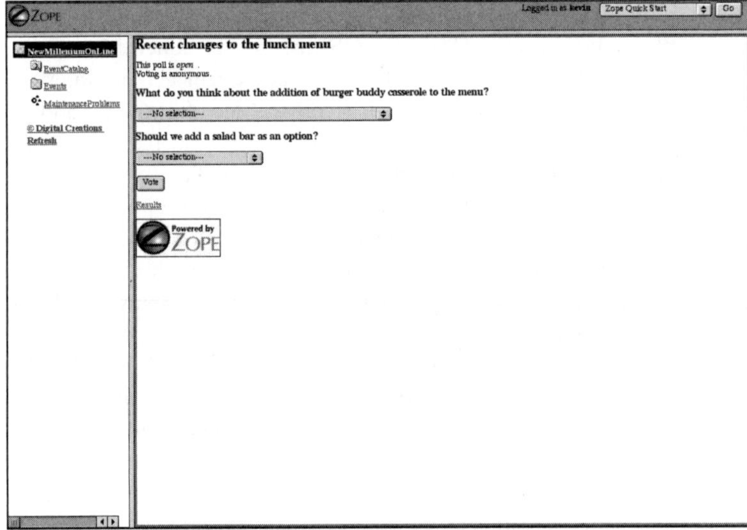

Figure 6.4 Example of a two-question poll.

Type the URL of the LunchMenu poll into your browser and answer the questions. When you do, you will be told that your votes were accepted. Click the OK button, and you will be shown the Results screen. One strange thing that you might notice is that, if PIL is installed, the product includes broken icons. If PIL is not installed, the product seems to detect that situation and doesn't attempt to use any icons. Assuming that PIL is installed, you will notice to the left of each question a broken image icon. The source code appears to be looking for images in a nonexistent directory. You have two options at this point. You can either jump into the source code located at $ZOPEROOT/lib/python/Products/Poll/Poll.py, which is where the `drawGraphics` method is defined, or you can edit the method that display this results screen. Let's take a look at how to edit out the `img` tag from the results screen. We'll leave the debugging and editing of the Poll.py source to you. Refer back to the section on IMapClient included in Chapter 5 for more information on how to work with the source code of a product.

Go back to the Zope management interface and click the LunchMenu poll object. You will see a tab called Documents along the top of the screen. Click it. You will see two DTML documents listed. The first is the index_html object for this poll (the default display), and the second is the object that is called to display the results. Ah ha! That's the one you want. Click this method, and you'll see the default code that is included with the Poll product (see Listing 6.3).

Listing 6.3 **Default DTML for Results Page of Poll Object**

```
<!--#var standard_html_header-->
<H2><!--#var title_or_id--></H2>
<p>
This poll is <em><!--#if open-->open<!--#else-->closed<!--#/if--> \
    ➥</em>.<br>
Voting is <em><!--#if anonymous--><!--#else-->not<!--#/if--></em> \
    ➥anonymous.<br>
</p>
<!--#if "objectItems(['Poll Question'])"-->
<!--#in "objectItems(['Poll Question'])"-->
    <H3><!--#var question--></H3>
    <TABLE BORDER=0>
    <TR>
        <!--#if fancy_graphics-->
            <TD><IMG src="<!--#var sequence-key-->/drawGraph? \
            ➥size:int=200&dummy=<dtml-var "ZopeTime().time">"></TD>
        <!--#/if-->
        <TD><!--#var pollLegend--></TD>
    </TR>
    </TABLE>
<!--#/in-->
<BR>
<a href="<!--#var URL1-->">Vote</a>
<!--#/if-->
<!--#var standard_html_footer-->
```

You can edit this code to your heart's content, making it fit in nicely with your overall web site design. This code uses some of the older style DTML, but you can easily see what it is doing. Most importantly, you can see the only place where an image tag is located. Simply remove that tag, and the broken image icon will disappear from your results display.

You can see how quickly a poll can be constructed using this tool and how easily it can be incorporated and customized for your own web sites.

# Tools to Build Tools

In this final section of this chapter, we take a look at two products that help simplify two web development tasks that are important and ubiquitous but are often tedious.

## Web Forms to Make Web Forms

One of the most often performed tasks in web-page development is the production of web forms to collect information. In the days before the fancy visual HTML authoring tools such as Adobe GoLive!, Dreamweaver, and HomeSite, designers usually resorted to writing HTML by hand. The creation of web forms was generally not difficult; more than anything, it was time-consuming.

A nice drop-in Zope product designed to solve this very problem is called *Formulator*. Formulator was created by Martijn Faassen, a highly active and talented participant in the Zope community. This book uses version 1.0.1.

## Installing Formulator

To install Formulator, complete the following steps:

1. Download the Formulator-1.0.1.tgz file located at **`http://www.zope.org/Members/faassen/Formulator`** to your Zope server.
2. Copy this file to the $ZOPEROOT/lib/python/Products directory.
3. Unzip the Formulator-1.0.1.tgz file. Type `gunzip Formulator-1.0.1.tgz`.
4. Now untar the resulting Formulator-1.0.1.tar file. Type `tar -xvf Formulator-1.0.1.tar`. This produces a directory called Formulator in the Products directory.
5. Restart Zope from the Control Panel.
6. Make sure that Formulator is installed and that it doesn't show a broken product icon.
7. Remember to check the user-support mailing lists on zope.org if any problems occur.

## Creating a Web Form Using Formulator

In this section, you use the Formulator product to produce the beginnings of a web form that parents can fill in and submit online, providing basic information about incoming students.

Go to the root of your school project and create a new folder in which to put your web form. Give the folder the ID of `StudentInfo`, and give it a title of Student Info Form. Click into the newly created folder and select Formulator Form from the pop-up list of objects that can be added. As with most object instantiations, you will be asked to provide an ID and an optional `title`. For this demonstration, give the new Formulator object an ID of `MyForm`. Click the Add button.

A Formulator object acts very much like a folder object. You can open it, and it can contain other objects. The major difference between a Formulator and a folder is related to the kinds of objects that can be added to them. You already know most of the kinds of objects that can be added to a folder. Most of those objects *cannot* be added to a Formulator. A Formulator restricts the objects to a special set of objects created specifically for Formulator. In fact, these objects cannot be added anywhere else but a Formulator. The list of objects that can be added to a Formulator includes the following:

- CheckBoxField
- DateTimeField
- EmailField
- FileField
- FloatField
- IntegerField
- LinesField
- LinkField
- ListField
- MultiCheckBoxField
- MulitListField
- PasswordField
- PatternField
- RadioField
- RawTextAreaField
- StringField
- TextAreaField

To see how Formulator works, you need to add some of these objects to your MyForm object. Start by adding a simple *StringField* object selecting it from the pop-up list inside your MyForm formulator. Give it an ID of `FirstName`. Now create another one and give it an ID of LastName. You should now have a screen that looks like the one shown in Figure 6.5.

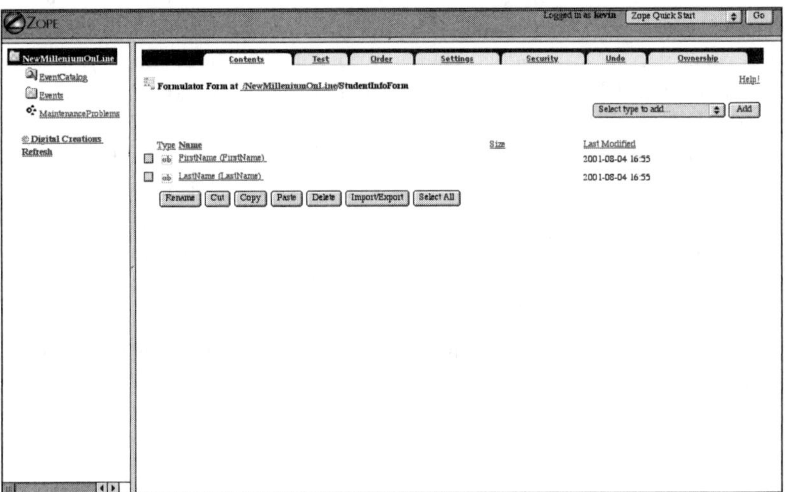

**Figure 6.5** Formulator object containing two subobjects.

### The Test Tab

Now experiment with some of the tabs associated with Formulator. Currently, you are in the Contents area of your Formulator object. Click the Test tab and observe the results. You will see a screen like the one shown in Figure 6.6.

Notice that the two fields that you just created are displayed as string entry fields. The text next to each is the ID of the field that you entered when you created them. Below the two string entry fields you will notice a Test button. Click the Test button to see what happens. The form is redrawn, but above it you will notice that an error banner has been included. The errors indicate that the contents of the fields FirstName and LastName are required fields and that no data was entered for them. Not only did Formulator create the HTML (simple as it may be in this particular case), but it also set up validation code to make sure that content was included for each string. Now enter the string "Richard" into the "FirstName" string, and "Hammond" into the "LastName" string. Press the Test button again, and you will see the message "All fields were validated correctly."

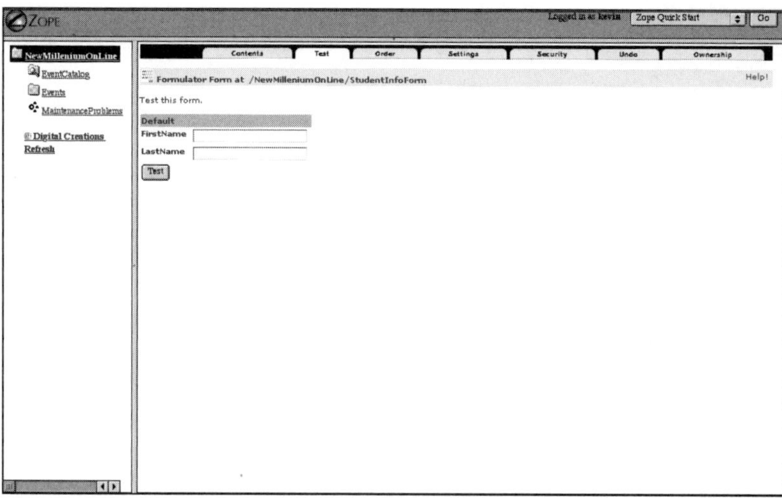


Figure 6.6 Formulator object being tested.

Okay, now add another StringField object to the Formulator and give it an ID of `MiddleName`. To do this, you'll need to click the Contents tab along the top to get you back to the screen where you can add objects. Choose StringField from the pop-up list, and add the new object. Now select the Test tab, and once again use `Richard` in the FirstName field and `Hammond` in the LastName field. But don't put anything in the MiddleName field. (Hey, maybe Richard doesn't have a middle name—it happens.) Click the Test button. You probably can guess the result. A warning banner is displayed above the form that informs you that a required field did not contain data. Now this is a problem. Some students might not have middle names. You can't require parents to give their kids middle names just so that your information form will work. You need some way to tell this MyForm that you don't want to require the MiddleName field to be filled in. Click the Contents tab again. When you see the list of StringField objects in your Formulator, click the MiddleName object. You will now see the screen shown in Figure 6.7.

### The Title Property

The first property listed for this StringField object is called `Title`. The contents of `Title` consist of the text that will appear next to the string entry field on the rendered form. Notice that the word `Title` has an asterisk following it. This indicates that the property requires a value. In fact, if you remove the title completely and hit the Save Changes button at the bottom of the screen, you will find that the last value the property had will be returned. There must always be a value in the Title field. If you look farther down the list, you will also see that the property `Display width` also includes an asterisk after it. Once again, a value for this property is required. For now, concern yourself only with the `Title` property and the check box farther down the screen that says Required.

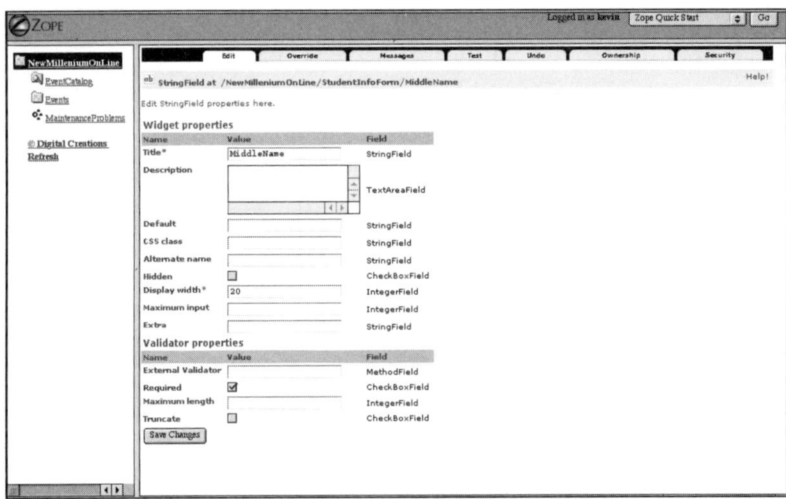


**Figure 6.7** Edit StringField object.

Currently, the Required check box is checked. Uncheck the box. Now the field will not be required to contain something for the form to be valid. Also, while you're editing this thing, change the `Title` to Middle name. In fact, for a more pleasing display, change all three titles to First name, Last name, and Middle name. This will make them more readable when they are rendered in the web browser. Notice that this simply changes the `Title` property and, consequently, the text that is rendered next to the field when it appears on the screen. It does not change the ID.

Now click the Test tab along the top of the screen and enter data for the First name field and the Last name field, but leave the Middle name field blank. Now when you click the Test button, everything will be acceptable. You might want to establish some standard method of informing your users what fields in your forms are required. Upon looking at the test rendering of the current MyForm object, an end user would have no idea that a first name and last name are required while a middle name is not. You might include an asterisk with the title of each field that is required. Make sure that somewhere on your form you indicate what the meaning of the asterisk is.

Now add a *MultiCheckBoxField* object to your Formulator. Give it an ID of `MedicalConditions`. If you click the Add and Edit button instead of the Add button, you will be taken immediately to the management screen for this new object. Notice that its default `Title` is the ID property that you just typed. Change that to be a more readable Medical Conditions. Also, uncheck the `Required` property because you don't want to require your students to have a medical condition as a prerequisite for admission. Another of the properties of the MultiCheckBoxField is the `Items` property. This is a list of the items that you want to be associated with the object MedicalConditions. For now, just give it a few for example. You certainly can add a whole list when you really implement this form. Include in the list Allergies, Diabetes, Heart Disease, and Sickle Cell Anemia. More can be added later. Your screen should look like Figure 6.8.

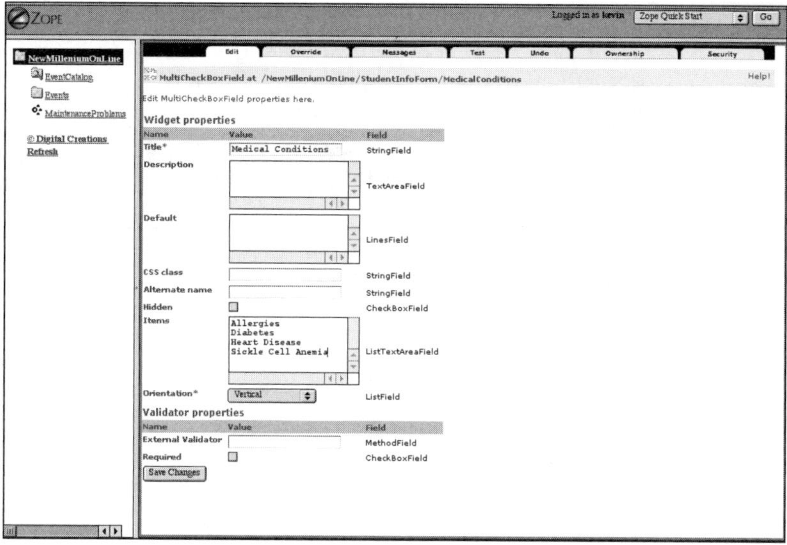


Figure 6.8 Edit MultiCheckBoxField object.

Click the Save Changes button. Now you can test this new object by itself or in the context of the other data entry objects that you have created. To test this object in isolation, simply click the Test tab along the top. This will display the new object and allow you to interact with it. Make sure that the object is not required, by clicking the Test button while no boxes are checked. The Formulator should indicate that the test was successful and should show an empty list ([]) as the value. To see this object in context with the other objects, click MyForm and click its Test tab. The entire Formulator object will be displayed, allowing you to interact with it and see the values that are produced.

### The EmailField Object

Now add an *EmailField* object to your Formulator. Give it an ID of `ParentEmail` and, instead of waiting until you edit this object, give it a `Title` of Parent/Guardian Email Address. Click Add and Edit. The EmailField object is very much like a regular StringField object, except for the validator method that is used. In the case of an EmailField object, the string that is included must "appear" to be a valid email address. In other words, it must have a string followed by the symbol "@" and must be followed by a string that contains at least one period (.). Unless this convention is followed, an error will be raised.

Go to MyForm and click the Test button to take a look at it. Suppose now that you decide that you really want the ParentEmail field to be directly beneath the MiddleName field. What do you do? You really don't want to delete the

MedicalConditions object and then re-create it so that it will appear in the right order. It would be nice if there were an easier way. There is. Click the Order tab along the top of the screen. You will see the screen shown in Figure 6.9.

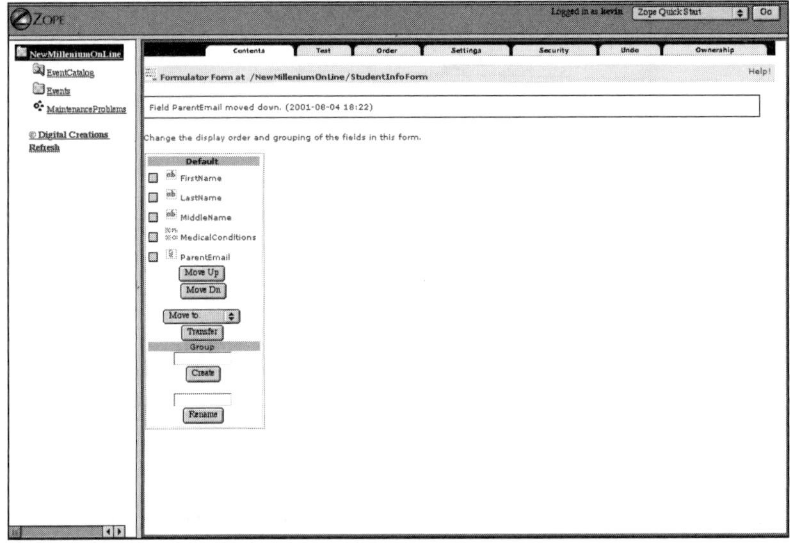

Figure 6.9 Setting the order of objects in a Formulator.

Put a check in the check box next to ParentEmail, and then click the Move Up button. The result will be the result you were hoping for. The ParentEmail will now show up directly beneath the MiddleName field in the list. Click the Test tab to confirm that this is the case when the form is rendered as well. Although multiple boxes can be checked at one time, it does not appear that, at this time, multiple objects can be moved up or down together. One way to do that, however, is to "group" the objects and move the entire group.

### Grouping Two or More Objects Together

To group two or more objects together, you must first create a group. Type the name that you want to assign to the group into the field just above the Create button. Use the name "Name" for this example. Click the Create button, and you will see the screen shown in Figure 6.10.

You now see that you have two groups available into which to place your objects, Default and Name. Put checks in the check boxes next to FirstName, LastName, and MiddleName. From the pop-up list called Move to:, select the Name group. Now press the Transfer button below it, and you will see that the three objects have been moved to the new Name group. Okay, but now how do you know where the groups will appear on the rendered screen? Click the Test tab, and you will see the result shown in Figure 6.11.

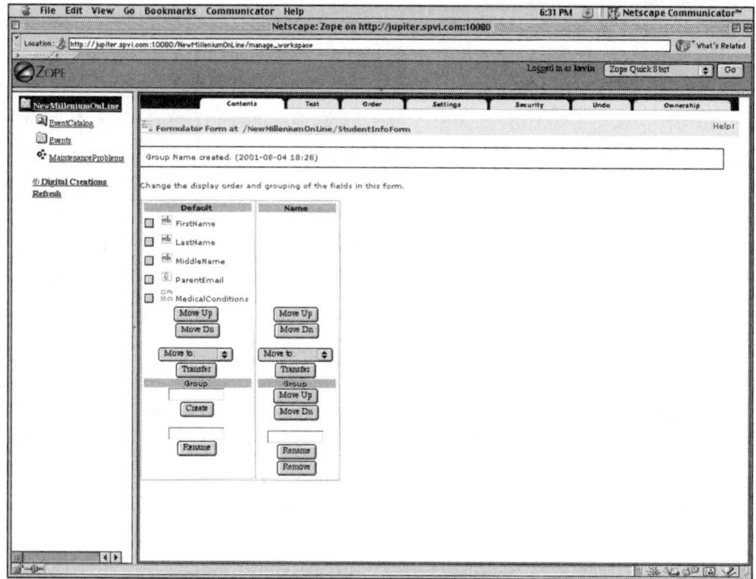


Figure 6.10 Multiple object groups in a Formulator.

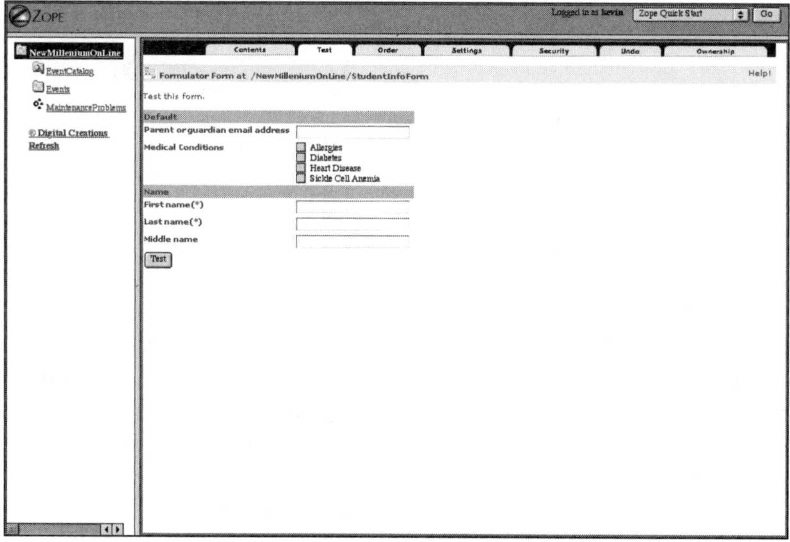


Figure 6.11 Multiple groups in Formulator rendered on the screen.

Notice that the two groups are highlighted by two banners giving the name of the group and then displaying the objects within each group. You probably want to change some things. First of all, the name of the Default group probably should be changed to something more informative. Also, it makes sense to ask for name information before jumping into other information such as medical conditions. Click the Order tab again and notice the Rename buttons at the bottom of each group definition. Above the Rename button in the Default group, type the word `Medical` and click Rename. You can imagine a final form that would include questions about the shots that a student has had and when, and medications that the student is currently taking, prescription and nonprescription.

Things are improving, but you still have a problem. The Medical group still appears first on the rendered screen. Notice that beneath the Name group there are Move Up and Move Dn buttons beneath a Group banner, as well as the Move Up and Move Dn buttons directly beneath the objects list. Click the Move Up button under the Group heading, and voilá—nothing happens. What? Unfortunately, the first group in the list has special precedence, and it can't be moved in the list. This is one small irritation with Formulator. The solution is to rename the groups so that the Medical group becomes the Name group, and vice versa. Then you can select each of the objects within the groups and move them to the newly named groups where they belong. You won't be able to change the name of Medical to Name because there is already a group called Name. You will need to create intermediate names as you work this order thing out. When you have finished, you should have the groups in the desired order with the correct objects in each. There is still one lingering problem, though. The ParentEmail object really doesn't fit in the Medical group, but it doesn't fit in the Name group, either. You know the solution. Create another group called Address, and move ParentEmail to it.

### The DateTimeField Object

Also create StringField objects and put them into the Address group for Address, City, State, and ZipCode. Make sure that if you are requiring these fields that you take a look at one of the other objects that can be added to a Formulator, the *DateTimeField* object. Select DateTimeField from the pop-up list of available objects. Give it an ID of `LatestTetanusShot` and a `Title` of "Date of Latest Tetanus Shot." When you click the Add and Edit button, you will see the screen shown in Figure 6.12.

This screen contains a number of different properties from the ones that you've already seen with the StringField and MultiCheckBoxField objects. Focus your attention on a couple of these properties that you will find interesting. The first is the Default to now field. If this is checked, then whenever the form is rendered the current date is inserted as the default value. This feature is not particularly useful in this particular case, but you can easily imagine cases where the current date is, while not the only answer, certainly the most probable. Take, for example, a form that is used by teachers to request a repair to a computer in the classroom. A field could be added that asks "when" the repair is needed. In most cases, the teacher would like the repair made today, if possible. This is the most likely answer, however, maybe today is a very busy day for the students and the teacher would like the classroom not to be interrupted for a computer repair. In this case, the default answer of today's date would not be appropriate, so the teacher could easily change it. Today's date would be appropriate for most situations thus, saving the teacher from having to enter the date. But because some cases will be better suited by a different date, the field is included as an editable value. This kind of feature saves users time and makes them very happy with your design.

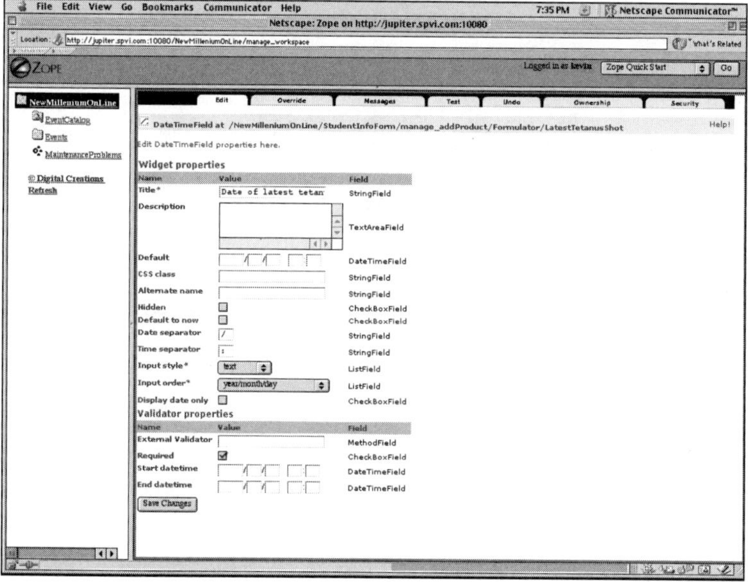


**Figure 6.12** Edit DateTimeField object.

Another property of the DateTimeField object is the `Display date only` property. This box is checked if you want to leave the time off the display and entry. In this case, you will want to check this box because you don't want to require the parents to include the exact time when the tetanus shot was administered. The date is sufficient. Another neat feature of the DateTimeField object is in the Validator properties at the bottom of the screen. You can set a minimum and maximum date between which the entered date must fall. Once again, this is not particularly useful for your example, but you can certainly think of situations in which this could come in pretty handy. Finish creating your LatestTetanusShot field object, and click Save Changes. Go back to the Order tab and move the new object to the Medical group. The result is shown in Figure 6.13.

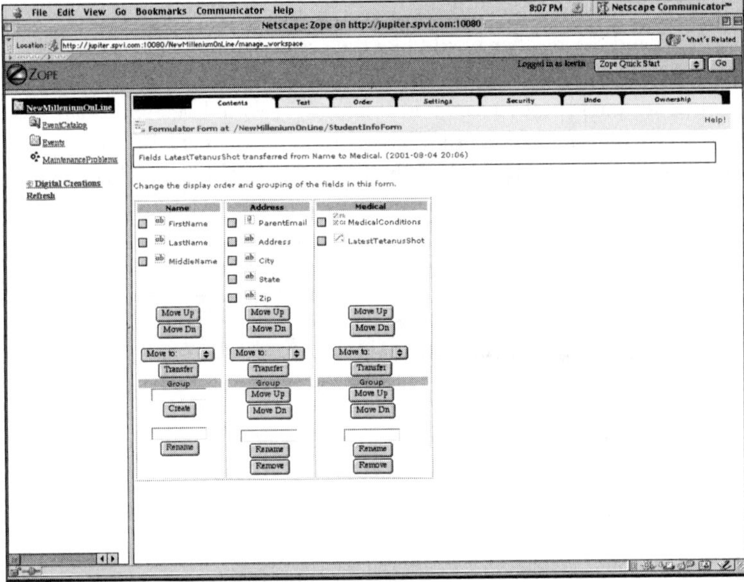

Figure 6.13 Three populated Formulator groups.

### Processing the Form

Another very important thing that you need to provide to any HTML form is the name of the method or function that is designated to handle the form when it is submitted. You can specify this and related properties using the Settings tab at the top of the screen. The first property specifies the layout of groups on the Order screen. If your screen size does not show the groups the way you want when you are editing them, you can adjust the display here. This has no effect on the way that the form is laid out.

The next two properties are the important ones. The first Form Action is where you provide the path to the object that will handle the form when it is submitted. The second Form Method selects between the two types of HTTP methods used with forms, POST and GET. Briefly, a GET method includes the form data in the actual URL itself. The URL is followed by a question mark (?), and then the form fields follow in sequence after that in the format `key=value`. Each key/value pair is separated from the others with an ampersand (&). A GET method is okay with short forms, but if the number of fields gets too high, then it can create problems by producing a very long URL line. In these cases, a POST method is used. A POST encodes the field values right in the actual http message that is sent. POST methods generally are used when the URL refers to a process instead of a static resource. In general then, it is best to use a POST method for processing forms.

Take a look at how your developing form is looking. Click the Test tab once again, and you will see the screen shown in Figure 6.14.

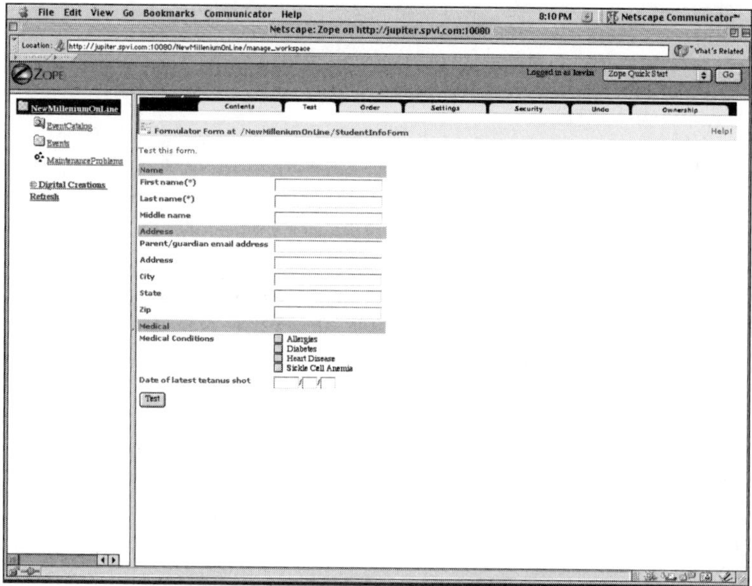


Figure 6.14 Rendered Formulator.

If you look at the source for the rendered page, you'll see that it is laid out using an HTML table. The elements are sized in a pleasing way so that the screen is organized and easy to read. However, you still might be feeling that you need to add a few things to the display to make it fit in better with your overall web site design. If the Formulator had a View tab that would render it like it renders with the Test tab, then you could simply drop it into the middle of a design with a `<dtml-var MyForm>` tag. Unfortunately, there is no standard view of the Formulator. However, another way is provided by the Formulator. If you dig through the source code for Formulator (Form.py), which is located in the $ZOPEROOT/lib/python/Products/Formulator directory, you will find a method of the Form product called `render` that a comment line states is used to provide a default rendering of the Formulator. This default rendering lays out the groups in the same order as you created them and provides the group names above each in a larger font.

Listing 6.4 shows how to drop the default layout of the Formulator right into a simple DTML method. Obviously, you could make the basic layout much more intricate. As an example, create a DTML method called StudentInfo and include the code from Listing 6.4.

Listing 6.4 **Default Formulator Rendering in DTML Method**

```
01  <dtml-var standard_html_header>
02  <center>
03  <table>
04      <tr>
05          <td align=center>
06              <h1><dtml-var title_or_id></h1>
07          </td>
08      </tr>
09      <tr>
10          <td>
11              This form must be completed and returned by the \
                ➥start of school.  When you have finished entering \
                ➥all of the required information, press the "OK" \
                ➥button at the bottom of the screen to automatically \
                ➥send this form to the school.  Thank you.
12          </td>
13      </tr>
14      <tr>
15          <td>
16              <dtml-var "MyForm.render()">
17          </td>
18      </tr>
19  </table>
20  </center>
21  <dtml-var standard_html_footer>
```

Line 16 in Listing 6.4 makes a call to the `render` method of the MyForm object. When the DTML method from Listing 6.4 is viewed, the result is as shown in Figure 6.15.

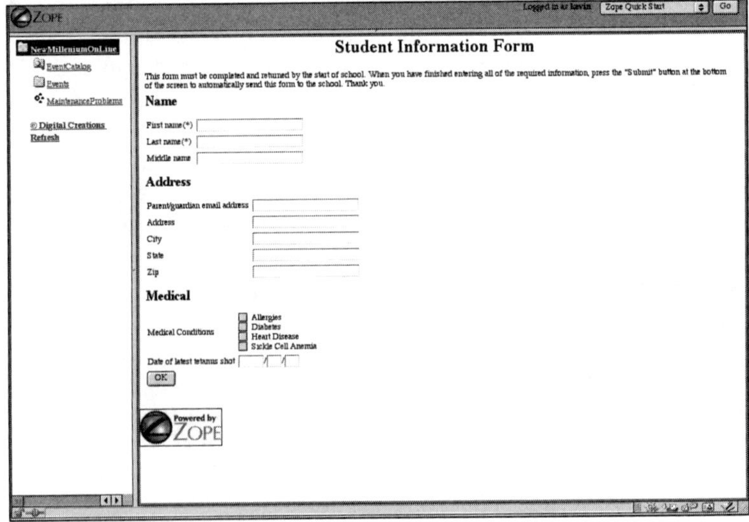


**Figure 6.15** Default Formulator displayed from DTML method.

This should do, for most cases. You can use the Formulator management interface to alter or create groups of fields, change the names of the groups for display purposes, and alter the order of the fields within each group. However, if you're still not satisfied with the way the form looks, Formulator gives you another way to gain access to the fields that it controls and thereby incorporate them differently in your web site. Look at Listing 6.5.

Listing 6.5 **Access to Formulator Field Objects in DTML**

```
01  <dtml-var standard_html_header>
02  <center>
03  <table>
04      <tr>
05          <td align=center>
06              <h1><dtml-var title_or_id></h1>
07          </td>
08      </tr>
09      <tr>
10          <td>
11              This form must be completed and returned by the \
                ➥start of school.  When you have finished entering \
                ➥all of the required information, press the "OK" \
                ➥button at the bottom of the screen to automatically \
                ➥send this form to the school.  Thank you.
12          </td>
13      </tr>
14      <tr>
15          <td>
16              <dtml-var "MyForm.header()">
17              <dtml-in "MyForm.get_fields()">
18                  <dtml-let theField=sequence-item>
19                      <dtml-var "theField.get_value('title')"> \
                        ➥<dtml-var "theField.render()">
20                      <br>
21                  </dtml-let>
22              </dtml-in>
23              <input type="submit" value="Submit Registration">
24              <dtml-var "MyForm.footer()">
25          </td>
26      </tr>
27  </table>
28  </center>
29  <dtml-var standard_html_footer>
```

Most of the Formulator work is accomplished between lines 16 and 24 in Listing 6.5. Line 16 calls the `header` method of the Formulator object, which inserts the `<FORM>` tag with the action and method properties that you set earlier. Line 17 calls the `get_fields` method of the Formulator, which returns a list of its field objects. Now lines 18 through 21 are applied to each field object in the Formulator. Keep in mind that the list returned from the `get_fields` method is a list of "objects." These objects also have methods that can be called. You can peruse the source code in $ZOPEROOT/lib/python/Products/Formulator/Field.py to find more information.

One of the methods of the field object is the `get_value` method. You pass the name of a property into this method, and it returns the value of that specified property. Line 19 uses that method to obtain the value of the `Title` property and then prints it out. The final part of line 19 makes use of the `render` method of the field objects. The `render` method produces the necessary HTML code to draw the correct type of field on the screen with the appropriate name and default value, if one exists. Line 23 is necessary to produce a button to submit the form to the designated method. Finally, line 24 calls the `footer` method of the Formulator. This method simply includes the `</FORM>` tag, although in future releases, this method might do more, so use it instead of ending the form yourself.

You can easily extrapolate from the example in Listing 6.5 to create a form that is visually appealing as well as functional. Still, it feels like you are trapped into including the form fields in the order in which they are returned to you in the list. Without a lot of hard work, the fields will appear in this order on the screen. It would be nice if you could access the fields when you needed them in the context of a layout. Well, you can. Formulator gives you access to the field objects on a field-by-field basis so that you can easily use them in any order.

Although this way of displaying the fields gives you more flexibility, it comes at the price of reuse. The code in Listing 6.5 can be used by any Formulator object. The code has no references to form-specific names. This code could be placed at the root of your school web site project in a `DTML Method` called renderForm. Each Formulator that you create could then be placed in its own folder, making sure that each Formulator object has the same ID of `MyForm`. The enclosing folders will carry the load of differentiating among the various forms. Each folder could be given an ID that reflects the use of the enclosed Formulator; plus, the title that you want your web form to display would be included as the `Title` property of the folder. Furthermore, you could include a file called index_html within each folder so that the folder would have a default render method. This index_html file could simply call the acquired `renderForm` method. This would cause the `renderForm` method to be called in the context of the folder; therefore, the resulting display would be reflective of the enclosed Formulator.

Still, you might be willing to give up reuse for the flexibility provided by direct access to the field objects. In that case, let's walk through the procedure for doing that. Listing 6.6 shows direct access to the Formulator fields.

Listing 6.6 **Direct Access to Formulator Field Objects in DTML**

```
<dtml-var standard_html_header>
<center>
<table>
    <tr>
        <td align=center>
```

```
            <h1>Student Information Form</h1>
        </td>
    </tr>
    <tr>
        <td>
            This form must be completed and returned by the \
            ➥start of school.  When you have finished entering \
            ➥all of the required information, press the "OK" \
            ➥button at the bottom of the screen to automatically \
            ➥send this form to the school.  Thank you.
        </td>
    </tr>
    <tr>
        <td>
            <dtml-var "MyForm.header()">
            <dtml-var "MyForm.FirstName.get_value('title')"> \
            ➥<dtml-var "MyForm.FirstName.render()">
            <br>
            <dtml-var "MyForm.LastName.get_value('title')"> \
            ➥<dtml-var "MyForm.LastName.render()">
            <input type="submit" value="Submit Registration">
            <dtml-var "MyForm.footer()">
        </td>
    </tr>
</table>
</center>
<dtml-var standard_html_footer>
```

Notice that the code in Listing 6.6 could not be used like the code from Listing 6.5 because it makes specific reference to field names (such as FirstName and LastName). Although this way gives you more direct access to the field objects, it makes the code much less portable.

If you render the code from Listing 6.5 or Listing 6.6 and then attempt to submit the form without providing the required fields of information, you would expect that an error would be generated because that is what happened during the testing phase. However, if you try this little experiment, you will see that no errors are generated. What happened to all of that powerful form validation that was going on when you tested this Formulator? Well, the validation methods are still there; you just have to invoke them. The validation methods are invoked from the method that you have designated to be the "action" method for your form. You must modify your action method to make the call to the validation method and act upon any errors that are noted.

### Form Validation

The action method should make a call to the `validate_all_to_request` method of the Formulator. This method takes one parameter, the `REQUEST` object. If any errors are caught, then a FormValidationError exception is raised. Therefore, the proper way to use this `validate_all_to_request` method is to include it in a try/except clause. The except clause can catch the FormValidationError and act upon it. When an exception is thrown, a variable is available that can be used to display the causative error. The variable is *error_value.errors*. This variable is a list of the errors that occurred in the validation process. Use the list in a `<dtml-in>` loop, and print out the errors. Each error has an associated field object and error_text. Listing 6.7 shows a simple form handler that makes use of the validation code provided with Formulator.

Listing 6.7 **Simple Action Script to Handle Validation**

```
<dtml-var standard_html_header>
<dtml-try>
    <dtml-var "MyForm.validate_all_to_request(REQUEST)">
<dtml-except FormValidationError>
    <dtml-in "error_value.errors">
        <dtml-var "field.get_value('title')">
        <dtml-var error_text><br>
    </dtml-in>
<dtml-else>
<!--
    Do something with the form data
-->
</dtml-try>
<dtml-var standard_html_footer>
```

The code in Listing 6.7 will produce a list of the field names and the associated error if any of the fields do not contain valid data.

So now you have seen how to create forms quickly and powerfully using a nifty Zope product called Formulator. You've also looked at how to render these web forms after they are built. It's time to look at some other products that make web design quicker and easier.

## Making a Web Page Visually Appealing—Fast!

Most of the products covered so far in Chapters 3–5 and in this chapter are products that perform some "necessary" task with respect to providing dynamic information to end users or accepting and logging information back to you, the web manager. Before ending Part II, however, we thought that it would be nice to show you a product that is strictly "window dressing." This is certainly not to belittle the product; it is a very useful product. What we mean is that sometimes you want to do things in your web application that are strictly to make it look fancy or exciting. The *ActiveImages* product does just that. It makes extensive use of JavaScript, so you must assume that your end users have systems that support JavaScript. But these days, most of the browsers have built-in support for JavaScript.

The product ActiveImages produces several effects with images that can be written in JavaScript (if you know how to write it) but are much more easily implemented by just incorporating this product into your Zope installation. ActiveImage is a folder-like object that allows you to produce several tricks with images including rollovers, sticky images, and linkages. These features will easily make your sites more visually appealing to an end user.

## Installing ActiveImages

To install ActiveImages, complete the following steps:

1. Download the AcitveImagesV4.tar.gz file, located at **http://www.zope.org/Members/admin/ActiveImages**, to your Zope server.
2. Copy this file to the $ZOPEROOT directory (*not* the products directory).
3. Unzip the ActiveImagesV4.tar.gz file. Type `gunzip ActiveImagesV4.tar.gz`.
4. Now untar the resulting ActiveImagesV4.tar file. Type `tar -xvf ActiveImagesV4.tar`. This produces a directory called ActiveImages in the products directory.
5. Restart Zope from the Control Panel.
6. Make sure that ActiveImages is installed and doesn't show a broken product icon.
7. Remember to check the user-support mailing lists on zope.org if any problems occur.

## Instantiating and Using ActiveImages

To play around with this product, you'll need some images on your machine to work with. Make sure that you have a supply of images to test with before proceeding. You probably should have a minimum of four images. Create a folder at the root of your school system project, and give it the ID `images`. Now locate some images (preferably all the same size) and load them into the images folder that you just created.

Now, at the root of your school system web site, select ActiveImages from the pop-up list of objects. Provide the new object with an ID and an optional `title`. Use the highly creative and unique ID of `TestActiveImages`. When you click the Add button, you will have a new object that looks very much like a folder. This ActiveImages object will contain the actual ActiveImage objects that you will create.

Click down into the TestActiveImages folder. You will see that you have only one option for what kind of objects can be added to this folder, ActiveImage objects. Click the Add ActiveImage button to create an ActiveImage object. Give it an ID of `LogoFun`. Now click the newly created LogoFun object, and the configuration screen shown in Figure 6.16 will appear.

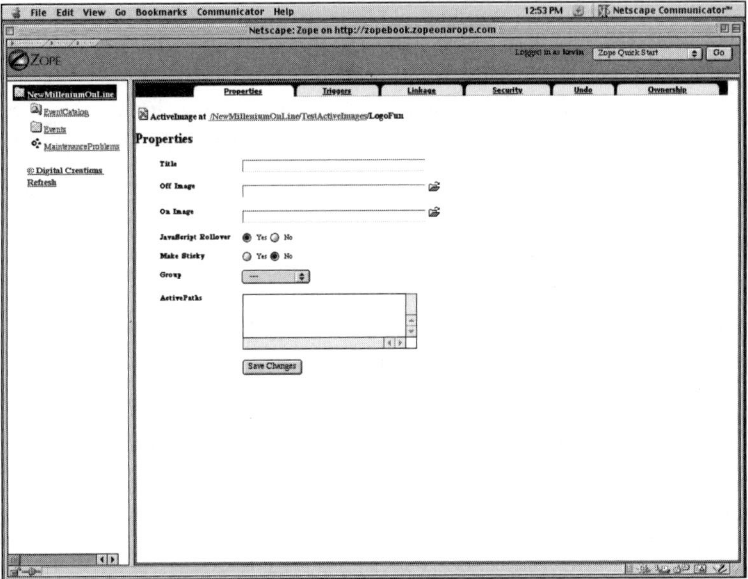

Figure 6.16 ActiveImage configuration.

As you can see from the configuration screen, an ActiveImage object really comprises two images, an Off Image and an On Image. To set either image, click the open folder icon to the right of the field or type the URL for the desired image into the blank field. If you click the open folder icon, you will be presented with a browser-like view of your current web site. Click down into the "images" folder and then click the radio box next to the desired image. Click the Choose button at the bottom of the screen to finalize your selection. Set both the On Image and the Off Image before proceeding to the next step.

For this first example, let's implement a simple JavaScript rollover. For this, make sure that the `JavaScript Rollover` property is checked Yes and that the `Make Sticky` property is checked No. Actually, when the `JavaScript Rollover` property is checked Yes, it doesn't seem to matter which way the `Make Sticky` property is set. It might be clearer if the four radio buttons were mutually exclusive. Maybe they could be labeled JavaScript Rollover, Sticky Image, and Neither.

For this example, no `Group` needs to be set and no `ActivePaths` need to be listed. Click the Save Changes button and then click back up to the TestActiveImages folder object. You will notice that one of the tabs on the TestActiveImages object is labeled Preview. Click this tab, and you will see the Off Image that you chose. Now pass your cursor over the image, and you will see it change to the On Image that you chose (provided, of course, that there *is* a visible difference between the two images). This is a simple image rollover that you have created without having to write a single line of JavaScript! You've seen this effect on numerous web sites, and now you can easily add it to yours.

For the next example, you are going to modify the parameters of the existing LogoFun image and produce a slightly different effect. Click the link next to your rollover image, and it will bring you back to the configuration screen for your LogoFun object. Now toggle the `JavaScript Rollover` property to No and the `Make Sticky` property to Yes. Click Save Changes, and once again click into the TestActiveImages and then click its Preview tab. Now, however, when you move your cursor over the Off Image, you will see that it doesn't change to the On Image. Bummer! Well, maybe not. Try clicking the image. Voilá! The On Image appears. If you click the image again, it returns to the Off Image. Once again, you have created a nifty little visual effect with very little effort.

Now let's get a little more fancy with your images. For this, you'll need to go back and follow the procedures listed previously to create another ActiveImage object. Give it an ID of `RemoteControl`. To help demonstrate the power of this next feature, you should choose two different images for this new ActiveImage object than the ones you used for LogoFun. Set up RemoteControl to be a JavaScript Rollover type. Now go back to the LogoFun object. Leave its properties alone this time, but click the Triggers tab at the top of the screen. You will be informed that no triggers currently exist, and you will be presented with three buttons, New Trigger, Save Changes, and Delete Triggers. You also will notice a pop-up that, when selected, shows the name of the other ActiveImage object that you just created. Select it. What you are doing is telling the ActiveImages object that you want to have the LogoFun object trigger the RemoteControl object into action whenever the LogoFun object is activated. Next to the pop-up, you'll see another field for entering an image object. Choose an image for this. To see the real power of this feature, choose a different image here than the one you chose for the Off Image for RemoteControl. In other words, RemoteControl has its On Image, its Off Image, and the image that you chose to be activated by the LogoFun object. Click the Save Changes button.

It's getting a little convoluted here, but a visual demonstration will help clear things up. Click into the TestActiveImages object and then click its Preview tab.

Now you will see both Off Images displayed on the screen. Pass your cursor over the Off Image of the LogoFun object that you create first. Nothing will happen to it. However, notice that the second object changes to the image that you selected in the trigger just as if you had activated it. The reason the first image doesn't change is that it is still set to be a sticky image. Click this first image, and you will see it change also. Now, lest you think that's it, run your cursor over the second image and you'll see it immediately turn to its Off Image state. In other words, your RemoteControl object actually has three states!

Now this is all pretty interesting, except that you are probably once again in the position of seeing exciting things in the testing mode but are left wondering how to incorporate this new invention into an actual working web site. Listing 6.8 shows some code that does just that.

Listing 6.8 **DTML Script Incorporating ActiveImages Objects**

```
<dtml-var standard_html_header>
<head>
    <dtml-with TestActiveImages>
        <dtml-var JavaScript>
        <dtml-var js_header>
        <dtml-in "objectValues('ActiveImage')">
            <dtml-var js>
        </dtml-in>
        <dtml-var js_footer>
    </dtml-with>
</head>
<body>
    <dtml-var "TestActiveImages.LogoFun">
    <dtml-var "TestActiveImages.RemoteControl">
</body>
<dtml-var standard_html_footer>
```

Create a new DTML method and insert the code from Listing 6.8 into it. If you render the new DTML method, you'll see both of the Off Images that you specified for these ActiveImages. You also will see that when you place your cursor over the LogoFun image, the RemoteControl image will change. If you move your cursor over the RemoteControl, image it will change to its On Image. All of this works just like it did in the preview.

Two other features of the ActiveImages object will be touched on briefly here: linkages and sticky image groups. Linkages basically provide you with an easy way to make an image act as a button to take you to another URL. You can instruct the linkage to open the URL in a new window, and you can specify several of the new window's parameters. Go back to the management view of your TestActiveImages object, and then click the LogoFun object. Now click its Linkage tab. To create a linkage for this ActiveImage, you first give it a URL to link to. Make sure that you use a complete URL and include the `http://` at the beginning if you are trying to go to an URL outside of your Zope site. Next, you give a name to the window in which the page will be displayed.

Next you will see a set of radio buttons that purport to allow you to determine whether you want the URL to be displayed in the current window or a new window. It appears that these buttons really do not do what they were intended for. To control what window the URL appears in, you need to use the previous field for the window name. If you choose any name other than _top, you will get a new window. If you call the window _top, then it will use the current window.

Finally, you can specify the following six parameters of your window. These parameters are applied to either the new window that is created or the current window, if it is used:

- Navigation Toolbar
- Location Toolbar
- Status Bar
- Menu Bar
- Scrollbars as Needed
- Resize Handlers

Set your desired parameters and then click the Preview tab of the TestActiveImages object. You will now see that when you click the LogoFun image, your specified URL appears in your main browser window or in a new window (depending on what you specified in the Linkages management screen.)

The final feature of the ActiveImages object is called Sticky Image Groups. Sticky image groups are groups of images that act like radio buttons. In other words, only one image at a time can be in its On state. If you click one and it toggles to its On `Image` state, then any other image in the group that might be in its On state is toggled off. To see this better, you should change the activity of the RemoteControl object from JavaScript Rollover to Make Sticky. Now both objects will toggle on and off when clicked with the mouse.

Next you need to group them together, and, to do that, you will need to create a group inside the TestActiveImages object. From the management screen of the TestActiveImages object, click the Properties tab. You will see a list box that allows you to type in the names of the groups that you want to have associated with the items in the current ActiveImages object. For now, just type in one group name, `Group1`. Go to the management pages of both ActiveImage objects and select Group1 for their group settings. Now both objects are considered to be grouped together. When you preview their behavior, you will see that only one of these objects can display its On image at one time. They are linked together like radio buttons.

As you can see, the ActiveImages object is an extremely powerful tool for helping you build dynamic and visually appealing web sites. The greatest utility of this product is that you don't have to learn a single line of JavaScript. The ActiveImages object does all the code writing for you.

## Summary

This chapter looked at a number of different kinds of products that can be dropped into your existing web sites to provide useful and fancy features with relatively little effort. It looked at ways to access constantly changing content from other web sites for incorporation into your own site. In particular, this chapter discussed the RDF/RSS format, which is used to syndicate information among web sites, and it explored how the Zope product RDFSummary makes integration of this kind of data easy.

The chapter also looked at creating online polls using the Zope Poll product, which will be especially useful in your role as IT manager of the fictional New Millennium school district. Finally, the chapter looked at two products that provide two of the basic needs of most web sites, web form creation plus fancy graphics.

Although the products looked at in the past four chapters have covered a wide range of uses, they are by no means exhaustive of the products available to you as a Zope developer. Keep connected with the Zope community. Read the bulletin boards and follow the email lists. More products are coming out everyday that will make your development life a lot easier.

# Site and Content Management

# 7

# Delegation, Databases, and Users

IN THIS CHAPTER AND THE REST OF PART III, "Site and Content Management," you will find answers to questions that every web master faces sooner or later. Are you looking ahead to a time when the amount of content on your web site exceeds your ability to maintain it? Have you been dreading the day when the responsiveness of your site begins to suffer noticeably from the side effects of its own success? Rising traffic volume and relentless growth of site content can drag down the performance and impact the manageability of any site. Dynamic object publishing is no less vulnerable. The wise web master plans and prepares for the inevitable, before the symptoms become obvious.

## User Management

Up to this point, your efforts have been directed toward putting facilities in place that meet the immediate needs of New Millennium Schools users. As this process has unfolded and the usefulness of the web site has been recognized, the number of frequent visitors has steadily increased. Likewise, the number of individuals and groups who are eager to post their information is rapidly rising. Even if the speed of your web site hasn't slowed down yet, the concept of delegating content creation and updates to topical experts is becoming more attractive by the day. Realistically, you can't keep up with the workload, and you know that it will only get worse the longer you try.

A prerequisite of delegation is identifying those eligible to perform each task. A hierarchy of users and the roles that they play can be established so that as new content providers are brought into the system, the web master can be relieved of the duty to personally add them to the content provider list. Not only will you delegate the ability to create and manage site content, but you will be delegating the task of delegation itself. This is the reason Zope has built-in access control lists (ACL).

In simplest terms, the ACL is a list, but in the form of a "tree" structure. The familiar tree is the organizational model of most computer files systems, with their folders and subfolders, sometimes called directories/subdirectories. This is the same framework that the Zope ACL is based upon, although it has considerably broader flexibility. Recall when you installed Zope and signed on as admin. The first thing you did was to add your own name to the acl_users folder of the Root Folder, with the "role" of manager. Although it might have seemed that you were giving yourself access to that folder and its contents, the effect was to allow access to everything that was to be created under that Zope installation. At least, that is the default setting. Now you'll see what that means and how to adjust things for scenarios that aren't properly served by the common case.

## Exploring Roles and Permissions

Think back to the very first exercise in Chapter 2, "Point and Click Web Building," when you created the top_folder object and carefully checked the box marked Create User Folder (refer to Figure 2.2). You were already starting to use the Zope ACL features, although it wasn't explained in detail at that time. There were enough new concepts to master at that point, without dwelling on the intricacies of users, roles, and permissions. Now we can no longer gloss over the details, and you are ready to learn about delegation and user management as the means to distribute a burgeoning work load. Open the top_folder now in the ZMI, and take a closer look.

Click the acl_users folder, and notice that there are no names listed. Of course, you have access to the top_folder and the site_folder because you are assigned the manager role of the Root Folder. Therefore, you have access to everything in the Root Folder, which is indeed "everything." Select the Ownership tab and you will see that you are listed as owner of the top_folder. That is because you created it during the first exercise in Chapter 2. Notice the explanation that appears on the Ownership page:

> Almost all Zope objects can be owned. When you create an object, you become its owner. Ownership matters for method objects since it determines what roles they have when they are executed. See the Proxy Roles view of method objects for more information.
>
> **(copyright 1998, 1999, 2000, 2001 Digital Creations, Zope Corporation)**

This means that because you have been assigned the role of manager, any methods that you create will run as if they were being run by someone with total access to the entire Zope system. This might be exactly what you intend, but not always. At any rate, it is very important that you understand that the ownership of an object determines the influence of that object on the system.

In Chapter 4, "Zope Discussion Tools," there is a brief introduction to Zope security and a bit more in Chapter 13, "User Management: Interfacing with External Systems." At this point, you will learn how to apply roles and permissions to content management. Click the Security tab, and notice that the check boxes along the left side are all selected, but none of those under the Roles section are selected (see Figure 7.1).

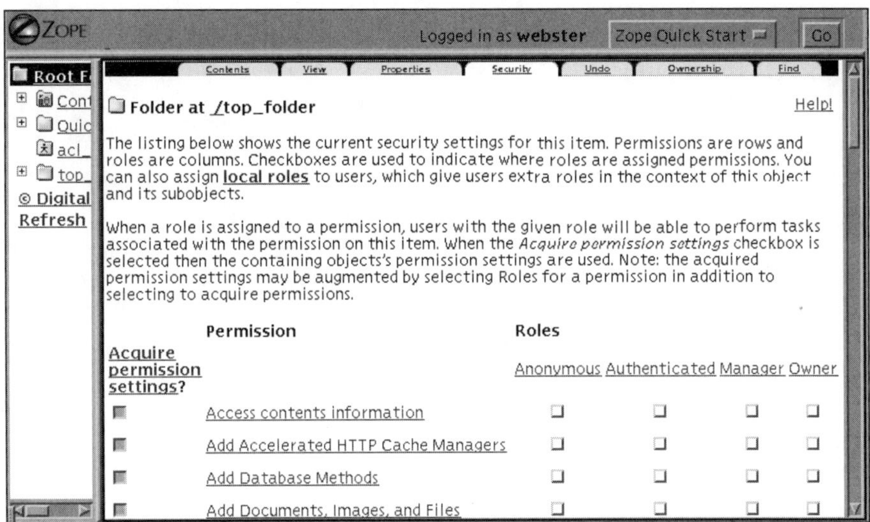


**Figure 7.1** Top folder Security tab.

This is the default setting for a newly created folder; because you didn't change anything (yet), it is still in the default state. The heading over that leftmost column asks, "Acquire Permission Settings?" Because all the check boxes are selected, the answer to this question is set to True, for all the options. This means that unless another selection has been made for an option, the settings of the parent folder will also hold for this folder. This is the form that acquisition takes with respect to security settings of folders, and this is similar for other object types. Keep in mind that, in the default case, you can't be certain what the actual security settings of a folder are without examining the security settings of the parent folder. It will be best to establish some standards early, to keep this form of acquisition as simple and consistent as possible. To make the implications clear, now take a look at the Security tab of the Root folder (see Figure 7.2).

The first thing that you will see is that the Acquire Permission Settings? column is "missing." Of course, this is reasonable because the Root folder has no parent folder to acquire from. The next point is that the first option is selected from the Anonymous column, along with a few others that you can see if you scroll farther down, but notice what types they are. The permissions selected for Anonymous are all very basic and don't involve creating and updating objects. In fact, the permissions that Anonymous users have are only for accessing and using objects, not for making changes to the site or objects. They have names like "view," "use," and "search," which is to say that any web surfer who can access the site at all can do these things. The role of the Anonymous user is the lowest "permission" level in terms of site security, and it defines the individual who can simply see and use the site, but nothing else.

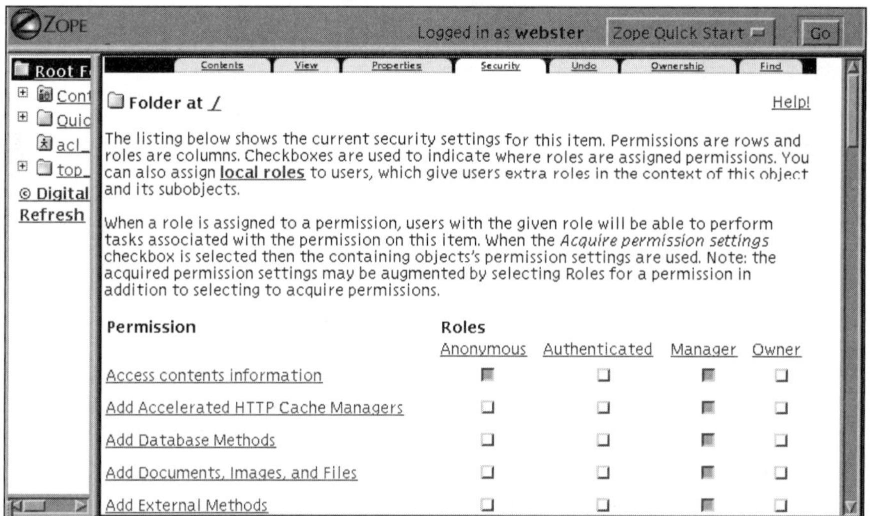


**Figure 7.2** Root folder Security tab.

## Built-in Security

The next security level is the role of the Authenticated user, which is where site security truly begins. As mentioned in Chapter 4, "Zope Discussion Tools," the Authenticated role is a new feature as of Zope 2.4. The need to improve security for all web-based systems is the driving force behind this change. Like all new features, there will be a period of adjustment for those accustomed to "the old way," but most folks realize that the ultimate goal is worth the effort. Every Zope "page" has a built-in property named `AUTHENTICATED_USER`, which, in the case of an anonymous user, is `empty` or `false`. The only way for this value to be set to `true` is for the user to be identified as an individual, usually through some form of sign-on process. This is exactly what happens when you use the ZMI and fill in your username and password to access the Zope TTW management interface. You identify yourself, and the value assigned to `AUTHENTICATED_USER` is set to your own username. To see this for yourself, create a new `dtml-method` with the contents shown here:

```
<dtml-var "REQUEST">
```

### The REQUEST Object

In the HTTP protocol, the term "request" refers to the entire set of data elements that are sent to a web site when a page is requested or "hit." Zope captures all of this data in an object named REQUEST, along with a few of its own touches, including the AUTHENTICATED_USER property. Because you are signed on to the ZMI, your own username appears among the values stored in the REQUEST object (see Figure 7.3) along with many other useful bits of information. Study the entire REQUEST data set to get an idea of what is possible in terms of identifying a site user, protocols, and paths, including the IP address of the user and even the browser type and version being used to view the web.

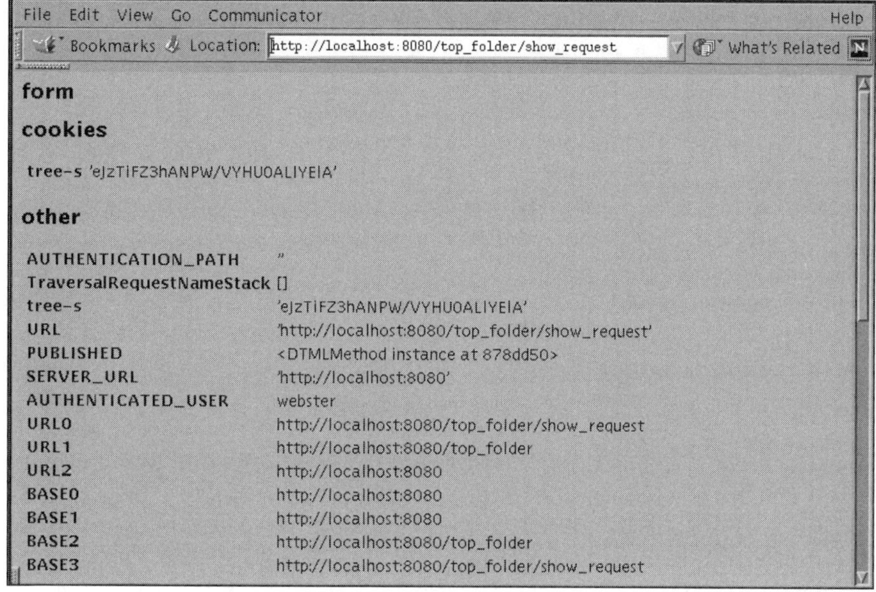


Figure 7.3 Display REQUEST data.

### For More Information

For a more in-depth look at the kind of information contained in an HTTP request, which, in turn, is captured and made available to Zope in the REQUEST object, see these links:

**http://hoohoo.ncsa.uiuc.edu/cgi/env.html**

**http://www.ombomb.org/mission/sw/cgivars.html**

**http://hopf.math.nwu.edu/docs/appendixD.html**

Unfortunately, some browsers do not adhere to the standard, so you might see some data items out of place when you inspect the Zope REQUEST object. This complicates things, but at least Zope helps you see where the problems lie. You can detect malfunctioning browsers (check the data labeled HTTP_USER_AGENT) and develop workarounds in your site objects so that your users aren't inconvenienced.

The quickest way to leverage Zope's own security features is just as you have been doing, using the acl_users folder, via the ZMI. You should need to adjust the Security tab settings only to suit special cases. What makes this approach quick is the simple fact that the features are built in, so you don't have to create anything new to delegate content- and user-management tasks to others. You can see how this works in a simple exercise.

### First Delegation Exercise

Create a new folder with the ID `new_folder` and title of New Folder in the site_folder that you created during an exercise from Chapter 2. Select both Public Interface and User Folder. Add a username to the acl_users folder in the newly created folder with the role of Manager. You will now need to end your own ZMI session and sign on as the newly created user. At the top of the ZMI display, select Logout from the drop-down menu. You should see a dialog box saying something like, "Authorization failed, retry?" Select Cancel. Some browsers don't work correctly with this form of ZMI logout, but if yours does, it is the easiest way. You might need to shut down your browser and restart it because you are already signed on in the current session. Restarting the browser forces a new user authentication step when you "hit" the ZMI. Some browsers won't require you to shut down completely, but instead you will need to start a new browser by clicking the browser icon or selecting the browser from an Applications menu. Opening a new browser window from a running browser menu usually won't work because the new window is really just another display area of the current browser session where you are already signed on as yourself. In the location bar of the browser window, enter the URL **`http://localhost:8080/top_folder/site_folder/new_folder/manage`**. Don't sign on as yourself, instead sign on as the new user that you just added.

When the ZMI appears, notice that it seems as if the new folder is the highest-level folder, where you're accustomed to seeing the Root Folder (see Figure 7.4). From the new user's perspective, this is correct. The new user has no access to the higher folders within the ZMI. If the new user tried to "hit" the ZMI at a higher level, an authentication error would occur. You can see how delegation of ZMI access is isolated to a subset of the Zope site. The new user has complete access and rights to create and update any standard Zope object in the new folder and any subfolders, but he cannot make any changes to folders above this level.

You can further restrict the new user's access by adjusting the permissions options shown in the Security tab of the new folder. Sign back on as yourself to carry out the following examples of setting custom permissions.

In a ZMI window showing that you have "logged in as" yourself, select the Security tab. Slide down through the list of options and notice that the first set all start with "Add." Find Add External Methods and deselect the Acquire Permissions Settings? option. Select the Owner option. Now slide to the bottom of the page and click Save Changes. Remember, because you created this folder, you are the owner, and not even the manager will have the right to add an external method after this change, although you will still be able to.

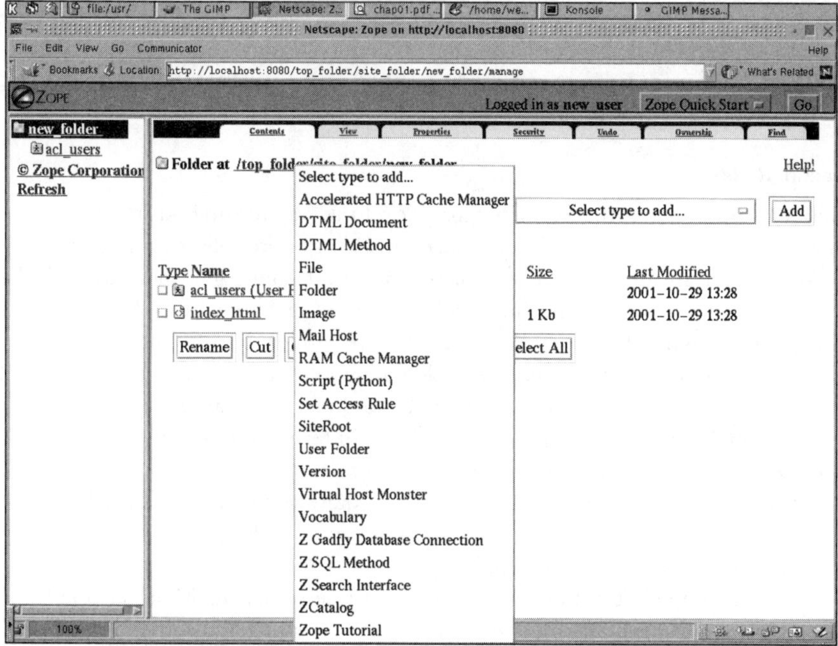


**Figure 7.4** External Method is not an option.

To see how this works, select the new folder from the ZMI navigation tree, and click the Select Type to Add drop-down menu choice. Notice that between DTML Method and File, you can select External Method object. However, when you sign on as the new user, notice that the external method is missing from the Select Type to Add list. Adding an external method is no longer an option for the new user, even though that user has the role of Manager (see Figure 7.4).

Select the Security tab again, and look at more of the options listed there. Below the first bunch that all start with "Add" is a second set that start with "Change." Usually, if you deselect a permission such as Add External Methods, you will also want to deselect Change External Methods. By continuing to adjust permissions, you can delegate a limited subset of very safe and simple content-management and update functions that will empower users to take over certain content-management tasks. Even after you begin to delegate certain responsibilities to users, the full range of options remains available to you.

Thanks to the default settings of new folders, you do not need to adjust the permissions of every single folder that you add. Because Acquire Permission Settings? is selected for all permissions of a new folder, once you adjust permissions for a folder, any subfolders under that level will have the same behavior as the adjusted folder. Entire branches of your site can be easily managed this way by adjusting only the "top" folder of each branch. An easy way to replicate custom setting combinations is to create a "master" folder object with the predefined settings and simply copy/paste/rename as needed. You might want to create a master_objects folder in the top_folder to keep these in one place.

### Special Roles

While you are studying the Security tab, slide all the way to the bottom of the browser window. There you will see advice on adding more roles that, in turn, might be assigned special rights to add and change objects. It's not a good idea to push the hierarchy of roles much beyond the four default roles of Anonymous, Authenticated, Manager, and Owner. There are already more types of permissions here than can be easily kept track of, and every time you add a new role, you are adding an entire column to the Permissions tab. You can see that additional roles can quickly turn out to be more trouble to manage than they are worth, in terms of flexibility. Even so, you might want to consider adding at least one extra role, to designate a type of user with limited add and change permissions, but still not quite at the full Manager level. A single new role of Editor offers a good compromise and clearly identifies a user with permission to make changes to (some) objects.

The most compelling reason to add an Editor role is that the Manager role has specific meaning in terms of method objects—the ones that "do something." Granting full Manager status to users gives them broad control over the folders and subfolders where that status applies. At the very least, an auxiliary role, such as Editor, will add a safety factor to protect your site from sudden upheaval resulting from experiments of inexperienced users. You and your users are both beginning to explore delegation, so a touch of precaution is in order.

### Proxy Roles

To wrap up this discussion of user roles and delegation, here's a final tip regarding permissions and methods. Sometimes it seems that for every new rule, you need yet another to counteract it. The cautionary advice in the prior section mentioned the unique relationship between method objects and the Manager role. It turns out that certain methods *must* behave as if they have Manager status, for those methods to carry their proper functions. Sometimes that turns out to be a conflicting requirement, and the Proxy role is the solution. Take a look at the Proxy tab of a DTML method object (see Figure 7.5).

You now recognize the four standard roles, including Manager. Some objects must have a Manager role associated with them to run correctly, such as the `<dtml-sendmail>` tag.

To achieve a facsimile of Manager status, assign a Proxy role by selecting the Manager option in the Proxy tab of the object's ZMI, as shown in Figure 7.5. There are examples of using email within Zope in Chapter 5, "Web Mail," but for more details about the handy `<dtml-sendmail>` tag, see **http://www.zope.org/Documentation/Guides/DTML-HTML/DTML.16.html**.

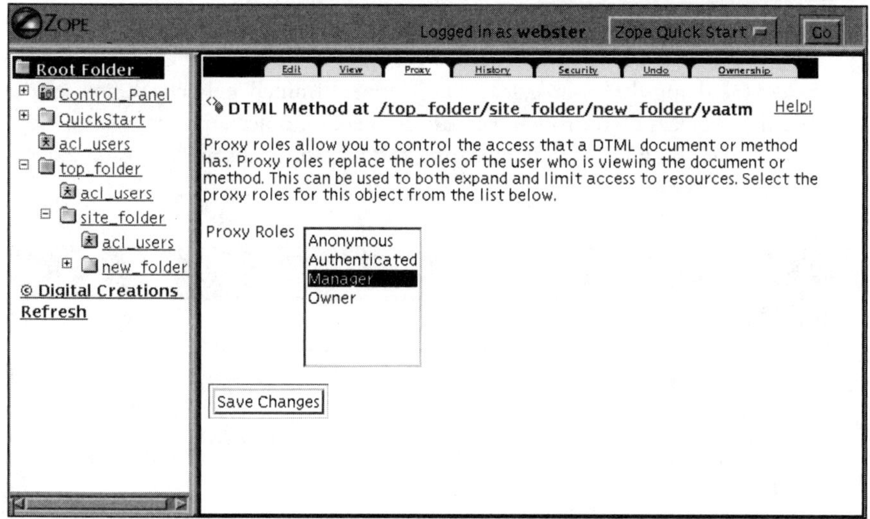


**Figure 7.5** Proxy role options.

# Choosing the Right Tools

As mentioned previously, ever-increasing volumes of content and rising user traffic can have an unfortunate side effect on the speed of a web site returning pages to users. To prevent disappointing results, you must choose components well suited to handle specific types of data, possibly in large amounts. One very commonly used tool for managing tabular data, such as labeled numeric values and catalogs of items, is the Relational Database Management System (RDBMS). You might not have noticed that there is a simple but quite useful RDBMS available within Zope, the Gadfly system. Gadfly is very handy for testing and prototyping, which is one reason that Zope comes with Gadfly built in. However, in most cases Gadfly won't be used in a working Zope site, except perhaps for very small "read-only" databases. You have seen the Z Gadfly Database Connection object listed in the Select Type to Add drop-down list. In the exercises that follow, you will try your hand at creating tables and accessing tabular data stored in Gadfly. You will use Gadfly again in Chapter 12, "Integrating Applications with ZPatterns."

## Setting Up a Connection

To create a connection object, do the following:

1. Select the top_folder as the location for your first Z Gadfly Database Connection object.

2. Pick Z Gadfly Database Connection from the Select Type to Add drop-down list, and give it an ID of `zGadflyRDBM` and a title of Gadfly Data.
3. Select the demo data source, leave the Connect Immediately check box selected, and then click Add. Your new database connection object appears (see Figure 7.6). You are now ready to start storing and accessing tabular data using Zope's ZSQL methods.

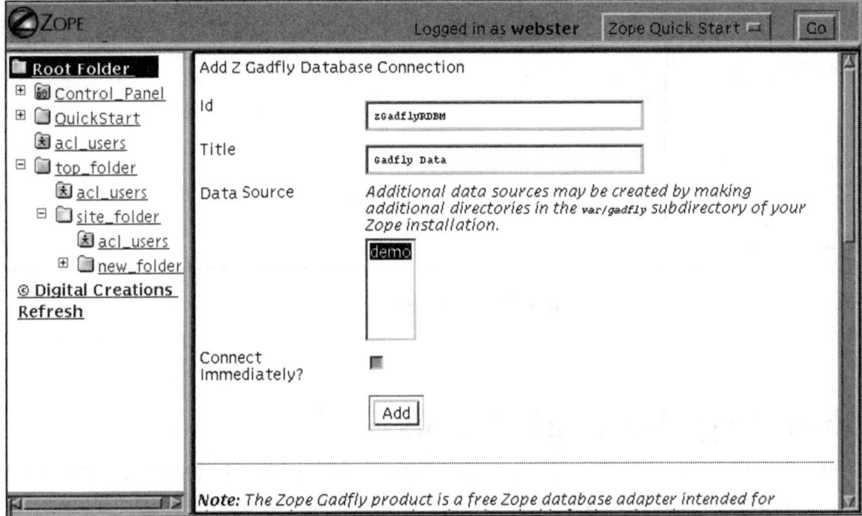


**Figure 7.6** Create a Gadfly database connection.

## ZSQL Methods

Another Zope object type that might have caught your eye is the ZSQL Method. The ZSQL Method type is a Zope object that makes it easy and safe for data to be stored and retrieved from an RDBMS, through Zope, and to display that data within a Zope "page." SQL, which stands for Structured Query Language, is the programming syntax for interacting with many RDBM systems. The examples to follow are all very generic SQL and should work with nearly any standards-compliant RDBMS, although this is by no means guaranteed.

Stay in the top_folder to create your first ZSQL Method, which you will use to create a data table with your new database connection object. Choose ZSQL Method from the Select Type to Add drop-down list. Give your new object an ID of `create_user_contacts`, and select zGadflyRDBM as the data source. Leave Connect Immediately? selected, and click Add. Now enter the SQL `create table` command in the text box of your new ZSQL method, as shown in Listing 7.1 (also see Figure 7.7).

Listing 7.1 **Create a Table, with Two Columns**

```
create table user_contacts (
  user_id varchar(56),
  user_email varchar(56)
)
```

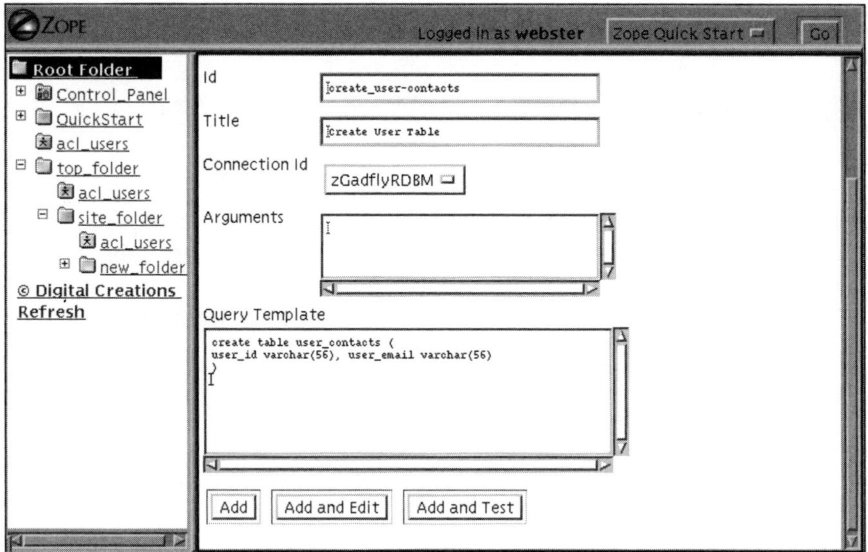


**Figure 7.7** Create a ZSQL Method.

Select Add and Test. In the next screen, choose Submit Query. Successful completion of the command is indicated by a screen with the message, "This statement returned no results." If you have made a typographical error, the command might fail. In this case, you cannot use the Back button of your browser to correct your error. You must return to the top_folder and select the new ZSQL Method object for updating. Make the correction, and select Change and Test. When this process is complete, you will have a newly defined data structure ready to receive data. Another possible cause of an error testing this method is trying to run it again after it has succeeded. In this case, the command is asking to create the same table again, which isn't allowed because it already exists. To assure yourself that the command has in fact succeeded, select the `zGadflyRDBM` object and click the Browse tab. Select the `user_contacts` object to see the structure of the new table. A create table command is unusual because you use it only once, but you might want to copy it to another folder for safe keeping. If you forget how you created the table in the first place, you will still have the original method to review.

To add your first user to the new table, create another ZSQL Method with an ID of `insert_user_contact`. In the text box of the new ZSQL Method, type the SQL insert command shown in Listing 7.2.

Listing 7.2 **Insert a Row**

```
insert into user_contacts values (
'Webster W. Weaver',
'webweaver@newmilleniumschools.org'
)
```

To retrieve the contents of your newly populated table, create yet another ZSQL Method, with an ID of `sql_select_user_contacts`, with the SQL Select command shown in Listing 7.3.

Listing 7.3 **Retrieve Table Data**

```
select user_id, user_email
from user_contacts
```

Click Add and Test, and then click Submit Query. To display the data in an HTML table, create a DTML Method that calls the `sql_select_user_contacts` object, like the example shown in Listing 7.4.

Give your new DTML Method object an ID of `show_all_user_contacts` and the contents shown in Listing 7.4.

Listing 7.4 **Displaying Table Data**

```
<table border=1>
  <tr>
    <th>User ID</th>
    <th>E-Mail</th>
  </tr>
  <dtml-in sql_select_user_contacts>
    <tr>
      <td>&dtml-user_id;</td>
      <td>&dtml-user_email;</td>
    </tr>
  </dtml-in>
</table>
```

**For More Information**

See these links for a tutorial on incorporating Z SQL Methods within your web site, more tips, and related How-To documents:

**http://www.zope.org/Documentation/Guides/ZSQL-HTML/ZSQL.html**

**http://www.zope.org/Members/teyc/howtoSQLVariables**

**http://www.zope.org/Members/spinwing/ZSQL_Results**

**http://www.zope.org/Members/fquin/zsqlmethods**

**http://www.zope.org/Members/rbickers/cataloganything**

**Living with the "Standard"**

The beauty of SQL is that it is a widely supported standard for database programming. Every database vendor that boasts SQL support has added its own unique flavor and diverged from the standard in the process.

The saving grace is that the closer you stay to the simplest forms of generic SQL queries, the easier it will be to change your RDBMS platform, if and when the time comes. If all of this is new to you, here are some links where you can continue your adventure:

**http://w3.one.net/~jhoffman/sqltut.htm**

**http://www.w3schools.com/sql/default.asp**

## Swapping the ZopeDA

The SQL examples in Listings 7.1, 7.2, and 7.3 are very generic and should work unchanged with nearly any SQL-compliant database. The reason this has been mentioned, referred to, and hinted at is that you very well might need to move the data that is available through your Zope web site at some point. In fact, odds are good that it will happen sooner than you imagine. Fortunately, if you have wisely kept true to generic SQL syntax, the move can be very straightforward.

Exporting data from one RDBMS and importing to another is well beyond the scope of this book, but switching from one Zope database adapter to another is right on target. When you have moved your data and adjusted your SQL to compensate for any name changes, very little is required to change the Zope DA that a ZSQL Method interacts with. You will need to install the appropriate Zope DA and select the new Zope DA in the Connection ID drop-down list in the ZMI for each method. That's all there is to it.

Zope DAs are numerous, including options for ODBC and even JDBC as a route to RDBMS/Zope cooperation.

**For More Information**

These links point to sources for the entire range of Zope DAs:

**http://www.zope.org/Products/external_access**

**http://www.zope-treasures.com/sybSQL/Treasures/found.html?rating=word&word=database+adapter&BKat=Search%21&my_srch=word&num=25&word=All&rating=cat&my_srch=category**

# Industrial-Strength Database

The RDBMS model has been found to have a narrow range of features that are unmatched in other technologies. Two that stand out as pre-eminent are the capability to process ad hoc queries and the elimination of redundant data. By strictly adhering to the relational model, very large data sets can be maintained with absolute integrity because there will be a single row that contains each discrete data item. The possibility that two records will hold contradictory data is eliminated because there will be no duplicate data. The data is not guaranteed to be correct, mind you, but it should be unquestionably *consistent*. The same model that ensures robust integrity also ensures unlimited flexibility in querying. If you can imagine a question that you'd like to ask about a relational data set, there is almost certainly a way to structure a query or series of queries to extract that information.

For the promise of the RDBMS to hold true, certain restrictions must be upheld in the practice of capturing and updating the data in question. Beyond diligent creation and maintenance of the data itself, by applying the principles of normalization and data modeling, the RDBMS engine must have certain intrinsic features that ensure integrity. The prevailing "ACID test" that identifies an RDBMS as being suitable for the most demanding applications refers to the four properties of Atomicity, Consistency, Isolation, and Durability. These refer to the necessity of data integrity to be maintainable during normal processing but also during times of intense processing loads, and even in the case of system failures.

**For More Information**

For further studies into the intricate details of RDBMS systems, see these links:

`http://ccism.pc.athabascau.ca/html/courses/comp200n/errata/section4.htm`

`http://www.phpbuilder.com/columns/barry20000731.php3`

`http://www.odbmsfacts.com/articles/acid_properties.html`

`http://www.odbmsfacts.com/articles/atomicity.html`

## More SQL Than a Webbie Wants to Know

As you have no doubt surmised, we can't dwell on the details of SQL and assorted RDBMS systems in this book. However, there are several remaining points worth mentioning simply because they can make an amazing difference in the performance of your web site, even though they have nothing to do with Zope itself.

### Indexing and Foreign Keys

When you design a table structure, or "schema," for use with a SQL-based interface, creating indexes of the most frequently requested data items can drastically improved performance. An index of the students of New Millennium Schools, for instance, should have one index ordered by last name and another by grade. If a certain query that yields a large result set is run everyday or even more frequently, consider adding an index that is custom-made for just that purpose. If you start to see a performance problem, especially as a data set grows, think about what order the data is queried for, and try an index on for size.

### Balancing Normalization and Performance

The rules for normalized data are just that, and we all know what rules are for. Sometimes overly zealous adherence to "third normal form" places enormous processing burdens on a system, with very little benefit. Especially when used in the context of a Zope-based system, don't feel that you are duty-bound to follow every rule in every case. Sometimes Zope can step in to make up for some minor deviation from a "pure" relational model, by post-processing at the data display stage. You will need to experiment to find the best balance of features and performance relative to the systems that you are working with.

### Transactions and ACID

By all means, follow the rules when it is important! If you are processing online purchases through a Zope-based e-commerce "Web Store," choose an RDBMS that has been fully validated for ACID compliance. Zope supports secure, reliable transactions very well, but Zope can't make up for an inadequate RDBMS.

# External Authentication

When you sign on to the ZMI, you are confirming your identity by comparing your user ID and password to two corresponding data items stored within Zope. It's just a way to prove that you are who your user ID says you are. This is fine for a small handful of Zope administrators, managers, and content providers. If this matches your situation, then don't be too concerned about the need to coordinate with an external authentication system. However, like most large organizations, New Millennium Schools already has at least one directory and user authentication system in place. Every time another standalone system is brought online, another ID and password is added for every user. Certainly, it is ideal to cooperate with an existing system in such a case, with the goal of achieving a "single sign-on" so that each user needs to remember only one password at a time.

## Directories and Protocols

Like RDBMS systems, directory services abound. Luckily, there are Zope modules that provide the capability to interact with the most common systems. The link listed next was generated using Advanced Search at the Zope.org site, by entering `ldap OR nis OR nds OR smb OR radius` in the Google Search form at the bottom of the page. This link will show you virtually every page at Zope.org with a reference to any of the popular directory services: **`http://www.google.com/custom?q=ldap+OR+nis+OR+nds+OR+nis+OR+radius+OR+smb&sa=Google+Search&cof=T%3A%23000000%3BLW%3A78%3BL%3Ahttp%3A%2F%2Fwww.zope.org%2FImages%2Fzbutton%3BLC%3A%23000066%3BLH%3A77%3BBGC%3A%23ffffff%3BAH%3Acenter%3BVLC%3A%23606060%3BGL%3A0%3BAWFID%3A7f13e3c1e82f098d%3B&domains=www.zope.org%3Blists.zope.org&sitesearch=www.zope.org`**.

Whether or not any of these modules will be of help to you depends entirely on which directory service your web site needs to interact with. More details on enabling Zope to interact with an external authentication service are included in Chapter 16, "Backup, Disaster Recovery, and Distributed Processing."

**For More Information**

The most widely used directory systems include these:

- NIS, the venerable Network Information System, originally developed by Sun Microsystems (**http://iroi.seu.edu.cn/books/whatis/nis.htm**)
- LDAP, Lightweight Directory Access Protocol, a widely supported standard (**http://www.kingsmountain.com/ldapRoadmap.shtml**)
- NDS, Netware Directory Services, a proprietary directory system from the Novell folks (**http://foldoc.doc.ic.ac.uk/foldoc/foldoc.cgi?NDS**)
- SMB, the LAN Manager–style system based on NetBIOS, used on SAMBA LANS and others (**http://geowww.uibk.ac.at/~bernd/unix/Samba-Server-FAQ-2.html**)
- RADIUS, the Remote Access Dial-In User Service, for direct LAN access via modem (**http://www.sans.org/infosecFAQ/authentic/radius.htm**)

# Summary

You have seen how to delegate content-management tasks to users, who are, after all, the true experts with regard to the topical materials that they need to publish. Next, you found out about storing tabular data in a database, both internal to Zope and in a separate RDBMS system. Another type of interaction with external systems that ties delegation and user management together is the need to refer to an existing user authentication service for password verification. As with many subjects, each of these areas can grow into a book. You no doubt have come to expect that even when we can't cover every point in fine detail, you have been provided with enough to get started, including some timely tips and plenty of pointers to a World Wide Web of additional information.

# 8

# Getting Content Under Control

A ZOPE APPLICATION IS DEFINED by the set of requests that a browser can reasonably make and the responses that Zope can provide to those requests. The first section of this chapter discusses in detail the request/response process and how it fits into the application as a whole. Then you'll consider the concept of "acquisition" and how it works at the Python level so that you can understand its operation at the lowest level of Zope. With these tools firmly in hand, you'll take another look at the logical composition of web pages. Next you'll explore the *Content Management Framework* (*CMF*) and see how it uses all these ideas and more to create a certain class of Zope application that is especially adept at handling content managed by a collective group of contributors. Finally, this chapter considers one of the most recent additions to the Zope tool chest, *Zope Page Templates* (*ZPT*), and shows how they make the job of template building easier.

## HTTP Request and Response

Every time a user "clicks" a button or a link of your Zope application, the same basic process occurs. The user's browser collects any information needed, encodes it in an HTTP request, and transmits it to Zope, with a particular Zope object targeted by the URL specified. Zope decodes the information sent by the browser and puts it all in a single Zope object called the REQUEST object, as you saw in Chapter 7, "Delegation, Databases, and Users." This object is available to all methods and templates so that they can react to the information passed from the browser. At the same time, Zope supplies a RESPONSE object that can be used to modify the results that are sent back to the browser.

To illustrate how this works in detail, the following set of examples will start from very basic interactions and build from there to give you a more sophisticated understanding of the whole process. The process itself is represented in Figure 8.1.

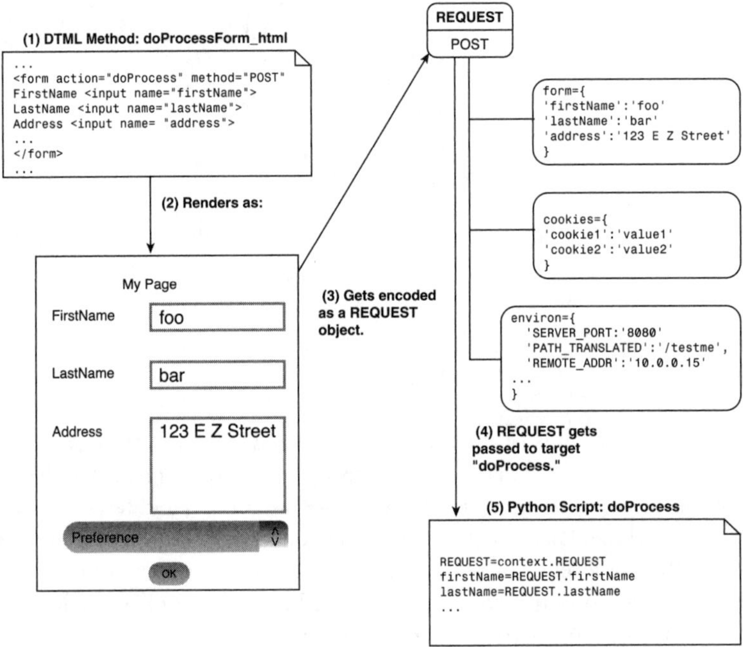


**Figure 8.1** Diagram of REQUEST submission process.

Figure 8.1 illustrates the basic process of a web-based form being "submitted" to a method—in this case, a Python script in Zope. The process has several steps:

1. A method—in this case, a DTML method called `doProcessForm_html`—is used to provide HTML for a form with `<input>` tags that define variables that need to be filled in by the user.
2. This HTML is rendered by the user's browser to produce a screen with input boxes corresponding to the variables defined in step 1.

3. When the user clicks the Submit button, the data that the user typed in is encoded as a REQUEST object by Zope and is passed to the "target" method—in this case, a Python Script called `doProcess`.
4. Finally, when `doProcess` is executed, it can retrieve anything from the form via the REQUEST object.

All of this happens automatically in Zope so that you, as a developer, don't need to handle the details manually. However, it's sometimes useful to *understand* what's going on so that you can more easily diagnose problems that can occur. Because most of the user-supplied input for each transaction comes with the REQUEST object, Zope often looks in the REQUEST object to resolve references made by Python scripts, DTML methods, ZSQL methods, and other "target" objects.

## Manually Testing a "Target"

In Zope, a URL is the address of a method or function that operates on an object. You can think of this method as a "target" that gets "executed" when the REQUEST is received by Zope. Let's make up a target method, called `testTarget`, and test it.

The first simple target is shown in Listing 8.1.

Listing 8.1 **A Very Simple Zope Target Method**

```
<dtml-var standard_html_header>
<h2><dtml-var title_or_id> <dtml-var document_title></h2>
<p>
<pre>
Checking: firstName = "<dtml-var firstName missing>"
 and lastName="<dtml-var lastName missing>"
</p>
<dtml-var standard_html_footer>
```

If you put this into a DTML Method called `testTarget`, you'll see an output something like this:

```
Checking: firstName = ""
and lastName=""
```

There was no Name Error because you included the "missing" parameter in the `dtml-var` tag, which basically says, "If there is nothing called firstName, then display nothing". Now try supplying the parameters by using a `QUERY_STRING` and the end of the URL by using a URL like this: **`http://127.0.0.1:8080/testTarget?firstName=foo&lastName=bar`**.

You should see a screen that looks like this:

```
Checking: firstName = "foo"
and lastName="bar"
```

### REQUEST and RESPONSE Objects

The REQUEST and RESPONSE objects both have special attributes and methods. This is a short summary. You can find a complete reference on the zope.org site, **`http://www.zope.org/Members/michel/ZB/AppendixB.dtml`**

The REQUEST object is an encapsulation of everything that comes from the browser on each transaction.

REQUEST:

- **`PARENTS`:** A list of the objects traversed to get to the published object.
- **`PUBLISHED`:** The actual object published as a result of URL traversal.
- **`RESPONSE`:** The RESPONSE object.
- **`URLn`:** The absolute URL of the request with *n* path elements removed. If *n* is 0 or is missing, then the entire URL is the value. Example: If URL = `http://test.com/a/b/c`, then URL1 = `http://test.com/a/b`.
- **`BASEn`:** The base of the absolute URL, with *n* path elements added. BASE0 is the absolute URL up to but not including the Zope application object.
- **`form`:** A dictionary-like object that represents the contents of any "form" that has been submitted.
- **`environ`:** A dictionary-like object that represents the contents of the environment variables defined in the Common Gateway Interface (CGI) specification.
- **`get_header(name, default=None)`:** Gets a particular HTTP header.
- **`items()`:** Gets (key, value) pairs for all keys defined.
- **`keys()`:** Gets all the keys defined.
- **`values()`:** Gets all values defined.
- **`set(name, value)`:** Sets a (key, value) pair.
- **`has_key(key)`:** Is key defined?

The RESPONSE object is used to modify the HTTP response sent to the browser. You can set cookies and headers and actually stream data to the browser.

RESPONSE:

- **`setHeader(name, value)`:** Sets a particular header in the HTTP response to the browser (such as RESPONSE.`setHeader('Content-Type','text/plain')`).
- **`appendHeader(name, value, delimiter=',')`:** Appends a value to an existing header using an adjustable delimiter.

- **`setCookie(name, value, **kw)`:** Sets a cookie in the response headers. The optional keywords recognized are `expires`, `domain`, `path`, `max_age`, `comment`, and `secure`. These can be used to modify the duration or scope of the cookie set.
- **`appendCookie(name, value)`:** Adds an additional value to an existing cookie.
- **`expireCookie(name, **kw)`:** Removes a cookie from the browser after this response.
- **`setStatus(status, reason=None)`:** Sets the status code returned to the browser.
- **`write(data)`:** Sends "data" directly to the browser. This forces headers to be sent, if they have not been sent already. Error handling must be finished before streaming output is started.

Using the REQUEST and RESPONSE objects, it's fairly easy to get directly involved in the details of communication with the browser, if necessary.

## REQUEST Subobjects

The REQUEST object has a number of subobjects that can be used to specify where you want to look for information about the actual request. Notice that, in the last example, it was not specified *where* Zope was supposed to get `firstName`. Using acquisition (see the next section), Zope could get the value of `firstName` as a property of the folder, or the REQUEST, or some enclosing namespace through which testTarget was being called. If you really want to know that some variable comes from the REQUEST, you'll need to be more specific. The REQUEST object has a subobject called form that represents the fields in the form as a Python dictionary. See the sidebar "The Behavior of Zope Dictionaries" to review the methods of dictionaries—they can come in quite handy! Note, however, that just because an object supports some methods of a "normal" dictionary, it might not support all the methods (for example, it might be a read-only dictionary). Try changing the DTML method to something like Listing 8.2.

Listing 8.2 **Displaying All the Variables from a Form**

```
<dtml-var standard_html_header>
<h2><dtml-var title_or_id> <dtml-var document_title></h2>
<p>
<pre>
Checking: <dtml-var "REQUEST.form">
</p>
<dtml-var standard_html_footer>
```

And then reload the same URL. You should see something like this:

```
Checking: {'firstName': 'foo', 'lastName': 'bar'}
```

So, the `form` attribute of the REQUEST object is really a dictionary that you can treat like any other dictionary. There is also a `cookies` attribute and an `other` attribute that work similarly.

### The Behavior of Zope Dictionaries

Because the REQUEST object has several dictionaries bound to it, you should review some of the methods and properties of Python dictionaries. Dictionaries are mappings of keys to values. Most of the methods are pretty obvious, but here are some examples, in the form of in interactive Python session, to show how they work:

```
python

Python 2.1 (#4, 05/17/01, 18:34:21)
[GCC Apple DevKit-based CPP 6.0alpha] on darwin1
Type "copyright", "credits" or "license" for more information.

>>> x = {}  # create an empty dictionary

>>> dir(x)  # ask it for its methods

['clear', 'copy', 'get', 'has_key', 'items', 'keys',
'popitem', 'setdefault', 'update', 'values']

>>>
>>> x['a'] = 7       # set a value
>>> x                # check it
{'a': 7}
>>> x['b'] = 3       # set another value
>>> x                # check it
{'b': 3, 'a': 7}
>>> x.update({'z':2, 'a':4})  # use "update" to change a value and set another
>>> x
{'z': 2, 'b': 3, 'a': 4}

>>> x.keys()         # get the keys of the dictionary
['z', 'b', 'a']

>>> x.get('z',4)     # get the value of z
2
>>> x.get('w',4)     # there is no 'w' so we get the default
4
>>> y = x.copy()     # make a copy
>>> y
{'b': 3, 'z': 2, 'a': 4}
>>> y['b'] = 1
>>> y                # changing the copy doesn't modify the original
{'b': 1, 'z': 2, 'a': 4}
>>> x
{'z': 2, 'b': 3, 'a': 4}
>>> x.has_key('w')  # check for a particular key
0
```

```
>>> x.has_key('z')
1
>>> x.items()        # get a set of tuples (key, value)
[('z', 2), ('b', 3), ('a', 4)]
>>> x.values()       # get the values
[2, 3, 4]
>>> z = x.setdefault('r',0) # like "get" but also sets
>>> z
0
>>> x
{'r': 0, 'b': 3, 'z': 2, 'a': 4}
>>> x.popitem()      # pop a random (key, value) pair
('z', 2)
>>> x.clear()        # clear out the dict
>>> x
{}
>>>
```

## Form Names and Marshalling

As you saw in Chapter 7, the REQUEST is rich with information about the REQUEST, but by focusing on the `form` object, you can just look at variables sent in the form (or in the `QUERY_STRING` of a `GET` request). Notice that both `firstName` and `lastName` ended up as strings in the REQUEST. What if you want an integer or a date? Zope can do that! Just append a type-conversion flag to the end of the field name in the form or in the QUERY_STRING, and Zope will take care of the rest. Try the `testTarget` with the following QUERY_STRING: **`http://localhost:8080/testTarget?firstName=foo&age:int=36&birthday:date=2001/3/4`**.

You should see output like this:

```
Checking:
{'firstName': 'foo', 'birthday': DateTime('2001/03/04'), 'age': 36}
```

Note that Zope automatically converted the date into a `DateTime` object and the age into an integer. This process is called "marshalling," and Zope has more tricks up its sleeve. Suppose that instead of setting a `QUERY_STRING` manually in the URL, you used a form to set up some variables. You probably know enough HTML to build a simple form. Here you're going to focus on the capability of Zope to manage some of the tedious parts of getting what you want from a form. As you just saw, Zope can handle conversion of data from your form, which always arrives as character type to int, float, date, and so on. The REQUEST can also be organized in collections (list, record, and records). You can get this conversion by adding a conversion flag to the end of the "name" of an input type. For example, Listing 8.3 shows such a form that uses the "records" collection format to collect the inputs into a series of records. Each record has a name and an age. The age is also an integer (so that you can combine collection converters and type converters on a single field).

Listing 8.3 **A Form to Exercise Your Target**

```
<dtml-var standard_html_header>
<form action="testTarget" method="post">
<table>
<tr><th colspan="2">Person 1</th></tr>
<tr><th>Name:</th><td><input name="persons.name:records"></td></tr>
<tr><th>Age:</th> <td><input name="persons.age:records:int"></td></tr>
<tr><th colspan="2">Person 2</th></tr>
<tr><th>Name:</th><td><input name="persons.name:records"></td></tr>
<tr><th>Age:</th> <td><input name="persons.age:records:int"></td></tr>
<tr><th colspan="2">Person 3</th></tr>
<tr><th>Name:</th><td><input name="persons.name:records"></td></tr>
<tr><th>Age:</th> <td><input name="persons.age:records:int"></td></tr>
<tr><th colspan="2">Person 4</th></tr>
<tr><th>Name:</th><td><input name="persons.name:records"></td></tr>
<tr><th>Age:</th> <td><input name="persons.age:records:int"></td></tr>
<tr><td colspan="2" align="center"><input type="submit" value="OK"></td></tr>
</table>
</form>
<dtml-var standard_html_footer>
```

What does `name="persons.name:records"` do? First of all, it creates a list of records in the form object called `persons`. Then it sets the value of the corresponding `name` element of the record to the string input in the browser. It's best to see an example. Modify the `testTarget` to iterate through the person records, as shown in Listing 8.4.

Listing 8.4 ***testTarget* Is Modified to Handle a List of Person Records**

```
<dtml-var standard_html_header>
<h2><dtml-var title_or_id> <dtml-var document_title></h2>
<p>
<pre>
Checking:
<dtml-in "REQUEST.form['persons']">
<dtml-var sequence-index> : <dtml-var sequence-item html_quote>
</dtml-in>
</p>
<dtml-var standard_html_footer>
```

Notice that the `persons` element of the form is now a list, each element of which is a person record. When you view the form created in Listing 8.3, you should see a screen like that in Figure 8.2.

When you click the OK button, you'll see this:

```
Checking:
0 : age: 10, name: joe
1 : age: 12, name: jim
2 : age: 28, name: sue
3 : age: 23, name: sally
```

Just as you expected! Any HTML input type (such as SELECT, CHECKBOX, and RADIO) can be used to enter information, and you can use the marshalling converters to make sure that it comes in the most useful form to your method.

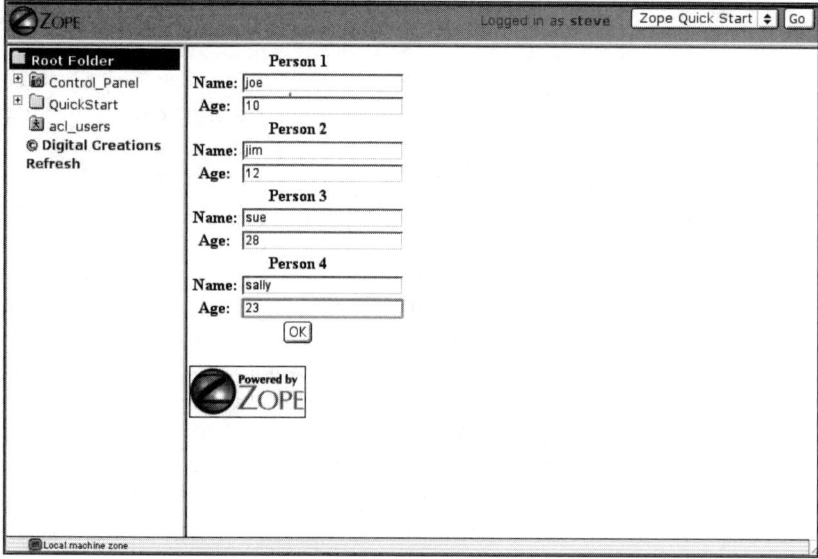


**Figure 8.2** Screen showing form of Listing 8.3.

# Why Acquisition Works

You've heard it said before that you can tell a lot about a person by the crowd he hangs around. This is also the case with objects in Zope. Many times the properties and behavior of a Zope object are affected by other objects in Zope based on their proximity to the original object. *Proximity* might mean an "actual" physical position in the hierarchy of objects, or it might mean an "imposed" location by virtue of mutual reference. In other words, Zope objects have an inherent relationship to other objects just by their location in the Zope directory structure, but they can also be "placed" in a relationship with other Zope objects by the careful construction of a URL.

In object-oriented programming, there is the concept of *inheritance*. Inheritance is the act of obtaining methods and properties from another object without having to re-create them. Inheritance is the idea of "not reinventing the wheel." When behavior that you want already exists in another object definition, inheritance enables you to declare your new object to be related to the existing object to automatically obtain some of its behavior and attributes. It's kind of like choosing your parents in advance. You look around and say, "Hey, those folks have lots of money and influence. That's something I want. I'll just declare myself to be a direct descendant, and I'll automatically inherit all of that." Well, it might not be quite that selfish, but you get the idea.

Acquisition is similar to inheritance, but it differs in one major respect. With inheritance, when an object is declared to be a subclass of another object, then it is locked into that relationship. With acquisition, the relationship is changeable in real time. In other words, acquisition allows an object to inherit on the fly. Inheritance is much like the "genetic" aspects of an object. When it is born, it has these genes with their resulting characteristics and behavior, and nothing is going to change that. This might be a bad example, considering the advances being made in genetics these days, but the idea is that inheritance is locked in when the object is created. It's very useful but not very adaptable. And although Darwin said that genes do get modified over time, the time is generally long. If you want the capability to adapt and change quickly, then acquisition is the way to go.

Acquisition allows objects to behave as chameleons. Genetics (inheritance) dictates that a chameleon should be a reptile and have four legs and scaly skin. The chameleon can't easily change those things when different situations arise. If temperatures suddenly drop, the chameleon can't automatically switch from being a reptile whose body temperature can't be regulated to a mammal who can tolerate the lower temperatures. It would be nice if it could, but it can't. However, if a chameleon goes from a green tree to a sandy beach, it can change its coloration to better match its surroundings, thus providing it some protection from hungry predators. This capability to quickly change a characteristic to better assimilate into a situation is what acquisition is all about. Acquisition means that objects can change characteristics based on their environment or *context*.

## Context Versus Containment

You've worked with Zope enough to know that many objects are designed to contain other objects. Folders are the most obvious example, but ZCatalog are also objects that can contain other objects. These kinds of objects are generally subclassed from the base class objectManager. They "manage" other objects that are contained within them. And you've certainly seen Zope sites where there are objects containing several objects, some of which are containers for other objects. When an object is placed inside another object, it is said to be *contained* by the other object. The container object is often called the *parent*, while the object being contained is called a *child*.

Containment is one method of acquisition. This is the location aspect of acquisition mentioned previously. In addition to containment, there is the concept of *context*. An object can be placed in the context of other objects without actually changing the physical location of the object within the object hierarchy. Even if an object does not acquire characteristics by virtue of a containment scheme, you can force acquisition by referencing an object "through" other objects. This is accomplished through a URL. Acquisition via containment takes precedence over acquisition by context. You can augment with context, but you can't override with it.

## Simple Example of Context Versus Containment

Let's take a real, although somewhat silly, example of these concepts. To work through this example, complete the following steps:

1. Create a folder called Animal in your Zope installation. At the same level, create a folder called Environment.
2. Go down into the Animal folder, and create two folders: one called Mammal and one called Reptile.
3. Click down into the Reptile folder, and create two folders: FourLegged and Legless.
4. Go down into the FourLegged folder, and create a folder called chameleon.
5. Step back up to the Environment folder that you just created, and create three folders inside: Beach, RainForest, and RockyMountain.
6. Now you're ready to add some properties to these folders:
   A. Start with the FourLegged folder. Give it the property `variety` with a value of `four-legged`.
   B. Give the same property to the Legless folder, but give it the value `legless`.
   C. Step up to the Mammal and Reptile folders, and give them each a `type` property. For the Mammal folder, give the `type` property a value of `mammal`; for the Reptile folder, give it a `type` of `reptile`.
7. Go down into the Environment folder and, for each of its three subfolders, give them properties: `location` and `color`.
   A. For the Beach folder, give the `location` property a value of `on the beach`, and give the `color` property a value of `sandy white`.
   B. For the Rainforest folder, give the `color` property a value of `bright green` and the `location` property a value of `in the rain forest`.
   C. Finally, for the RockyMountain folder, give its `color` property a value of `dark brown` and its `location` property a value of `on the rocky mountain side`.
8. Now that all the properties are set, you need to create a couple of DTML methods:
   A. Start at the root folder (where you created Animal and Environment), and create a method called `tellAboutMe`.
   B. Place the code from Listing 8.5 into it.
9. Finally, drop down into the chameleon folder and create a DTML method called `index_html` as the default method for this folder. For the contents of `index_html`, use the single line `<dtml-var tellAboutMe>`.

Listing 8.5 **Acquired DTML Method for Displaying Properties**

```
<dtml-var standard_html_header>
<center>
<h3>I am a <dtml-var title_or_id></h3>
I am a
<dtml-try>
```

*continues*

Listing 8.5 **Continued**

```
     <dtml-var variety>
<dtml-except KeyError>
</dtml-try>
<dtml-try>
     <dtml-var type>
<dtml-except KeyError>
    generic
</dtml-try>
 type of animal.<br>
<dtml-try>
    When I live <dtml-var location> I am <dtml-var color> in color.
<dtml-except KeyError>
</dtml-try>
</center>
<dtml-var standard_html_footer>
```

Whew! That's a lot of work for this little demonstration, but hopefully it will help make context and containment clear to you. To access the `chameleon` object, you simply type its URL into your browser window. The URL is something like **`http://127.0.0.1:8080/Animal/Reptile/FourLegged/chameleon`**.

When you type the URL of the `chameleon` object into your browser window, the message in Figure 8.3 appears.

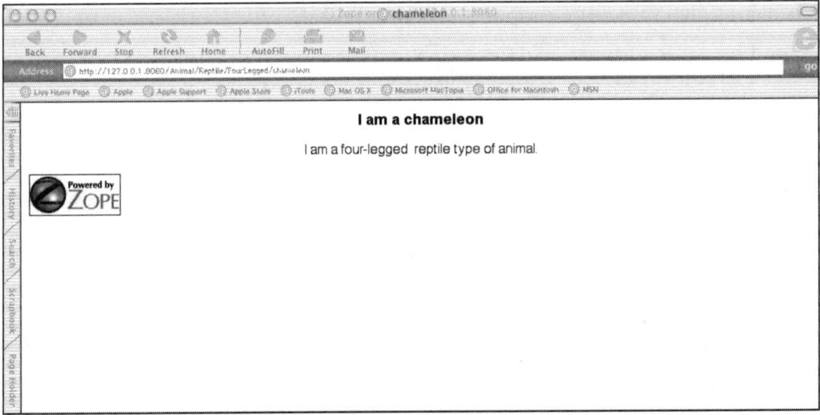


**Figure 8.3** Simple output resulting from the acquisition of properties.

## Analyzing the Example

Let's briefly analyze what is happening. First of all, when you access a folder type of object, the default behavior is to look for a file with the ID `index_html` and render it. The chameleon folder's file called index_html makes a simple call to an object called tellAboutMe. Well, the chameleon folder doesn't contain any objects with that name, so acquisition tells you to start looking in the containing objects for an object with the desired ID. The chameleon folder is contained by the FourLegged folder. The FourLegged folder doesn't contain an object called tellAboutMe either, so you should continue to look up the containment ladder. The FourLegged folder is contained by the Reptile folder. Still no object named tellAboutMe. Next, the Reptile folder is contained by the Animal folder, and you discover that there still is no object called tellAboutMe. Finally you reach the root level and locate an object called tellAboutMe. Therefore, chameleon *acquires* this object as its own and renders it. Keep in mind that the tellAboutMe object is essentially transported down into the chameleon folder so that its world view is the same as the chameleon object's. This is important when it starts to render.

Take a look at the acquired code from Listing 8.5. Line 03 attempts to print the title_or_id property. Even though the tellAboutMe object is physically located up in the Animal folder, it is acquired by the chameleon object, so it sees the namespace from the chameleon folder's point of view. From that perspective, title_or_id gives the title or ID of the chameleon folder, *not* the Animal folder. Do you see the difference between "acquiring" and "having access to"? Having access to an object would mean that you could make use of it but that it would remain in its own location. Acquiring an object means that the object is transported, in a sense, into the environment of the acquiring object.

Now take a look at lines 05 through 08 of Listing 8.5. This series of lines attempts to render an object or property called variety. Again, you have to look for the variety object or property because chameleon has neither. Stepping up to the FourLegged folder you immediately locate a property called variety and render its value, which is four-legged. That was easy. You surrounded the rendering of this value in a try/except clause just in case the property was not located. You don't want to generate an error; you just don't want it to print anything.

Next, lines 09 through 13 attempt to render an object or property called type. Again, this action is encased in a try/except mechanism to avoid printing an error if the desired object is not found. The chameleon folder does not have an object or property with that name, so you step up to the FourLegged folder. You still find no type object. The next container up is the Reptile folder, and here you happily find a property called type. Its value is reptile, so you print it. The except clause of this section prints the word "generic" if no type property is found.

Finally, lines 15 through 18 attempt to render a location and color. If they both are found, then they are rendered to the screen; otherwise, nothing is printed. If you follow the containment tree up to the top, you'll find that no property called location or color is found. The result is, therefore, the display shown in Figure 8.3.

### A Change of Scenery for a Different Look

Now you've seen a simple example of container acquisition. Various properties and objects were acquired by the `chameleon` object simply by the hierarchical containment method. To further see how location in the containers is important, you're going to change the rendering of the `chameleon` object simply by moving it to a different location. You won't change a bit of code or a single property, yet the `chameleon` will render differently.

Complete the following steps:

1. Go down into the FourLegged folder and cut out the chameleon folder.
2. Move over to the Legless folder and paste the chameleon folder into it.
3. Now type the new URL for the chameleon folder (**`http://127.0.0.1:8080/Animal/Reptile/Legless/chameleon`**). The screen shown in Figure 8.4 will appear.

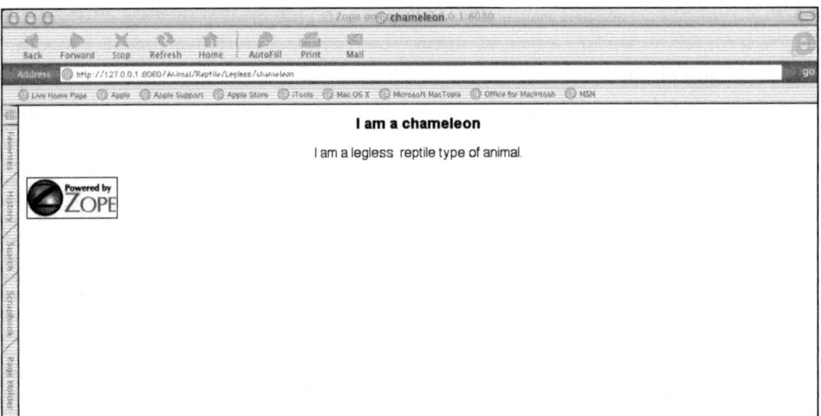


**Figure 8.4** Modified output resulting simply from a change of containers.

Notice that the screen is essentially the same, but now the message tells us that the chameleon is a legless reptile instead of a four-legged reptile. Although the zoology is completely incorrect, the programming ramifications are exciting. You changed the default rendering of this object simply by where you placed it in the containment hierarchy. If you carry this one step further and move the chameleon folder all the way up and place it in the Mammal folder and then type the address **`http://127.0.0.1:8080/Animal/Mammal/chameleon`**, the result is shown in Figure 8.5.

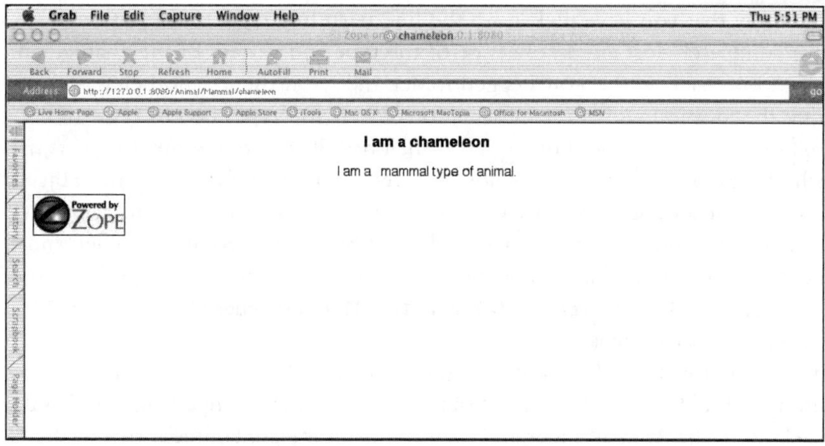


Figure 8.5 More rendering differences due to containment.

Again, the genealogy is a mess, but the containment idea is supported. For now, put the chameleon folder back in the FourLegged folder. Notice that you've traversed the containment hierarchy all the way to the top and have never located an object or property called `location` or `color`. The `tellAboutMe` method would love to include that information, if it could, so let's see how to provide it with some. You know that you have specified those properties for the folders within the Environment folder, but how do you get to them? You could move the chameleon folder over into one of those folders and see what happens. Move it to the Beach folder. The result of rendering the chameleon in its new environment is shown in Figure 8.6.

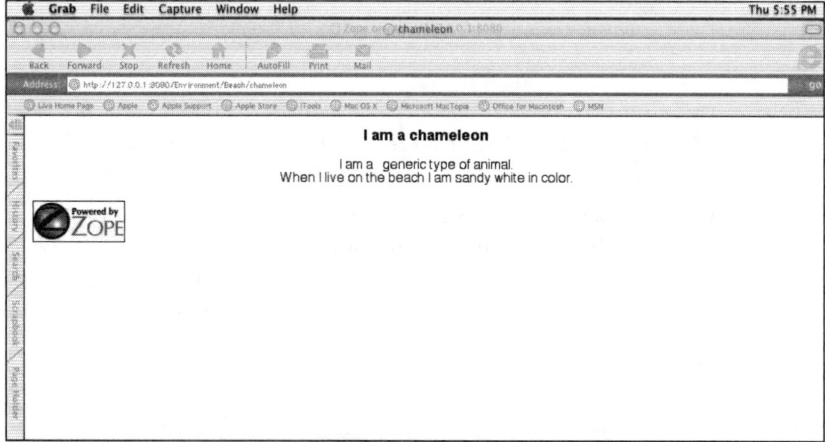


Figure 8.6 Rendering `chameleon` in a new environment.

Notice now that you have picked up the line regarding color and location, but you've completely lost any knowledge of the type and variety of the chameleon. Let's put him back in the FourLegged folder and see if there's another way to acquire the location and color information. When you type the URL for the `chameleon` object, you will notice that it includes all the containment objects in which `chameleon` is nested. That's how you tell Zope where to locate the object that you want to access. Suppose that you fool Zope for a minute and start telling it that the `chameleon` is down in the Beach folder within the Environment folder, and then you change your mind and give it the correct location. The resulting URL would look something like this: **`http://127.0.0.1:8080/Environment/Beach/Animal/Reptile/FourLegged/chameleon`**.

If you read this URL from left to right, it's almost like you start down in the Environment folder and get to the Beach folder, and then change your mind and go back up to the Animal folder and then on down the containment tree to the `chameleon` object. The result of this somewhat bizarre-looking URL is the shown in Figure 8.7.

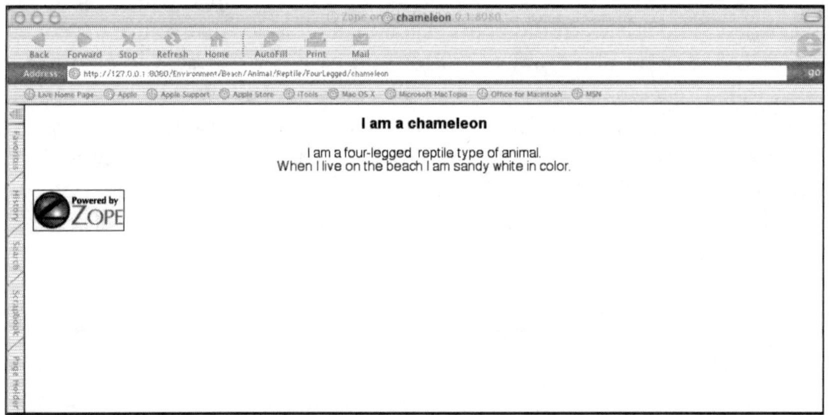


**Figure 8.7** Rendering `chameleon` with context acquisition.

Ah ha! That's what you want. The `chameleon` object hasn't lost sense of its place in the Animal chain, but it has acquired the concept of environment with its associated color change. By simply changing the name of the folder after Environment in the URL, you'll see the color change to match the environment. Now that's a chameleon for you!

### Containment Before Context

One final piece of this is demonstrated by giving both the Environment and Animal folders a property called `controllingFeature`. For Environment, give this property a value of `location`; for Animal, give it a value of `genetics`. Now, if you add this line to the `tellAboutMe` object, which value is `chameleon` going to acquire?

```
The dominant controller of my behavior is <dtml-var controllingFeature>
```

The Environment folder appears first in the URL, so maybe the answer will be `location`. When the `chameleon` is rendered, however, you'll see that the answer is `genetics`. The `chameleon` object acquired its `controllingFeature` property from the Animal folder. Maybe if you move the Environment folder portion close to the `chameleon` in the URL, that will cause its property to be acquired instead. But if we change the URL to **`http://127.0.0.1:8080/Animal/Reptile/FourLegged/Environment/Beach/chameleon`**, you find that the answer is still `genetics`. The `chameleon` object still acquires its `controllingFeature` property from the Animal folder. This is because containment acquisition has a higher priority than context acquisition. It's more important where an object is physically located than what objects it is associated with via a URL.

We hinted a few paragraphs back that you were going to try to fool Zope into thinking that `chameleon` was in one place when it actually was in another. In reality, you aren't "fooling" Zope at all. This is the mechanism that Zope gives you to further specify where you want acquisition objects and properties to come from. As you can see from this example, the combined use of containment acquisition and context acquisition is extremely powerful.

One of the tools available to you to help you visualize acquisition is Shane Hathaway's Acquisition Understander. It is an external method that can be added easily; a short description and the source are located at **`http://www.zope.org/Members/chrisw/showaq`**.

## Acquisition at the Python Level

Ultimately, all of the Zope objects are Python-based; therefore, it is instructive to take a brief look at the concept of acquisition from Python's perspective. In many cases, it is necessary, or at least prudent, to create class descriptions in Python instead of using ZClasses through the web. Most of the time, these new objects are subclassed from one of several existing base classes. One common base class used is called SimpleItem. These base classes provide nice starting points for Zope product design because they already have many of the features that you've come to expect from Zope products built it. One of those "expected" features is acquisition.

SimpleItem actually encompasses a lot of things, but one of those things is the acquisition piece. By subclassing from this existing class, you automatically obtain the acquisition capability without explicitly including it. In fact, if you take a look at the source code from SimpleItem.py, located in $ZOPEROOT/lib/python/OFS, you'll see that the class definition for SimpleItem (found at the bottom of the file) includes several base classes. One of those is Acquisition.Implicit. This is one of the base classes available that provides acquisition.

Here's a little test that you can perform on the Python command line to experiment a bit with acquisition. Create two classes: class Reptile and class Chameleon. Define them as shown in Listing 8.6. For the code in Listing 8.6 to work, you need to be in the $ZOPEROOT/lib/python directory, or you need to have this directory on your Python path.

Listing 8.6 **Classes to Test Acquisition**

```
import ExtensionClass, Acquisition

class Reptile(ExtensionClass.Base):
    genus = 'reptile'
    color = 'N/A'

class Chameleon(Acquisition.Implicit):
    pass
```

Now, if you type `aReptile = Reptile()` and then type `aReptile.genus`, you'll get `reptile` as the return value. If you type `aReptile.color`, you'll get `N/A`. Now type `aChameleon = Chameleon()`; when you type `aChameleon.genus` or `aChameleon.color`, you'll get an `AttributeError`. So, things that are declared as being Reptile objects have a `genus` property associated with them, but objects declared as being Chameleon do not.

What if you declare a subobject of `aReptile` to be a Chameleon object by typing `aReptile.myFavoriteAnimal = Chameleon()`. Because the `myFavoriteAnimal` subobject is declared to be a type Chameleon and you've already shown that Chameleon objects don't have a `genus` property, you might expect that if you type `aReptile.myFavoriteAnimal.genus`, you would get an `AttributeError`. However, you'll find that you actually get the answer `reptile`. The new object `myFavoriteAnimal` has properties `genus` and `color` just by being a subobject of an object that does have these properties.

If you explicitly give the `myFavoriteAnimal` object a property value for `color` by typing `aReptile.myFavoriteAnimal.color = 'multifarious'`, then it will be used instead of `N/A`. However, if you type `aReptile.color`, it still shows `N/A` for its `color` property. In other words, the `myFavoriteAnimal` subobject now has its own `color` value, which doesn't affect the `color` value for the parent `aReptile` object.

Two types of acquisition are defined by the Acquisition module, implicit and explicit. When an attribute is requested from an object that is subclassed from Acquisition.Implicit and the attribute is not found in the object or through inheritance, then the attribute can be obtained automatically from the environment (context). In the case of Acquisition.Explicit, an attribute is not automatically obtained from the environment and can be acquired only using the `aq_acquire` method (as in `aReptile.myFavoriteAnimal.aq_acquire('genus')`).

When an object that has been subclassed from an Acquisition base is referenced as a subobject of another object, a new object is returned that is called an *acquisition wrapper*. The reference `aReptile.myFavoriteAnimal` actually creates a new object that contains references to both the `aReptile` and `myFavoriteAnimal` objects. The acquisition wrapper takes care of deciding where properties and methods come from when referenced.

Use the built-in Python `type` method on the object, and see what type of object Python believes the `aReptile.myFavoriteAnimal` is. If you enter the following on the command line,

```
type(aReptile.myFavoriteAnimal)
```

the result is something like this:

```
<extension class Acquisition.ImplicitAcquirerWrapper at 28220920>
```

Notice that Python believes this object to be of a type `Acquisition.Implicit AcquirerWrapper` instead of being of the type `chameleon` like it was declared. If you had typed this,

```
type(aReptile)
```

you would have gotten back this,

```
<extension class __main__.Reptile at 80dab80>
```

which is what you expect.

The `type` method is a good one to use to make sure that both you and Python are in agreement about what types of objects you are working with.

Acquisition wrappers provide a couple methods that permit direct access to the objects involved in the wrapping. One method, called `aq_parent`, provides direct access to the object parent object involved in the wrapping process. In this case, `aReptile.myFavoriteAnimal.aq_parent` returns the object `aReptile`. On the opposite end of things is the `aq_base` method that returns the object that is left after all wrappers are removed. In some cases, wrappers are further wrapped by other objects and `aq_base` unwraps all the wrappings and delivers the bottom object. The method `aq_self` is similar to `aq_base` but might differ in a multiply wrapped system.

As a final example of containment and context, look at the Python program shown in Listing 8.7.

Listing 8.7 **Showing Acquisition with Python**

```
import Acquisition

class DummyClass(Acquisition.Implicit):
    pass

a = DummyClass()
a.b = DummyClass()
a.b.c = DummyClass()
```

*continues*

Listing 8.7 **Continued**

```
a.d = DummyClass()
a.d.e = DummyClass()
a.d.e.f = DummyClass()
a.d.e.f.g = DummyClass()

a.name = 'a'
a.b.name = 'b'
a.b.c.name = 'c'
a.d.name = 'd'
a.d.e.name = 'e'
a.d.e.f.name = 'f'
a.d.e.f.g.name = 'g'

a.d.e.color = 'red'
a.d.e.f.color = 'green'
a.d.e.f.g.color = 'blue'

a.b.c.x = DummyClass()

print "my name is: ",a.b.c.d.e.f.g.x.name
print "my color is: ",a.b.c.d.e.f.g.x.color
```

Also refer to Figure 8.8.

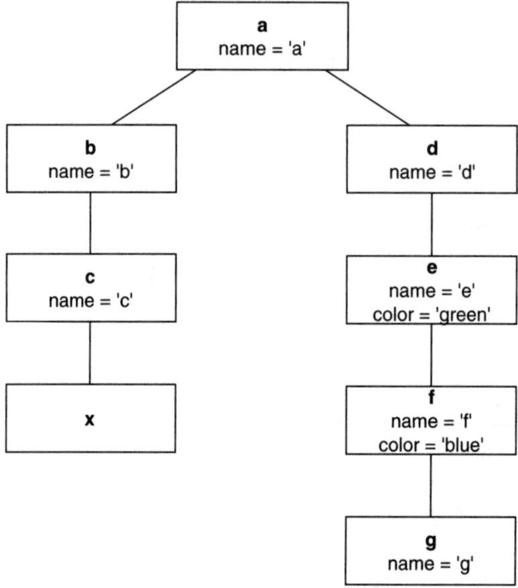


**Figure 8.8** Object acquisition flowchart.

When this Python program is executed, the output is the following:

```
My name is: c
My color is: red
```

Because all the objects have, `name` properties except `a.b.c.x`, looking at the chain of objects in lines 28 and 29, it's hard to see why the object `c` is chosen as the one that shares its name. To discover that, you need to refer back to the containment scheme established in lines 06 through 12. Another way is to refer to Figure 8.8, which visually presents the containment structure. When `a.b.c.x` is found not to have a `name` property, then the parent object is checked. As you can clearly see from Figure 8.8, the immediate container for `a.b.c.x` is `a.b.c`, so `a.b.c` shares its `name` property.

The situation is a bit different for the `color` property. When it is noticed that `a.b.c.x` does not have a `color` property, then you move up the list of containers looking for a `color` property. None of the containing objects has this property, so you now have to look elsewhere. From the context string, you see that the objects `a.d`, `a.d.e`, `a.d.e.f`, and `a.d.e.f.g` are included as a context for the `x` object. In the case of context, you travel up the containment tree to the top and then start back *down* the containment tree for the other objects included in the list. You already know that object `a` does not have a `color` property, so you start down this other branch that you've been permitted to descend because of context. The next object that you reach is `a.d`. It does not have a `color` property, so you continue down the tree to the next object, `a.d.e`. This object does have a `color` property, so you can stop there. Your job is finished. So, even though `f` and `g` are physically closer to `x` in the context string that you used in lines 28 and 29, context acquisition goes from left to right on the context string.

If you added another branch to the main object `a` (`a.h`, `a.h.i`, and `a.h.i.j`) and gave its subobjects `color` properties, the situation would be complicated even further. However, the same rule applies. When containment searching is exhausted, context searching begins, and it moves from left to right along the context string. If the new branch were listed first in the string (`a.b.c.h.i.j.d.e.f.g.x.color`), the color of the `h` object would be acquired (if it has one). If not, then `i` is given an opportunity to donate, and so on along the string. However, if the new branch were listed last (`a.b.c.d.e.f.g.h.i.j.x.color`), then `x` would still acquire the `color` property from `e` as before.

Let's briefly review the high points. When acquisition occurs, it starts with containment type acquisition first; then, if the desired property or method is not found, context acquisition comes into play. Containment comes before context. Sometimes it's easier to see things if you make a quick sketch of the containment scheme before trying to figure out what's acquiring from what.

## Building Consistent Templates

In Chapter 2, "Point and Click Web Building," you got your first hands-on look at treating Zope objects as page elements and wrappers. Wrappers assemble a set of references to page elements into a package that can be included on any web page. Now turn your attention back to the concerns that any web master must feel when facing a rising deluge of web content. That basic concept of "decomposing" a page into components is the foundation of Zope content management.

With a storm surge of content threatening to swamp the tidy web coastline that you have painstakingly built for New Millennium Schools, now is the time to take full advantage of dynamic object publishing. Zope objects are the individual sandbags that work together as a larger structure to channel the flood of web content.

## Objects Are Building Blocks

When you look at the "source" of a typical HTML page, it can be difficult to see it as a set of components. Still, underneath the apparent hodge podge, there is a structure based on a defined sequence:

- Head
  - Title
  - Metatags
  - Libraries
  - Styles
- Body
  - Banner
  - Navigation
  - Unique content

That last item might have been labeled simply Content, but from the web designer's point of view, all the elements are content. It's just that most of the other elements are not unique to a single page, but they are shared components, appearing on many other pages as well. Taking this notion one step further leads to the web portal concept, where few elements are unique to any page. The specific combination and ordering of a set of common elements is the only truly unique aspect of most portal pages.

## Start at the Top

In the wrapper-style template model that the examples in Chapter 1, "The Object of the Web—Optimizing Web Development," and Chapter 2, "Point and Click Web Building," are based on, the first element to be involved in the object publishing process is the DTML document, which sets up the `page_body` variable and provides the title property that the wrapper (DTML method) acquires. You will now "build out" that simple example in preparation for more advanced content-management techniques presented later in this chapter.

When you last saw that initial DTML document, now called the title object, it looked very much like Listing 8.8.

Listing 8.8 **Title Object of the "Object of the Web" Home Page**

```
01 <html>
02   <head>
03     <title>&dtml-title;</title>
04   </head>
05   <body>
06     <dtml-let page_body="'my_home.stx'">
07       &dtml-standard_dtml_wrapper;
08     <dtml-let>
09   </body>
10 </html>
```

The purpose of the title object is to "initialize" the page, which means that it should "set up" any truly unique aspects of a single page and to "call" or "include" additional common elements. This is exactly what is happening at line 06 of Listing 8.8, where the value of the variable `page_body` is set to the name of the second DTML document. Next, at line 07 of Listing 8.8, the common element `standard_dtml_wrapper` is inserted into the page.

That is a simple, clean way to define a page, but perhaps it's a little too simple for the "real world." What other elements might you need to add to arrive at a more complete prototype for a title object?

Starting with the `<head>`, unique metatags are certainly a candidate, such as topical information that search engines use for identifying a page by subject. What about more general metatags, though? There could very well be a set of descriptive words that apply to a section of your site that this page is part of, and another with topical hints about the site in general.

### Metatag as Objects

All the metatags required by a page can be organized within the `<head>` section of the title object, but the section- and site-related metatags should be isolated as shared elements. The `head` section could start to look like Listing 8.9.

Listing 8.9 **Including Metatags as Shared Elements**

```
01 <head>
02   <title>&dtml-title;</title>
03   <meta name="keyword" content="Web, content, management, Zope, object" >
04   <meta name="description content="Web development with Zope">
05   <dtml-var local_metatags>
06   <dtml-var global_metatags>
07 </head>
```

At line 05 of Listing 8.9, an object with an ID of `local_metatags` is called. Then, at line 06, another with the ID `global_metatags` is included. Of course, those two objects don't exist yet, but you can see that the technique of inserting shared components can be applied to build up to a complete page template, just as the `standard_dtml_wrapper` was included in the earlier example.

It might occur to you to remove the reference to `global_metatags` and place it inside the `local_metatags` object. This is exactly the sort of thought process that you need to start developing. The ease of maintaining your site can be greatly improved simply by "refactoring" the distribution of objects. In this case, the advantage is to reduce the number of items that must be referred to directly within the title object.

It doesn't look like much when you are considering a single page, but every page that follows this model will have one shared metatag reference, or two, depending on how efficiently the objects are "nested." Because you know that every page will need both objects, it does make sense to reduce the number of direct references in all the title objects by moving a reference to a shared object.

### Objects for Dummies

Before you go about creating your `local` and `global` objects, there might be a nagging question lingering. Take a moment to ask, "How do I *know* that every page will need both objects?" In case of an exception, when the unique content of a single page is related to the other pages in a section but the normal metatags don't really apply to that specific page, you need a way to "override" the default behavior.

In that case, you have several options, the most obvious being to simply leave the reference to `local_metatags` out of the title object of that page. Another way to approach this sort of thing is to create a "dummy" object with the same ID as the object that should be disregarded and place it in a location where the title object will acquire it. If you place that one very special page in a separate folder, you can also place an empty DTML method named `local_metatags` in the same folder.

However, if you are going to have a separate folder just for one page, there is an even easier way to solve the puzzle. Instead of going to the trouble to add a blank DTML method, you can just add a blank property to the folder itself with the same name (ID) as the object to be overridden.

Add your new folder object, and then select it when it appears. Click the Properties tab of the folder. At the bottom of the screen, type `local_metatags` in the Name box. Click Add. You now have a "dummy" `local_metatags` object.

### How to Find an Object

Z Publisher doesn't know or care whether an object is supposed to be a document, a method, or even a simple text value (in this case, an empty string). Acquisition is based on locating an object with a particular name (ID), and the first one that turns up will be applied.

If there is no object with the correct name (ID) in the same folder with the DTML document that refers to the object, the next place that ZPublisher looks is at the folder itself. If your keys aren't in your briefcase, where you usually keep them, look in your pockets!

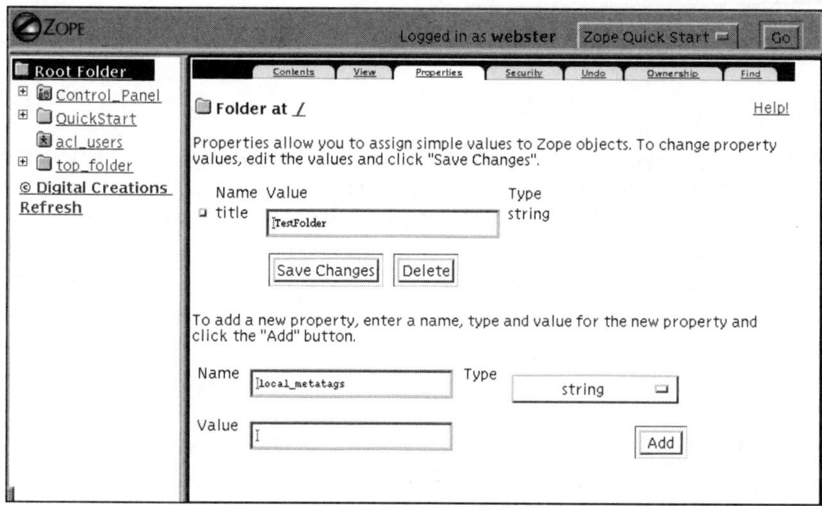


**Figure 8.9** Folder properties.

## A Head-Level Wrapper

Before you move the reference to `global_metatags` to the `local_metatag` DTML method, pause for a moment to consider what this decision implies. If the `local_metatags` object is going to be adapted for use as a wrapper for another object, by including a reference to that object, is it still just a `local_metatags` object, or has it evolved into something else? You are starting to treat it as a wrapper.

The first pass at a `standard_head_wrapper` object might look like Listing 8.10.

Listing 8.10 **Page Head Wrapper v.01**

```
<dtml-var global_metatags>
```

The new name (ID) has the advantage of being clearer about the purpose of this object to anyone who sees the reference, including yourself. Sometimes more precise naming can help you understand the true nature of things more readily. Would you have considered adding a reference to your standard JavaScript library in a `local_metatags` object? It seems perfectly reasonable to add that same reference in a `standard_head_wrapper` because that's exactly the kind of thing that wrappers are for.

The second version of the `standard_head_wrapper` object might look like Listing 8.11.

Listing 8.11 **Page Head Wrapper v.02**

```
<dtml-var global_metatags>
<script src="/scripts/standard_lib.js" type="text/javascript"></script>
```

If a custom .js script is unique to a page, the reference to that element can be included directly in the head, just like the unique metatags.

### Styles Cascade

Style sheets can be included in exactly the same way as metatags and .js references, but special care is needed in some cases. Keep in mind when designing style sheets that the full name of these handy bits is Cascading Style Sheets. The "Cascading" part means that the order in which the references to style sheets appears affects their behavior. If two style sheets have the same style name, the one that is read into the browser last "wins." The styles are applied to the page in reverse order, last to first. So, if you intend to include a style sheet in your page that overrides the standard one, the reference to that custom style sheet *must* appear *after* the reference to the standard style sheet.

### The Caching Conundrum

While you're looking at the sort of thing that should become part of your `standard_head_wrapper`, this is a good time to address an annoying paradox of web development, the user-friendly cache. Caches are intended to make life on the web more pleasant by eliminating the need to repeatedly download the exact same page that you already waited 127 seconds for, every time you hit the Back button.

The bad news is, many web designers took this as the sign that every full-page graphic background and flashy complex plug-in script was fair game because the user needed to download it only once. A little restraint on the part of web designers can provide you with perfectly presentable pages that download quickly without the need for caching. For a dynamic publishing environment, that is especially important because the page that you were on a few minutes ago might have been updated by the time you get back to it. Always try to keep your pages "lightweight." For pages that must be viewed in the most current edition due to frequent updates, use special pragma metatags to label them as noncacheable to make certain that your users get the full benefit of dynamic object publishing.

Start building your `global_metatags` object with two metatags to tell browsers not to cache Zope pages (see Listing 8.12).

Listing 8.12 **Global Metatags Object v.01**

```
<meta http-equiv="expires" content="0">,
<meta http-equiv="pragma" content="no-cache">
```

Even with these clear signals in place, some browsers will still cache whatever passes across the screen. This can be very confusing to a web designer working with Zope because each dynamic update requires a page refresh to display properly. Usually holding down the Shift key while you click on the browser's Refresh button will force a browser to display the current page.

### Back to the Top

Along with all this concern over what to put and which object to put it in, you need to consider where these new objects should be in the site hierarchy. One reason that you created that top_folder back in Chapter 2 was to provide a universal location for all common elements.

When you create the elements that you expect every page will include, such as the `global_metatags` and `standard_head_wrapper` objects, they belong at the very top of the tree. That way, any page can acquire them from the moment the page is created. If you need to override the generic version for a special section of your site, just put a new custom object with the same name at the top of that branch. Then all the pages below that point will acquire the custom version rather than the universal one.

### Templates Are Consistent

When your users first sit down in front of a WYSIWYG "web processor," they might very well be caught up in the same euphoria that led clerical workers around the globe to include every single font that they could get their hands on in a five-line memo. This, too, shall pass, but it's better for the quality of your site if you can set some guidelines ahead of time. Templates are a great way to provide a frame where those memos can find a comfortable home—and where they don't feel obliged to show off so much.

> **For More Information**
>
> You can find some great "design for usability" sites on the web. Here are a couple that you might find useful:
>
> **`http://www.asktog.com`**
>
> **`http://www.useit.com`**

As you experiment with the ideas that have started popping up after seeing these template examples, always keep in mind that the goal is to facilitate effective communication. Dynamic object publishing with page templates helps keep the nonessential details in the background so that content topic experts can focus on sharing their knowledge.

## Exploring CMF

The CMF is a major new undertaking of the Zope Corporation and is deserving of a book in its own right. You had a brief introduction to the CMF in Chapter 4, "Zope Discussion Tools." What follows is more in-depth treatment of certain aspects of the CMF, but it still represents only another layer of a very big onion. For the latest complete documentation of the CMF, you'll want to visit the CMF dogbowl (**`http://cmf.zope.org`**), which is a CMF site. You'll start by reviewing the tools of the CMF that govern policy of the CMF site. Then you'll learn about content and how content is managed in a CMF site. Finally, you'll create your own content type and configure it so that members can work with it.

## CMF Tools

You already know how to add and set up a CMF site from Chapter 4. If you inspect the highest level of your CMF, you'll see several tools there, as shown in Figure 8.10.

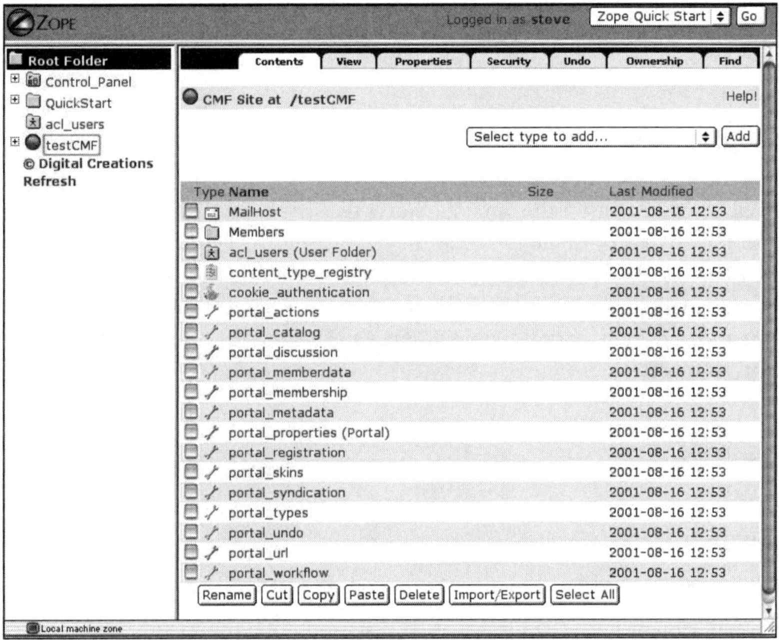


**Figure 8.10** The tools in CMF.

There are lots of tools here, and we won't be able to analyze each of them in detail. A few key tools handle most of the site policy, and we'll focus our attention on those. As you can see, the tools are as follows:

- **portal_actions**—This is a manager of "things members can do." The actions tool is where you would go to ask, "What can this member do now?"
- **portal_catalog**—This is the catalog that keeps track of all the portal's content.
- **portal_discussions**—The discussions tool manages the way "replies" to content are managed in the portal.
- **portal_memberdata**—The memberdata tool configures what data is kept for each member.

- **portal_membership**—The membership tool keeps track of how authentication is handle for the portal.
- **portal_metadata**—The metadata tool keeps track of portal policy about content metadata (for example, what subjects are allowed for documents or other content types).
- **portal_properties**—The properties tool keeps track of portal-wide properties.
- **portal_registration**—The registration tool configures portal registration policy.
- **portal_skins**—The skins tool keeps all the skin folders for all the content types in the portal. A skin folder is like a layer of an onion. As content is being acted on by some method, it visits one skin folder after another, looking for methods to satisfy references made by that method. The order of the skin folders (referred to as "layers" in the portal_skins preferences) is defined in the skins tool preferences and also by the users selection of a site skin. This way, the display of content is a question of site policy (which skins are put in the skins tool preferences) rather than the content object developer. We'll discuss this in greater detail in the following section, "User-Selectable Skins."
- **portal_syndication**—The syndication tool sets policy for publishing content from the CMF to external syndication clients (such as RSS).
- **portal_types**—The portal types tool sets site policy on how all the various content types are created, displayed, and published. We'll go into greater depth with this tool.
- **portal_undo**—The undo tool provides an interface to Zope's "undo" facility.
- **portal_url**—This is an interface to get the portal's URL.
- **portal_workflow**—The workflow tool provides "workflows" that govern the steps in the publishing process and how content moves from one step to the next.

These tools are a key concept in the CMF, and they represent a new way of thinking about Zope applications. In a CMF site, content objects have no inherit display capability, nor any internal concept of workflow or policy. All the work of handling workflow, searching, viewability, and display is provided by service-oriented tools that manage the processes and the policy behind the processes, separate from the content itself.

## User-Selectable Skins

It's worth browsing around in the skins tool for a bit. You'll notice that there are subfolders there that have a "green" lock. These are skins that are stored on the filesystem and come installed with the CMF. If you update the CMF products to a newer version, these skins will be updated automatically. There is another folder however, called custom. This is a "normal" Zope folder. This is a "normal" Zope folder. You'll store customized methods and scripts here. If you update the CMF product, this folder remains untouched. In this way, updates to the CMF don't break any skin customizations that you make to the site.

Look at the Properties tab of the portal_skins tool in Figure 8.11. You'll see a list of skin selections.

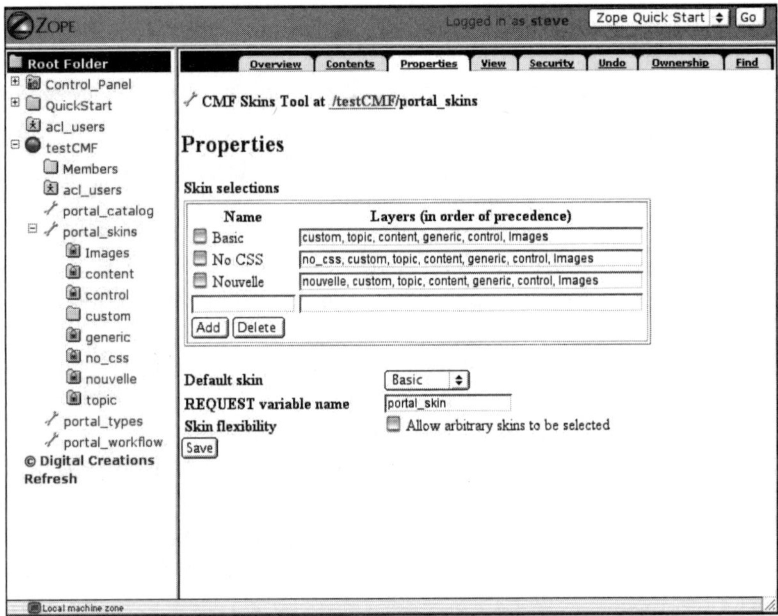


Figure 8.11 The Properties tab of the skins tool.

These are options presented to members in their Preferences area. If a member picks Basic, for example, it means that when content is displayed, a search for display methods goes through the skins folder in this order: custom, topic, content, generic, control, Images. If the member chooses No CSS, on the other hand, then when content is displayed, the skins folders is visited in this order: no_css, custom, topic, content, generic, control, Images. In this way, a user setting a preference can completely change the look of the CMF site. For example, you might have a Flash and a NoFlash version.

You can create as many skin folders in the skins tool as you like, and you can modify the order of the folders used by each skin to taste. The default setup is a good starting place.

## Customizing a Method

Let's say that you want to do the following:

- Change the logo of the site
- Display recent items that *aren't* news items in a box below news items

You can do this by "customizing" the default skins that are installed with CMF. After snooping around a bit, you'll find that the menu is built in `standard_top_bar`, defined in the generic skin folder. If you click `standard_top_bar`, you'll notice that it is not editable. It's a filesystem-based object, so it's *not* editable through the web. You can, however, customize it easily by clicking the Customize button. A list to the left of the button shows all the skin folders that you've added with the portal_skins tool. If you've not added any, you should at least have the custom folder that was created when you installed the CMF site. Click the Customize button. You'll be instantly faced with an editable version of `standard_top_bar`, now located in the custom folder under portal_skins.

Put your own logo in the custom folder, and call it customLogo. Then you can edit the `standard_top_bar` so that the logo is referred to like this:

```
<td class="PortalLogo" align="left" valign="top" width="1%"><a
    href="&dtml-portal_url;"><img src="customLogo"
    alt="Custom Logo" border="0"></a></td>
```

Now you should see your new logo on the site. Notice that this method also defines the menu and the title display in the masthead of the site.

Look at the `news_box` method in generic. Notice that it displays *only* the news box. You can use this as a starting point for your recent items. Create a new DTML method called `recent_box` in the custom folder and a Python script called `getRecentChanges`. Listings 8.13 and 8.14 show what these should contain.

Listing 8.13 **Python Script *getRecentChanges*: Get the 10 Most Recent Changes**

```
## Script (Python) "getRecentChanges"
##bind container=container
##bind context=context
##bind namespace=
##bind script=script
##bind subpath=traverse_subpath
##parameters=
##title=
##
theList = []

for item in
➥context.portal_catalog.searchResults(sort_on='bobobase_modification_time',
➥sort_order='reverse', review_state='published' ):

    if item.id != 'index_html' and item.meta_type != 'News Item':
        theList.append(item)

    if len(theList) > 10:
        break

return theList
```

Listing 8.13 shows a way to use the portal_catalog to find content that has changed recently. By setting the sort order to reverse and the `sort_on` to `bobobase_modification_time`, you can get items in reverse time order. Then, when you have enough, you can "break" out of the loop (see Listing 8.14).

Listing 8.14 **DTML Method *recent_box*: Display the 10 Most Recent Items in a Box**

```
01 <table class="NewsItems" cellspacing="0" cellpadding="0" border="0"
   ➥width="100%">
02 <tr>
03 <td class="NewsBorder" width="1" rowspan="13" bgcolor="#6699CC">
04 <img src="spacer.gif" alt=" "
05 width="1" height="2" border="0">
06 </td>
07 <td valign="top" class="NewsTitle" width="100%">
08 <b>Recent Changes</b>
09 </td>
10 </tr>
11 <dtml-let theList="getRecentChanges()">
12 <dtml-in theList>
13 <tr class="NewsItemRow">
14 <td valign="top">
15 <a href="<dtml-var "getURL()"
16 >"> &dtml-Title;</a><br>
17 <dtml-var Date>
18 </td>
19 </tr>
20 <dtml-else>
21 <tr class="NewsItemRow">
22 <td valign="top">
23 No Recent Changes.
24 </td>
25 </tr>
26 </dtml-in>
27 </dtml-let>
28 </table>
```

Notice that in line 11, you call the Python script `getRecentChanges`, and it takes care of deciding what has changed recently. The `getRecentChanges` script checks to make sure that you're not showing members pages or news items (which have their own box). Finally, to add this to the CMF, you'll need to customize the `index_html` method. All you need to do is add `recent_box` after the `news_box`, like this:

```
<td valign="top" width="20%">
<dtml-var news_box><br>
<dtml-var recent_box>
</td>
```

So that's it. You have a customized CMF portal.

## Adding Your Own Content Type

It is possible to create completely new content types using ZClasses or Python products. There are several How-Tos on zope.org that describe this (see, in particular, **`http://cmf.zope.org/search?SearchableText=howto`**). In a subsection of a chapter, we can't hope to accomplish anything quite so ambitious (although it's not altogether different from creating ZClasses and Python products in general, both of which *are* discussed in detail in Chapter 3, "Web Event Publishing," and Chapter 12, "Integrating Applications with ZPatterns"). What you can easily do is create your own content type based on an existing content type.

Let's say that you want to create new content type called a Foo (it could be any simple variation on an existing content type that you want to treat with a different site policy for viewing, workflow, editing, metadata, and so on).

To start, follow these steps:

1. Visit the portal_types tool.
2. Click the Contents tab.
3. Select Add Factory-Based Type Information. This is best for simple new types. You're going to create a variation on document.
4. Choose CMFDefault:Document as the type to use to fill in the defaults for the type tool.
5. Change the description of the Foo type to be Foos Are Like Documents, as shown in Figure 8.12.

The Types Tool interface should look like Figure 8.12 when you create this new type.

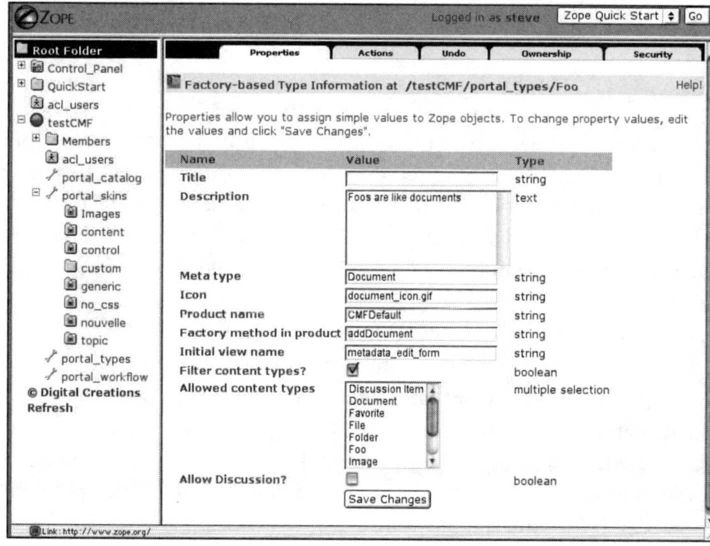


**Figure 8.12** Creating a new type in the Types Tool.

You can leave the constructor and everything else the same. you will still be creating documents, really. It's just that they will be treated with different policies because they will have a different portal type. Now go to the Actions tab.You want to change the way that Foos are displayed. So, in the View action, rather than use the `document_view` method, you're going to create a new method called `foo_view`. In the View action, change the Action to `foo_view`. Next, go to the portal_skins tool and create a new DTML method called `foo_view`. Copy the current DTML from document_view into it. Now you can customized it to display your Foo differently (so that you'll know that it worked). Listing 8.15 is the new foo_view that we used on our testCMF site.

Listing 8.15 **DTML Method foo_view for Displaying Custom Content Type**

```
<dtml-let relative_to_content="1">
<dtml-var standard_html_header>
</dtml-let>
<div class="Desktop">
 <div class="Document">
  <dtml-var content_byline>
  <hr>

  <table>
  <tr><td bgcolor="blue">
  <dtml-var CookedBody>
  </td></tr></table>

  <div class="Discussion">
   <dtml-var viewThreadsAtBottom>
  </div>

 </div>
</div>

<dtml-var standard_html_footer>
```

Notice that the only change is to wrap the CookedBody in a table with a blue background. If you now log in as a member and go to add some content to your area, you'll notice, as illustrated in Figure 8.13, that there is a new content type available. When you add it, edit it, and view it, you can see that it is indeed displayed in a table with a blue background, as shown in Figure 8.14, with the View Source window beside the browser window.

Finally, if you inspect the portal_workflow tool, you'll see that each content type can have its own workflow.You can create new workflows (see DCWorkflow, **http://cmf.zope.org/Members/hathawsh/DCWorkflow-0.2.tar.gz/view**) with their own rules and states, and assign different workflow policies to different content types. In general, the CMF gives you incredible flexibility in determining who can do what with each different content type.We hope that, if nothing else, we've piqued your interest in the CMF for your application!

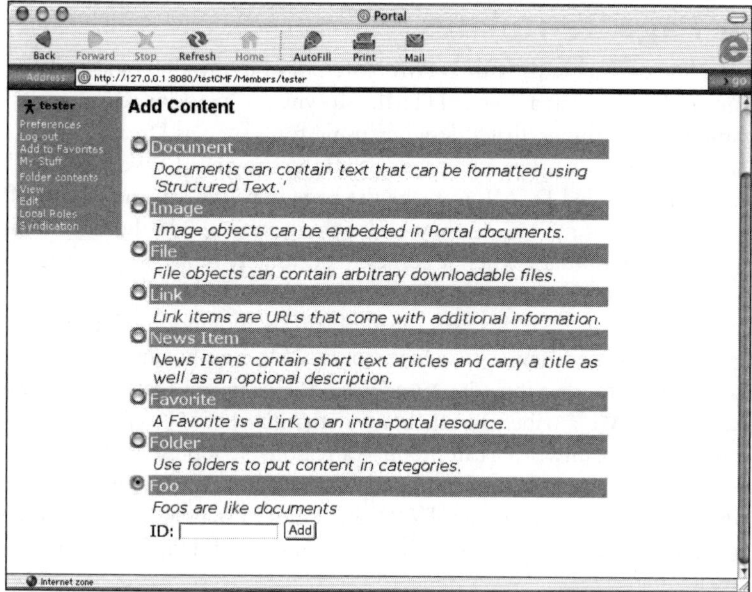

Figure 8.13 New content type Foo is available.

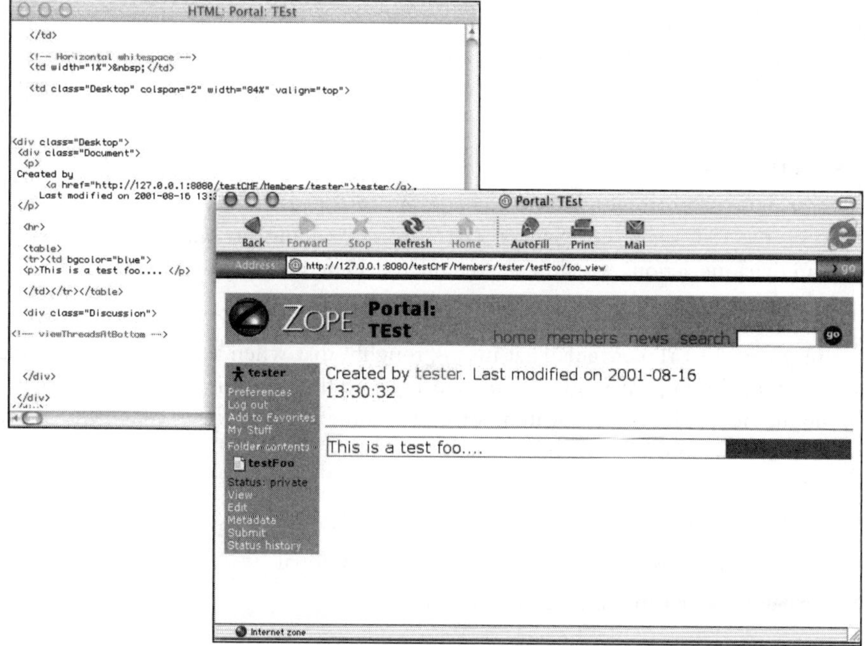

Figure 8.14 Foo content type displayed with its own display method.

# Zope Page Templates

One of the biggest problems with DTML, JSP, Cold Fusion, PHP, and a plethora of other similar efforts is that a special HTML-ish syntax is used for templates. This means, among other things, that a designer, using tools such as Dreamweaver or GoLive, cannot edit a "marked-up" page without destroying the work of the developer who painstakingly added DTML to make the page dynamic. In general, HTML-aware tools know nothing of DTML, so they can't be expected to "do the right thing" when it comes to editing, *especially* when it comes to accurately rendering the page outside its "native" environment.

A *Zope Page Template* (*ZPT*) solves this problem by moving the dynamic markup from new custom *tags* to new custom `attributes`. Most authoring tools will ignore but preserve attributes that they don't understand. This means that you can embed instructions in HTML attributes in such a way that the HTML will still *render* correctly. A tool like Dreamweaver can produce a reasonable representation of the page that a designer can modify however he likes. At the same time, programmers can embed dynamic content using special ZPT attributes in standard HTML tags. This allows for full "round-trip" editing, with programmers and designers both working on the same document.

This is wonderful news to application developers who work with groups of talented people who use different sets of tools to get their job done. Artists with fine artistic sensibility can work productively with developers who understand the technology without "stepping on toes."

You can find Zope Page Templates at **http://www.zope.org/Members/4am/ZPT** along with lots of useful supporting information, tutorials, documentation, and examples.

## TAL and TALES

The first thing to learn with ZPT is the concept of *Template Attribute Language* (*TAL*). TALES is the TAL Expression Syntax. TAL works by adding attributes to HTML tags to perform dynamic actions when they are rendered. Here is a simple example:

```
<title tal:content="here/title">Page Title</title>
```

The magic is the `tal:content`. That means, roughly, that when this is rendered, change the *content* of this tag (currently set to Page Title) to the dynamic value that you get by looking up `here/title`. The meaning of "here" is the current context, and the title is an attribute looked up in that namespace.

You can use six special TAL attributes:

- **define**—Used to define a variable to be used later in the scope of the current tag
- **condition**—Used to make an entire tag conditional
- **repeat**—Used to render a tag repetitively

- **`content`**—Used to replace the *contents* of a tag
- **`replace`**—Used to replace the tag itself
- **`attributes`**—Used to set the attributes of a tag

You can combine these attributes in any way that you like, with the following caveats:

- No matter how you write the attributes, they are always evaluated in the order given.
- You cannot use content and replace it in the same tag because their behaviors are mutually exclusive.
- You cannot use any one attribute more than once in a single tag.

Even with these restrictions, ZPTs are extremely flexible, although it does take some practice to "see" how to do things. There are lots of wonderful examples and lots of details about TAL and TALES on the ZPT Wiki at Zope.org (**`http://dev.zope.org/Wikis/DevSite/Projects/ZPT/FrontPage`**).

Listing 8.16 is an example called showPopup that renders items from a TinyTable so that it can be used as a pop-up display on a form.

Listing 8.16 **Example ZPT That Renders a *select* Control**

```
<html>
  <head>
    <title tal:content="template/title">The title</title>
  </head>
  <body>
    <form tal:define="checkName string:check">
       <select name="checkName">
           <option value="dummyValue"
             tal:repeat="aType here/popupItems"
             tal:attributes="value aType/name;selected
             ➥python:aType.name==checkName"
             tal:content="aType/value">A Dummy Option</option>
        </select>
    </form>
  </body>
</html>
```

The TinyTable is named popupItems and has content as follows:

```
columns: name, value

data:

    "test1", "one"
    "test2", "two"
    "check", "three"
    "ok", "four"
```

When rendered, this template produces the following:

```
<html>
  <head>
    <title></title>
  </head>
  <body>
    <form>
       <select name="checkName">
           <option value="test1">one</option>
           <option value="test2">two</option>
           <option value="check" selected>three</option>
           <option value="ok">four</option>
       </select>
    </form>
  </body>
</html>
```

There are lots of things to notice here, but several deserve special mention

- This template is a complete HTML page. Templates must be acceptable HTML. If there are missing tags or quotes, ZPT will not render the template. When you view such a template through the ZMI, you'll see an error message in the edit view.
- You can have more than one attribute in a `tal:attributes` definition. You need to separate them with a semicolon. This goes for most of the other attributes (where it makes sense).
- The `repeat`, `define`, and `attributes` definitions take two elements, a name (for example, the repeat variable) and the value that defines the name.
- If you can't use an existing tag, you can probably "force" a tag using either `<div>` or `<span>` to add content (as in, `<span tal:replace="foo">Something to be replaced</span>`).
- Within an expression, there are some special keywords that affect how the expression is interpreted. `python:` means that the expression is interpreted as a Python expression. `string:` means that the expression is interpreted as a literal string, with `${var}` used to substitute the variable `var`.
- The keyword `structure` is used to prevent HTML encoding of the result of an expression (pass HTML through to the browser).
- The keyword `nocall` is used to prevent callable functions from being called in a definition so that you can use it later as a function; the default is to call anything that's callable to render it in the template.

## METAL

The *Macro Expansion Template Attribute Language* (*METAL*) is where the real power comes in. You can define a macro in one template that is reused in many other places. If you change the macro, its new definition is replicated everywhere that it is used.

The main new concept here is the notion of a "slot." A macro is like a defined layout with some "empty spots" that you can fill in dynamically later, when you use the macro.

Listing 8.17 is a macro for a main page look and feel called look.html.

Listing 8.17 **Simple Macro Using METAL**

```
<html metal:define-macro="lookNFeel">
    <head>
        <title tal:content="template/title">The title</title>
    </head>
    <body bgcolor="lightblue">
        <div metal:define-slot="bodySlot">
        </div>
    </body>
</html>
```

Notice that the whole page is a macro, with one slot defined called bodySlot. If you now create a new template called form.html and at the top, in the html tag, add `metal:use-macro="here/look.html/macros/lookNFeel` and then hit Save, you will be rewarded immediately with a page that matches the look.html template. You'll notice that the slot has been changed to a fill-slot rather than a define-slot, as shown in Listing 8.18.

Listing 8.18 **Using a Macro in Another Template**

```
<html metal:use-macro="here/look.html/macros/lookNFeel">
  <head>
    <title tal:content="template/title">The title</title>
  </head>
  <body bgcolor="lightblue">
  <div metal:fill-slot="bodySlot">
   </div>
  </body>
</html>
```

Now, let's make a macro out of your select box. Edit showPopup as shown in Listing 8.19. All you do is add a `div` tag with a `metal:define-macro` attribute.

Listing 8.19 **Defining a Macro for a Form Control**

```
<html>
  <head>
    <title tal:content="template/title">The title</title>
  </head>
  <body>
    <form tal:define="checkName string:check">
     <div metal:define-macro="popup">
       <select name="checkName">
           <option value="dummyValue"
```

*continues*

Listing 8.19 **Continued**

```
                tal:repeat="aType here/popupItems"
                tal:attributes="value aType/name;selected
                ➥python:aType.name==checkName"
                tal:content="aType/value">A Dummy Option</option>
            </select>
          </div>
        </form>
      </body>
    </html>
```

Notice that it's still a fully valid HTML file, but it now has a macro for the pop-up. You can use this macro from another page, such as form.html, shown in Listing 8.20.

Listing 8.20 **Using a Macro for a Form Control**

```
<html metal:use-macro="here/look.html/macros/lookNFeel">
  <head>
    <title tal:content="template/title">The title</title>
  </head>
  <body bgcolor="lightblue">
  <div metal:fill-slot="bodySlot">
  <form tal:define="checkName python:path('request/checkName') or 'test2'"
        action=""
        tal:attributes="action template/absolute_url"
        method="post">
  <div metal:use-macro="here/showPopup/macros/popup">
       <select name="checkName">
          <option value="dummyValue"
            tal:repeat="aType here/popupItems"
            tal:attributes="value aType/name;selected
            ➥python:aType.name==checkName"
            tal:content="aType/value">A Dummy Option</option>
        </select>
      </div>
  <input type="submit" value="OK">
  </form>
   </div>
  </body>
</html>
```

The `form` tag deserves a little attention. It attempts to get the value of `checkName` from the REQUEST; failing that, it sets it to the default value of `test2`. Notice that the *action* of this form is the template itself. So, when you change the pop-up and hit OK, it remembers where it was. The great thing about the macro is that as soon as you type in the following and hit Save, the macro magically fills in all the code for the macro itself:

```
<div metal:use-macro="here/showPopup/macros/popup"></div>
```

Even better, if the owner of the macro changes it, the change automatically is reflected in the templates that *use* the macro.

You've now used TAL, TALES, and METAL in some example Zope Page Templates. These are very powerful and promising technologies, and, at the time of this writing, they are becoming much more stable. We expect to see a lot more of these as Zope continues to mature.

If you decide to learn ZPT, you'll want to read the documentation and examples available at zope.org. You will probably miss some DTML features at first, until you figure out how to "do the same thing" in ZPT. Some utilities (ZTUtils) can help with support functions (such as batching) and work much like their DTML counterparts. There are also examples with DMTL and ZPT compared (see **http://dev.zope.org/Wikis/DevSite/Projects/ZPT/FrontPage**).

# Summary

In this chapter, you investigated the HTTP request/response mechanism in detail, paying particular attention to the mechanisms that Zope uses to make the developer's job easier. Understanding exactly how this works is key to building a content-management system with flexibility and elegance. You then looked at acquisition from the Python level to show how you can understand what's happening behind the scenes to make your content easier to share. Next, you took a more detailed look at some finer points of basic page templates. Armed with these new insights, you can dig even deeper into Zope's Content Management Framework, this time creating a new content type of your own and adding it to a CMF site. Finally, we considered Zope's new answer to templates: Zope Page Templates, a solution to the "round-trip template" problem.

# 9 Time Management and ZCatalogs

THE WHOLE CONCEPT OF CONTENT MANAGEMENT implies that the content is changing. Otherwise, why would it have to be managed beyond its initial publication? In the very early days of the web, primarily static content was developed and then placed on the web for others to view. Very little management of that content needed to occur except for occasional updates to phone numbers, email address, or physical addresses. All of that has changed. A lot of the content on the web is now dynamic, changing at a very rapid pace. Content management is the act of keeping that changing content under control.

Time is a critical part of content management. For that reason, it's important to understand how Zope deals with time. You learned about time back in Chapter 3, "Web Event Publishing," and Chapter 5, "Web Mail," in particular, when you created an online calendar and event objects. In this chapter, you'll look at a much more powerful way to deal with time in Zope. You'll also look more at the ZCatalog product and how it can be used to help manage content that is rapidly changing, not only within a local Zope installation but on other, non-Zope sites as well. You'll learn how your Zope site can reach out into the wider world of the web and help your users take control of information over which you don't have direct control.

# Dates and Times in Zope

In working with dynamic-content web sites, an important requirement is keeping that content current. The word *current* implies the concept of time, or, more specifically, date and time. Back in Chapter 3, you created events objects that were then connected to a calendar display object. Those event objects were given a date that was represented by a simple string object. To make things work correctly, the format of the string was very strictly controlled. While you specified the format that the date string should be in, there was nothing really in place to prevent the person designated to manage the calendar from violating that format. If the calendar manager inadvertently used the wrong format for a date, the associated event object would not be located by the various methods that you designed to retrieve it. This problem applies to the situation in which the date string was used as the ID of the objects or when the date string was used as a column in the TinyTable. The limitation even applied when you created a brand-new ZClass object as your event object. Because the date was represented as a string, it was very important for catalog-searching purposes that the string satisfy a strict format.

## The DateTime object

In this chapter, you're going to modify your CalendarEvent ZClass definition to take advantage of another Zope component that will make working with dates and times much easier. The object is called *DateTime*.

DateTime objects represent a single instant in time. Because they are objects, they have properties and methods. DateTime objects consist of three parts:

- A date
- A time
- A time zone

All DateTime objects store their times in *Coordinated Universal Time (UTC)*, which is widely called *Greenwich Mean Time (GMT)*. Each DateTime object also has the concept of a time zone. While the internal storage of the time remains based on UTC, the external representation of the date/time is always in the context of its time zone.

In working with DateTime objects, it is important to understand the concept of *epoch*. An epoch is an arbitrary starting point in time used as a reference point. Although an epoch is arbitrary, the one used by the DateTime object is the one used by UNIX systems, January 1, 1970. The concept of the epoch is important because many of the methods of the DateTime object make use of the epoch. We'll come back to the epoch in a moment.

DateTime objects can be created from numeric or string data in many different combinations, or they can result from an operation on or manipulation of another DateTime object. To experiment a bit with DateTime objects, create a Python script somewhere in your Zope installation. Give it an ID of `TestDateTime`. Use this script to try out some of the following examples.

If the DateTime object is instantiated with no parameters, then what is created is an object that represents the current time. The time zone is selected to be that which the server is using. Verify this by typing the following code into your `TestDateTime` object and clicking the Test tab:

```
print DateTime()
return printed
```

The string that is printed will resemble the following:

```
2001/09/15 17:03:04.41501 GMT-6
```

If the DateTime object is instantiated with a single numeric value, it assumes that this number is a floating-point number representing the number of seconds past the epoch (January 1, 1970). Be careful, however! If you type `DateTime(1)`, don't expect to get back a DateTime object that is "January 1, 1970 00:00:01." Unless you live in the Greenwich time zone, you will see something earlier or later. Because you didn't specify a time zone, DateTime uses the time zone of your server.

Try this by entering this code into your `TestDateTime` object and clicking the Test tab:

```
print DateTime(1)
return printed
```

The string that is printed will resemble the following:

```
1969/12/31 19:00:01 GMT-5
```

When you click the Test tab, you will see a string representation of your new DateTime object. Again, unless you live in the Greenwich time zone, you will see a date/time that differs from the epoch, depending on your location.

If you create a DateTime object by passing two numeric values, then the DateTime initialization code expects that the first number is an integer representing the year and the second is an integer number of days from the start of that year. As an example, consider this:

```
print DateTime(2001,254)
return printed
```

The result is this:

```
2001/09/11
```

Notice the difference in the output format between the results of this example and the results of the previous ones.

If the year is a single- or double-digit number, then for numbers less than 70, it assumes the 21st century. For numbers equal to or greater than 70, it assumes the 20th century (again, the epoch shows its face). `DateTime(59,57)` gives an output of `"2059/02/26"`, whereas the line `DateTime(71,57)` gives `"1971/02/26"`.

If three or more numeric values are passed, then DateTime assumes that the first represents the year, the second represents the month, the third represents the day, the fourth represents the hour, the fifth represents the minute, and the sixth represents the seconds (see Table 9.1). The first five are assumed to be integers, while the last one is assumed to be a floating-point number. If any of the last three parameters is omitted, then it is set to 0. One additional optional parameter string can be included. If so, it should be one of the valid time zone strings.

Table 9.1 **DateTime Parameters**

| **Parameter** | **1** | **2** | **3** | **4** | **5** | **6** | **7** |
|---|---|---|---|---|---|---|---|
| Assumed Role | year | month | day | hour | minute | second | timezone |
| Expected Type | integer | integer | integer | integer | integer | floating point | string |

If a single string (as opposed to numeric) parameter is passed to the DateTime initialization function, then things get more interesting and a bit more complex. If the string is a simple string representing a valid time zone, then a DateTime object is created that represents the current time in that specified time zone.

Here's a brief example:

```
print DateTime('US/Eastern')
return printed
```

The output is something like this:

```
2001/09/15 18:02:15.8851 US/Eastern
```

A full list of valid time zone strings can be found in "$ZOPEROOT/lib/python/DateTime/DateTime.py."

In addition to time zone information, year, month, day, hour, minute, second, and AM/PM data can be included in the initialization string. Exactly how that information is included is very important, as we'll discuss next.

## Going to the Source with DateTime Objects

To better understand the DateTime object, it is very useful to take a look at the source code. Often the source code is the best way to learn about Zope objects, especially new ones that might not include sufficient documentation. In the file system of your Zope server, go to "$ZOPEROOT/lib/python." In this directory you will see a directory named "DateTime." Go down into this directory, and you will find several files. Use your favorite editor and open the file DateTime.py. Search down into the file to find the definition for the DateTime object. Search for "class DateTime:" which starts the definition of the DateTime object. The first part of the class definition provides details on how the DateTime object works. It's a good idea for you to read through this description. The description, which is included with the object definition, is very useful but seems to be a bit inaccurate in some areas.

When the DateTime object is instantiated with a single string containing the desired date/time information, the individual parts or *date/time elements* (year, month, hour, and so on) are separated from each other with the use of a character delimiter.

In the source code, search for the word delimiter. You will find it several times, but locate the reference where the `delimiter` variable is defined as a string. You will see the following:

```
delimiter = '-/.:,+'
```

This establishes the six characters listed as possible delimiters for separating the elements of the date and time string that is passed in. Any of those six characters can be used. It turns out that the space character can also be used as a valid separator. Because the date string separator is not limited to the forward slash character (/) and the time separator is not restricted to the colon (:), the DateTime object must make some assumptions about the parameters that are included when a DateTime object is instantiated. What date/time would you think this code would produce?

```
print DateTime("10:06 03/05/01 US/Eastern")
return printed
```

It certainly appears that you are trying to represent March 5, 2001, at 10:06 in the morning Eastern Standard Time. In general, that's the meaning that would be associated with this string. However, the resulting DateTime object is **`2003/10/06 05:01:00 US/Eastern`**. In other words, the DateTime object took the **`10`**, **`06`**, and **`03`** and created a date. The remaining **`05`** and **`01`** were then left as time values. Another way to look at this is to imagine that the numbers from the string were assembled into a list. All of the separators are removed. The resulting list is `["10","06","03","05","01"]`. Without the separators, how does the DateTime object deal with these individual numbers? It doesn't; therefore, it makes the assumption that the first three items in the list are parts of the date. Anything remaining is part of the time.

Now modify this line

```
print DateTime("10:06 03/05/01 US/Eastern")
return printed
```

a bit to this:

```
print DateTime("10 06 03 05 01 US/Eastern")
return printed
```

This new string is just the individual components from the previous code, using the space as a common separator. What this tells you is that, while there are seven separators that you can choose from when forming your input strings for DateTime creation, the choice is simply for your own ease of reading. The choice of separator has *no* bearing on the resulting DateTime object. In other words, colons don't automatically mean time, and forward slashes don't automatically mean date. The following is very uncommon and not readily recognizable, but it is very usable by the DateTime object:

```
"01:02:03 04/05/06 US/Eastern"
```

This string "appears" to represent April 5, 2006, at 2 minutes and 3 seconds after 1 in the morning. What it represents to the DateTime object is this:

```
2003/01/02 04:05:06 US/Eastern
```

The choice of separators is irrelevant in this case. What is important is the order in which the elements appear. It takes the first three elements in the string (remember, elements are separated by *any* of the seven delimiters) and attempts to resolve those to a date. If it is not successful, it takes the current date from the server. In either case, after the first three elements are used, it takes the next elements (up to three) and tries to create a valid time. The first element is assumed to be the desired hour, the second is the minutes, and the third is the seconds. The last element is the time zone string. If it is used, it must be the last element in the initialization string.

The only other element that can be added is the meridian specifier element, *am* (ante meridiem) or *pm* (post meridiem). This element can use any combination of uppercase and lowercase letters (such as am, Am, AM, aM, and so on) and can appear anywhere in the initialization string except last. That spot is reserved for the time zone element.

When analyzing the first three elements of the string to create a date, the DateTime initialization code uses conventions recognized in the United States. The reference to the United States is to clarify the fact that when a date of 5/11/2001 is entered, it is interpreted as May 11, 2001. In most other parts of the world, this is interpreted as November 5, 2001. The DateTime object assumes U.S. ordering. In spite of that, the DateTime object is fairly flexible with its interpretation of what is a valid date element. All of the following would be considered valid:

- 1/5/01
- 01/05/2001
- 2001/1/5
- 2001/01/05
- 2001.1.05
- 1.5.01

Although it is acceptable to use a two-digit year, it is probably something that you should avoid. What date does the string `"69/01/05"` represent? Is it January 5, 1969, or January 5, 2069? It turns out that this string represents January 5, 2069. However, `"70/01/05"` represents January 5, 1970. The cut-off point is `70`. Remember the epoch concept we talked about earlier. It returns here. When a year is specified with only two digits, it is assumed to mean the earliest year "after" the epoch. For 69, it must mean 2069 because 1969 is before the epoch. The number 70, however, can mean 1970; because 1970 is earlier than 2070, that is the date used. In general, it is safer to fully form the year string to make sure that the actual date that you are wanting is properly created. The discussion at the beginning of the initialization code for the DateTime object states that all two-digit years are assumed to be in the 20th century. If you do a simple test, however, you'll see that this is not the case because 69/01/02 returns the date 2069/01/02, clearly a 21st-century date.

## DateTime Mathematics

DateTime objects exhibit some pseudonumeric behavior. You can add or subtract numbers from DateTime objects and obtain new DateTime objects. One DateTime object can be subtracted from another DateTime object to obtain the number of days between them. The answer is returned as a floating-point number. Also, a floating-point number representing a number of days can be added or subtracted from a DateTime object to produce a new DateTime object the specified number of days before or after the original date and time.

The description in the source code indicates that a DateTime object can be converted (cast) to a float, integer, or long, and that this number represents the number of days past January 1, 1901. However, simple testing seems to indicate this is not the case and that, in fact, the result represents the number of seconds past the epoch. In general, the starting point is irrelevant, so this doesn't matter much. Most of the time you are casting to find the difference between two DateTime objects; when you take a difference, the base time drops out anyway. In addition, the number of seconds past a specified point is a lot more useful than the number of days past a point.

DateTime objects also have a number of built-in methods that allow you to use the objects in many different circumstances. Continue looking through the source code, and you'll see them. Many of them, such as `isFuture`, `isPast`, `isCurrentYear`, `isCurrentMonth`, `isCurrentDay`, `isCurrentHour`, and `isCurrentMinute` are comparative methods comparing the calling DateTime object with the DateTime object representing the current date and time. There are still further comparative methods such as `greaterThan`, `lessThan`, and `equalTo` that compare two DateTime objects.

Dozens of methods also return various string representations of the DateTime object. Some return all of the information, while others return only the day of the week or the month name (full name, abbreviated name, initial cap, and so on). One very important method, `ISO()`, returns the International Standards Organization (ISO, as in ISO 8601) representation of the DateTime object. The ISO representation is widely recognizable around the world and, for that reason, should be strongly considered for development of web sites that are to service a worldwide audience. It's probably a good idea when displaying date/time objects to specify the layout that you are using, to eliminate any confusion.

A couple of the methods will be particularly useful for your CatalogEvent object, and you'll make use of them later in this chapter. They are `earliestTime` and `latestTime`. They return DateTime objects that represent the absolute earliest time in the specified day and the absolute latest time in the specified day, respectively. You'll see how to use those in a moment in the section "ZCatalogs, a Deeper Look."

## Adding DateTime to the CalendarEvent ZClass

Back in Chapter 3, you created a CalendarEvent Z Class object for use with your online calendar. You created these objects so that you could use a ZCatalog to search on these events. Take some of the knowledge that you've just gained about DateTime objects and modify the CalendarEvent object to take advantage of this knowledge. Go to the Control_Panel of your Zope installation and then go to the Products folder to edit the CalendarEvent ZClass. Click on its Propertysheets tab and then click the Fundamental property sheet. You will notice that you have, as your first property, the `dateEvent`. This property is a string object. This is the property that is currently being used as an index for searches and for associating the event with the Calendar object.

So as not to disturb anything, leave the `eventDate` property alone, but add a new property. Give the new property the ID `startDateTime`. Select date as the type for this property. You will immediately receive a message indicating that you have entered an invalid Date-Time string. A date property is a DateTime object. It must have a valid default value, and because a blank is not a date/time, the property can't be created. Click the Back button on your browser, and type `1900/01/01` into the Value field and then click the Add button. Your new property will now be added with a default value that is a valid date. Now follow the same procedure and create another date-type property and give it an ID of `endDateTime`.

Now for any existing CalendarEvent objects that you have, you will need to go in and edit them to add their new `startDateTime` and `endDateTime` properties. Make sure that when you combine the `startTime` and `endTime` properties with the `eventDate` property, you create valid DateTime strings.

# ZCatalogs, a Deeper Look

Chapter 3 introduced you to the basics of ZCatalogs. Now you need to return to ZCatalogs and look at some of the more advanced features. In particular, you'll look at how to apply these advanced features to the Calendar object and the CalendarEvent ZClass objects that you created.

## Advanced Searching

You'll need to go to the EventCatalog and make some changes to the indexes and the metadata that it includes. Go to your EventCatalog and click the Indexes tab. Add both `startDateTime` and `endDateTime` as indexes. Make sure, though that you make these indexes Field Index type indexes. The Text Index works well for individual word matching but does not work for numbers. Because the DateTime object contains numbers, you will have to make those indexes Field Index types.

You will also want to click the Metadata tab and add both of the new properties in as metadata so that they will be available for quick rendering to the calendar. Now click the Advanced tab and click the Update Catalog button. This will cause the indexes to be rebuilt and the new metadata to be included.

When you've updated all of the existing CalendarEvent objects and recataloged the objects, you'll need to modify the DTML methods that you created in Chapter 3 to take advantage of the new DateTime properties.

Back in Chapter 3, in the section "Between the Tags" you learned that during each iteration through the calendar tag, an object is available to you called date. We mentioned that it was an object and that it had day(), month(), and year() methods, but that was the extent of the discussion of the object. You can guess now that the date object is actually a DateTime object called date that represents the day currently being rendered on the screen. In line 08 of Listing 3.4 (in Chapter 3), you used a <dtml-let> tag to create the date string from the results of year, month, and day methods of the date object. You had to produce the string to create something by which you could catalog these objects. That was a lot of work. Let's look now at how you can make use of your knowledge of DateTime objects to make this job much easier.

Locate your ViewOnlyCalendar object, which should be in the root of your school system example (refer to the first half of Chapter 3). Take the code for the ViewOnlyCalendar from Listing 3.11, and modify it to Listing 9.1.

Listing 9.1 **ViewOnlyCalendar Using Advanced ZCatalog Searching**

```
<HTML>
<HEAD>
    <TITLE>New Millennium Event Calendar</TITLE>
</HEAD>
<BODY>
    <CENTER>
    <dtml-calendar>
        <dtml-var "date.day()"><br>
        <dtml-in "EventCatalog({'startDateTime':[date.earliestTime(), \
            date.latestTime()],'startDateTime_usage':'range:min:max'})">
            <dtml-var "startDateTime.AMPMMinutes()"> - \
            <dtml-var "endDateTime.AMPMMinutes()"><br>
              <dtml-var description>
            <br>
        </dtml-in>
    </dtml-calendar>
    </CENTER>
</BODY>
</HTML>
```

In Listing 9.1, you are making use of four of the built-in methods of the DateTime object: day(), earliestTime(), latestTime(), and AMPMMinutes(). You've already learned about all but the AMPMMinutes() method. If you look through the source code for the DateTime object, you can see this method along with several others that are used to extract and render the time portion of the DateTime object in various formats. This one seemed to be the best for this situation. In this version of the ViewOnlyCalendar code, we have eliminated the <dtml-let> altogether. You no longer need to extract the pieces from the date object and recombine them to form a string for searching the EventCatalog.

Line 09 of Listing 9.1 is where all the exciting stuff is happening. Take a look at it. It is calling the EventCatalog and passing it a Python dictionary, just like in Listing 3.11. However, the value that it is passing for the `startDateTime` index is actually a Python list of values instead of a single value. How is the ZCatalog supposed to make use of the list? The default way that a ZCatalog uses the values in a list is to perform a logical OR. All objects that match *any* of the values are returned. In this particular case, though, you're going to override the default action. Actually, you're going to tell the ZCatalog how to use this list. The next parameter that you pass in through the dictionary is called `startDateTime_usage`. Its value tells the ZCatalog how to *use* the values passed in for the `startDateTime` parameter. The value for `startDateTime_usage` is `range:min:max`. That means that the values passed in for `startDateTime`" should be used to define a range of values that will be used for the search. The first value in the list is used as the minimum value, and the second value is used as the maximum value for the range. If the `startDateTime` property for an object in the catalog falls within the range defined by the two values passed in, it will be considered a match and will be returned by the catalog.

Other ways to override the default, "exact match" behavior of a ZCatalog's search function include using the supplied value as a minimum value (`range:min`) or as a maximum value (`range:max`).

Because you are trying to match only a single day during each pass through the calendar loop, why didn't you just do a simple match on the date object itself? The reason is that the search would find only those events for which an *exact* match occurred, date *and* time. Because you are trying to find all events within the specified day, regardless of the time, and because the date object provided by the calendar tag has a default time of 00:00:00, you need to simulate a match on the date portion only. To set up the range to cover the entire day in question, use the `earliestTime` and `latestTime` methods of the date object. These methods create new DateTime objects that represent the first and last possible times within the given day. This produces a range that covers the entire day.

Finally, on the display side of things, you can make use of the `AMPMMinutes` method of both the `startDateTime` and `endDateTime` objects to render just the times associated with those DateTime objects. This particular method displays the time in only hours and minutes, eliminating the seconds. Several other methods will produce the time portion of the DateTime object in other formats. Choose the one that best suits your needs.

## Cataloging Almost Anything in a ZCatalog

ZCatalogs don't actually contain the objects that they are cataloging. That would be redundant. They maintain only enough information to allow rapid searches and to print small reports to help you identify the actual object that you are looking for. In addition, they maintain a "path" to each item that they have catalogued so that you can retrieve the real item if you want it. The information that facilitates the rapid searching is the index data that you included, and the report information is the metadata that you specified. To keep ZCatalogs from growing too large in size, it is advisable to include only the indexes and metadata that you really need. Metadata should be included only to give you the capability to uniquely identify objects that you might want to fully retrieve.

As an example, suppose that you are cataloging book objects in your ZCatalog. And suppose that each ZClass that describes the books has a field that contains all of the text of the book. If you included this book content as metadata, you can imagine that the ZCatalog would be huge! Instead, you might create a field in your ZClass description called summary and include a very short summary of the book. This way, when an end user searches for a book by topic, for instance, the search results report could easily include the summary to help the user determine whether the book would suit his needs.

When you do a search and get results back, the objects that you get back are just summarized representations of the actual objects. In addition to the metadata and indexes that you specified, these ZCatalog objects include a property called `data_record_id_`. This ID number can be fed back to the ZCatalog using its `getPath()` method. This method returns the actual path to the object that was catalogued. This is used when you need to retrieve more than just the metadata about an object.

The beauty of a ZCatalog is that you can catalog virtually *anything* in it. The things that you catalog don't have to even be in ZODB. They can be things on the local server's file system, or they can even be objects on a multitude of other machines that are accessible to the your Zope server. The main key is that they must be Zope objects before they can be added to the catalog. Initially, that sounds like it greatly limits the objects that you can catalog. It sounds like you can't catalog files and things from remote servers that aren't using Zope. And while you know how great and wonderful Zope is, a portion of the internet community still hasn't discovered Zope yet. In reality, the requirement that the objects be Zope objects when they are catalogued does not really restrict you from using remote, non-Zope things. You just have to create a Zope-object representation of the objects that you want to include in the ZCatalog. The Zope objects that you create to enable the cataloging of external data don't actually exist anywhere in ZODB. They are transient objects that allow you to pass the desired parameters into the ZCatalog. When the data is catalogued, the object disappears.

Let's look at a specific example with applications to your role as the IT manager for the fictional New Millennium school district. Suppose that there are a number of web servers that have HTML files on them whose content is constantly changing. Suppose that these files are things that you think your clients might be interested in. Some might be the policies and procedures for your school system. Others might be weekly newsletters from each of the classrooms in your school district. You might even include files on web servers that are not directly related to your school system, such as educational news services or government proceedings, or the results of ongoing scientific research projects. Because all of these resources are presented as HTML files, then the structure is fairly straightforward and easy to work with. If the remote web pages were selected carefully to make sure that their content was, in general, useful to your school community, you could imagine a simple search engine that is focused on the sites that you have deemed pertinent.

You might ask, why wouldn't someone just go to one of the Internet search engines, like Google, Yahoo!, or Infoseek and do a search? Certainly, there the scope of the search would be much broader. That's true, but the capability of these search engines to include up-to-the-minute information is limited by the sheer number of sites that they include. It takes a finite amount of time for new information to be included in these large search engines. In the ZCatalog example, the information could be updated as often as you like. You could update the ZCatalog every few minutes, thus providing a search of documents within seconds of their publication.

Certainly, there are limitations in this simple example, but you can see the possibilities. Let's implement this example so that you can see how it's done.

To get HTML files catalogued into a ZCatalog, you first need to create a ZCatalog. You can use Chapter 3 or *The Zope Book*, by Amos Lattier and Michele Pelletier, as a reference if you have trouble creating a ZCatalog and working with the indices and metadata. From the pop-up menu, instantiate a ZCatalog and give it an ID of `HTMLCatalog`. Look at the ZMI of HTMLCatalog now to create an index, and call it contents. There is already a default index on the `title` property. Next, check to make sure that the `title` property is included in the metadata. Also include a metadata field and call it source.

Now you have a ZCatalog with indices and metadata, the next thing that you need to do is to go to come up with a mechanism for keeping track of the web pages that you want to include in your ZCatalog. Again, you return to an object used earlier in the book, the TinyTablePlus. There are, of course, many different ways to accomplish this, and once the list gets long enough, a TinyTablePlus might not be the best choice, but for this example it will work fine. If you need help with your TinyTablePlus, refer back to Chapter 3. Instantiate a TinyTablePlus at the same level as your ZCatalog, and call it CatalogedURLs. For this TinyTablePlus, you'll need only one column of data; call it url. Into the TinyTablePlus you can type a list of URLs for web pages that you want to catalog. Pick a couple of test pages and type their URLs into the table. Make sure that the URLs are valid URLs (complete with the initial "http://" string) and that they are included in double quotes.

Now you need some way of going out to the specified web pages and reading in their content and then creating temporary objects in which to store this data for transfer to the ZCatalog. Let's look at the issue of reading data from a web page first.

## External Methods and ZPublisher/Client

Chapter 2, "Point and Click Web Building," touched on external methods, but you're going to actually create one here. Remember that one of the reasons for using external methods is to perform tasks that are restricted because of security issues. To write an external method, you need to have access to the file system of the Zope server; external methods cannot be created through the web interface. Folks who have access to Zope and who can create methods and objects through the Zope interface don't have access to most of the modules and services that could be destructive to Zope or its host system. An example of a module that can be misused by malicious users is *ZPublisher.* You can modify the source of PythonMethods to allow access to ZPublisher, but the negative effect of this is that it gives access to this module to anyone who has a role that allows him to write Python scripts. It's probably best to make use of ZPublisher through the use of an external method.

To write an external method, you need to be able to access the file system of the machine on which your Zope is running. You can create the External method online or offline and ftp it to the proper location within your Zope installation. External methods are located in the $ZOPEROOT/Extensions folder. Call your External method HTMLForCatalog.py, and include the Python code shown in Listing 9.2.

Listing 9.2 **External Method for Converting HTML Files to Objects**

```
01  from ZPublisher import Client
02  import string
03
04  class dummyObject :
05      pass
06
07  def createTitle(url,data):
08      aTitle = string.split(url,'/')[-1]
09      firstIndex = string.find(string.upper(data),'<TITLE>')
10      if(firstIndex <> -1):
11          secondIndex = string.find(string.upper(data),'</TITLE>')
12          if(secondIndex <> -1):
13              aTitle = data[firstIndex+7:secondIndex]
14      return aTitle
15
16  def getHTMLForCatalog(self,url):
17      x = dummyObject()
18      theFile = Client.call(url)
19      theData = theFile[1]
20      x.title = createTitle(url,theData)
21      x.content = theData
22      aSource = string.split(url,'/')[-1]
23      x.source = string.join(aSource,'/')
24      return x
```

In line 01 of Listing 9.2, you import the client piece from the ZPublisher module. There's a lot more to ZPublisher but this is all you need for this job. Next, in line 02, you import the string module that you'll use to manipulate the data being returned from the web. Next, in line 04, you create a class (an object) named dummyObject. The purpose of this object is to create an object structure into which you can plug the various pieces of the web page that you access so that it can be incorporated into the ZCatalog. Remember that the ZCatalog requires a thing to be an "object" to be used by the ZCatalog. The ZCatalog needs the data to be in the form of an object so that it can access the various pieces (index data and metadata) by name. The ZCatalog can't be responsible for trying to figure out from a mass of data what part of it is the title and what part is the content. The ZCatalog needs to be capable of saying to the object, "Hey, give me your content," or "Give me your title." This is the purpose of the object. You create the pieces that the ZCatalog is going to ask for and put them into an object form.

Not all indices and metadata need to be included with an object for it to be included in the ZCatalog; however, if indices are not present, then the associated item will not be found when a search involving that index is performed. In addition, if metadata is not included, then when the associated item IS returned by a search, it will not be capable of producing a proper report. In general, it makes sense to provide your object representation with properties that reflect *all* of the indices and metadata that the ZCatalog defines, even if they are empty.

The dummyObject definition that you create in lines 04 and 05 of Listing 9.2 is extremely simple. That's all it has to be. It doesn't need to define any methods; it simply needs to exist as a placeholder and structure for the data that you will be reading in from the web pages. Line 05, the pass line, is required if nothing else is included with the class definition, or it will not appear to be a valid class definition. Pass does nothing, exactly as its name implies.

Next, lines 07 through 14 define a method for creating a title. This method will be used by the main method to produce the best possible title for the new object. You'll return to this method in a moment. Finally, lines 16 through 24 are the main method that will be called by Zope. They define a method called `getHTMLForCatalog`, which is the actual external method. This method takes two parameters. The first is required by all external methods: the value `self`.

External methods are just that—they are methods that live externally to Zope. As methods, they do not have the concept of self and must be contained by another object. Remember, in the sidebar "DTML Method Versus DTML Document," in Chapter 3, we talked about the differences between DTML methods and DTML documents. We stated that DTML documents were complete Zope objects, whereas DTML methods were simply methods of another containing object. This is true of external methods as well. They are subobjects of another object and have no concept of self. When an external method is invoked, Zope passes in the containing object to the external method so that it has access to the namespace of that containing object. The containing object is passed in as the parameter `self`. For example, if an external method were contained by a folder called BigContainer, a reference by the external method code to the value `self.title` would produce the string `"BigContainer"`, *not* the name of the external method. Because this value of `self` is passed in automatically by Zope, your external method definition *must* include the parameter `self` in its definition. Any other arguments are optional. In this case, you will be passing in one argument, the URL of the web page that you want to catalog.

Line 17 creates an instance of the dummyObject, which was defined in Lines 07 through 14. Line 18 makes use of the Client module, which is included with the ZPublisher module. One of the methods defined by Client is called `call`, which is very simple and yet very powerful. The first argument that it takes is a URL. This is the URL of the object that you want to retrieve. The URL should be a fully qualified URL (including the "http://" or "ftp://"). The `call` method can also take an optional username and password as its second and third arguments.

The `call` method accesses the specified URL and returns the data in a Python tuple. The first element of the tuple is the header information, and the second element is the actual data. In your case, you are interested in only the actual data, so you need to extract the second element. This is done in line 19.

Line 20 passes the data chunk to the method that you define called `createTitle` to try to produce some kind of logical title for this data. You can obviously imagine many ways to augment this method; this one is just to give you a start. Notice that the `createTitle` method takes two arguments. The first is the URL that was passed in, and the second is the data retrieved from the site. Line 08 uses the imported string module to split the URL into parts wherever it finds a forward slash (/). If the URL that is passed in is a valid URL, it will at least have the two forward slashes required after the protocol and colon (as in http://, ftp://, afp://, and gopher://). In many cases of a web page, the domain name will be followed by a forward slash and a specific filename (as in **`http://www.newmillennium.com/importantFile.html`**). In either case, there will at least be two elements when the string is split at the slashes. Line 08 extracts the last element (filename or domain name) of the list that results from the "split" method. At this point, you have either a filename or the domain name. This will serve as your default title if another, more appropriate one can't be found.

The next few lines, lines 09–13, scan the data that was returned from the URL to see if an HTML `<title>` tag is included. Because these are HTML files, there is a reasonable chance that the writer of the file included a title tag in the document. Line 09 uses the string module's `find` method to see where the `<title>` tag starts. It casts the data to uppercase letter first and then looks for "TITLE" to make sure that it catches any combination of lowercase and uppercase letters (such as title, Title, TITLE, and so on). If it finds this string, it creates an index of the location where it located the string. It then attempts to do the same thing for the `</title>` tag. Again, if it finds the tag, it creates an index. If both tags are found, then it uses the indices to "slice" out the title information from between the tags. It adds 7 to the firstIndex to skip over the seven letters in the `<title>` tag. In any case, a title is returned in line 14.

In line 21, a `content` property is set to be the data that was returned from the URL. Next, in Line 22, a tuple is produced by breaking up the URL on its forward slash characters, like you did for the default title. In this case, the slicing is a little bit different, resulting in a tuple where the last element (what you used as the default title) is eliminated. A string is re-created from those tuple elements that is the original URL minus everything after the last forward slash. This is done in line 23. In the case of

URLs with specific filenames attached, this is a rough way of obtaining something close to the domain source. It won't work in a lot of cases, but it gives you something close, and you can certainly improve on this technique in future designs. Line 24 finishes everything up by returning `x`, which is your newly created object.

This method, therefore, has taken a URL and retrieved the data from it, created an object with the appropriate properties set for your HTMLCatalog, and returned this object. Now you're ready to connect this external method to Zope and tie it to the list of URLs in the CatalogedURLs TinyTablePlus.

To connect an external method to your Zope site, return to the web browser and navigate your way to the location in your site where you want to place the external method. Choose External Method from the pop-up list of objects, and give this one an ID of `GetHTMLForCatalog`.

When you create an external method, you will be asked to provide an ID (as always) and also a module name and a function name. The module name is the name of the Python file that you just created (HTMLForCatalog.py), *without* the .py extension. The function name is the name of the function within the file that you want to be the entry point. Remember that, in this case, you had two functions defined (`getHTMLForCatalog` and `createTitle`). You want this external method to call the `getHTMLForCatalog` method, so type that name into the module name field. That's all there is to it. When you say Add, the code will be read up into Zope (as long as the named file is in the $ZOPEROOT/Extensions folder and the specified function is defined with no errors). Any time you make changes to the Python file, you need to simply return to the external method object and click the Save Changes button, and the altered code will be uploaded again.

Well, you have this external method, but now you need to create something to "call" this method. Either a Python method or a DTML method will work. For this example, just create a simple DTML method called `addFilesToCatalog`. Place the code from Listing 9.3 in it.

Listing 9.3 **DTML Method to Read TinyTablePlus and Call External Method**

```
01  <dtml-var standard_html_header>
02  <dtml-in CatalogedURLs>
03      <dtml-let newObject="GetHTMLForCatalog(anURL)">
04          <dtml-call "HTMLCatalog.catalog_object(newObject,url)">
05      </dtml-let>
06  </dtml-in>
07  <dtml-in "HTMLCatalog()">
08      <a href='<dtml-var "getPath()">'><dtml-var title></a><br>
09  </dtml-in>
10  <dtml-var standard_html_footer>
```

Line 02 of Listing 9.3 retrieves the values in the CatalogedURLs TinyTablePlus and iterates through them. Line 03 creates an object called `newObject` by invoking the external method that you just created called `GetHTMLForCatalog`. It passes in the augmented URL string into this external method. Remember that the external method retrieves data from the specified URL, creates an object into which it puts the important information, and then returns the newly formed object. Line 04 takes this new object and calls the `catalog_object` method of the HTMLCatalog. It passes in the object itself plus the location of the object. The HTMLCatalog strips out the index data and metadata and then discards the object. There is not an object hanging around in Zope—only the catalog information about it. The real object resides elsewhere, potentially on another machine.

Lines 07 through 09 are included simply to show you that the information has gotten successfully into the catalog. It iterates through all of the items in the catalog (because no search parameters are specified) and then uses the `getPath` method of each object to retrieve the exact location of the original object. Line 08 uses the information to form a link to the original item and ties that to the title of the object. By choosing HTML files located on different systems around the Internet, you can see how well the `createTitle` method works.

Again, this is a very basic example of this capability, just enough to hopefully inspire you to think of numerous ways to modify this code to really create something useful.

One thing is still left to consider with regard to this example. We mentioned that this setup is good for cataloging files whose content is constantly changing, so you'll need to remember to run this `addFilesToCatalog` method fairly often to keep it up-to-date. Wouldn't it be nice if there were some way to automate this process? Think back to Chapter 5, and you'll remember that you did a similar thing with automating email reminders for events. The product that you used was called XRON. Go back to Chapter 5 and remind yourself how to use XRON, and then set up a XRON to execute the `addFilesToCatalog` method as often as you like. As the information in each document changes, the indices and metadata in the ZCatalog will change to reflect it. That way, searches of the ZCatalog will be current.

A summary of how to catalog almost anything is included here:

- Create a ZCatalog to hold the reference data.
- Decide what common aspects of the objects that you are cataloging should act as indices and metadata.
- Create indices and metadata for those aspects.
- Create some programmatic way to get to the data that you want to catalog. If you can get to the data from within Zope (Python script, DTML, and so on), then so much the better. If not, then you will probably need to write an external method.
- Create an object description for the data.
- Create a method of some kind to extract the pertinent data from the objects when they are retrieved and put them into the objects that you created in the previous step.
- Create an ID for each object that is a pointer to the original object.

- Use the ID that you created in the previous step and the object that you created in the step before that, and make a call to the `catalog_object` method of the ZCatalog.
- Create some search functions to test that your data are being properly catalogued.

## Summary

In this chapter, you learned about the DateTime object available to Zope through Python. You learned how the DateTime object could be combined with a ZCatalog to provide powerful searching over ranges of time instead of just specific times.

You also learned a great deal more about the wonderful ZCatalog. You learned how to catalog objects completely outside of Zope, even on distant machines over which you have no control.

In spite of what you learned here, we only skimmed the surface of the capabilities of the ZCatalog. We encourage you to take the knowledge that you've gained here and experiment and play. You'll be greatly surprised at the multitude of things that you can do with ZCatalogs. And remember to keep visiting the mailing lists and the Zope resources at places like **http://www.zope.org** and **http://zope.nipltd.com** for ongoing discussions about new developments in the Zope community.

# 10

# Survival Gear for Web Masters

PROBABLY ONE OF SINGLE MOST ASKED QUESTIONS on the Zope mailing list is, "How do I get Zope to work with Apache?", or something related to communicating with Zope in some configuration that isn't provided directly "out of the box." This chapter addresses exactly this sort of question. We'll start with setting up "virtual hosts" in Apache (different sections of a Zope instance that provide content for different domain names, www.xyz.com, www.def.com, and so on). Then we'll present various options for interfacing Zope with content stored on the filesystem. Finally, we'll tackle some of the issues relating to serving Zope securely via SSL.

## Hosting Virtual Sites

When you run Zope, the default port for the HTTP (web) protocol is port 8080. The standard default port for web servers is port 80. Why did Zope Corporation decide to ship a web server that doesn't even set its default web port to the standard value? As you might have guessed, there is a good reason. On most systems, a process needs to have full administrative privileges to access port numbers less than 1024. If Zope defaulted to port 80, then only users with full administrative privileges could run it! Also, because many systems already have a web server running at port 80, Zope would die if it tried to bind to port 80 when it was already being used. So, you have a web server that uses port 8080, and you need somehow to "map" it to port 80.

Next, you have another problem. Imagine that you have several Zope sites, and you don't want to run a full instance of Zope for each site that you host. You want wwwa.spvi.net to point to one folder in a Zope instance, and you want wwwb.spvi.net and wwwc.spvi.net to point to different folders in the same Zope instance—something like Figure 10.1.

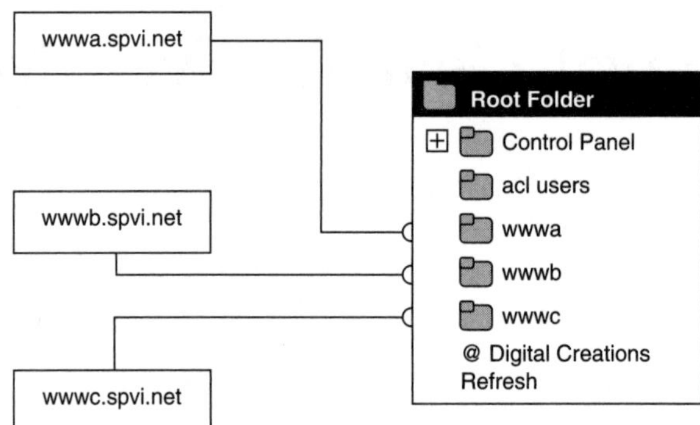


**Figure 10.1** Three domain names directed to VirtualHosts.

Both of these requirements occur for many Zope installations, so it makes sense that there should be a robust and flexible solution. Actually, there are several! Based on the nature of the questions that relate to these two issues on the Zope mailing list, it is our totally unscientific guess that most of these ask about a solution that involves Apache (go to **http://www.apache.org**). Apache is a highly robust, portable, open source web server that has an extremely flexible set of configuration options. Apache can be set up to listen on any port and to forward traffic from any port to any other port on the same system or different systems. These capabilities, coupled with Zope's capability to accommodate externally managed virtual hosts, makes this a workable, if not totally simple, solution.

## A Detailed Example

Suppose that you have three domains: wwwa.spvi.net, wwwb.spvi.net, and wwwc.spvi .net. You want to operate these three sites using only one instance of Zope running on port 10080 on the IP interface 10.0.0.1. First, you set up DNS so that all three domain names point to the same IP address, something like this:

```
wwwa            IN  A       10.0.0.1
wwwb            IN  CNAME   wwwa.spvi.net.
wwwc            IN  CNAME   wwwa.spvi.net.
```

The details of setting up DNS servers is a little outside of our scope, but we can recommend *DNS and Bind*, by Albitz and Liu (see **http://www.oreilly.com/catalog/dns4/**). The idea is that when someone types the URL **http://wwwa.spvi.net** into a browser, that person should be taken to the home page for that domain, which will really just be a folder in Zope (for example, the /wwwa folder).

The easiest way to set this up with Apache is to use a truly wonderful creature called a *Virtual Host Monster* (*VHM*), which is a beast that evolved from the SiteRoot object by of one of the ZC Geniuses, Evan Simpson (author of the Python Script object and zealot of Page Templates). Don't let the name scare you! There's really not that much monstrous about it, except for its apparently magical capability to grab URLS and warp them around to produce an elegant solution to the virtual hosting problem.

> **For More Information**
>
> There is another interesting product along these lines that you also might want to consider, at **http://www.zope.org/Members/sfm/SiteAccessEnhanced**.

For this example, set up a Zope at port 10080 on the host 10.0.0.1 (which is the same as wwwa, wwwb, and wwwc). You can do this by editing the "start" script to with a -P option, as in -P 10.0.0.1:10000, which will put web service on 10080, ftp on 10021, and monitor on 10099.

Start with an empty Zope, and select Virtual Host Monster from the Select Type to Add pop-up. You should see a screen like Figure 10.2.

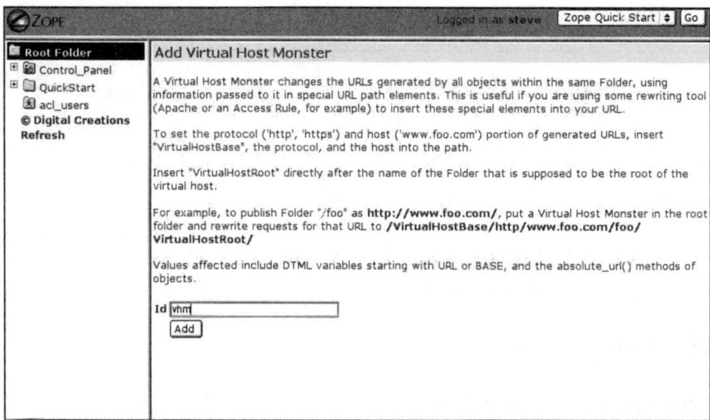


**Figure 10.2** Creating a Virtual Host Monster.

Set the ID to `vhm:`, for short, and click Add. You now have a VHM in your Zope. Don't fret. The great thing about VHM is that they awaken only under very special circumstances. The VHM uses a special "before traverse" hook in the folder where it's kept. If you attempt to traverse into a folder with a VHM and you use some "special" names in the path, the VHM takes over and uses the path to set various system variables, adjusts the path, and finally allows the traverse to continue (along the modified path).

Now create folders in your Zope for wwwa, wwwb, and wwwc. Don't select Create a Public Interface when creating them (because this creates DTML documents), but do create a default index_html DTML method in each one so that you'll be able to easily see that your virtual hosts are working. Be sure to use a title that distinguishes each folder so that the default public interface displays a distinctive headline for each domain.

When you're finished, your ZMI should look something like Figure 10.3.

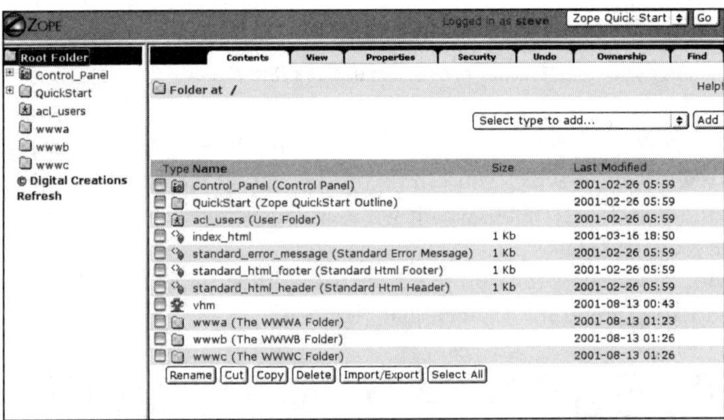


**Figure 10.3** ZMI after creating folders for three sites.

In your Apache configuration, you'll need to add a VirtualHost instance. In this case, it looks like Listing 10.1.

Listing 10.1 **Virtual Host Configuration for wwwa.spvi.net**

```
NameVirtualHost 10.0.0.1:80

<VirtualHost 10.0.0.1>

Serveradmin steve@spvi.net

ServerName wwwa.spvi.net
ErrorLog /var/log/wwwa.spvi.net_error_log
CustomLog /var/log/wwwa.spvi.net_access_log common

RewriteEngine on

# uncomment these next two lines to enable logging
```

```
14 # RewriteLog /var/log/rewrite.log
15 # RewriteLogLevel 2
16
17 Alias /icons/ "/usr/local/share/apache/icons/"
18 Alias /pil/   "/usr/local/share/doc/PIL/handbook/"
19
20 RewriteRule ^/icons - [l]
21 RewriteRule ^/pil - [l]
22
23 RewriteRule ^/(.*)
   ➥http://10.0.0.1:10080/VirtualHostBase/http/wwwa.spvi.net:80/wwwa/
   ➥VirtualHostRoot/$1 [P]
24
25 </VirtualHost>
```

There are several key points to notice here:

- Apache wants a NameVirtualHost definition for any IP address that's going to have multiple domains assigned to it (see line 01).
- The VirtualHost tag uses the IP address of the interface that is targeted for multiple domains (see line 03).
- The ServerName declaration tells which VirtualHost you're really defining (see line 07).
- Each VirtualHost can have separate log files (see lines 08 and 09).
- You're using the RewriteEngine to do most of the real work here. We'll get into details of this in the next paragraph.
- Unless you have unlimited disk space, you'll want to leave the RewriteLog commented out unless you're debugging a RewriteRule.

The main workhorse in this configuration is the Apache Rewrite Engine (see **http://httpd.apache.org/docs/mod/mod_rewrite.html**). The basic plan of the RewriteEngine is to map incoming URLs onto other URLs so that you can move things around on the server, and they'll "appear" to be in a consistent place to the web browser.

The basic syntax of the RewriteRule statement is as follows:

```
RewriteRule Pattern Substitution [flags]
```

The "pattern" is a regular expression that is compared to the requested URL. The "substitution" is the new path, after the RewriteRule is complete. The optional flags affect how the RewriteRule is interpreted. A more detailed description follows. The RewriteEngine makes extensive use of "regular expressions." We provide a quick overview of regular expressions (see Tables 10.1–10.4), but there is more detail on the Python web site and lots of other resources on the Internet (for example, see **http://www.python.org/doc/current/lib/re-syntax.html**) and in books, such as *Mastering Regular Expressions*, by Jeffery Friedl (O'Reilly & Associates, ISBN: 1565922573).

Table 10.1 **Text**

| Symbol | Description |
|---|---|
| . | Any single character |
| [chars] | One of a set of characters |
| [^chars] | None of a set of characters textA\|textB textA or textB |

Table 10.2 **Quantifiers**

| Symbol | Description |
|---|---|
| ? | 0 or 1 of the preceding text |
| * | 0 or N of the preceding text (N > 0) |
| + | 1 or N of the preceding text (N > 1) |

Table 10.3 **Grouping**

| Symbol | Description |
|---|---|
| (text) | Grouping of text (for reference) |

Table 10.4 **Anchors**

| Symbol | Description |
|---|---|
| ^ | Start of line |
| $ | End of line |

The flags of the RewriteRule are very powerful. We're just touching on a few that you might need:

- **R**—Redirect browser to substitution URL
- **F**—Send "FORBIDDEN" response
- **P**—Forward request as proxy
- **L**—Last rule (stop!)

There are three RewriteRules in this configuration. The first two just refer to static content on the filesystem, which is served directly by Apache, without even bothering Zope. The `-` is a substitution, which means that don't change anything. The `[l]` flag means, "When you match this rule, you're finished—just serve it up." So, the effect of these two rules is to make the /icons and /pil paths serve content without going through Zope at all. This technique also improves performance because Apache can deliver static content without bothering Zope; hence, you'll see this mentioned again in Chapter 15, "Scaling Up."

The last RewriteRule is the one that talks to Zope. What is all that crazy stuff in the substitution on line 21? Let's go through it step by step:

1. The pattern `^/(.*)` means to match anything after the first `/` in the path as $1.
2. The substitution starts with `http://10.0.0.1:10080/` and ends with the `[P]` flag. This is a proxy. When a request comes in on port 80, Apache gets it. If the hostname is wwwa.spvi.net, it fires this VirtualHost definition and hits the RewriteRules. If the rules on lines 18 and 19 don't match, the rule on line 21 has to match (because it's matching on `.*`).
3. Apache now acts as a proxy and forwards a request to Zope, but now with a completely different path! If you ask for `/index_html`, this substitution takes everything after the `/`and pastes it onto the end of this:

   `/VirtualHostBase/http/wwwa.spvi.net:80/wwwa/VirtualHostRoot/`

   Then it sends that as a path to Zope at **`http://10.0.0.1:10080/`**.

   This path wakes the Monster. The VHM sits silently waiting for a path to be requested that starts with VirtualHostBase. When it sees such a path, it swallows it, looks for a protocol in the next element (such as http), looks for a hostname: port combination in the second element (such as wwwa.spvi.net:80), and then looks for a VirtualHostRoot. If it finds it, it traverses to that target and then sets what's left after the VirtualHostRoot to the path, to be finally traversed by Zope in the normal way. In the process, the VHM sets the BASE tag to be the VirtualHostBase, plus whatever came after the VirtualHostRoot.
4. For example, if you asked your browser for **`http://wwwa.spvi.net/foo/bar/index_html`**, then Apache converts this to:

   **`http://10.0.0.1:10080/VirtualHostBase/http/wwwa.spvi.net:80/wwwa/VirtualHostRoot/foo/bar/index_html`**

5. VHM sets the BASE tag to:

   **`http://wwwa.spvi.net/foo/bar/`**

6. VHM traverses to:

   **`/wwwa/foo/bar/index_html`**

**For More Information**

The details of the Zope traversal are somewhat complex, but there are some excellent references on the Internet. One of the best is in the Zope Developers Guide, at **`http://www.zope.org/Documentation/ZDG/ObjectPublishing.dtml`**.

Basically, this does what you want it to do. It makes the wwwa folder look like the root of the wwwa.spvi.net site without demanding that it actually be at the root of Zope itself.

You can set up the other sites (wwwb and wwwc) completely in Apache, with no other modification to Zope at all. This is nice because it also means that you can use a browser to administer the server on port 10080 directly, and you'll never wake up the monster by accident.

There are other, more sophisticated options for VHM. There is also a related product, SiteAccess, that allows you to hook any callable method into the traversal process to do essentially arbitrary adjustment to the traversal process. Both of these are beyond the limits of the current book, but they are interesting and certainly worth investigating.

# Flexible File Access

Sometimes you need to serve data that lives on the filesystem, but you'd like to wrap it in a Zope application, with roles and permissions and other related metadata. We're going to illustrate this idea using a Zope product by jfarr (go to **http://www.zope.org/Members/jfarr**) called LocalFS. LocalFS basically sets up a "window" in to your filesystem. Suppose that you want to share the documents in your ~/public_html directory through Zope. You could set up a LocalFS object that points to that directory, as shown in Figure 10.4.

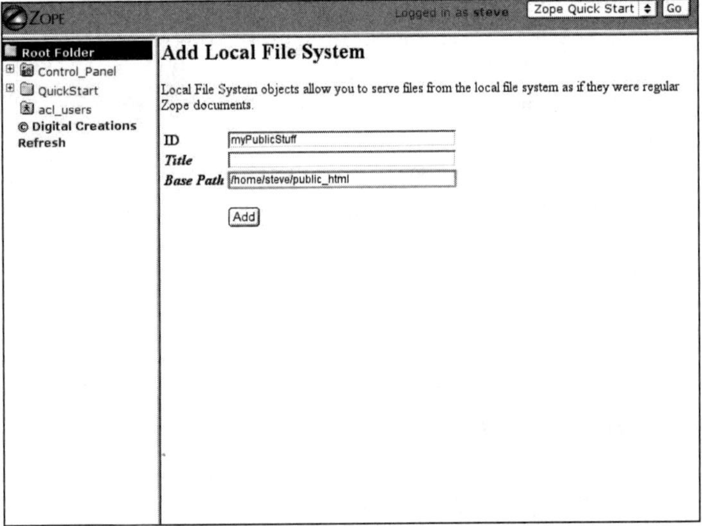


**Figure 10.4** Creating a LocalFS object.

After it's created, you will see the LocalFS object as a hard-disk icon in the folder where you created it, as shown in Figure 10.5.

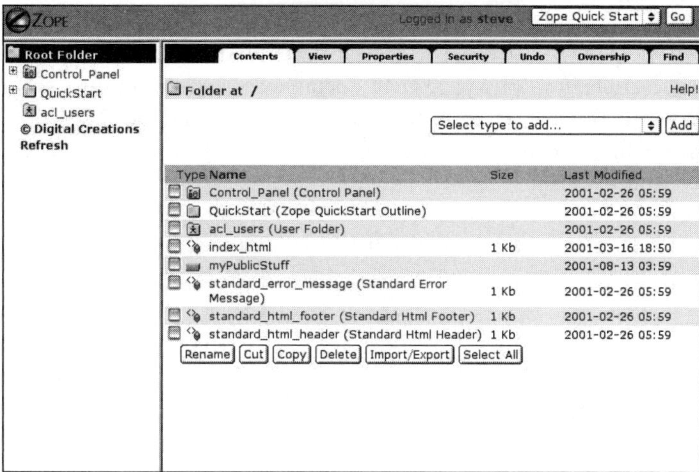


**Figure 10.5** LocalFS object as listed in the ZMI.

Finally, if you actually click the LocalFS object, you'll see a folder view such as Figure 10.6, not unlike the display of a "regular" Zope folder.

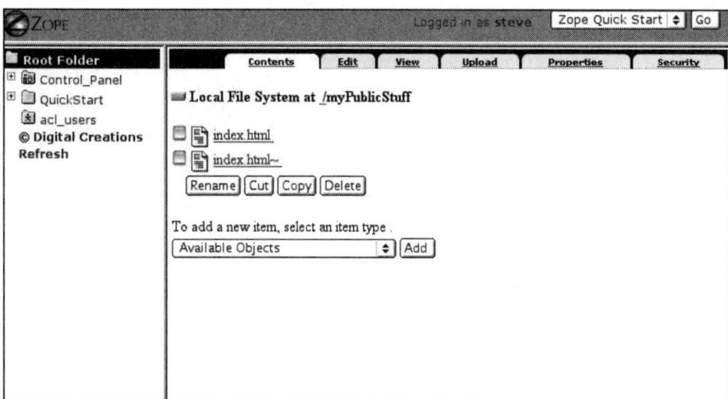


**Figure 10.6** Listing view of LocalFS object.

How does LocalFS know to show an HTML document as if it were a DTML document? If you click it, you'll see that you can edit it just like a DTML document! Notice that *unlike* a regular Zope folder, the LocalFS object has an extra tab: Edit. If you click it, you'll see an administrative screen where you can specify what files are mapped to what Zope types based on their filename extension. If you look at the list, you'll see an entry like this:

```
.html text/html DTMLDocument
```

This means, "Files that end in `.html` are published with a mime-type of `text/html` and are represented by DTMLDocument objects. When you "click" an HTML document in a LocalFS, by default a "proxy" DTML document is created on the fly to represent that object. When you publish it, it is literally published using the DTML document" object with the file content stuff in dynamically. Of course, you can change the mapping to anything you like.

Subfolders can be traversed and displayed. As an example, Listing 10.2 shows the DTML Method that we used to display the HTML rendering of this book as we worked on it.

Listing 10.2 **DTML Method to Display Content from LocalFS**

```
01 <dtml-try>
02 <dtml-var "fileValues('chapter_src.html')[0].getObject()">
03 <dtml-except IndexError>
04 <dtml-var standard_html_header>
05 Hmm.. I can't seem to find a chapter_src.html in this Area.
06 </dtml-try>
07 <br>
08 <dtml-in "objectValues('Local Directory')">
09 <dtml-if sequence-start>
10 <table>
11 <tr><th>sub-section</th></tr>
12 </dtml-if>
13 <dtml-if "meta_type=='Folder'">
14 <tr><td><a href="&dtml-id;/index_html">&dtml-title_or_id;</a></td></tr>
15 <dtml-else>
16 <tr><td><a href="&dtml-id;/displayBook_html">&dtml-title_or_id;</a></td></tr>
17 </dtml-if>
18 <dtml-if sequence-end>
19 </table>
20 </dtml-if>
21 </dtml-in>
22 <dtml-var standard_html_footer>
```

Lines 01–06 attempt to display a file from the local directory called chapter_src.html (which is a standard name that we use for the HTML rendering of all our chapters). The method `fileValues` is specific to the LocalFS Product; it returns a list of objects whose names satisfy the "glob" passed in (such as chapter*).

Lines 13–21 look for subfolders and display links to those with different targets depending on the meta_type encountered.

What good is all this? It's good because our book is maintained in CVS as structured text files. We can run a process that parses the structured text and converts it to HTML or other formats. For ease (and flexibility), we tend to use HTML a lot. The chapters are kept in a hierarchical structure that matches the basic structure of the book. This one DTML method allows us to browse around the book in Zope, while keeping the actual structured text/html on the filesystem where our command-line tools can get at them easily. This is the sort of thing that LocalFS is really good at, letting you use your traditional methods while simultaneously accessing some of the powerful features of Zope (such as deciding which users can see what content without granting Zope users command-line access to the server).You also can create multiple LocalFS objects with different security settings and different extension/object mappings so that users with one set of permissions see one mapping and users with a different set see another.

# Securing the Site

Sooner or later, you'll want to use SSL to encrypt some traffic to or from your Zope application. There are a number of approaches to this problem, but we're going to focus on one that leverages one of the existing implementations based on Apache. There is a set of patches to Apache available from **http://www.modssl.org/** that makes SSL a snap with Apache.

This set of patches gives Apache some new directives and permits you to set up an SSL connection by simply defining a new VirtualHost section in the configuration file.

The good news is that when you get Apache_modssl working for static files on the filesystem, it's easy to add SSL support to Zope; you can simply create a RewriteRule in the SSL portion of the configuration file that uses the same VHM, but with different settings:

```
RewriteEngine on
RewriteRule ^/(.*)
 http://10.0.0.1:10080/VirtualHostBase/https/10.0.0.1:443/VirtualHostRoot/$1 [p]
```

Notice, in particular, that the protocol is now https and the port number (in the VirtualHostBase) is set to 443 rather than 80 (because 443 is the correct default https port.)

You also can use RewriteRules on the http side that redirect (use the `[R]` flag) to the https protocol under certain circumstances (accessing a certain area, for example).

> **For More Information**
>
> There are other ways to get SSL/Zope together. In particular, you might want to consider the following sources:
>
> M2Crypto, at **http://www.post1.com/home/ngps/m2/**
>
> **http://www.zope.org/Members/Ioan/ZopeSSL**
>
> **http://www.zope.org//Wikis/DevSite/Proposals/ZServerSSLIntegration**

## Identifying Problems

The other thing that a web master—or developer, for that matter—needs to know is how to figure out what's happening when things are broken.You can turn on extra levels of logging by setting the -M switch or setting the STUPID_LOG_FILE environment variable (details in Chapter 15 when we discuss measuring performance), but these give only subtle clues to the handshaking that's going on between the browser and the server. To get a real handle on things, you need tools such as webdebug (go to **http://www.cyberclip.com/webdebug/**) or tcpwatch.py (see **http://www.zope.org/Members/hathawsh/tcpwatch**).

The tcpwatch.py program was written by the unstoppable Shane Hathaway, author of countless jewels of the Zope community. The program works by serving as a proxy for your browser but capturing everything that your browser sends the server and everything that your server sends back. It requires Tkinter (see **http://www.python.org/topics/tkinter/**). So, if your platform doesn't support it, you're out of luck (that's why we also mention webdebug).

When you get tcpwatch.py, it's easy to use. On the command line, run it as a python program. To start, just run without arguments: `python tcpwatch.py`. You'll see the following:

```
TCPWatch 0.9 (c) 2000 by Shane Hathaway, Digital Creations
http://www.digicool.com
Monitors TCP connections through a proxy connection. Requires Tkinter.
Usage: tcpwatch.py <local-port> <server-host> <server-port>
```

So, tcpwatch.py takes three arguments:

- The local port to listen on
- The server to contact
- The server port to use

Suppose that you are running Zope on port 10080 on 10.0.0.1. You could run tcpwatch.py on the same host, like this:

```
python tcpwatch.py 8000 10.0.0.1 10080
```

Then, as long as Tkinter is installed and working, you should see a display like Figure 10.7.

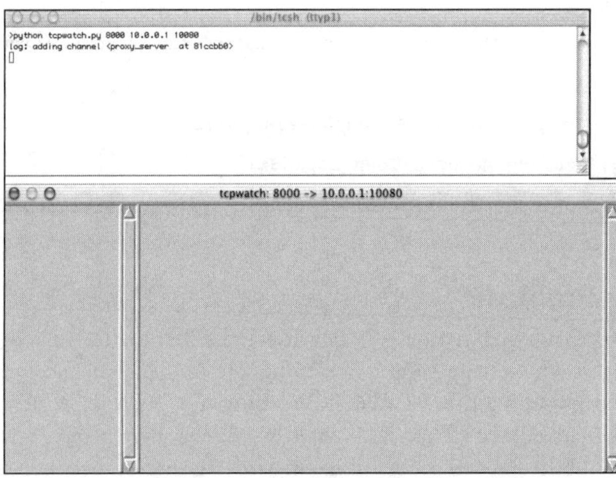


**Figure 10.7** Initial tcpwatch.py screen.

If you now make a request directly at tcpwatch.py (specifically asking for port 8000), it will forward it to Zope, as in **`http://10.0.0.1:8000/myPublicStuff`**, and you should see a result similar to Figure 10.8.

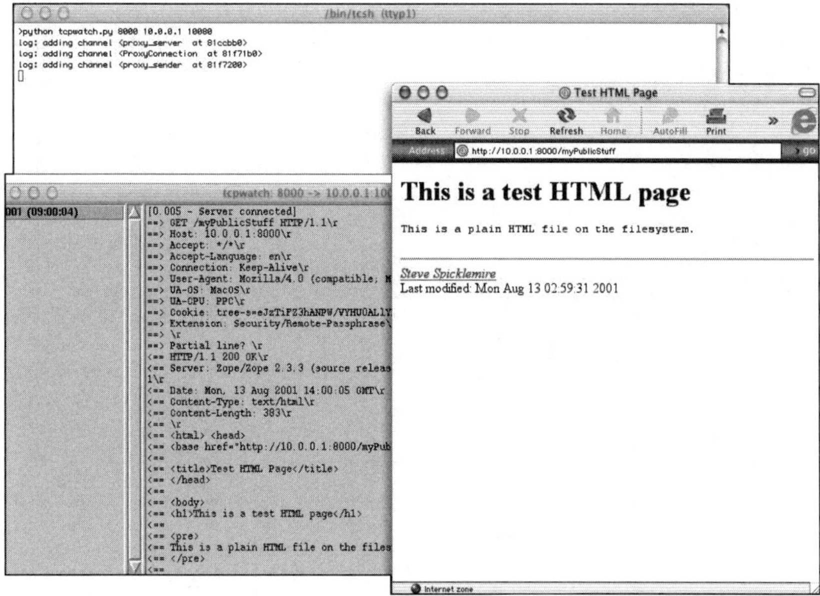


Figure 10.8 The tcpwatch.py program proxying a web request.

If you don't have Tkinter, you can run webdebug. It's quite similar, but rather than using a custom UI, it lets your web browser display the details. You set webdebug as "the" proxy for you browser and then browse anywhere you like. As you go, webdebug is capturing everything. You can see the results by visiting **`http://host.that.runs.webdebug:2001/WEBDEBUG`**. A sample of the output provided by webdebug is shown in Figure 10.9.

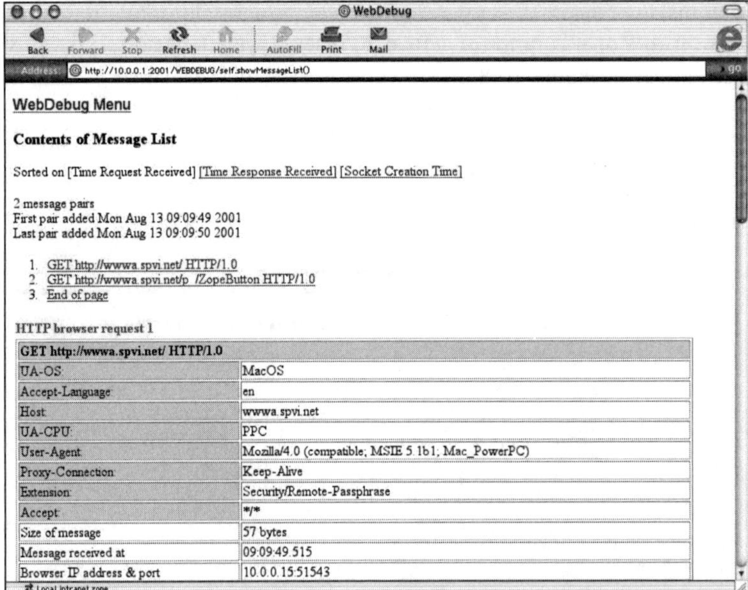


Figure 10.9 The diagnostic display of webdebug.py.

# Summary

In this chapter, we've discussed how to integrate Zope into an existing web server environment. We've worked out how to serve multiple domains from a single Zope instance using the incredibly flexible Virtual Host Monster. We've set up a Zope that gets its request through Apache's modssl module so that you can take advantage of SSL encryption. Finally, we presented a couple different strategies to get detailed diagnostic information about exactly what Zope is getting from a browser and what is being return by Zope to the browser.

# IV

# Web Application Development

# 11

# Design for Integration the ZPatterns Way

ZPatterns is an object-oriented application-development framework especially designed to allow for application reuse and integration of legacy data. This chapter introduces the basic ZPatterns components using a simple example of an application in which three object types interact to produce a simple "Deliverable" manager.

## Overview: The Purpose of ZPatterns

Lots of open source applications are available on the Internet. If you browse the products that have been submitted to the Zope.org web site (**http://www.zope.org**), you'll see a tremendous breadth of possibly useful products. This is a goldmine of potential code reuse that theoretically could be leveraged to allow anybody to create fantastic integrated applications by plugging various applications together to form a working whole. Unfortunately, it's not really that easy, for a number of reasons.

### Object-Oriented Programming Is Not Enough

One of the most often cited promises of object-oriented programming is the ease with which software can be "reused." In practice, this is a very difficult problem because reuse can take on many different forms and meanings. Often reuse means, "copy the source code for an object or set of objects, and then paste it into a different project and modify to taste." This might be valuable, but it's probably not the intention of object reuse. In Zope, reuse could mean, "create an instance of an existing object in your application and use it!" Each instance becomes a case of code reuse. However, this form of reuse usually involves some type of customization so that the object works in your particular application. If the object has any inherit visibility in the user interface, it can mean that you have to do a lot of work to make the object "fit in." The object also might make assumptions about where related data is stored, which limits its appropriateness in other circumstances. (For example, one software developer uses ZODB to store object attributes, whereas another needs to use a RDBMS. How can their code cooperate sanely?) As you will see, ZPatterns is an object-oriented framework that aims to mitigate many of these reuse/integration problems by providing the tools needed to assign arbitrary data storage for objects and connections between components.

## ZPatterns Gives Objects New Life

ZPatterns was developed by Phil Eby and Ty Sarna, and was shared with the Zope community. One of the basic ideas of ZPatterns is to allow programmers to cleanly separate program logic from the storage system used to provide objects with attributes. This allows for better object/system reuse because different complex systems can be integrated by remapping attributes and methods to work with one another *after* systems are designed. ZPatterns can be found on the Zope site (**`http://www.zope.org/Members/pje/ZPatterns`**) along with a Wiki (**`http://www.zope.org/Members/pje/Wikis/ZPatterns`**) with lots of documentation. ZPatterns gives objects new life by allowing them to pose as different characters in different situations. In this way, an online shopping application can see a "shopper," whereas the newsletter system can see a "subscriber," but both are really supplied by the user management system as a "member."

## Basic ZPatterns Ideas

ZPatterns is deep and complex because, in addition to modifying the behavior and properties of objects on the fly, it contains a fair amount of new jargon that can take a while to get used to. Having said that, if you look at it from the right perspective, it's quite simple. Before getting into the grungy details, the 10,000-foot view will be presented so that you can sort out the forest from the trees.

Donald Knuth, author of the classic book *The Art of Computer Programming*, got it right when he called it the "Art" of computer programming.[1] What makes it art? "Art" has several meanings, one of which is: "High quality of conception or execution, as found in works of beauty; aesthetic value."[2] Beauty, of course, rests in the eye of the

1. Knuth, Donald E. *The Art of Computer Programming*. Reading, MA: Addison-Wesley, 1998.

2. *The American Heritage Dictionary of the English Language, Fourth Edition*. Boston, MA: Houghton Mifflin Company, 2000.

code reviewer, but there are certain aspects that mark high-quality code that most developers would probably accept:

- Simplicity is a virtue. Code *can* be too clever for its own good.
- Elegance, the happy coincidence of deep insight and clean implementation that ultimately leads to simplicity, is nice.
- One of the most important things to determine is what *not* to include in a solution or an implementation. Good judgment in this process also leads to simplicity in the end.
- Make sure that objects have a limited scope of responsibility. Each class of object should manage only a few things, delegating other responsibilities to other objects. This is also known as the "Law of Demeter."[3] See the section "ZPatterns Fits the Pieces Together," later in this chapter.

Keeping these four ideals in mind when developing models and using ZPatterns to implement those models will save a lot of frustration. Work out some basic ideas on paper first, and then go to objects.

Keep in mind that the very same skills that are important to modeling in other areas are the keys to good modeling in software. Questions include these:

- "What if we leave out this effect (or component or interaction)?"
- "How will this abstraction affect the rest of the system?"
- "Is this part fundamentally different from this other part?"

The goals of other fields that use modeling and software development can be fairly different, but the process and methodology share a great deal in common.

# A Concrete Example: ToDos/Deliverables/Doers

It's time for a specific example of using ZPatterns. You can start with high-level abstract objects and then move to classes when you get to the stage of producing a working implementation.

## Installing ZPatterns and the ToDo Example

To use ZPatterns, you've got to get it and install it in your Zope server. The following is a quick-start description of how that can be done.

3. "Law of Demeter." Available from Internet: **`http://www.ccs.neu.edu/home/lieber/LoD.html`**. Web page maintained by Karl J. Lieberherr, College of Computer Science, Northeastern University, Boston, MA. Page last updated: June 15, 2001.

### Getting ZPatterns

The companion web site has the ZPatterns products, and they can also be found at **http://www.zope.org/Members/pje/ZPatterns** and CVS access at **http://www.eby-sarna.com/**. The current version of ZPatterns and PlugIns was 0-4-3b2 at the time of printing with patches from various Zope community members. If you are running Zope on Linux or another UNIX variety, you can unpack the ZPatterns and PlugIns .tgz files in your Zope directory. You'll need to compile the shared library DynPersist.so. The Python script (a command-line script, not a Zope script!) in Listing 11.1 works well.

Listing 11.1 **Python Script to Build DynPersist.so on Linux/UNIX**

```
import os
import sys

os.system('cp %s/config/Makefile.pre.in .' % sys.path[1])
os.system('make -f Makefile.pre.in boot')
os.system('make')
```

If you are on Linux, you'll need a source install of Zope to run this script. We have prebuilt versions of DynPersist.so for Linux on the companion web site (**http://webdev.zopeonarope.com** or **http://www.newriders.com**).

If you are running Zope on Windows, you can simply unzip the ZPatterns and PlugIns .zip files in your Zope directory. We've already compiled DynPersist.dll for you and included it on the companion web site.

### Installing the Completed ToDo Example

If you want to explore the completed ToDo example described in this chapter, you can find it on the companion web site. The example comes in two files: ToDoProducts-X-X-X.zexp and ZPatternsExample-X-X-X.zexp—you should replace "X-X-X" with the actual version number of the version you find on the web site. You should use the most recent version available on the web site. You must install the ToDoProducts.zexp file *first*.

Put both of these files in the "import" directory of your Zope directory. Then do the following:

- Go to Control_Panel/Products in the Zope Management Interface (ZMI), and find the Import/Export button at the bottom of the screen. Click the button, and then type **ToDoProducts-X-X-X.zexp** (X-X-X is the version number) into the Import File Name field, and click Import.
- Find a spot in your Zope folder space where you want to install the ToDo example. Once there, find the Import/Export button and repeat the procedure. But this time, import ZPatternsExample-X-X-X.zexp.

That's it!

## Setting Up the Participants

Suppose that you have some "Deliverables" that are concrete expectations that must be met by a certain time. They each have a well-defined description and associated tasks that must be completed. These tasks are "ToDos." Naturally, for a ToDo to be done, there must be a Doer, an individual or organization that will actually do the thing specified in the ToDo. You want these objects to interact and behave correctly no matter how they integrate into some visible application. They might be part of a defect-tracking system, a school scheduler, or a project-management system.

You've identified Deliverables, ToDos, and Doers as objects in our system. Are you missing any? Probably. Who is responsible for each Deliverable? Is the Deliverable just a part of some larger project? What project? Who is responsible for it? Obviously, when you're really solving a *big* problem, these sorts of questions need to be asked at this stage, and the number of classes and interactions that you might wind up with could be quite large. To keep this example manageable, we resisted the temptation to make it completely realistic.

So for now, we'll stick to Deliverables, Doers, and ToDos. Next we'll go through each of the object types and determine what attributes and behaviors (methods) we'll need for them to have. We'll put actual method names in parentheses so that you can see which specific Zope methods are used to provide corresponding behaviors.

A few use cases should make this more clear:

- A *user* will need to list the ToDos in the system and have email links to the Doers so that she can contact them.
- A *manager* will need to create new deliverables.
- A *programmer* will need to modify a ToDo.

## Refining Attributes, Objects, and Interactions

This section goes through each class in detail. While you are reading this section, think about what they know (that is, their attributes), who they know (that is, their connection to other objects), and what they do (that is, their methods or behaviors).

Deliverables have attributes: name, date, description, status, and a list of ToDos. They also need to have certain abilities: to display themselves (`index_html`), change their values, (`editInstance`, `editInstance_html`), and display forms for users to manage them (`editInstanceForm_html`). Notice that "change their values" has *two* methods. Why? Because `editInstance` is a pure PD method, while `editInstance_html` is a UI method that *calls* `editInstance` to get the work done. This way the capability to modify values is separated from the default UI associated with that process.

ToDos have attributes: name, description, status, a Doer, and a Deliverable. ToDos also need methods to be able to display themselves (`index_html`), display a brief summary (`displayBriefInfo_html`), change their values, (`editInstance`, `editInstanceForm_html`) and display forms for users to modify their content. The methods/scripts `index_html`, `displayBriefInfo_html`, `editInstance`, `editInstanceForm_html`, and `editInstance_html` satisfy these needs.

Doers have attributes: name, email, and a list of ToDos. Doers also must be capable of displaying themselves, changing their values, and displaying forms for users to modify their content. Their methods/scripts `index_html`, `editInstance`, `editInstanceForm_html`, and `editInstance_html` perform these functions.

Notice that some of the attributes of one class relate to the other classes. A Doer has a list of ToDos, and a ToDo has a Deliverable. These are the connections between the classes. You also can think of them as lines of communication. The essence of the Law of Demeter is that you need to use direct lines of communication only. For example, if you find yourself, as a Deliverable, doing something *explicitly* with a Doer, then you need to know too much about the rest of the system. Deliverables don't have Doers; they have ToDos. They are allowed to work with ToDos; if they want to know something about the ToDos Doer, they need to ask the ToDo about it.

All these attributes and the relationships between the various classes are illustrated in UML notation in Figure 11.1.

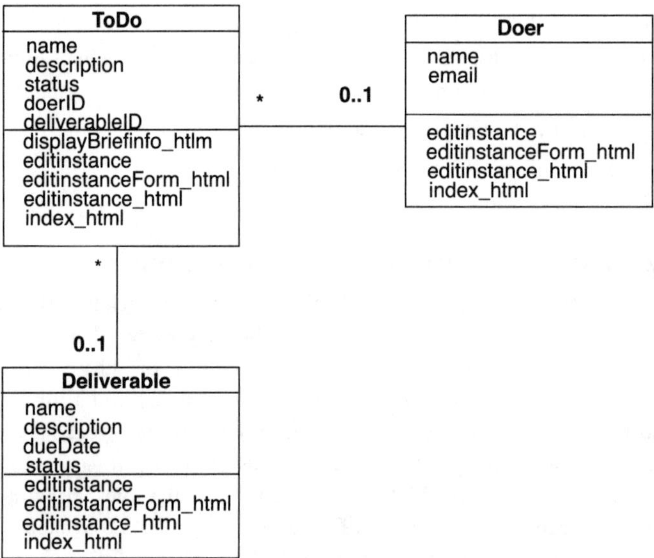


**Figure 11.1** ToDo object diagram.

## ZPatterns Tactics and Vocabulary

Now that you have an object model, you can tell which classes talk to which other classes to get things done. To create a real implementation of this model, you need to construct ZPatterns components that provide the services that enable your object model to work. This requires some thought and familiarity with the various components that ZPatterns provides. You can begin by creating the classes that will implement the roles in the object model.

### Classes and Their Domain of Responsibility

Each of our classes will be implemented as a ZClass.[4] This ZClass will have attributes and methods that match the attributes and methods from the object model. It's worthwhile to separate methods and attributes that reflect different application domains. For example, attributes such as `description` and `dueDate` are clearly problem domain (PD) attributes because they related directly to the real-life object represented by the Class. On the other hand, a method such as `index_html`, the default display method, is a user interface (UI) domain method because it generates the display seen in a web browser.

It's helpful to keep in mind a separation between the UI domain and the PD so that later you can freely modify the UI without concern for affecting the actual logic of the system. To clarify this distinction, we have adopted a convenient naming convention: We will name all UI domain methods with a trailing "_html" so that it's clear that they belong to the UI domain. It's also a good idea to group attributes by domain. So far, we've discussed only PD attributes, but you could envision some cases in which a single object might have UI aspects as well as PD aspects. One easy way to accomplish such a grouping is to put all related attributes into a single property sheet so that those properties can be managed together.

The connections between the classes are sometimes called references or relations. For example, the Deliverable has a list of ToDos. A ToDo has a Doer, and a Doer can have many ToDos. In the object model, these references are drawn as a line, with a name and some enumeration constraint (for example, 1 – n, or 1, or 0 – n). In ZPatterns, these lines are usually implemented "under the covers" so that the application logic doesn't need to know about them, but the application integrator does. The following sections show how you might implement these connections using the ZPatterns framework.

4. ZClasses are described in *The Zope Book*. See Chapter 12, "Extending Zope," at **`http://www.zope.org/Members/michel/ZB/CustomZopeObjects.html`**. Latteier, Amos, and Michel Pellatier. *The Zope Book*. Indianapolis, IN: New Riders Publishing, 2002.

## ZPatterns Vocabulary

The ZPatterns framework comes with a rich and sometimes mystifying vocabulary. Before the details of the ToDo example are described, you need to become familiar with the following terms:

- **DataSkin**—A DataSkin is a Python class that allows instances of DataSkin to get their attributes' data from a DataManager. The classes that we use to build a ZPatterns-based application will inherit from `ZPatterns::DataSkin`.
- **PlugIn**—A PlugIn is a configurable DataManager used to handle some aspect of the data sources for DataSkins (for example, a SkinScript plug-in can provide attributes to a DataSkin or events related to a DataSkin's data).
- **Rack**—A Rack is an object that manages DataSkins. It acts as their DataManager and a keeper of data "PlugIns" that are used to provide PlugIns for objects of a particular class.
- **SkinScript**—SkinScript is a simple language used to implement several important classes of data management. It is "documented" on the ZPatterns Wiki (**http://www.zope.org/Members/pje/Wikis/ZPatterns**). Also see the "SkinScript Syntax" sidebar for a brief summary.
- **Specialist**—A Specialist handles the interaction between the rest of the system in objects of a particular kind. When a Specialist is created, there is normally a Rack with the ID `defaultRack` created at the same time that is owned by the Specialist. Because a Specialist can have multiple Racks, the data associated with these objects can be highly diverse.
- **AttributeProvider**—An AttributeProvider is a type of DataManager PlugIn that has the job of getting the attributes of a DataSkin. An attribute provider can use any Zope object or method to retrieve the data associated with attributes of a DataSkin.
- **RuleAgent**—A RuleAgent acts as an event-based trigger that fires when certain conditions are satisfied. These can be used to carry out specific tasks when data needs to be stored, created, or deleted.

ZPatterns provides these tools so that an application developer can build application components that can be easily adapted to provide a consistent interface in a wide variety of circumstances.

### SkinScript Syntax

It's helpful to be familiar with the kinds of things that can be done in SkinScript. This is a very brief summary of SkinScript syntax. For more detail and lots of examples, see the ZPatterns Wiki at **http://www.zope.org/Members/pje/Wikis/ZPatterns/SkinScriptSyntax**.

There are six basic types of SkinScript Declaration:[5]

5. This is a short summary of the online help that comes with ZPatterns. Zope Corporation. The SkinScript Language Reference. June 2001. Available from Internet: **http://www.zope.org/Members/pje/Wikis/ZPatterns/SkinScriptSyntax**.

- Initialization: INITIALIZE OBJECT WITH *assignmentlist*
- Attribute provider referring to another source: WITH [QUERY] *expression* COMPUTE *nameorassignlist* [OTHERWISE LET *assignmentlist*] [DEPENDENT ON *dependencies*]
- Attribute provider referring to SELF: WITH SELF COMPUTE *assignmentlist*
- Rule Agent for storing attributes by calling another method: [WHEN eventspec] STORE *attributelist* USING *expression* [SAVING mementolist]
- Rule Agent for storing attributes in SELF: STORE *attributelist* IN SELF
- Rule Agent to call an arbitrary method: WHEN *eventspec* CALL *expression* [SAVING mementolist]

The following list, on the other hand, defines the meanings of the variable components:

- *expression* is a DTML-style Python expression.
- *assignmentlist* is a comma-separated list of assignments.
- *nameorassignlist* is a comma-separated list of assignments or simple names. This is used in the attribute provider when the result of *expression* has attributes that match the attributes being provided. In such a case, you don't need to specify `foo=foo` (as in `self.foo = RESULT.foo`), but you can simply write `foo`.
- *mementolist* is like a *nameorassignlist* but is used for saving values rather than providing attributes.
- *eventspec* is a specification of an event in the form of a clause such as OBJECT ADDED, CHANGED, DELETED, where ADDED CHANGED and DELETED can be combined in any way.
- *attributelist* is a comma-separated list of attribute names.
- *dependencies* is a comma-separated list of attribute names that will cause the attributes that depend on them to be recalculated when they are next fetched.

Using these statements in a SkinScript, you can create AttributeProviders and RuleAgents that create, retrieve, store, and delete data from any source that Zope can access as a natural part of object manipulation.

***Setting Up a ZPatterns Application from Scratch***

Before marching into the example application, it is probably worth setting up a simple ZPatterns application by hand to see where the pieces all fit in. This is pretty easy, assuming that you know about ZClasses and working in the ZMI. If you're not familiar with ZClasses, you'll need to review them! See Chapter 3, "Web Event Publishing."

To set up a ZPatterns application from scratch, do the following:

- Create a Product in the Products folder to hold your ZClass(es).
- Create a ZClass in your newly created Product that will implement one your object classes. Select `ZPatterns::DataSkin` as the only superclass.
- Create a property sheet for your ZClass. Notice that you now have a choice of two types of propertysheet. Choose a DataSkin Attribute Property Sheet.
- Create some simple properties for your ZClass.
- Create a DTML Method called `index_html` that displays some of your properties so that you can tell that they are working.
- Create a Specialist in any Zope folder where you want to set up your test app.
- Inside this Specialist, you will find a Rack (see the Racks tab) called `defaultRack` (see the Racks tab). Click the `defaultRack`. Click the Storage tab of the `defaultRack`. There is a pop-up there that sets the class of objects that this Rack will handle. Notice that it lists only classes that are subclassed from DataSkin. Choose the class that you just created. Leave the Store Persistent Data setting on "directly in this object." Click the Change Storage Settings button.
- Now you can create methods that make new objects of the type you defined in your ZClass by calling the `newItem( id )` method of the Specialist.
- You can retrieve objects that you create by calling the `getItem( id )`. After they are retrieved, they behave like any other Zope object.
- You can access methods of your objects through the web by traversing through the Specialist. For example, **`http://yourserver.com/YourProject/yourSpecialist/foo/fooMethod`** would call the method `fooMethod` of the object whose ID is `foo` in a Rack of the Specialist `yourSpecialist`, in the folder `YourProject`.
- You can delete objects from the Rack by calling the `manage_delete()` method of the objects. (They inherit this method from DataSkin.)

That's it! Now you have a very simple ZPatterns application. Some notes of interest: A Rack is associated with a particular class that must be a subclass of DataSkin. A Specialist can have multiple Racks and, therefore, can manage more than one class of object.

## ZPatterns Fits the Pieces Together

At this point, three basic classes and some concept of the relationships between them have been described. In an application, you need some "glue" to hold these classes together and make their interactions work. The relationships between the objects in an application can be nicely managed by instances of the Specialists class.

## Delegating Responsibility with Specialists

The name "Specialist" comes from the notion that each type of object will be managed by a single manager (Specialist) that is the keeper of all information related to objects of that type and only that type. To keep things simple, call each of the Specialists by the name of the objects they manage. (For example, "Doers" would be the name of the Specialist that manages objects of the "Doer" class.) Although it is possible to subclass "Specialist" in applications where special behavior is required, this example uses plain Specialist instances as created in the ZMI. Figure 11.2 illustrates how these appear in the ZMI.

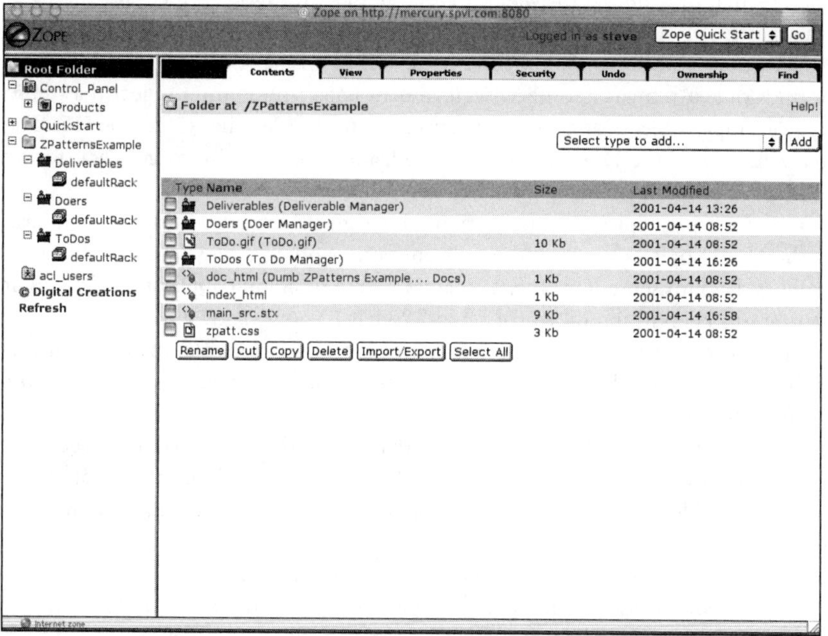


**Figure 11.2** Specialists used in the ToDo example.

Specialists have an extremely simple built-in API. Their primary methods are `getItem` and `newItem`. The `newItem` method accepts an ID (a unique string that identifies a particular item that the Specialist will manage) and returns a new instance of such an item. The `getItem` method also requires an ID, but it either returns the existing instance with that ID or returns `None` if no such instance is found. Of course, you can easily add methods to a Specialist to handle more specialized needs (such as `getToDoIDsForDeliverable( deliverable_id)`).

Specialists usually have one or more Racks that are the *real* DataManagers for the DataSkins that the Specialist manages. Racks use PlugIns to implement data management (for example, getting and setting various attributes, and handling certain events for the DataSkins). For example, Doers have names and email addresses. How are those names and addresses actually stored? In "non-ZPatterns" Zope development, developer would decide ahead of time how the attributes would be stored, and then she would include the appropriate connections to carry out that plan. But what if someone else wanted to *reuse* her code but they had a different idea of where the data should be stored? (For example, Joe likes SQL, Walker wants LDAP, and Sue prefers ZODB). ZPatterns deliberately separates the application logic from the grungy details of data storage. When the application wants a Doer, it asks the "Doers" Specialist for a Doer with a particular ID (such as `thisDoer = Doers.getItem(theDoerID)`). The Doers Specialist then goes to its Rack(s) and tries to find a Doer that can satisfy the request. If it finds one, it returns it; otherwise, it returns `None` (the Python object that represents a null or empty object), and the application has to decide what to do about it. The Rack knows how the Doers are really stored, and it has PlugIns to get data (for example, email addresses or names) for the Doers attributes.

One of the principles of object-oriented design is Law of Demeter, which basically says that each object/class should touch only other objects/classes that are "nearby" in an object diagram sense. This means that, as you're designing applications/classes, it's important to keep in mind "who I know," "what I know," and "what I do" as guiding principles that determine what information is kept in various classes and what methods those classes provide. In simplest terms, this means that objects should talk to only their nearest neighbors in an object diagram.

Following this principle, it's easy to see that things that relate to the collection of all the Deliverables belong to the Deliverables Specialist, while things that relate to a particular deliverable belong to the Deliverable object itself. For example, say that you're a ToDo and you need to show a list of the possible Doers in the form that you provide to edit yourself. You should call the Doers Specialist and ask it to give you a snippet of HTML that would display such a list. In this way, even if the Doers implementation is completely changed, as long as it can still respond to the same method (for example, `getDoersSelectHTMLSnippet()`),you still have a hope of getting a reasonable widget to display a choice of Doers in the editing form of a ToDo.

## Making Connections Behind the Scenes: Attribute Providers

You can see how this works by implementing the code needed to handle a concrete use case—for example, the first use case: "A *user* will need to list the ToDos in the system and have email links to the Doers so that she can contact them."

In the object diagram, you can see that a ToDo has zero or one Doer.

The realization of this implementation should result in a display that could appear on a web page as shown in Figure 11.3.

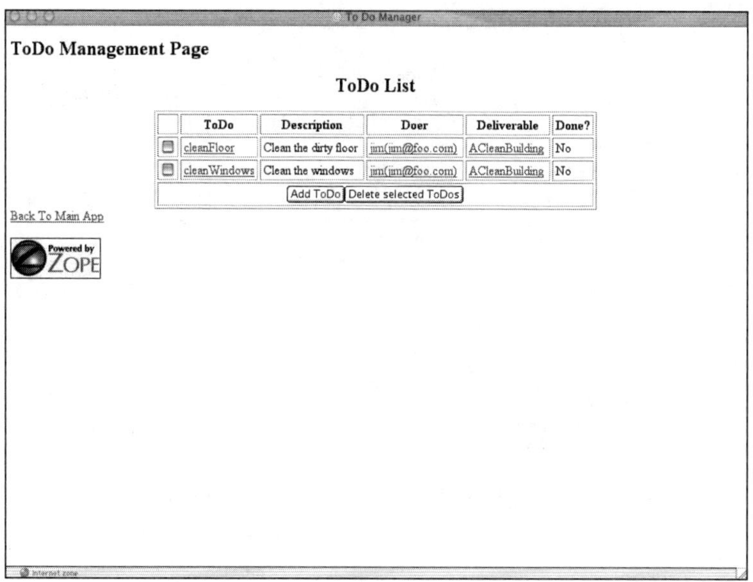


**Figure 11.3** Tabular display of ToDos.

This requires the ToDos Specialist to iterate through its ToDos and display information about each one. For example, you'll want to display the email address of each Doer as you display each row. To get the email address, you'll need to get a reference to the Doer. Figure 11.4 shows an interaction diagram for this process.

Of course, the display of the ToDos would be a natural default display for the ToDos Specialist, so it's only natural that you call the method (a DTML Method) `index_html`. As you list the ToDos, it makes sense that you also should list the Doers and Deliverables associated with that ToDo. The ToDo class has a very simple set of properties, shown in Figure 11.5.

Notice in particular that although the object diagram (refer to Figure 11.1) shows attributes `myDoer` and `myDeliverable`, the actual implementation has no such attributes. You will need to get the Doer associated with a ToDo so that you can display information about the Doer, such as an email address, as you list the ToDos. The property that relates a ToDo object with its Doer is `doerID`. So, at first glance it appears that a ToDo needs to ask the Doers Specialist for the Doer that has the ID given by the ToDos `doerID` property. In other words, you might think that you would need to write code like this:

```
theEmail = Doers.getItem(aToDo.doerID).email
```

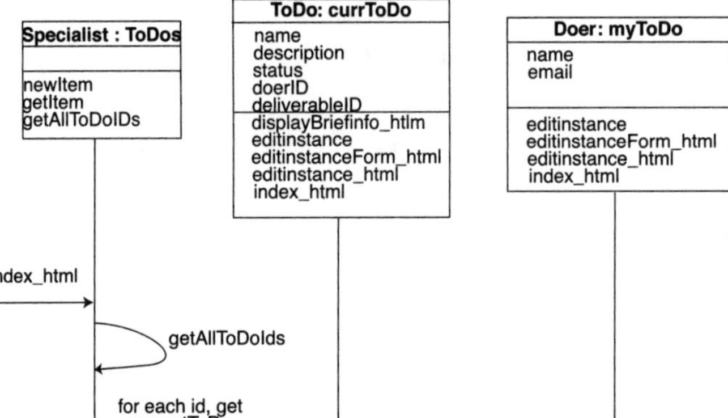

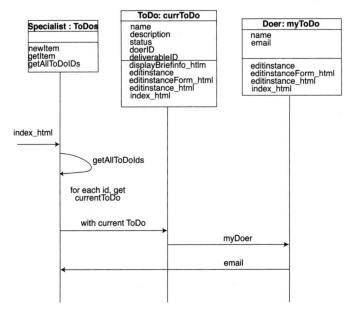


Figure 11.4 ToDos Specialist displays ToDos.

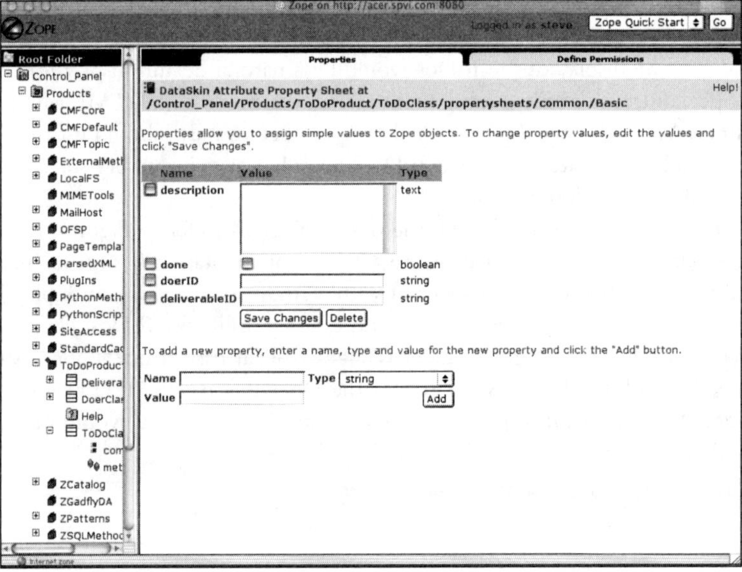


Figure 11.5 Propertysheet of ToDo class.

A straightforward implementation based on this approach might look like Listing 11.2.

Listing 11.2 **First Pass: Displaying a List of ToDos**

```
<dtml-var standard_html_header>

<!-- index_html DTML Method of ToDos Specialist -->

<h2><dtml-var document_title></h2>
<p>
<div align=center>
<h2>ToDo List</h2>

<dtml-in getAllToDoIDs sort> <!-- go through all the ToDos -->

    <dtml-if sequence-start>  <!-- draw the table header -->
        <form action="." method="post">
        <table cellspacing=3 cellpadding=3 border=1>
        <tr>
            <td> </td>
            <th>ToDo</th>
            <th>Description</th>
            <th>Doer</th>
            <th>Deliverable</th>
            <th>Done?</th>
         </tr>
    </dtml-if>

    <dtml-let currID="_['sequence-item']">
        <dtml-with "getItem(currID)">
            <dtml-let myDoer="Doers.getItem(doerID)"
                      myDeliverable="Deliverables.getItem(deliverableID)">
                <tr>

                <!-- the first column is the checkbox -->
                <td><input type=checkbox name="ids:list" value="&dtml-
                ➥currID;"></td>

                <!-- the second column is the ToDo link -->
                <td><a href="<dtml-var currID url_quote>"><dtml-var
                ➥currID></a></td>

                <!-- the third column is the description -->
                <td><dtml-var description> </td>

                <!-- the fourth column is the Doer link -->
                <td>
                    <dtml-if myDoer>
                        <a href="<dtml-var "Doers.absolute_url()">/<dtml-var
                        ➥doerID url_quote>">
```

*continues*

Listing 11.2 **Continued**

```
                            <dtml-var doerID></a>
                        <a href="mailto:<dtml-var "myDoer.email">"><dtml-var
                        ➥"myDoer.email"></a>
                    </dtml-if> 
                </td>

                <!-- the fifth column is the Deliverable link -->
                <td>
                    <dtml-if myDeliverable>
                        <a href="<dtml-var "Deliverables.absolute_url()"
                        ➥>/<dtml-var deliverableID url_quote>">
                            <dtml-var deliverableID>
                        </a>
                    </dtml-if> </td>

                <!-- the sixth column is the 'done' status -->
                <td><dtml-if done>Done!<dtml-else>No</dtml-if></td>

                </tr>
            </dtml-let>
        </dtml-with>
    </dtml-let>
    <dtml-if sequence-end> <!-- draw the control buttons at the end -->
        <tr><td colspan=6 align=center>
            <input type=submit name="addNewToDoForm_html:method" value="Add
            ➥ToDo">
            <input type=submit name="deleteInstances_html:method" value="Delete
            ➥selected ToDos">
        </td></tr>
        </table>
    </dtml-if>

<dtml-else>
Sorry.. no "to do"s!
<br>
<form action=".">
<input type=submit name="addNewToDoForm_html:method" value="Add New ToDo">
</form>
</dtml-in>

</div>
</p>

<a href="&dtml-URL2;">Back To Main App</a>
<dtml-var standard_html_footer>
```

This implementation works. That's the good news. The bad news is that it requires the implementer to know a lot about how the rest of the application is connected. Wouldn't it be nice if a programmer working with a ToDo object didn't have to know about the Doers and Deliverables Specialist? In this code, the programmer had to use `myDoer=Doers.getItem(doerID)` in line 27. But this is *ugly* and error-prone because it requires the programmer to refer to the Doers Specialist. As a rule, if you have to know so much about the global connections in the application to do something simple, such as display an email address, it's probably a bad thing.

In the best of all possible worlds, each ToDo could get its Doer just like getting its description, as a simple property of itself. If this *were* possible, you could implement the display of the ToDo list as the `index_html` method of the ToDos Specialist, as shown in lines 08 through 13 of Listing 11.3.

Listing 11.3 **Displaying a List of ToDos**

```
01 <dtml-with "getItem(currID)">
02 <tr>
03
04 <td><input type=checkbox name="ids:list" value="&dtml-currID;"></td>
05 <td><a href="<dtml-var currID url_quote>"><dtml-var currID></a></td>
06 <td><dtml-var description> </td>
07 <td>
08   <dtml-if myDoer>
09     <a href="<dtml-var "myDoer.absolute_url()">">
10      <dtml-var doerID></a>
11     <a href="mailto:<dtml-var "myDoer.email">>
12       (<dtml-var "myDoer.email">)</a>
13   </dtml-if>  
14 </td>
15
16 <td>
17   <dtml-if myDeliverable>
18     <a href="<dtml-var "myDeliverable.absolute_url()">">
19       <dtml-var "myDeliverable.id">
20     </a>
21   </dtml-if> 
22 </td>
23
24 <td><dtml-if done>Done!<dtml-else>No</dtml-if></td>
25 </dtml-with>
```

Note in particular that when a ToDo needs its associated Doer, it just says `myDoer`. This would the most natural way to access the related Doer, and it makes creating templates much easier.

Can you achieve the simple logic of the previous display code without having to know so much about how the internals of the application are wired? This is one of the coolest things about ZPatterns. You can create a "generic attribute provider" in the form of a SkinScript PlugIn. In the PlugIns tab of the ToDos Rack, the SkinScript can be set up like Listing 11.4.

Listing 11.4 **Using SkinScript to Provide an Attribute**

```
WITH Doers.getItem(self.doerID) COMPUTE myDoer = RESULT or NOT_FOUND
```

A graphical representation of the action of this attribute provider is given in Figure 11.6.

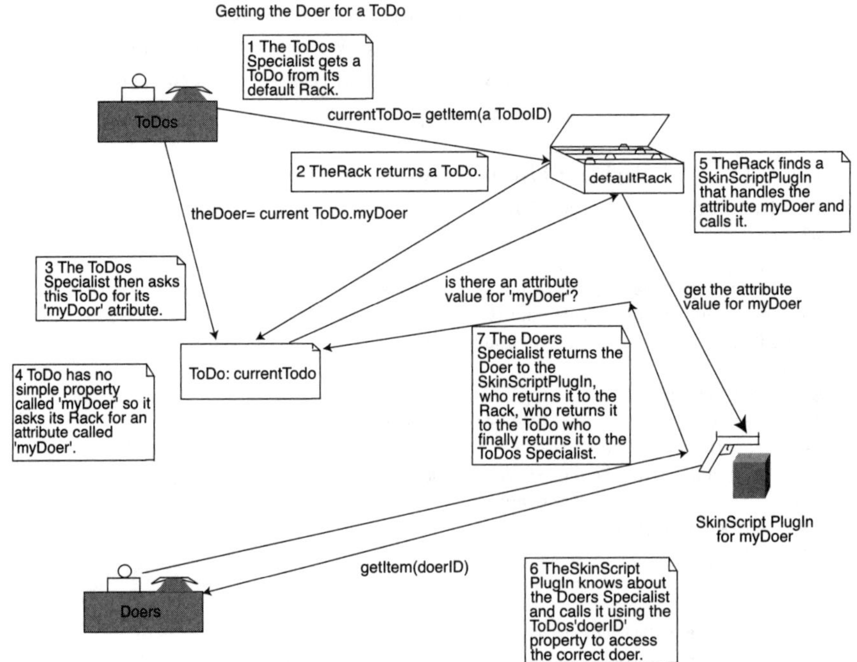


**Figure 11.6** Specialist ToDos gets the `myDoer` attribute.

When the "ToDo" DataSkin instance is asked for an attribute called `myDoer`, it sees that it has no simple attribute called `myDoer`. It then checks with its Rack to see if there is a PlugIn that provides values for `myDoer`. The SkinScript PlugIn sees that it has a line of SkinScript that assigns a value to `myDoer`. So, it calls `Doers.getItem(self.doerID)` to satisfy that request. Because this is a PlugIn of the Rack, neither the Specialist nor the DataSkin itself knows or cares exactly *how* it is happening. So, if you later change how data is stored (for example, you may switch the data from ZODB to LDAP), the only change you'll need to make is a single line of SkinScript that refers to the correct data source. This same idea can be used to provide `myDeliverables`, `myDoers`, and similar properties for each of these object types so that the developer doesn't need to bother with exactly how these things are connected but rather just worries about getting the problem domain logic and web presentation working.

## Relationships with Higher Degrees of Multiplicity

The one line of SkinScript works well when you want a reference in one instance (such as `doerID`) to produce what appears to be a simple attribute (`myDoer`), but what about references with higher degrees of multiplicity? For example, according to the object model, each Deliverable can have multiple ToDos. One approach would be for each Deliverable to keep a list of associated ToDos. But this would be cumbersome because this list would need to be maintained every time a ToDo was added or deleted. Another approach, which requires much less bookkeeping, is to let the ToDos Specialist keep track of the ToDos (that is its job, after all!). The Specialist in this case needs a method that will deliver objects under its control that satisfy various constraints. It usually works best to give these methods very clear names such as `getAllFoosForBar` or `getRecentFoosForBar(date)`. Of course, the Specialist could delegate these methods to a Rack, or to a ZCatalog, or to an SQL Query—or whatever makes sense to the Specialist for that object type. The main point is that the Deliverable object itself shouldn't have to know anything *but* the name of the attribute that it needs to reference to retrieve the object(s) in question.

The Deliverable Specialist needs a list of ToDos. Therefore, it would ask the ToDos Specialist for all the ToDos that belong to that Deliverable (that is, the ToDos that have that `deliverableID`)—something like `getToDosForDeliverable(deliverableID)`. One possible implementation of `getToDosForDeliverable` is shown in Listing 11.5.

Listing 11.5 **Method (Python Script) of Retrieving ToDos for a Deliverable**

```
## Script (Python) "getToDosForDeliverable"
##bind container=container
##bind context=context
##bind namespace=
##bind script=script
##bind subpath=traverse_subpath
##parameters=deliverable_id
##title=
##

hits=[]

for id in container.getAllToDoIDs():
    theToDo=container.getItem(id)
    if theToDo:
        if theToDo.deliverableID == deliverable_id:
            hits.append(theToDo)

return hits
```

Of course, this is just a naive way to satisfy the basic requirement that this method actually work. It's naive because it accesses *all* the ToDos in the Rack and inspects their `deliverableID` property. This is a relatively expensive—and usually unnecessary—operation.

In a *real* application, you would use a ZCatalog or an SQL Method to do the work of finding all the right ToDos and getting only those ToDos from the Rack. We will demonstrate this technique in Chapter 12, "Integrating Separate Modules with ZPatterns," when we work out the details of the back end of the Academic Data System.

But you certainly don't want to have to do that explicitly every time you need the list of ToDos or the ToDoIDs! How can you get this list? You can make the conversation with the ToDos Specialist happen behind the scenes by using a SkinScript Attribute Provider to make the list appear as a simple attribute of the Deliverable object. Listing 11.6 shows how two lines of SkinScript can provide attributes `myToDos` and `myToDoIds` by calling methods of the ToDos Specialist. You can find this SkinScript in the `defaultRack` of the ToDos Specialist in the downloadable version of this example. These commands are actually entered on one line each in the SkinScript text box. They are presented in Listing 11.6 on two lines to enhance readability.

Listing 11.6 **Providing List Attributes in SkinScript**

```
WITH ToDos.getToDosForDeliverable(self.id) COMPUTE
       myToDos=RESULT OTHERWISE LET myToDos=[]

WITH ToDos.getToDoIdsForDeliverable(self.id) COMPUTE
       myToDoIds=RESULT OTHERWISE LET myToDoIds=[]
```

# Sharing UI Elements Between Objects and Specialists

Specialists can get more from one another than just objects. They also can provide display code. This is nice because the Specialist knows best how to provide a sensible UI for its objects.

## Assigning a Doer to a ToDo

Let's say you're editing a ToDo and you need to adjust the Doer associated with a particular ToDo. For this, you need a UI snippet in the form of a DTML Method, such as Listing 11.7.

Listing 11.7 **Doers Specialist Providing a UI Snippet**

```
<select name="doerID"><option value="">Nobody
    <dtml-in "Doers.getAllDoerIDs()" sort>
       <option
          value="&dtml-sequence-item;"
            <dtml-if "_.has_key('doerID') and doerID==_['sequence-item']">
                selected
            </dtml-if>>
         &dtml-sequence-item;
    </dtml-in>
</select>
```

In the example, this is implemented as the DTML method `doerSelectTag` in the Doers Specialist.

When a ToDos Instance needs to render a widget that will allow a user to change the Doer for that ToDo, it can call the Doers Specialist (which knows all about the Doers) and ask for a "UI snippet" that will represent a list of Doers that can be chosen for the ToDo. This is implemented as a DTML Method of the ToDo, in the methods of the ToDo ZClass definition, as shown in Listing 11.8.

Listing 11.8 **ToDo Instance Requesting a UI Snippet**

```
<dtml-var standard_html_header>
<center>
<h2>Edit ToDo Item</h2>
<form action="editInstance_html" method="post">
    <table cellspacing=3 cellpadding=3>
        <tr><th>Name</th><td>&dtml-id;</td></tr>
        <tr>
            <th>Description</th>
            <td>
                <textarea
                    name="description"
                    wrap="soft"
                    cols=60
                    rows=15>&dtml-description;</textarea>
            </td>
        </tr>
        <tr>
            <th>Doer</th>
            <td><dtml-var "Doers.doerSelectionTag_html(Doers, _)"></td>
        </tr>
        <tr>
            <th>Done?</th>
            <td><input type=checkbox name="done" <dtml-if done>checked</dtml-
            ➥if>></td>
        </tr>
        <tr>
            <td colspan=2 align=center><input type=submit value="Edit
            ➥ToDo"></td>
        </tr>
    </table>
</form>
</center>
<dtml-var standard_html_footer>
```

In this case, the Doers Specialist chooses to provide a pop-up with the `DoerIDs` as the values. If the Doers implementation changes, this method could easily change without requiring any modification of the ToDos instance editing frame.

## Summary

We've only touched the surface of ZPatterns, but we've discussed a lot already. We can implement abstract object models using ZPatterns and can have the connections between objects provided by Specialist, which acts only when those connections are actually needed. If we were to "grow" this application, we could add new SkinScript that would allow objects to be stored in a relational database, or we could add new Specialists and objects to our object model without disturbing the relationships that already exist.

Now that we've implemented a simple application using ZPatterns we're ready for a more sophisticated example that can stretch the use of ZPatterns to include more advanced concepts such as event triggers and virtual instances. Chapter 12 covers these concepts in the context of an e-commerce application.

# 12

# Integrating Applications with ZPatterns

IN THE LAST CHAPTER, YOU USED ZPATTERNS to build a simple example system using persistent objects that interacted with one another to form a complete application. In this chapter, you'll encounter a different situation in which ZPatterns provides the tools needed to allow one application to work with another. You'll also use ZPatterns to implement a set of objects that store their attributes outside of Zope storage as another step in the journey toward ZPatterns Zen. This technique can be used to bring any kind of external or "legacy" data into a new ZPatterns-based application in a natural and seamless way. Finally, we'll present some general Zope techniques that can be used to help you automate much of the tedious duplication that is often required when dealing with complex applications. If you haven't read Chapter 11, "Design for Integration the ZPatterns Way," it would probably be best to read it first, before starting this chapter.

## Application Integration Is Difficult

Application programmers can't think of everything! Even if they could, applications must deal with a limited subset of the "universe of problems" so that they can be finished quickly enough to be useful. This often leads to difficulty. Although applications need to have a well-defined scope to be shipped, users have no such constraint on their imagination or their needs. So, it often happens that applications don't do all the things that users feel they should. If one application developer is unable to fulfill all of a user's needs, the user can simply acquire another application. Often users will accumulate several applications to handle all their various needs.

When an organization is using multiple applications to handle different aspects of its work, the issue of interapplication integration looms. Questions arise such as, "How can we get access to the data in our accounting system as we run the online support application so that we know whether an end user (as identified by the support app) is a customer (as identified by the accounting app) with an overdue balance?" Answers to these questions are usually that it will be difficult or impossible. Some application-development technologies make solutions to this problem intractable by creating monolithic executable programs that cannot be easily adapted. Figure 12.1 shows the basic situation.

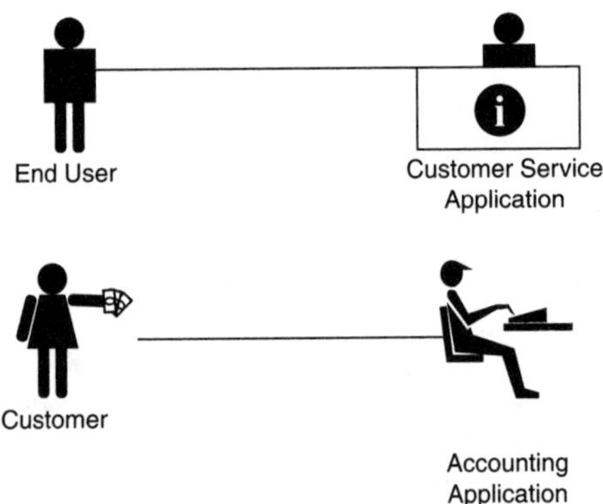


**Figure 12.1** Two applications with different objects.

Zope applications often ship with some objects that are *meant* to be modified by the application installer/integrator. This helps because it means that, at least at the user interface (UI) level, you can easily add links/displays that relate to other parts of the system. In fact, it makes the previous question sound pretty easy, as long as both applications identify users with the same ID; a few well-placed links in the customer support UI probably should do the trick. Unfortunately, other kinds of questions are not so easily answered: "How can we synchronize the end users in the customer support application with the customers in the accounting package?"

One of the goals of ZPatterns is to allow external data to appear in an application as if it were fully integrated. So, the ZPatterns answer is, in a Zope Zen-sounding phrase, "Grasshopper! There is no need to synchronize the two. On the surface they appear to be two, but if you see clearly, you will understand that they are one."

This is one of the core concepts of this chapter. There is data—an entry in a database somewhere for an actual person who calls up and asks for help. There are "objects" that the applications understand—for example, customer (if you are the accounting package) or end user (if you are the online support package). The same data may apply to *both* objects, and there is no need to have the data duplicated just because two different applications use different objects to represent that one person.

## Object Participation/Role Depends on Context

This design pattern occurs frequently in application integration, and it's closely related to the *Person-Participant* pattern. The idea is that we have a single *Person*, the user who calls and asks for help. This one person plays different *roles* in relation to the two different applications. This person's relationship with an application is a way of participation in that application, so the person is a *Participant* in relation to that application, as illustrated in Figure 12.2.

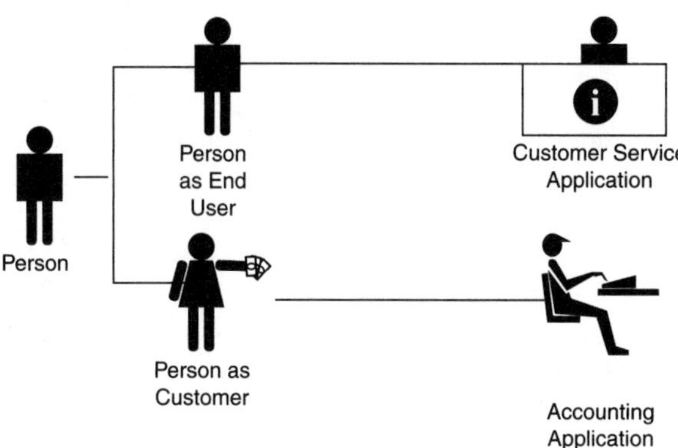


**Figure 12.2** Person-Participant pattern applied to application integration.

> **Person-Participant Pattern**
>
> The Person-Participant pattern reflects the idea that there are properties and actions that relate more to a person's role in a certain situation than they do to the person themselves. A woman can participate in the family as a mother, in the marriage as a wife, and in the auto parts store as a customer. There are certain aspects of her that are common to all of these because they are about the *person* (for example, age, weight, gender) as basic properties of an actual person. Other aspects relate only to the participation of that person in a particular context (for example, customer_id, wedding_date, childrens_names). You can think of the participant object as a sort of object-oriented "hat" that a person wears that helps the person to operate in a particular environment or context. Often the participant can be implemented so that it obeys the person interface by delegating all "person" responsibilities to its person object.

The beauty of ZPatterns is that neither the customer service application nor the accounting application needs to know about the internal details of the other. An application integrator might need to edit a display method or two in the applications, and he probably will need to adjust the PlugIns of the Rack that manages the data for the customer and end user objects. The application integrator might even *add* some utility methods to various objects to facilitate the process, but these will not change the internal structure of the original application.

# ZPatterns Remaps Objects Behind the Scenes

Application integration is basically the art of fitting a square peg into a round hole, or maybe, more accurately, putting two sets of puzzles together into a single bigger picture where the pieces of the two puzzles are completely different. At first it appears that the pieces don't fit at all, but ZPatterns allows you to change the shapes of the objects to fit into the patterns of the other puzzle. There are three main stages to this process:

- Understanding and connecting the object models for the two applications
- Creating any new classes or methods that are required to fulfill the interface requirements of the two applications' objects
- Creating and adapting the Data Managers (PlugIns) to actually do the dynamic mapping that allows the objects to seamlessly interact with one another

## Interfacing Two Object Models

When two different applications are merged, their object models should be inspected to discover classes that might be used to satisfy various roles in the other application. When they are identified, these classes can be "mapped" onto classes in the other application with attribute providers and triggers (to keep things in sync).

Before digging into the gory details of a full-blown case of multiapplication integration, consider a simpler case in which one application is essentially embedded in another. This is an actual case from our consulting experience, so you know that this can happen in real life!

Imagine that you have already created a web-based catalog of books. These books use an existing Book object with various properties:

- `title`—The actual book title.
- `id`—The ISBD number for the book.
- `price`—The retail store price for the book.
- `shortDescription`—A one- or two-sentence description of the book.
- `description`—A multiparagraph description of the book.

After this application is "finished," it is decided that the books need to be made a available for sale over the Internet. Rather than start a *new* application from scratch, it is also decided that an existing online shopping framework should be employed. You discover EMarket (**`http://www.zope.org/Members/sspickle/EMarket`**). EMarket is just such a framework, written by us using ZPatterns, to make it easy to integrate into most existing situations. EMarket has three primary classes: MarketItem, Shopper, and Basket. Roughly, these are a thing to sell (MarketItem), a participant (Shopper) to buy the thing, and a container (Basket) to keep track of all the different things in a single order.

Of the three primary EMarket classes, only one, MarketItem, has any peer in the existing Book Catalog application. A MarketItem has similar but not identical attributes:

- `name`—A simple name used for UI listings.
- `id`—Any unique identifier.
- `price`—The actual online price of this "thing."
- `description`—A short description for UI listings.
- `available`—Boolean that is "true" if the item is ready for sale.

These lists show that the MarketItem and Book classes don't match. Book uses the `title` attribute, while MarketItem uses the `name` attribute. Book uses `shortDescription`, while MarketItem uses the `description` attribute. Also, the `price` attribute for the MarketItem is the online price of a thing, but for the Book class, the `price` attribute is the retail price. It so happened that the book publisher wanted to give an "online discount" for customers who use the web page to purchase books. How can you calculate the discount? That problem is handled by the Book class! It has a method called `discountPrice` that calculates the correct online price of a book. Finally, there is no concept of "available" for books. If they are in Zope, they should be "available."

## Virtual Instances Are Object-Oriented Impersonators

In Chapter 11, when you selected the classes that would be stored in the various ZPatterns Racks, you used the default storage setting: "Objects are: stored persistently." The alternative was "Objects are: loaded by accessing attribute X," as shown in Figure 12.3. Making the choice "stored persistently" meant that objects were encoded into a "flat" data format, called a "pickle," and were stored in a data file (Data.fs) on the filesystem where the Zope server runs. In this chapter, you will be working with objects that are stored in one of two places:

- Stored outside of Zope in a relational database (such as SQL Server, MySQL, or Gadfly) or in something similar (such as LDAP)
- Stored elsewhere in Zope, but not persistently in the Rack that uses the object (for example, in some other folder or Specialist's Rack)

To do this, you need to select the alternative to "stored persistently" and have the objects "loaded by accessing attribute X." To really understand how this works, you need to have a good idea of what's going on in a Specialist/Rack when an object is accessed.

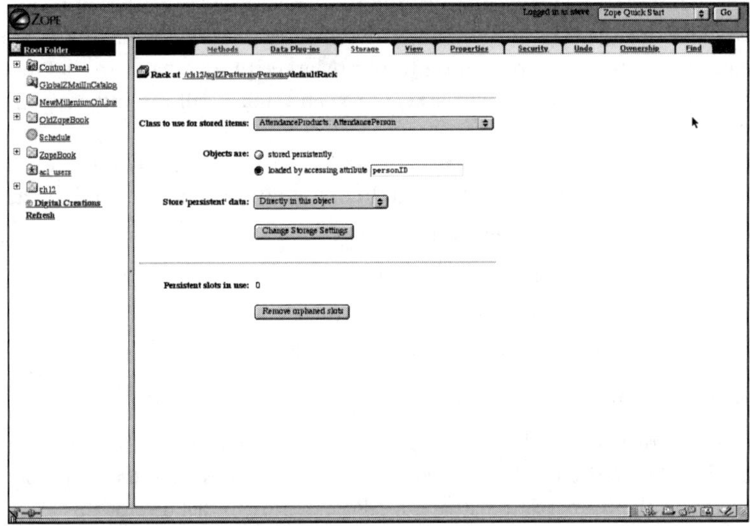

**Figure 12.3** Storage tab of a Rack with loadAttribute set.

When a Rack's `getItem` method is called, the Rack checks to see if there is a load attribute set. If not, the object is pulled from the Rack's persistent storage. If there *is* a load attribute set, a new empty instance of the object type set in the Storage tab of the Rack is created. An attempt is made to access the `loadAattribute` attribute of this newly created but *empty* instance. The idea is that this attempt will trigger a SkinScript PlugIn that will actually do the work of accessing the external data needed to fill in the empty object instance with "real" data. In this way, you get the following:

- The object type that you need, set in the Storage tab of the Rack
- The data that you need (set up by the skin script that retrieves the data from any arbitrary source available to Zope)

This concept can now be applied to the Book/MarketItem example from the "Interfacing Two Object Models" section.

## ZPatterns PlugIns Do Most of the Work

In the case of the Book/MarketItem integration, you can simply set the MarketItem's Rack to access objects by accessing a fictional attribute called `theRealThing`. This attribute will actually be the Book object from the Catalog. Then when you ask for a

MarketItem whose ID is `foo`, the Rack will create an empty MarketItem and then attempt to access an attribute of the empty instance called `theRealThing`. Then you can use the following SkinScript PlugIn to get the marketItem's Rack to retrieve the Book object with the same ID as is shown in Listing 12.1.

Listing 12.1 **SkinScript to Retrieve a *Book* Object**

```
WITH BookSpecialist.getItem(self.id)
      COMPUTE theRealThing = (RESULT is _.None)
      and NOT_FOUND or RESULT
```

The `COMPUTE` clause looks complex, until you realize that the `and` and `or` parts are just taking advantage of the way Python handles logical combinations. This technique is summarized in the sidebar "Python Logical Evaluation Simplifies Expressions."

**Python Logical Evaluation Simplifies Expressions**

You can use your knowledge of the way Python evaluates logical expressions to simplify logic and can eliminate extra functions. When Python sees an expression like:

```
x = a and b
```

it checks the logical value of a. If a evaluates to `true`, it returns b.

When Python encounters an expression like:

```
x = a or b
```

it checks the logical value of a. If a evaluates to `false`, it returns b.

This leads to the following results:

```
Python 2.1 (#92, Apr 24 2001, 23:59:43)  [CW CARBON GUSI2 THREADS] on mac
Type "copyright", "credits" or "license" for more information.

>>> print 1 and 'hello'
hello

>>> print 0 or 'goodbye'
goodbye
>>>

>>> print 1 and 'it is true' or 'it is false'
it is true

>>> print 0 and 'it is true' or 'it is false'
it is false
```

So, `condition and result1 or result2` is basically the same is a function that performs the logic:

```
def foo(condition):
    if condition:
        return result1
            else:
        return result2
```

But, as you can see it's much more compact. If you're familiar with C, you can think of this as `condition ? result1: result2`. If you see an expression like this:

```
theRealThing = (RESULT is _.None)
    and NOT_FOUND or RESULT
```

you can see it's basically shorthand for this:

```
def foo(RESULT):

    if RESULT is _.None:
        return NOT_FOUND
    else:
        return RESULT
```

but as a simple expression rather than a function. You'll see this form often in SkinScript because each SkinScript attribute provider must be expressed as a single line of SkinScript. SkinScript can call methods and functions, but for simple logic such as if/else, an external function is cumbersome. This technique of using the logical evaluation strategy of the Python interpreter comes in handy in situations like this.

When we have a Book object as an attribute of the MarketItem, it's easy to use a SkinScript PlugIn to compute the other attributes based on the Book, as is shown in Listing 12.2.

Listing 12.2 **SkinScript to Compute the Other MarketItem Attributes**

```
WITH self.theRealThing
       COMPUTE price=RESULT.discountPrice(),
       name=title, description=shortDescription,
       available=1, origPrice=price
```

Inspect the two lists of attributes for MarketItem and Book, and see how the SkinScript in Listing 12.2 handles the mapping of Book attributes to those of the corresponding MarketItem. Notice a couple things in particular:

- `available` is unconditionally set to 1. This is a consequence of the fact that Books have no concept of "availability."
- `price` is computed using the discountPrice method of the Book object.

Because the EMarket application never has to change the attributes of a Book object, this is all there is to it. Pretty simple! Notice that this means you've *extended* a "legacy" application to perform new functions without changing a *line* of the old program. Amazing!

# Academic Data System Integration: Attendance and Lunch Programs

To see how complete application integration can work, we need a "real world" example. The examples that we've chosen are a school attendance application and a school lunch application. Both of these can be implemented separately, and they are in the sections that follow. Then they are integrated into a single application. To be complete, we'll use an external relational database for the data in one application and a mixture of persistent and "stolen" data for the other.

## A Complete Example: Are You Here? (Attendance)

Keeping track of a student's attendance is basically a bookkeeping problem. Everyday the student is either absent, tardy, or not absent. If the student is tardy or absent, he either has an excuse or does not have one. In the following three sections, we'll implement a simple, complete, but not quite "finished" school attendance application using externally stored relational database data mapped on to an object-oriented application. Although this application is not "finished," the framework is here to create a full-featured application with a little UI design and some better data validation.

You can find get the Zope objects for this example from the companion web site (**http://webdev.zopeonarope.com** or **http://www.newriders.com**) or from the Zope site (**http://www.zope.org/Members/sspickle**). You should get and install these objects in a Zope of your own so that you can follow along with this example. To install the example, you need to place the .zexp files in your Zope's Import folder on the filesystem, and then use the Export/Import button in the ZMI to import them into Zope. You'll need to import the Products first and the application second.

### Setting Up the Object Model

The simplest object model that we could come up with that allows for a reasonable representation of the problem looks like Figure 12.4.

As you can see, there are five classes: Persons, Attendees (Students and Teachers), Events, Homerooms, and Records. The multiplicities are set up so that each Participant can attend multiple events. Events can occur in any homeroom. The model is a little more complex than you might imagine, but it's flexible enough to handle most situations.

### Implementing the Model with Specialists

The straightforward implementation of the object model in ZPatterns requires the use of one Specialist for each class. Each class can be implemented as a ZClass, similar to your last project with ToDos. One major difference is that, this time, you're going to use external data. The data for this implementation will be stored in a relational database. To make this example most useful, you're going to use Gadfly. Gadfly is a simple, memory-based relational database that supports a fairly large subset of standard SQL.

It's free and comes already installed with every copy of Zope. It's not intended for production environments, but only for testing and development. It's good for this situation because it requires no installation. Because it's implemented purely in Python, it runs on every platform that can run Zope.

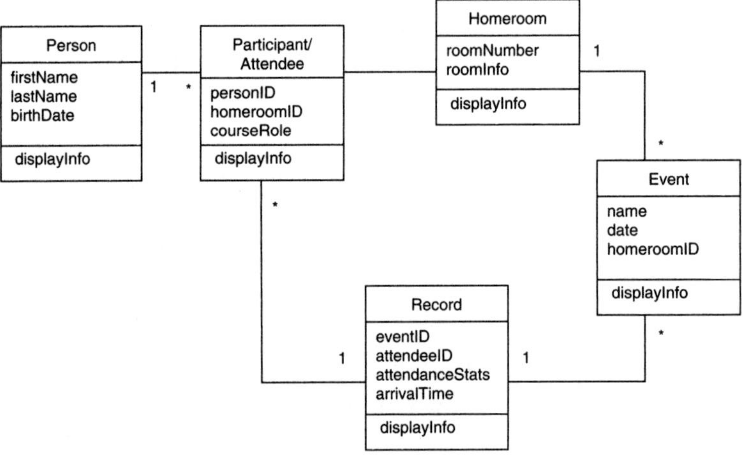


**Figure 12.4** UML model of attendance application.

Gadfly doesn't implement all of "standard" SQL. One problematic issue is its lack of any DateTime data type. To remedy this, you'll use ZPatterns to map DateTime objects back and forth between Zope and the database, where DateTimes will be stored as floating-point numbers.

Each Specialist will handle the management of one of the core classes. For example, there will be an Events Specialist to keep track of the events for which to track attendance. Specialist automatically support the getItem/newItem API. You'll add triggers to handle the insert/update/delete queries that need to happen to keep the database in sync with the application.

From the object model, you can see that an Event has properties: `name`, `date`, and `homeroomID`. These are entered into the Basic propertysheet of the AttendanceEvent ZClass. You can get there in the ZMI by clicking:

- Control_Panel
- AttendanceProducts
- AttendanceEvent
- PropertySheets
- Basic

They are entered with the types string, date, and string, respectively, as shown in Figure 12.5.

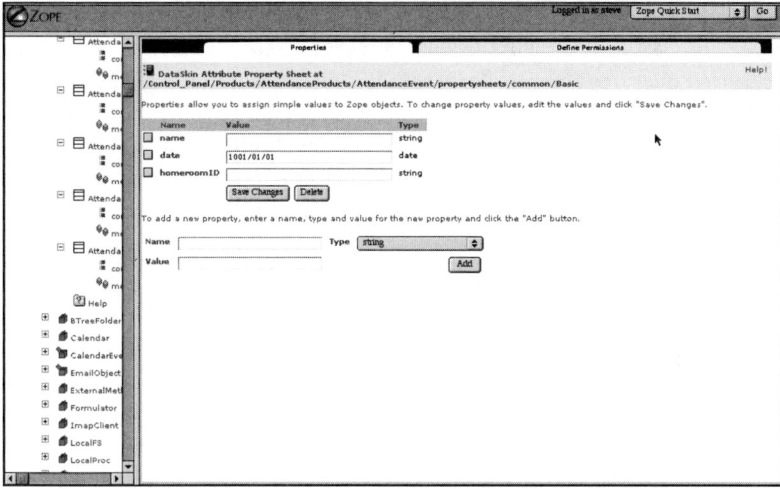

Figure 12.5 Basic propertysheet of Event class.

Each of the other core classes has a similar Basic propertysheet with its properties defined there.

Examine the methods of the Event's Specialist. It's located in the folder where you installed the attendance application. You should see a list of queries and Python scripts that looks like Figure 12.6.

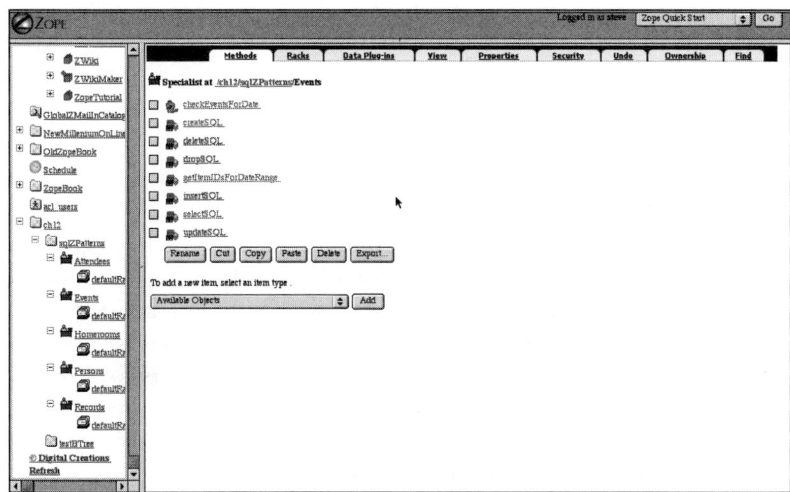

Figure 12.6 Queries and methods of the Events Specialist.

Notice that there are six fairly general queries and one specialized query. The general queries are `createSQL`, `deleteSQL`, `dropSQL`, `insertSQL`, `selectSQL`, and `updateSQL`. The one specialized query, `getItemIDsForDateRange`, makes sense only for a Specialist whose objects have some data property.

If you look at the listing of the `selectSQL` query—Listing 12.3 in the Events Specialist, for example—you will see that although it is a general function, choosing records from the database, it is specialized for the Event object class:

Listing 12.3 **ZSQLMethod *selectSQL* of the Events Specialist**

```
select eventID, name, date, homeroomID from Events_Basic
<dtml-sqlgroup where>
        <dtml-sqlgroup>
        <dtml-if eventID>
        <dtml-sqltest eventID type=string>
        </dtml-if>
        </dtml-sqlgroup>
<dtml-and>
        <dtml-sqlgroup>
        <dtml-if name>
        <dtml-sqltest name type=string>
        </dtml-if>
        </dtml-sqlgroup>
<dtml-and>
        <dtml-sqlgroup>
        <dtml-if date>
        <dtml-sqltest date type=float>
        </dtml-if>
        </dtml-sqlgroup>
<dtml-and>
        <dtml-sqlgroup>
        <dtml-if homeroomID>
        <dtml-sqltest homeroomID type=string>
        </dtml-if>
</dtml-sqlgroup>
</dtml-sqlgroup>
```

This select query takes full advantage of ZSQLMethod's capability to include extra conditions on a query, depending on the availability of qualifying arguments. If only `eventID` is defined, the query will return all records with a certain `eventID`. This query will be used a *lot* because you will need to look for particular events belonging to certain homerooms or times. Because this query is customized to query for Event records, it needs to live in the Events Specialist. If you look in every Specialist, you will see versions of these exact queries that work with the database records that represent objects of the kind managed by that Specialist.

Having a separate query object is nice because it means that you can test the query independently from the application. If you click the Test tab of the `selectSQL` ZSQLQuery object in the Events Specialist, you should see a screen with the four parameters: eventID, name, date, and homeroomID. You can leave them blank, and the query will return all the data in the Events_Basic table. If you fill in one or more of the blanks, then ZSQLQuery object will add a `where` clause to the query that filters on those parameters that you fill in, as shown in Figure 12.7.

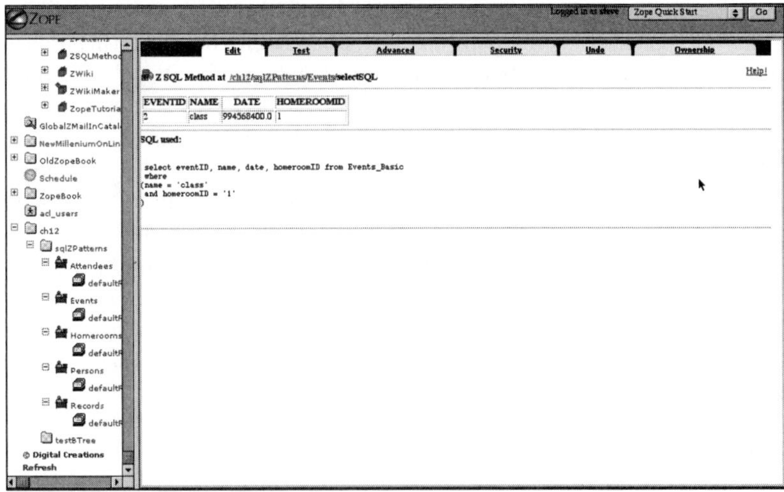


**Figure 12.7** Filtering the `selectSQL` query with parameters.

If you dig a little deeper, you will notice that there is a SkinScript PlugIn defined in the defaultRack of the Events Specialist. The PlugIn is called `dataScript`, and its purpose is to act as a set of triggers that provide attributes for existing Event objects, and also to create, delete and update records in the database as objects are changed in Zope. The SkinScript is shown in Listing 12.4.

Listing 12.4 **SkinScript to Handle Data for Events**

```
WHEN OBJECT ADDED CALL insertSQL(eventID=self.id,
 name = self.name, date = self.date.timeTime(),
 homeroomID = self.homeroomID)

WHEN OBJECT DELETED CALL deleteSQL(eventID=self.id)

WHEN OBJECT CHANGED STORE name, date, homeroomID
USING updateSQL( eventID=self.id, name = self.name,
date = self.date.timeTime(), homeroomID =
self.homeroomID)

WITH QUERY selectSQL(eventID=self.id) COMPUTE
eventID=EVENTID, name=NAME, date=ZopeTime(DATE),
homeroomID=HOMEROOMID
```

Notice in particular that this SkinScript is specialized for the Event object. Also, you can see that the SkinScript is dynamically converting between the floating-point representation of dates in Gadfly (because Gadfly has no DateTime data type) and the "native" DateTime/ZopeTime objects of Zope. Finally, notice that this is where the database fields are mapped to the object attributes.

If you poke around some more in the Specialists, you will see that in addition to the six general queries, each Specialist has a SkinScript PlugIn called dataScript in its defaultRack with similar code, but specialized to handle the correct object type for each Specialist.

Notice also that we chose to put the data-dependent SQL queries in the Specialist, while the data-dependent SkinScript was stored within the Rack. This is largely a matter of taste. In general, you should create a *data-independent* API for your Specialists that they use to communicate with one another. The Events specialist method `checkEventsForDate` presents such an API. But internally, it's okay for Specialists to use data-dependent techniques to manage their objects. Naturally, if you *change* the storage, you'll need to modify the data-dependent code. It makes sense, then, from a portability perspective, to keep the data dependent-code to a minimum and particularly isolated from the primary application logic.

### Filling in the UI/Admin Gaps

There are a lot of methods in the attendanceZPatterns folder. In general, there are three different types of objects located there, which are shown in the three tables that follow. The first group of Methods are meant to be acquired by a Specialist and used to perform a generic task, but using the Specialized generic queries in that particular Specialist. These include the methods listed in Table 12.1.

Table 12.1 **Generic Methods**

| Method | Description |
|---|---|
| `createNewItem` | Creates a new instance for a Specialist. Sets new properties according to REQUEST. |
| `createNewItemForm` | Displays a form to call `createNewItem` calls `displayInsertForm_html` to render form fields. |
| `createNewItem_html` | UI that calls `createNewItem`. |
| `createNewNumericID` | For Specialists who just have simple numeric IDs, finds a new unused one. |
| `deleteSelectedItems` | Deletes items in `ids`. |
| `deleteSelectedItems_html` | UI for `deleteSelectedItems`. |
| `displayInsertForm_html` | Displays form fields for insert. |

| Method | Description |
|---|---|
| `displayUpdateForm_html` | Displays form to update existing record. |
| `getAttributeList` | Gets list of attributes for this Specialists. |
| `getItemIds` | Performs a query to find Ids that match conditions. |
| `index_html` | Either redirects to `display_app` or calls `quickDisplay`. |
| `quickDisplay_html` | Displays admin UI for objects in the Specialist. |
| `updateItem` | Actually updates an item based on REQUEST. |
| `updateItem_html` | UI for updateItem. |

Next is a Method that is meant to display something from the context of the attendanceZPatterns folder (see Table 12.2).

Table 12.2 **Default Display Method**

| Method | Description |
|---|---|
| `display_app_html` | Main app display page |

The third group is Housekeeping methods that are used to manage all the specialized general queries and SkinScript used by the various Specialists, as well as creation and dropping of database tables (see Table 12.3).

Table 12.3 **Housekeeping Methods**

| Method | Description |
|---|---|
| `createSQLLever` | Lever to generate `createSQL` |
| `deleteSQLLever` | Lever to generate `deleteSQL` |
| `dropAllTables_html` | Drops all database tables |
| `insertSQLLever` | Lever to generation `insertSQL` |
| `dropSQLLever` | Lever to generation `dropSQL` |
| `runAllLevers` | Runs all the levers |
| `runLever` | Runs a particular lever |
| `selectSQLLever` | Lever to generation `selectSQL` |
| `skinScriptLever` | Lever to generation `dataScript` |
| `updateSQLLever` | Lever to generation updateSQL |

Methods in Table 12.1 allow you to have a very crude but functional administrative UI without having to specifically code it for each Specialist. For example, `createNewItem` is a method that creates a new item in any of the Specialists, as shown in Listing 12.5.

Listing 12.5 ***CreateNewItem* Is a General Instance-Creation Method**

```
newID = context.REQUEST.get('id',context.createNewNumericID())
newItem = context.newItem(newID)
newItem.propertysheets.Basic.manage_changeProperties(context.REQUEST)

return newItem
```

As you can see, `CreateNewItem` doesn't specifically refer to any particular object type. Because it uses `context.newItem()`, it can be acquired by any Specialist and used to create new items for that Specialist. The other members of the generic methods (see Table 12.1) work the same way so that you can create, edit, and delete the basic objects in all the Specialists using a crude "one size fits all" UI. You would never want to subject a normal user to this UI, but it is enough to allow you to navigate and modify various objects and to experiment with the application design.

The Housekeeping Methods (see Table 12.3) also deserve special comment. These are a group of methods that might collectively be called "a lever." These methods are used to automatically build default queries and SkinScript for the various Specialists. They base all their output on the propertysheets used by the ZClasses. The basic assumption is that all the ZClasses have a single propertysheet called Basic and that each property will be represented in the database by a field. Each class belongs to a Specialist, and for each Specialist there is a Table. A "lever" snoops through the properties of a fabricated instance and generates the SQL or SkinScript to operate with objects with those properties. For example, Listings 12.3 and 12.4 were actually generated using the selectSQLLever and the dataSkinLever shown in Listings 12.6 and 12.7. These levers normally are created on an application-by-application basis. Someday, it may be that a "General Purpose Super Lever" is created, but while the rest of us need to get work done, this idea is still quite powerful, if not totally elegant.

Listing 12.6 **Python Script: selectSQLLever to Create *selectSQL* ZSQLQuery**

```
## Script (Python) "selectSQLLever"
##bind container=container
##bind context=context
##bind namespace=
##bind script=script
##bind subpath=traverse_subpath
##parameters=primaryKey='', sqlName='selectSQL', dbName='testDB'
##title=
##
#
# Python Script to create "select" type ZSQLMethods
#
# First create an 'example' instance of our ZClass
#

import string
newObj = context.newItem('foobie' + `container.idCount`)
```

```
#
# increment idCount property of container to avoid ConflictError when
# running this lever multiple times in a single transaction
#
container.manage_changeProperties(idCount = container.idCount + 1)
#
# Map between Zope and DB types
#
typeMap = {'string':'string', 'date':'float'}
#
# if there is no primary key assigned, make something up
#
if not primaryKey:
    primaryKey = string.lower(context.id[:-1]) + 'ID'
#
# initialize the lists of arguments, and conditional variables, and the
➥template
#
argumentList = ['%s=""' % primaryKey]
itemList = [primaryKey]
typeList = ['string']
templateString = ''
#
# go through the propertysheets of the ZClass and add to the lists the
# appropriate thing for each property we see.
#
for item_pair in newObj.propertysheets.items():
    if item_pair[0] != 'webdav':
        name, ps_value = item_pair
        pm = ps_value.propertyMap()
        templateString = templateString + "\n select "
        for item in pm:
            itemList.append(item['id'])
            typeList.append(item['type'])
            argumentList.append('%s=""' % item['id'])
```

*continues*

Listing 12.6 **Continued**

```

        templateString = templateString + string.join(itemList,', ')

#
#  Zap the 'example' instance.
#
newObj.manage_delete()

#
# create the argument string
#

argumentString = string.join(argumentList,' ')

#
# create templates for the "where" clause, and "groups". Initialize the "whereList"
#

whereClause = """
<dtml-sqlgroup where>
%s
</dtml-sqlgroup>
"""

simpleGroup = """
<dtml-sqlgroup>
<dtml-if %s>
<dtml-sqltest %s type=%s>
</dtml-if>
</dtml-sqlgroup>
"""

whereList = []

#
# iterate through the itemList, mapping the type, and building the "where" clause.
#

for i in range(len(itemList)):
    item = itemList[i]
    theType = typeMap.get(typeList[i],'string')

    whereList.append( simpleGroup % (item, item, theType))

whereTemplate = string.join(whereList,'<dtml-and>')

templateString = templateString + " from %s_%s " % (context.id, name)
```

```

templateString = templateString + whereClause % whereTemplate

#
# The text of the ZSQLMethod is now in the templateString. So create it!
#

if not hasattr(context,sqlName):
    fc = context.manage_addProduct['ZSQLMethods']
    fc.add.manage_addZSQLMethod(sqlName,'', connection_id=dbName,
    ➥arguments=argumentString, template=templateString)

else:
    theSQL = getattr(context, sqlName)
    theSQL.manage_edit( '', connection_id=dbName, arguments=argumentString,
    ➥template=templateString)

#
# We're finished.
#

return "OK"
```

Notice that the query automatically is generated with the correct types based on the types in the propertysheet of the corresponding ZClass. All the levers also have an `if` statement at the end that checks to see if a ZSQLMethod of the right name is already in existence or needs to be created as new object. Listing 12.7 shows that the same idea can be applied to generating SkinScript methods. This lever is not as thoroughly commented because the pattern is almost identical to Listing 12.6.

Listing 12.7 **Python Script: skinScriptLever to create *dataScript***

```
## Script (Python) "skinScriptLever"
##bind container=container
##bind context=context
##bind namespace=
##bind script=script
##bind subpath=traverse_subpath
##parameters=primaryKey='', skinName='dataScript', rackName='defaultRack'
##title=
##
import string
newObj = context.newItem('foobie' + `container.idCount`) # create a bogus temp
➥instance..
container.manage_changeProperties(idCount = container.idCount + 1)

if not primaryKey:
    primaryKey = string.lower(context.id[:-1]) + 'ID'

addedString = 'WHEN OBJECT ADDED CALL insertSQL('
```

*continues*

Listing 12.7 **Continued**

```
deletedString = 'WHEN OBJECT DELETED CALL deleteSQL(%s=self.id)' % primaryKey
changedString = 'WHEN OBJECT CHANGED STORE '
computeString = 'WITH QUERY selectSQL(%s=self.id) COMPUTE ' % primaryKey

computeList = ["%s=%s" % (primaryKey, string.upper(primaryKey))]
saveList = ["%s=self.id" % primaryKey]
storeList = []

for item_pair in newObj.propertysheets.items():

    if item_pair[0] != 'webdav':
        name, ps_value = item_pair

        pm = ps_value.propertyMap()


        for item in pm:
            if item['type'] == 'date':
                saveList.append("%s = self.%s.timeTime()" % (item['id'],
                ➥item['id']))
                computeList.append("%s=ZopeTime(%s)" % (item['id'],
                ➥string.upper(item['id'])))
                storeList.append(item['id'])
            else:
                saveList.append("%s = self.%s" % (item['id'], item['id']))
                computeList.append("%s=%s" % (item['id'],
                ➥string.upper(item['id'])))
                storeList.append(item['id'])

changedString = changedString + string.join(storeList, ', ') +
                     ' USING updateSQL( ' + string.join(saveList,', ') + ') '
computeString = computeString + string.join(computeList, ', ')
addedString = addedString + string.join(saveList,', ') + ') '

newObj.manage_delete()

if not hasattr(getattr(context,rackName),skinName):
    fc = getattr(context,rackName).manage_addProduct['ZPatterns']
    fc.manage_addSSMethod(skinName,'')

theScript = getattr(getattr(context,rackName), skinName)
theScript.manage_edit( title='', text=addedString + '\n\n' +
                                deletedString + '\n\n' +
                                changedString + '\n\n' +
                                computeString + '\n\n')

return "OK!"
```

Notice that this lever creates a SkinScript PlugIn that automatically converts dates to and from floats so that Gadfly (with no DateTime datatype) can work with Zope objects with `date` attributes.

So, when the smoke clears, you can see that 90% of the methods in this application are *shared* by all the Specialists either to *use* in the course of the application or as building blocks to generate specific methods that are based on the properties of the ZClasses that implement the core classes of the application.

There are still some custom methods that need to be hand-coded to make the application work. These are methods that can't be automatically generated from a propertysheet but that are related to the internal logic of the problem domain. These are where the real dynamics of the object model come into play. A good example of one of these is `getStudentIDsForHomeroom`, shown in Listing 12.8.

Listing 12.8 **Python Script: *getStudentIDsForHomeroom***

```
## Script (Python) "getStudentIDsForHomeroom"
##bind container=container
##bind context=context
##bind namespace=
##bind script=script
##bind subpath=traverse_subpath
##parameters=homeroomID
##title=
##
conditions = {}
conditions['homeroomID'] = homeroomID
conditions['courseRole'] = 'student'

return container.getItemIds(conditions=conditions)
```

The good news about a method like this is that it can leverage the ubiquitous `getItemIds()` to select only the attendees who both are students and belong to the given homeroom. Another that requires problem domain logic is the Events Specialists `checkEventsForDate`, shown in Listing 12.9, which is used to create new Events, if necessary, and check for existing events, if not:

Listing 12.9 **Python Script *checkEventsForDate* Creates a New Event, If Necessary**

```
## Script (Python) "checkEventsForDate"
##bind container=container
##bind context=context
##bind namespace=
##bind script=script
##bind subpath=traverse_subpath
##parameters=timeToCheck, homeroomID
##title=
##
if same_type(timeToCheck, 0.0):
```

*continues*

Listing 12.9 **Continued**

```
    timeToCheck = DateTime(timeToCheck)

early = timeToCheck.earliestTime().timeTime()
late =  timeToCheck.latestTime().timeTime()

results = container.getItemIDsForDateRange(early=early,
                      late=late, homeroomID=homeroomID)

resultList = []

for item in results:
    resultList.append(item.EVENTID)

if len(resultList)==0:
    newID = container.createNewNumericID()
    newEvent = container.newItem(newID)
    newEvent.propertysheets.Basic.manage_changeProperties(
        homeroomID=homeroomID, date=timeToCheck.earliestTime(), name='class')
    resultList = [newID]

return resultList
```

The last clause in `checkEventsForDate` checks to see whether there were any dates in the checked range. If there were not, the method creates a new Event in the right range and returns its ID.

There is really only one other thing to discuss with this application, and that's the display method that renders the current attendance of a particular homeroom. Although we won't be able to discuss every line of this page, it's worth hitting some of the highlights. The method in question is the `index_html` method of the Homeroom class shown in Listing 12.10 (/Control_Panel/Products/AttendanceProducts/AttendanceHomeroom/).

Listing 12.10 **Display Method for a Homeroom Object**

```
<dtml-var standard_html_header>
<div align="center">
<h1>Homeroom &dtml-roomNumber; (&dtml-roomInfo;)</h1>

<dtml-call "REQUEST.set('attendanceDate',ZopeTime(REQUEST.get
➥('attendanceDate',ZopeTime().timeTime())))">

Attendance for Date: <dtml-var attendanceDate fmt="%m/%d/%Y"><br><br>

<dtml-let homeroomID=id
        studentIDs="Attendees.getStudentIDsForHomeroom(id)"
        instructorIDs="Attendees.getTeacherIDsForHomeroom(id)"
        eventIDs="Events.checkEventsForDate(attendanceDate.timeTime(), id)">
<h2>Instructors:</h2>
```

```
<dtml-in instructorIDs>
<dtml-let    theId=sequence-item
            theInstructor="Attendees.getItem(theId)"
            thePerson="Persons.getItem(theInstructor.personID)">
Name:    <dtml-if thePerson>
            <dtml-var "thePerson.firstName">, <dtml-var "thePerson.lastName">
        <dtml-else>
            <dtml-var theId>
        </dtml-if>
</dtml-let>
</dtml-in>
<br><br>
<dtml-in eventIDs>
    <dtml-let    eventID=sequence-item
                theEvent="Events.getItem(eventID)">
        <h2>Students for <dtml-var "theEvent.name"> on <dtml-var
        ➥"theEvent.date" fmt="%m/%d/%Y"></h2>
        <dtml-in studentIDs>
        <dtml-if sequence-start>
        <table border=1 cellpadding=2 cellspacing=2>
        <tr><th>Name</th><th>Status</th><th>Arrival Time</th></tr>
        </dtml-if>
            <dtml-let    theId=sequence-item
                        theStudent="Attendees.getItem(theId)"
                        thePerson="Persons.getItem(theStudent.personID)">
            <tr><td>     <dtml-if thePerson>
                        <dtml-var "thePerson.lastName">, <dtml-var
                        ➥"thePerson.firstName">
                    <dtml-else>
                        <dtml-var theId>
                    </dtml-if></td>

                    <dtml-in "Records.getRecordIDsForEventAttendee
                    ➥(eventID=eventID, attendeeID=theId)" sort>
                        <dtml-let    theRecordID=sequence-item
                                    theRecord="Records.getItem(theRecordID)">

                            <dtml-if "theRecord.attendanceStatus == 'OK'">
                               <td bgcolor="#ccffcc">
                            <dtml-else>
                               <td bgcolor="#ffcccc">
                            </dtml-if>

                                <dtml-var "theRecord.attendanceStatus">

                            </td>

                            <dtml-if "theRecord.attendanceStatus == 'OK'">
                                <td>On Time</td>
                            <dtml-else>
```

*continues*

Listing 12.10 **Continued**

```
               <td><dtml-var "theRecord.arrivalTime" null="N/A"
              ➥fmt="%I:%M %p"></td>
              </dtml-if>
              </tr>
            </dtml-let>
          <dtml-else>
            <td colspan="2">
              <form action="<dtml-var "Records.absolute_url()">/
              ➥createNewAttendanceRecord_html" method="POST">
              Status:
                <select name="attendanceStatus">
                  <option value="OK">OK</option>
                  <option value="Late">Late</option>
                  <option value="Absent">Absent</option>
                </select><br>
              Arrival Time = <input name="arrivalTime:date"
              ➥value="<dtml-var "ZopeTime()">"><br>
              <input type="hidden" name="eventID" value="&dtml-
              ➥eventID;">
              <input type="hidden" name="attendeeID"
              ➥value="&dtml-theId;">
              <input type="hidden" value="<dtml-var URL1>"
              ➥name="backURL">
              <input type="submit" value="Set Attenance">
              </form></td>
            </tr>
          </dtml-in>
      </dtml-let>
      <dtml-if sequence-end>
      </table>
      </dtml-if>
    </dtml-in>
  </dtml-let>
</dtml-in>

</dtml-let>
</div>

<dtml-var standard_html_footer>
```

There are a few things that are especially worth noting in this method:

- You can use methods from other Specialists by simply invoking their name in the method: `Attendees.getStudentIDsForHomeroom()`.
- If no Event is found for the date/homeroom, then a new Event object is automatically created.
- If no Record is found for a student, a form is supplied whose action will create a Record with the attendance details filled in.

- If a Record object *is* found, it is used to display the attendance details for that student, including color coding so that absences are easy to spot.

In summary, when the object model is defined and the ZClasses are in place, most of the work of generating this application is done by levers that automatically create queries and SkinScript to manage the object-database mapping. After that is finished, the problem domain logic can be focused on a relatively small number of methods. You'll use the same basic approach in the next application, although you'll have different classes.

## A Complete Example: Are You Hungry? (Lunch)

This application deals with keeping track of which students ordered which lunch on which days with what sort of payment. The basic mechanics of this application are the same as those of the attendance application, except that you will be using a filesystem-based product to illustrate how you can get even more control over the inner workings of your application.

You can find get the Zope objects for this example from the companion web site (**`http://webdev.zopeonarope.com`** or **`http://www.newriders.com`**) or from the Zope site (**`http://www.zope.org/Members/sspickle`**). You should get and install these objects in a Zope of your own so that you can follow along with this example. Note that this example uses a Python product (LunchBase) and that this needs to be installed on the filesystem. Zope must be restarted for the Python product to be recognized by Zope. Next, you need to put the LunchProducts.zexp (the ZClass definitions) into your Import folder and then import the ZClasses into your Control_Panel/Products area. Finally, put lunchZPatterns.zexp into your Imports folder and import it to a "test" area in your Zope (any folder should work).

### Setting Up the Object Model

The lunch application object model has some clear similarity with the attendance application. You still have Attendees, Person, and Homeroom classes. But there are no Events or Records. Now you have new classes:

- Lunch (a lunch that occurs on a particular date)
- LunchItem (something on the menu of a particular lunch)
- LunchItemContent (a component of a lunch, such as milk)
- Subscription (a student signs up for a lunch)
- Payment (a possibly partial payment for a lunch)

These are related to one another as shown in Figure 12.8.

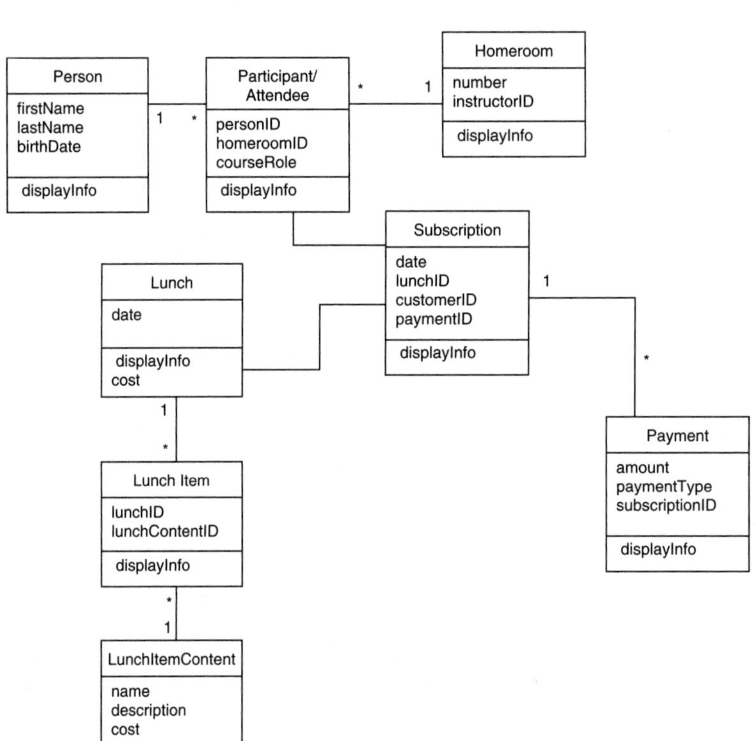


**Figure 12.8** Lunch application object model.

## Implementing the Model with Specialists

To keep things simple and allow your levers/shared code to work easily, you'll simply implement one Specialist for each of these classes. You're going to implement the Lunch object as a filesystem-based product. This will be an opportunity for you to see how a filesystem-based product can be used in a ZPatterns application.

The Lunch object doesn't have a `cost` attribute, but rather a `cost` method. This method will need to iterate over the lunch items in the lunch and calculate a cost based on that. With Zope, you can use Python to do the things that Python does best: logic and dynamic properties. You can use ZClasses to do the things that ZClasses do best: maintain TTW UI and property management. Using this strategy, you'll implement a LunchBase class as a filesystem product and subclass from that to form a ZClass Lunch that you'll use as the storage class for the `Lunchs` Specialist. (`Lunchs` is deliberately misspelled to match the naming convention used by the various levers.)

The complete source of the LunchBase class is shown in Listing 12.11.

Listing 12.11 **Lunch Base Source File**

```
#
# LunchBase
#

from OFS import SimpleItem

__doc__ = "A LunchBase"
__version__ = '0.0.1'

class LunchBase(SimpleItem.Item):

    "Simple Lunch Base Class"

    meta_type = 'LunchBase'

    def index_html(self):
        "display yourself to the world"
        return '<html><body>I am a LunchBase</body></html>'

    def cost(self):
        """ calculate the cost of yourself.. """

        totalCost = 0.0
        for lic in self.LunchItems.getLunchItemContentsForLunch( self ):
            totalCost = totalCost + lic.cost

        return totalCost

def initialize(context):
    context.registerBaseClass(LunchBase)
```

As you can see, it's quite simple. The good news about being defined on the filesystem is that developers can use "conventional" development tools and methodologies to test, edit, and control the object(s) source code. The only nontrivial method defined in this class is the `cost` method. It simply adds the cost attributes of all the LunchItemContent objects associated with this particular lunch. You can see the `cost` method being called by creating a Lunch object and associated LunchItems and LunchItemsContents. Then display the lunch by clicking the View tab of the lunchZPatterns folder. The last section of this chapter describes the process of creating Python-based products in much greater detail, if you're interested.

### Filling in the UI/Admin Gaps

Because you're using the same strategy with shared admin UI methods and levers as you used in the attendance application, there is little new to discuss with the lunch application. Of course, if you want to finish this application, you would need to add some custom queries and methods (such as `getPaymentsForCustomer` and `getSubscriptionsForLunchID`), but most of these can be made with simple customizations of `getItemIds`. The truly amazing thing about this application is that you can throw it together with shared methods and levers, and have something more or less blinking its eyes in a day!

## Integration of Two Separate Apps

Now you have two separate applications for attendance and lunch. How can you make these two applications work together? You're lucky that they are so similar! They can share the homeroom and person objects more or less directly. You can use the `theRealThing` trick from earlier in this chapter (see Listing 12.1), or, because they are *so* similar, you could just use the same table in the same database.

### Deciding How to Integrate

The first objective is to create a combined object model. Such a combination is shown in Figure 12.9.

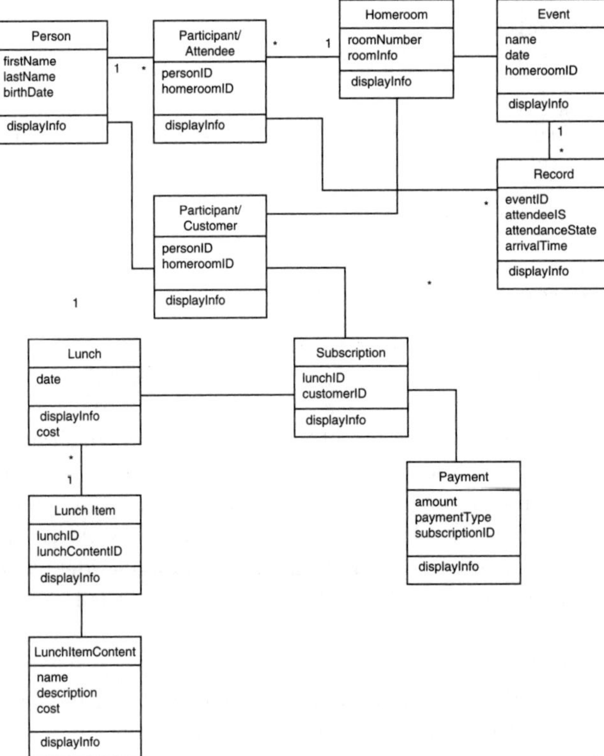


**Figure 12.9** Combined object model.

As you can see, this new model is basically a natural combination of the two separate object models. Because the Person and Homeroom classes are exactly the same in the two applications, they are used unchanged. There are two participant classes: Customer for the lunch application, and Attendee for the attendance application. It makes sense to keep these separate because there might be data related to lunch that's not relevant to attendance. Also, not all students participate in lunch, while attendance is required to have the status of student to begin with!

Storage of data is another question. Are there two databases already? Should the data be shared, or should you keep two separate databases in sync? Generally, keeping data sources, such as two separate databases, synchronized is very difficult. Other applications may be created that use one of the data sources, and they might not know (or care) about your synchronization issue. If they make a change that is not synchronized, all of your careful programming will be for nothing. If at all possible, you should use a single database for each attribute in the system. It doesn't mean that participants and persons have to come from the same database, or even that lastName and birthDate need to come from the same database! However, birthDate for an individual should be stored only in one place. All other applications that use that information should get (and set) it from (or to) that single data source.

There's another trade-off that should be mentioned before finishing this chapter. Usually when two applications are integrated, one application becomes the "host" and the other becomes the "guest." For example, you could make the attendance application the "host" and modify its UI to allow parts of the lunch application to "bleed" through, such as a link in the Homeroom view of the attendance application that allows the teacher to handle lunch preferences, or possibly even inline with the attendance display. Depending on how much work you want to do, you can move the nonoverlapping Specialists into the same application folder with the attendance application, or you can keep them separate and use Zope's acquisition machinery to get to them. The difference is mostly one of style. By keeping them separate, you can be sure not to pollute the acquisition namespace with objects that you don't know about, but you will have to do more typing to hook things up.

If you move both applications Specialists into the same combined application folder, you can type things like this:

```
<dtml-in "Lunchs.getItemIds(conditions={'date':today})">

... display the lunches..

</dtml-in>
```

while keeping the applications separate results in code, like this:

```
<dtml-in "LunchApp.Lunchs.getItemIds(conditions={'date':today})">

... display the lunches..

</dtml-in>
```

Generally, moving the applications together results in simpler code and fewer scope problems, while keeping them apart reduces the risk of accidentally acquiring the "wrong" method. If you keep them separate, you will also have two Persons Specialists, one for each applications. You need to be especially careful here that your Persons ultimately talk to the same database. This can be done by using the `theRealThing` trick from Listing 12.1, by using a shared database, or by modifying the methods and SkinScript of the Rack to refer to the other application's Specialist for database querying. This is a useful approach, so we'll show it in more detail. Try this: Delete all the queries from the lunch application's Persons Specialist (to be sure that you don't accidentally acquire the wrong query), and change the SkinScript as shown in Listing 12.12.

Listing 12.12 **Modified SkinScript to Defer to Attendance Persons Specialist**

```
WHEN OBJECT ADDED CALL
      attendanceZPatterns.Persons.insertSQL(personID=self.id,
      firstName = self.firstName, lastName =
      self.lastName, birthDate =
      self.birthDate.timeTime())

WHEN OBJECT DELETED CALL
      attendanceZPatterns.Persons.deleteSQL(personID=self.id)

WHEN OBJECT CHANGED STORE firstName, lastName,
      birthDate USING attendanceZPatterns.Persons.updateSQL(
      personID=self.id, firstName = self.firstName,
      lastName = self.lastName, birthDate =
      self.birthDate.timeTime())

WITH QUERY
      attendanceZPatterns.Persons.selectSQL(personID=self.id)
      COMPUTE personID=PERSONID, firstName=FIRSTNAME,
      lastName=LASTNAME, birthDate=ZopeTime(BIRTHDATE)
```

You can see that all we've done is to use acquisition to refer to the ZSQLQuery objects in the Attendance Specialist rather than our own (because we just deleted all our own!). This way, if you move the data for Persons to a different database, you will need to change the attendance application to talk to the new database, but the lunch application uses the Persons Specialist to get its Person objects, so it's okay. Notice that this also frees you to make a LunchPerson with different methods and appearance from an AttendancePerson, but they ultimately depend on the same data source. Unfortunately, changing SkinScript alone won't work. You've been using `getItemIds` a lot, and it assumes that each Specialist has ZSQLMethods with standard names to query the database. Because the lunch application's Persons Specialist no longer has these queries, `getItemIds` won't work anymore. Solution? Let's create a custom `getItemIds` that is contained in the lunch application's Persons Specialist that knows about deference to the other application's Persons Specialist, as shown in Listing 12.13.

Listing 12.13 **Customized *getItemIds* Knows About Attendance Application**

```
## Script (Python) "getItemIds"
##bind container=container
##bind context=context
##bind namespace=
##bind script=script
##bind subpath=traverse_subpath
##parameters=primaryKey='', conditions=''
##title=
##
import string

if not primaryKey:
        primaryKey = string.lower(context.id[:-1]) + 'ID'

theIDs = []

if conditions == '':
      conditions = context.REQUEST


for result in context.attendanceZPatterns.Persons.selectSQL(REQUEST =
➥conditions):
      theIDs.append(getattr(result, string.upper(primaryKey)))

return theIDs
```

Because all the other methods that you use to manage or list Persons use `getItemIds`, the rest of the application works as expected. Note that you have two applications that were originally separate but that now work together. It's true that they were fairly similar to begin with, and that made your job easier. But it's also true that they could've been much different, and you could still manage to get them to cooperate (as shown in the first example of this chapter). The main point is that ZPatterns allows you the flexibility to blend applications at the lowest level, with relatively little impact on higher-level logic and processes. This is a tremendously powerful tool that can be brought to bear on many kinds of legacy or externally imposed data-oriented problems.

# An Example Python Filesystem-Based Product

You've seen that you can create complete applications using Through the Web (TTW) ZClasses with Scripts and DTML Methods. Sometimes there are good reasons to create objects on the filesystem. These objects are sometimes called Python objects because they are defined in Python source files stored on the filesystem of the Zope server rather than in persistent ZODB storage. This case study takes you step by step through the process of creating a simple filesystem-based Zope product.

Your filesystem-based product will be defined here:

```
$ZOPEHOME/lib/python/Products/
```

Let's call the new Product TotallySimpleProduct. You'll start out as simple as we can make it and get a little more sophisticated as you go. Create a directory in Products called TotallySimpleProduct. In the directory, create a file called TotallySimpleProduct.py. First look at the entire file shown in Listing 12.11, and then you can follow as we explain each bit.

Listing 12.14 **Complete Source to TotallySimpleProduct.py**

```
#
# TotallySimpleProduct
#

from OFS import SimpleItem
from Globals import HTMLFile

def manage_addTotallySimpleProduct(self, id=None, REQUEST=None):
    "Add a TotallySimpleProduct."
    self._setObject(id, TotallySimpleProduct(id))

    if REQUEST:
        return self.manage_main(self, REQUEST, update_menu=1)

manage_addTotallySimpleProductForm = HTMLFile('addInstance',globals())

__doc__ = "A TotallySimpleProduct"
__version__ = '0.0.1'

class TotallySimpleProduct(SimpleItem.SimpleItem ):

    "Totally Simple Product"

    meta_type = 'TotallySimpleProduct'
    message = 'Hello World!'

    manage_options = ( {'label': 'Properties', 'action': 'manage_main'},
                       {'label': 'View', 'action': 'index_html'},
                     )

    def __init__(self, id):
        "Set the id of the TotallySimpleProduct"
        self.id = id

    def index_html(self):
        "display yourself to the world"
        format = '<html><body>I am a TotallySimpleProduct<br><br>My message is
        ➥"%s".</body></html>'
        return format % self.message

    manage_main=HTMLFile('editPropertiesForm',globals())

```

```
42      def manage_edit(self, message, REQUEST=None):
43          """ edit the message.. """
44          self.message = message
45          if REQUEST:
46              message="Saved changes."
47              return self.manage_main(self,REQUEST,manage_tabs_message=message)
48
49  def initialize(context):
50      context.registerClass(
51          TotallySimpleProduct,
52          constructors=(manage_addTotallySimpleProductForm,
            ➥manage_addTotallySimpleProduct),
53          icon='TotallySimpleProduct.gif',
54          )
```

That's basically it. Now we'll explain each part of this file before we go on to discuss the other support files that make up this very simple product.

The first element in the file, lines 01–03, is an optional comment to document the name/purpose of the product. In this case, it's pretty self-explanatory.

Next, in line 05, import the SimpleItem base class from which you will subclass your new Product. You will need some DTML-based objects to provide a simple UI to add new instances of TotallySimpleObject. You can use the HTMLFile class, imported on line 06, to create these instances.

You need to define a constructor that will create new instances of TotallySimpleObject and add them to a folder. This allows an application integrator/installer to create TotallySimpleProduct instances from the ZMI programmatically. Notice from lines 08–14 of Listing 12.14 that `manage_addTotallySimpleProduct` takes a folder as its first argument. It creates a new TotallySimpleProduct and adds it (using the `_setObject` method of the folder). It then checks to see if REQUEST is `None`. If it's *not* `None`, this means that it was called through the ZMI (as the target of the add form) and that it should return a UI but with an indication that the add was successful.

You need to create an instance of the HTML form for the ZMI to create instances of the Product—see line 15 of Listing 12.14. HTMLFile is a constructor that gets a file from the filesystem—addInstance.dtml, in this case—and loads it into a DTML Method object stored in the current Python context; in this case, that's a variable called `manage_addTotallySimpleProductForm` in the Python module TotallySimpleProduct.py. The same constructor, HTMLFile, is used to create the `manage_main` method in line 40.

__doc__ and __version__ are set on lines 17 and 18, and are used by Zope to display this information in the ZMI.

Finally, you need to define the actual TotallySimpleProduct class. If you are familiar with object-oriented programming in Python, then this will look familiar. First, on line 20, we are subclassing the SimpleItem class, which is a good base class for non–folderish objects in Zope (anything that doesn't need to "contain" any other objects as subobjects).

The class variable `meta_type`, set on line 24, needs to be unique in Zope because it is used by containers to decide what sort of object this is. The class variable `message` is set on line 25 to a default value for all instances.

**For More Information**

Persistence with Python filesystem-based products is a little tricky. There is a great reference in the Zope developers guide, at **`http://www.zope.org/Documentation/ZDG/Persistence.dtml`**.

The main issue is that if an object has a mutable attribute (such as a list) then, for the persistence machinery to work properly, that variable must be handled *as if it were immutable* so that the storage of the changed value can be detected by the Persistence base class. Normally, when you need to append to a list for example, you might just do something like this:

```
def push(self, value):
    self.aList.append(value)
```

However, if this is a method of a persistent object, it's best to treat the list as if it were an immutable attribute:

```
def push(self, value):
    l = self.aList
    l.append(value)
    self.aList = l
```

Note especially that it's the assignment at the end of this method that triggers the persistence machinery to save the new state of the `aList` attribute.

`manage_options` is similar to Views in a ZClass. It defines the label and action of the management tabs in the ZMI in lines 27–29 of Listing 12.14.

If you are familiar with Python classes, you will recognize lines 31–33 as a simple Python constructor. Note that the attribute `id` is not optional. Zope uses the `id` attribute of Zope objects to look them up in their container. No two objects in a single container can have the same value for their `id` attribute.

Any object with an `index_html` method, in lines 35–38 of Listing 12.14, can be displayed. This is the default display for objects of this type.

You will want an interface for editing this sort of object. In `manage_options`, it was called `manage_main`. On line 40 it is defined as an HTMLFile pulled from the file system when the Product is initialized.

Lines 42–47 implement a method that actually edits the properties of the object: `manage_edit`.

Notice that there is a strong similarity here between the constructor and the edit method in that REQUEST is checked; if it is not `None`, a UI is returned.

Finally, there is a "module-level" definition of `initialize` in lines 49–50. The idea of a "module-level" implementation is that this method needs to run to register the existence of these Products to Zope even if there is no instance defined. Like the factory, this needs to be defined outside of the class definition of TotallySimpleProduct.py.

Notice that the indention of `initialize` is such that it is not included as a method of a TotallySimpleProduct class, but of the TotallySimpleProduct module.

All of the other support files need to be placed in the TotallySimpleProduct folder, in the $ZOPEHOME/lib/python/Products folder of your Zope instance. There are a few other files as well. Listing 12.15 shows the __init__.py file:

Listing 12.15 **Initializer __init__.py for TotallySimpleProduct**

```
import TotallySimpleProduct

__doc__ = TotallySimpleProduct.__doc__
__version__ = TotallySimpleProduct.__version__

def initialize(context):
    TotallySimpleProduct.initialize(context)
```

This pulls __doc__ and __version__ from the TotallySimpleProduct.py file, as well as forwards the initialize call (when Zope handles Product registration at startup) to the method of the same name. Listing 12.16 shows the addInstance.dtml file, which defines the source for the form to add TotallySimpleProduct instances in the ZMI.

Listing 12.16 **addInstanceForm.dtml for Adding Instances in ZMI**

```
<!DOCTYPE HTML PUBLIC "-//W3C//DTD HTML 4.0 Transitional//EN"
➥"http://www.w3.org/TR/REC-html40/loose.dtd">
<HTML lang="en">
<HEAD>
<TITLE>Add TotallySimpleProduct</TITLE>
</HEAD>
<BODY BGCOLOR="#FFFFFF">
<H2>Add TotallySimpleProduct</H2>

<FORM ACTION="manage_addTotallySimpleProduct" METHOD="POST">
<TABLE CELLSPACING="2">
<TR>
  <TD ALIGN="LEFT" VALIGN="TOP">
  <STRONG>Id</STRONG>
  </TD>
  <TD ALIGN="LEFT" VALIGN="TOP">
  <INPUT TYPE="TEXT" NAME="id" SIZE="40" VALUE="">
  </TD>
</TR>
<TR>
<TD></TD>
<TD>
<BR><INPUT TYPE="SUBMIT" VALUE=" Add ">
</TD>
</TR>
</TABLE>
</FORM>
</BODY>
</HTML>
```

Finally, editPropertiesForm.dtml is shown in Listing 12.17.

Listing 12.17 **editPropertiesForm.dtml for Editing Instances in the ZMI**

```
<html><body>
<dtml-var manage_tabs>
<form action="manage_edit" method="post">
<table cellspacing="0" cellpadding="2" border="0">
  <tr>
      <td>Id</td>
      <td> &dtml-id; </td>
  </tr>
  <tr>
      <td>Message</td>
      <td><input name="message" value="&dtml-message;"></td>
  </tr>
  <tr><td align="center" colspan="2"><input type="submit" value="Save
  ➥Changes"></td></tr>
</table>
</form>
</html>
```

This is the form for the Properties tab of the ZMI interface for TotallySimpleProduct instances. Notice that every aspect of a Product can be defined in filesystem-based Python files. We haven't included the security system in this example, but there are good examples of that on the Zope site, as well as the Zope Developers Guide, if you need to create more sophisticated filesystem-based products.

If you need to create only a ZClass base class, you can dispense with these UI type files and create only the Python files and a simpler registration. You can see an example of this in the LunchBase class used in the lunch application.

# Summary

In this chapter, you've seen many of the powerful features of ZPatterns applied to the problem of application integration. You've seen how one application can be embedded in another after the first is "finished." You also saw how object models can be merged and several different strategies for making what were originally separate applications work together using shared resources.

# 13

# User Management: Interfacing with External Systems

AT THIS POINT, YOU'VE DEVELOPED a number of Zope applications involving multiple object types that get at least some of their data from "outside" sources. This chapter introduces a new Zope product, LoginManager, that uses the same ZPatterns technology applied to the singular task of managing a special class of objects called User Objects. User Objects deserve special attention in Zope because the security system and User Objects interact strongly. Of course, Zope comes with a built-in class for User Objects, but these objects have no other function than to authenticate users and, when authenticated, to provide users with certain default roles and allowed domains from which they can access Zope. LoginManager uses ZPatterns to allow essentially arbitrary generation of User Objects based on any available source of relevant information (for example, LDAP, /etc/passwd, SQL datbases, and so on).

**Getting LoginManager**

LoginManager is available at **www.zope.org** and on the companion web sites (**http://webdev.zopeonarope.com** and **http://www.newriders.com**). As of this writing the most recent version is LoginManager 0.8.8 beta 1, which works with versions of Zope up to 2.3.3. Later versions of Zope currently need patches from the ZPatterns mailing list (**http://www.eby-sarna.com**), but it seems pretty clear that 2.4.*x*–compatible versions of ZPatterns and LoginManager will be published soon. When compatible versions are released, we'll be sure to keep our companion web sites up-to-date with the latest information.

# Users, Permissions, and Roles

It's hard to imagine a system that does anything useful that doesn't somehow require the concept of a "user." After all, if anybody ends up "using" the system, that person will be some sort of "user." Anonymous users, those that haven't somehow authenticated with Zope, should have very limited rights to perform actions in the system; otherwise, the system would be exposed to possible exploitation or deliberate attack by malicious users. To grant different rights to different users, users are given special "roles" that permit them to perform tasks associated with those roles. You can allow a role to perform a task by granting that role a specific "permission" to perform the give task.

## Users Are the Keys to Security

You can think of Zope's security system as a hierarchy of roles and permissions. Users have roles, and roles have permissions to perform actions. If some method or content requires a special permission before it is executed or viewed, that permission needs to be mapped to a role. A role is like a "hat" worn by users that need to perform a task associated with the method or content in question. Any user that has the hat (role) can perform the method or view the content protected by that permission. Whether or not a particular user has a role determines what that user can do or cannot do in any context. Because the user object is the main mechanism by which users get roles, it is the user object that maintains most of the burden of keeping Zope secure.

## Authentication: Proving Your Identity

Before a person using a web browser can gain access to the methods and content protected by Zope, that person needs to become *authenticated* as a particular user. Based on the credentials supplied to the authentication system, the user will be recognized as a particular user, and the corresponding user object will be created to provide Zope with the roles that this user is allowed to "wear."

The default means of authentication is the HTTP Basic Authentication mechanism. When someone first accesses Zope, that person is, by default, effectively associated with the user object known as Anonymous, with no roles. When this user attempts to access any asset that does not permit access by the current user, determined by lack of the appropriate "role," the security system raises an "Unauthorized" exception, which results in an HTTP response of "Unauthorized." Most browsers then present the user with an authentication dialog that allows them to authenticate as a different user, presumably with the role that permits access to the resource in question. When this dialog is submitted, the browser tries the request again, but this time with the "Authentication" header set based on the input supplied by the user.

There are also methods that involve the use of cookies for authentication rather than the HTTP Basic Authentication mechanism. We'll get to these as we work out some examples with LoginManager.

## Roles, Permissions, and the Zope Security Model

Before Zope 2.2, the Zope security system was accessed by defining a Python dictionary in each Product's class that indicated what methods and subobjects were protected by what permissions, if any. Fairly recently, the Zope Corporation updated the security API to make it more flexible and simpler for programmers to use. To use this API, a programmer needs to access classes from the AccessControl module. For the product developer, the most important class is the `ClassSecurityInfo` class. Instances of this class are used by the new security machinery to protect Zope classes. Listing 13.1 illustrates its use by modifying the TotallySimpleProduct from Chapter 12, "Integrating Applications with ZPatterns."

Listing 13.1 **New Version of TotallySimpleProduct with Security Declarations**

```
import AccessControl

class TotallySimpleProduct(SimpleItem.SimpleItem ):

    "Totally Simple Product"

    meta_type = 'TotallySimpleProduct'
    message = 'Hello World!'

    manage_options = (  {'label': 'Properties', 'action': 'manage_main'},
                        {'label': 'View', 'action': 'index_html'},
                         )

    security = AccessControl.ClassSecurityInfo()

    security.declareObjectProtected('View')

    def __init__(self, id):
        "Set the id of the TotallySimpleProduct"
        self.id = id

    security.declareProtected('View', 'index_html')

    def index_html(self):
        "display yourself to the world"
        format = '<html><body>I am a TotallySimpleProduct<br><br>My message is
        ➥"%s".</body></html>'
        return format % self.message

    security.declareProtected('Change TotallySimpleProducts', 'manage_edit',
    ➥'manage_main')

    manage_main=HTMLFile('editPropertiesForm',globals())

```

*continues*

Listing 13.1 **Continued**

```
33     def manage_edit(self, message, REQUEST=None):
34         """ edit the message.. """
35         self.message = message
36         if REQUEST:
37             message="Saved changes."
38             return self.manage_main(self,REQUEST,manage_tabs_message=message)
39
40 def initialize(context):
41     context.registerClass(
42         TotallySimpleProduct,
43         permission='Add Totally Simple Product',
44         constructors=(manage_addTotallySimpleProductForm,
           ➥manage_addTotallySimpleProduct),
45         icon='TotallySimpleProduct.gif',
46         )
```

There are several things to notice in Listing 13.1 relating to security. Line 14 is the first change from the earlier "open" implementation from Chapter 12. It calls the constructor ClassSecurityInfo of the AccessControl module. This creates an instance of the `ClassSecurityInfo` class and assigns it to the TotallySimpleProduct class as its `security` attribute. All instances of TotallySimpleProduct will inherit this class attribute. When instances of this class are published, the Zope security machinery (ZSM) will inspect the `security` attribute of the instance to determine whether the action being requested should be allowed. Line 16 uses `declareObjectProtected` to associate the permission "view" with this object. As you can see, lines 22 and 31 declare that the `index_html` method is protected with the view permission, and the `manage_edit` method and manage_main document are both protected with the "change TotallySimpleProducts" permission. This means that if a user wants to use those methods, he needs to have a "role" that has those permissions, respectively. Finally, in the `initialize` method, the permission argument is explicitly set to a literal string (line 43) that defines the permission needed to create a new TotallySimpleProduct instance in the ZMI. In this way, it's easy to associate a particular permission to any of the methods, or subobjects, of a Zope product. With these changes made, you can see the effect on the Security tab of any folder, as shown in Figure 13.1.

As you can see, the two permissions Add Totally Simple Product and Change TotallySimpleProducts are both visible in the security tab. Of course, to change which roles actually get which permissions, you'll need to uncheck the Acquire Permission Settings check box (unless you are setting the security policy in the root folder), and then click the check boxes for the roles that you want to have each permission.

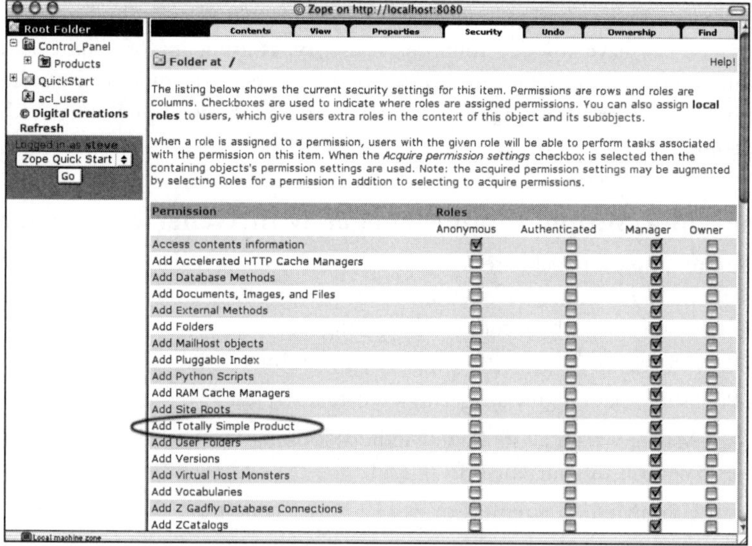


**Figure 13.1** Security tab of a folder after changes made in Listing 13.1.

The business of assigning roles to users is the main function of a User Folder. Zope comes with a very simple User Folder object built in. Many applications require something more flexible. Lots of User Folder substitutes are posted to the zope.org site. Most of them are specialized to get users from a particular data source (for example, LDAP, SQL, /etc/passwd, and so on). Because you spent a lot of time in Chapter 11, "Design for Integration the ZPatterns Way," and Chapter 12, "Integrating Applications with ZPatterns," becoming acquainted with ZPatterns, it makes sense to introduce what is arguably the most universal and flexible User Folder substitute available. It uses ZPatterns to make it possible to plug in any source of user data and any authentications scheme that you like, in combination. It's called Login Manager.

# ZPatterns and Users: LoginManager

Login Manager was designed to solve the so-called N × M problem: If you have *N* sources of users and *M* ways to authenticate/transmit authentication data, then you need N × M kinds of user folders to handle all the combinations. LoginManager is a subclass of Specialist that keeps track of login information. It contains two distinctly different sets of objects: UserSources and LoginMethods.

- UserSources are objects that can check for the existence of users and (when asked) can return instances of user objects given the user ID of a user.
- LoginMethods are responsible for extracting authentication information from a REQUEST and invoking some method to perform authentication.

Because a single LoginManager can have multiple UserSources and multiple Login-Methods, you can have any of a finite set of user types using any of a finite set of login/authentication types. This means that one kind of User Folder can handle an essentially arbitrary array of sources of user data and methods of providing credentials for those users.

## Setting Up a Simple LoginManager with GenericUserSource

To create the simplest possible setup, you will store your user data in a TinyTablePlus object (see the "TinyTablePlus" section in Chapter 3, "Web Event Publishing"). This way, you can easily see where the data is coming from.

The flow of LoginManager goes something like this:

1. ZPublisher asks LoginManager to validate a request.
2. LoginManager tries all its LoginMethods looking for one that recognizes the user based on the current REQUEST.
3. Each LoginMethod attempts to extract a username from the REQUEST and then checks with the UserSource to see if such a user can be found.
4. If a UserSource produces a real User Object, the LoginMethod calls that User Object's `authenticate` method.
5. If the User Object doesn't implement its own `authenticate` method (and there are some good reasons why it shouldn't, although it is allowed—see the "User Objects *Can* Authenticate Themselves (But Beware!)" sidebar), it delegates the actual authentication to the UserSource.
6. The Generic User Source that you'll be using further delegates the authenticateUser to a Through the Web (TTW) method that should be supplied by the application integrator called `userAuthenticate`.
7. The result of `userAuthenticate` is returned to ZPublisher as the result of `validate()`. At the same time, the `AUTHENTICATED_USER` element of the REQUEST object is set to the found and authenticated User Object.

**User Objects Can Authenticate Themselves (But Beware!)**

If a User Object implements `authenticate` directly, it brings back the N × M problem because users of that class would be confined to one type of authentication (the one that they implement). By delegating to the UserSource, any multiple UserSources that you set up can authenticate any way they like, while all using the same User class. Of course, for situations in which there is only one way to authenticate, it's perfectly okay for user classes to authenticate and get roles/domains themselves.

This process is illustrated graphically in Figure 13.2.

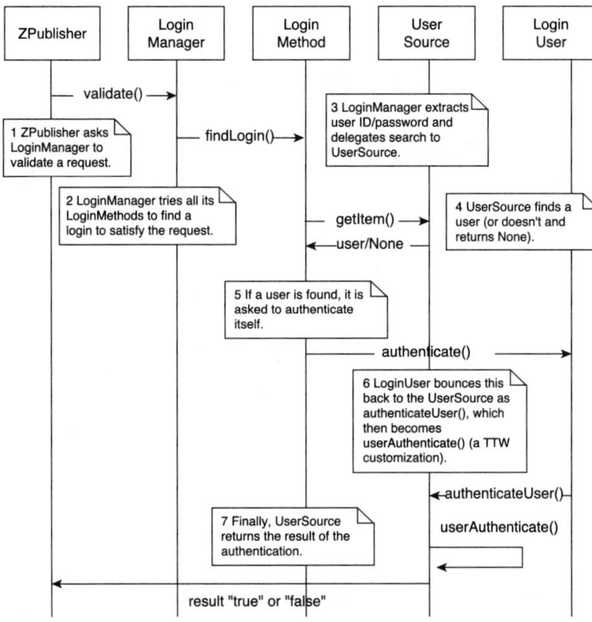


**Figure 13.2** The default process of authentication in LoginManager.

You can test this process by creating a test folder—in this case, we'll call it testFolder, just to be original. Inside this test folder, create a LoginManager; keep the default options as shown in Figure 13.3.

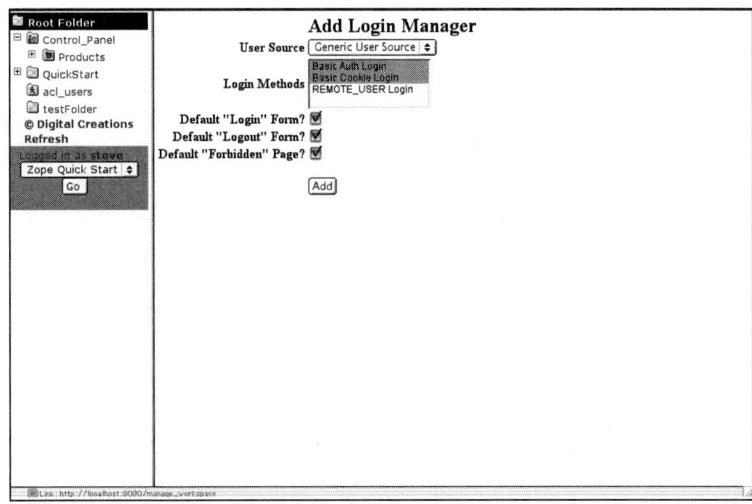


**Figure 13.3** Creating a LoginManager in testFolder.

When the LoginManager is instantiated (it's called `acl_users`, just like the built-in Zope UserFolder), put some content in the folder (such as a DTML method called `index_html`). In the `index_html` method, put some clever message, such as "You made it!", to let the user know that he successfully authenticated. When you're ready to test the LoginManager, you'll restrict viewing of this page so that users will need to authenticate to see it. Next you'll create four Python scripts in your UserSource, plus a source of data (in this case, a tiny table).

### Tread Carefully with User Folders

Before you begin creating methods and data sources in your UserSource, it's wise to strategize a bit. Playing with UserFolders is a little bit like playing with fire. It can be a lot of fun, but you can get burned if you're not careful! Let's glance at a few lines of the LoginManager source to see how that can be. Listing 13.2 is from LoginManager 0.8.8b1 (the most recent version as of this writing). The method listed here, from $ZOPEROOT/lib/python/Products/LoginManager/UserSource.py, is the authenticateUser method of the GenericUserSource class (the default UserSource that you selected when you created your LoginManager).

Listing 13.2 ***authenticateUser* Method from GenericUserSource Class**

```
01 def authenticateUser(self,user,password,request):
02
03     name = user.getUserName()
04
05     if self.cacheGetAuth(name, password):
06         return 1
07
08     if not hasattr(self, 'userAuthenticate'):
09         return 0
10
11     old_au = setuid(self.REQUEST, _LoggingInUser)
12     try:
13         ok = self.userAuthenticate(
14             self, request, username=name, password=password)
15
16     finally:
17         setuid(self.REQUEST, old_au)
18
19     if ok:
20         self.cacheSetAuth(name, password)
21
22     return ok
```

A lot happening here has to do with efficiently caching the results of authenticateUser so that Zope LoginManager doesn't keep calling the `userAuthenticate` method many times after it has be successfully called once. The main point for now is the try/finally construct between lines 12 and 17. What happens if there is a coding error in the `userAuthenticate` method? The exception (if any) is silently ignored and the authentication fails! This has the unfortunate side effect of possibly locking you out of the folder you are trying to protect. To prevent this from happening, it's good to use a technique suggested on the Zope mailing list by Phil Mayers and documented in a HowTo by jok (see **http://www.zope.org/Members/jok/SQL_based_LoginManager**).

The idea is to initially name the methods that do authentication and user lookup something else (such as xuserAuthentication). Then, when they are tested and work correctly, rename them to match the LoginManager API (such as xuserAuthenticate renamed to userAuthenticate).

Another good idea is to make a copy of the testFolder before you change the names. Then if there is a problem, you can simply delete the "broken" folder and copy the backup to restore the version that has not been renamed (alternatively, you can just "undo" the rename using the Undo tab).

### Connecting with the User Data

With that caveat made clear, let's investigate the components that you need to set up a pretty simple LoginManager.

First, you'll need a source of user data—in this case, a TinyTablePlus called userInfo. You can see a screenshot of the userInfo TinyTable in Figure 13.4.

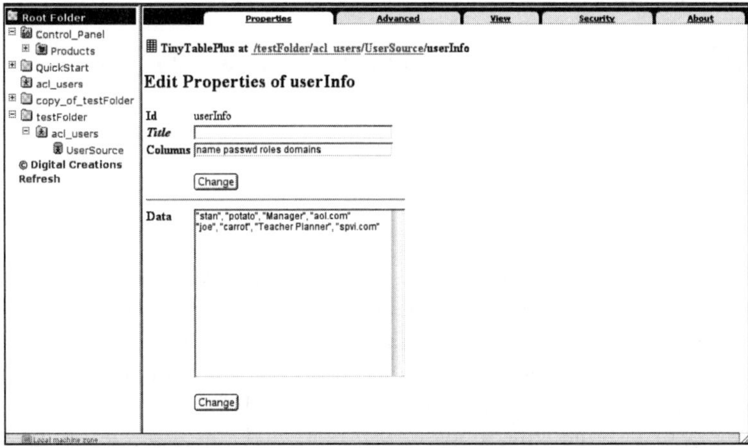


**Figure 13.4** TinyTable with user data.

One issue that deserves extreme care is that of the security of the data in userInfo. The problem is that before a user is authenticated, that user is generally Anonymous, which means that the user has no special roles, so he can't access anything that isn't available to all users. But if LoginManager needs to call a method to get data out of the userInfo TinyTable, then either that table needs to be readable by Anonymous or

LoginManager needs to "pretend" to be a privileged user while accessing userInfo. LoginManager uses a trick. It creates a special role called LoggingIn, and it temporarily logs you in as a generic user with this role. It does this only while it is in the validate method, so there is no way to get access to this role *except* while actually logging in to a LoginManager controlled resource. Notice that without this approach, a malicious user with access to the parent folder of the protected testFolder could write a DTML Method like that in Listing 13.3.

Listing 13.3 **Malicious DTML Attack on userInfo**

```
<dtml-var standard_html_header>
<h2><dtml-var title_or_id> <dtml-var document_title></h2>
<pre>
<dtml-in "testFolder.acl_users.UserSource.userInfo()">
<dtml-var name>
<dtml-var passwd>
-------
</dtml-in>

</pre>
<dtml-var standard_html_footer>
```

If userInfo were set up to allow anonymous users to query its data, this method would produce output like Listing 13.4.

Listing 13.4 **Results of Malicious DTML Attack on userInfo**

```
stan
potato
-------
joe
carrot
-------
```

To use this technique, go to the Security tab on the LoginManager folder (acl_users) in your testFolder. Make sure that the permission Query TinyTable Data is not set to acquire permissions from its parent and that the Anonymous role is not checked. *Do* check the role `LogginIn`. Then when the malicious user tries Listing 13.3, he'll be rewarded only by a "You are not allowed to access userInfo" message. However, while someone is actually attempting to log in, that user will be granted the role LoggingIn. This temporary role will be used while the user authenticates and gets the *real* roles and domains.

### The Authentication Process

How does the authentication actually happen? You need a script called userAuthenticate, located in the `UserSource` object of your LoginManager, as shown in Listing 13.5.

Listing 13.5 **Python Script *userAuthenticate* Checks a User's Password**

```
01 ## Script (Python) "userAuthenticate"
02 ##bind container=container
03 ##bind context=context
04 ##bind namespace=
05 ##bind script=script
06 ##bind subpath=traverse_subpath
07 ##parameters=manager, request, username, password
08 ##title=Authenticate a user
09 ##
10 #
11 # check password against data from TinyTable
12 #
13
14 # First try to get a record for this user
15 #
16
17 theUser = container.userInfo(username)
18
19 #
20 # Check password if we didn't get "None"
21 #
22
23 if (theUser is not  None) and theUser[0].passwd == password:
24     return 1
25 else:
26     return 0
```

As you can see, this is quite straightforward. Line 17 is a query of the `userInfo` TinyTablePlus object in an attempt to find the user. Line 23 checks to see that the result set is not `None`, and, if not, checks to see whether the `passwd` field of the first result (TinyTablePlus row) matches the password extracted by the calling LoginMethod. Remember that a TinyTable uses its first column as an index, so passing the username to the userInfo object is the same as saying, "Give me all the rows where the first column is the same as `username`." If the passwords match, then userAuthenticate returns a numerical value of `1`; otherwise, it returns `0`.

Pretty easy, eh? But LoginManager is smart! It doesn't want to call a (possibly) expensive authentication method if there's a chance that the user doesn't even exist. To make sure that there's really a user out there, it first looks for a method called `userExists`, located in the `UserSource` object of your LoginManager. The TinyTable version is shown in Listing 13.6.

Listing 13.6 **Python Script *userExists* Checks for Existence of a User**

```
## Script (Python) "userExists"
##bind container=container
##bind context=context
##bind namespace=
```

*continues*

Listing 13.6 **Continued**

```
##bind script=script
##bind subpath=traverse_subpath
##parameters=manager, request, username
##title=Check for existence of a User
##
#
# check for existence of user from TinyTable
#

# Try to get a record for this user
#

theUser = container.userInfo(username)

#
# Check if we didn't get "None"
#

if (theUser is not  None):
   return 1
else:
   return 0
```

The Python script `userExists` is similar to `userAuthenticate`, except that it doesn't worry about passwords. It just returns `1` or `0`, depending on the presence or lack of the user data itself.

### Getting Roles and Domains

Finally, Listings 13.7 and 13.8 are for the two Python scripts `userRoles` and `userDomains`, located in the `UserSource` object of your LoginManager. They are almost identical, except that one returns the roles field from the TinyTablePlus and the other returns the domain field.

Listing 13.7 **Python Script *userRoles* Returns Roles for User**

```
## Script (Python) "userRoles"
##bind container=container
##bind context=context
##bind namespace=
##bind script=script
##bind subpath=traverse_subpath
##parameters=manager, request, username
##title=Get Roles for a User
##
#
# check password against data from TinyTable
#

import string
```

```

# First try to get a record for this user
#

theUser = container.userInfo(username)

#
# Check roles if we didn't get "None"
#

if (theUser is not  None):
   return theUser[0].roles
else:
   return []
```

Notice that `roles` is just a string, while normally user objects have roles that are a *list* of strings. Happily, LoginManager notices when it gets a string from userRoles or userDomains, and it runs any string through `string.split`, which converts a space-delimited string into a list of its tokens. This is quite handy because it's hard to store a list in a TinyTablePlus field. Notice that if the user is not found, an empty list of roles is returned. Next you have the `userDomains` method in Listing 13.8.

Listing 13.8 **Python Script *userDomains* Returns Domains for User**

```
## Script (Python) "userDomains"
##bind container=container
##bind context=context
##bind namespace=
##bind script=script
##bind subpath=traverse_subpath
##parameters=manager, request, username
##title=Get Domains for a User
##
#
# check password against data from TinyTable
#

import string

# First try to get a record for this user
#

theUser = container.userInfo(username)

#
# Check domains if we didn't get "None"
#

if (theUser is not  None):
   return theUser[0].domains
else:
   return []
```

That's it! You have a LoginManager protected folder with user data stored securely in a simple TinyTable. In the next major section, "Integrating Enterprise Users (Lunch and Attendance Again)," you'll work on a more sophisticated case in which data is kept in an SQL database.

> ***Tips and Tricks***
> You can simulate multiple UserSources by simply copying your existing UserSource and giving it a new Name.
>
> Try this:
>
> 1. Navigate to the LoginManager (acl_users) and click the UserSources tab.
> 2. Add a new UserSource (called, for example, GUS2).
> 3. Copy the TinyTablePlus and all the methods from the original UserSource, and paste them into GUS2.
> 4. Edit the usernames in the userInfo TinyTablePlus in GUS2 so that they appear to be different users.
> 5. Quit your browser and log in to testFolder with one of the new names.
>
> It should work! This just points out that LoginManager will keep looking through all the UserSources until it finds one that works. You could mix SQL, LDAP, and NT types of users in a single LoginManager. It's amazingly powerful—and when you understand how it works, it's pretty easy.

# Integrating Enterprise Users (Lunch and Attendance Again)

You're going to revisit the applications from Chapter 12 now. You didn't worry much about security on the first pass, but after some thought, it's probably clear that you need to allow different users (Students, Teachers) to have different abilities when it comes to querying and changing data in both of these applications. In this section, you'll review the data that you maintained about the users of the system, and you'll set up some methods and displays that work with the security machinery to create an application that behaves reasonably from a security perspective. Because there's not much pedagogical benefit from the extra complexity of the combined Lunch/Attendance application, for the purposes of learning in this chapter, you'll discuss only the Attendance application. Applying these same ideas to the Lunch or combined application is straightforward, although more tedious.

## Attendance with Users

You should recall that the Attendance application already has the notion of users (Persons). You could use these Person objects and just store the password, domains, and roles there. However there is a security problem with that. If you include the password in the use object, it might be easier for someone who needs access to other Person data (such as home phone and birth date) to get at the password. So, it's best to keep the password in a separate table that you can protect with some additional permissions.

As in the last section, you'll need to store the data for these users to authenticate against somewhere. Because the rest of the application uses SQL tables to hold user data, you might create a new SQL table to hold the password information. Unfortunately, the levers that you used in Chapter 12 won't work directly because they are dependent on having a ZClass with propertysheets. Of course, you can create the tables the old-fashioned way: by hand. Listings 13.9 through 13.13 show all the SQL needed for maintaining the password data.

Listing 13.9 **Query to Create the User Table**

```
createSQL:

<params></params>
 create table Passwords_Basic (
 personID  varchar,
 passwd  varchar ,
 roles  varchar ,
 domains varchar    )
```

Listing 13.10 **Query to Delete User Records**

```
deleteSQL:
<params>personID</params>
 delete from Passwords _Basic where <dtml-sqltest personID type=string>
```

Listing 13.11 **Query to Create New User Records**

```
insertSQL:

<params>personID="" passwd="" roles="" domains=""</params>
 insert into Passwords_Basic  values (
   <dtml-sqlvar personID type=string>,
   <dtml-sqlvar passwd  type=string>,
   <dtml-sqlvar roles  type=string>,
   <dtml-sqlvar domains  type=string>
)
```

Listing 13.12 **Query to Find User Records**

```
selectSQL:

<params>personID="" passwd="" roles="" domains=""</params>
 select personID, passwd, roles, domains from Passwords_Basic
 <dtml-sqlgroup where>

 <dtml-sqlgroup>
 <dtml-if personID>
 <dtml-sqltest personID type=string>
 </dtml-if>
 </dtml-sqlgroup>
 <dtml-and>
 <dtml-sqlgroup>
 <dtml-if passwd >
 <dtml-sqltest passwd type=string>
 </dtml-if>
 </dtml-sqlgroup>
 <dtml-and>
 <dtml-sqlgroup>
 <dtml-if roles >
 <dtml-sqltest roles type=string>
 </dtml-if>
 </dtml-sqlgroup>
 <dtml-and>
 <dtml-sqlgroup>
 <dtml-if domains >
 <dtml-sqltest domains type=string>
 </dtml-if>
 </dtml-sqlgroup>

 </dtml-sqlgroup>
```

Listing 13.13 **Query to Change User Records**

```
updateSQL:

<params>personID passwd roles domains</params>
  update Passwords_Basic set
  passwd = <dtml-sqlvar passwd  type=string>,
  roles = <dtml-sqlvar roles  type=string>,
  domains = <dtml-sqlvar domains  type=string>

where <dtml-sqltest personID type=string>
```

You can create some users to match Persons in the application. Although it's beyond the scope of this particular chapter, you also could use all the techniques of Chapters 11 and 12 to teach your User Objects about the other information that you already have in the application, (for example, Person properties and Attendee properties can be mapped in SkinScript to corresponding properties in the User object). But just to get

SQL managed users, you still need some more Python scripts, like those from the last section, but now using queries to check for existence, roles, and so on. The four methods are still `userExists`, `userAuthenticate`, `userDomains`, and `userRoles`. These are listed here for your reference in Listings 13.14 through 13.17.

Note also that because you are keeping sensitive information in this table, these queries should be protected from anonymous use. In the Security tab of the LoginManager, be sure to uncheck the Acquire Permissions box for Use Database Methods, and grant the permission to users with the LogginIn role. This means that only users who are actually in the process of logging in can query the database.

First, you need to check for the existence of a user. This is best done with selectSQL. In fact, all of the authentication work is done with selectSQL. The other queries are really only useful for managing the user data. Such management is really off-topic for this chapter, but it clearly is an important part of the final application. The Python script `userExists` does the work of checking for existence; it is displayed in Listing 13.14.

Listing 13.14 **Checking for Existence of a User with an SQL Method**

```
01 ## Script (Python) "userExists"
02 ##bind container=container
03 ##bind context=context
04 ##bind namespace=
05 ##bind script=script
06 ##bind subpath=traverse_subpath
07 ##parameters=manager, request, username
08 ##title=Check existence of a user
09 ##
10 #
11 # Check for the existence of a user.
12 #
13
14 if container.selectSQL(personID=username):
15  return 1
16 else:
17  return 0
```

You can see how userExists calls on the SQL Method selectSQL to check the SQL database to see if there is a row defined with a personID equal to the username of the person attempting to log in. Line 14 just checks to see if the result of the query has a true Boolean interpretation (an empty result is returned as `None` and so evaluates to "false"). UserSource is looking for a numeric value of `1` to indicate success, and that is returned in line 15 if the result of the query is not false.

Next is userAuthenticate, which, like the TinyTable version, needs to get a value out of the database and use it to determine whether the password given is valid. The userAuthenticate script is displayed in Listing 13.15.

Listing 13.15 **Authenticate a User with an SQL Method**

```
## Script (Python) "userAuthenticate"
##bind container=container
##bind context=context
##bind namespace=
##bind script=script
##bind subpath=traverse_subpath
##parameters=manager, request, username, password
##title=Authenticate a User
##
#
# Get user information from Gadfly and check password given.
#

result = container.selectSQL(personID=username)

if result and result[0].passwd == password:
 return 1
else:
 return 0
```

This is quite similar to the TinyTable experience, except that, this time, rather than querying a TinyTable, you're using a SQL Method.

Finally, Listings 13.16 and 13.17 show the `userDomains` and `userRoles` methods.

Listing 13.16 **Getting a User's Domains with an SQL Method**

```
## Script (Python) "userDomains"
##bind container=container
##bind context=context
##bind namespace=
##bind script=script
##bind subpath=traverse_subpath
##parameters=manager, request, username
##title=Get Users domains
##
#
# check SQL Database for user's domains.
#

result = container.selectSQL(personID=username)

if result:
 return result[0].domains
else:
 return []
```

The script `userDomains` and `userRoles` are extremely similar. Basically, they just return the roles and domains fields from the database. The good news is that GenericUserSource automatically converts space-delimited strings to lists, so you don't have to do it here. The userRoles script is identical except that it returns the roles field (see Listing 13.17).

Listing 13.17 **Getting a User's Roles with an SQL Method**

```
## Script (Python) "userRoles"
##bind container=container
##bind context=context
##bind namespace=
##bind script=script
##bind subpath=traverse_subpath
##parameters=manager, request, username
##title=
##
result = container.selectSQL(personID=username)

if result:
 return result[0].roles
else:
 return []
```

### Allowing Parents to Check Attendance

Allowing parents to check attendance is an excellent use case for multiple UserSources. You know that student information is likely to be in a database somewhere with lots of gory details. What's the chance that you have access to data about parents in the same table? Maybe not that great. However, you can create a new UserSource that keeps its users in ZODB, or a TinyTable for those parents who want to check their children's attendance. This would work just like the second UserSource in the section "ZPatterns and Users: LoginManager." The management of the parent's data could be completely separate from the student and faculty data. Later, you might decide that you want parents in the primary database, but that's easy to change later. The logic of the application and the control of security policy is completely separate from the source of user data and the authentication process.

It's the capability to do just this sort of thing that makes LoginManager so powerful.

## Summary

In this chapter, you studied the details of Zope's security model at the Python product level. Given this low-level picture, it's pretty easy to see how the security model percolates through all the things that Zope does. The ZMI and ZClasses all use the same basic structures, but a lot of the "work" is already done for you. Knowing how things work internally can sometimes help a lot when things don't behave the way you think they should.

You also used the flexible and powerful LoginManager to create a UserFolder substitute that uses a TinyTablePlus to hold its authentication information. Then you applied the same concept to the Attendance application from Chapter 12 by getting your user data from an SQL database.

At this point, you've really hit a lot of the more difficult areas in application development. The next chapter covers how to handle application development in which there are many developers and when the application complexity reaches a state in which disciplined and deliberate testing is required.

# 14

# Multi-Developer Projects: Testing and Version Control

APPLICATIONS DEVELOPED IN ZOPE can vary tremendously in sophistication and size. They can be the product of a single developer working at home on the weekends or a team of many developers distributed around the world. This chapter brings together solutions to some of the most immediate problems that developers encounter when they try to tackle a large project that requires coordination among multiple people and Zope servers. First, we'll use Zope Version objects for simple version control, but you'll quickly see their limitations. Next we'll consider the more traditional version-control system: CVS. Wouldn't it be nice if we could use CVS with Zope? Sure! That's why we wrote ZCVSFolder. There's also ZSyncer—another area that affects large projects is systematic testing. We'll present PyUnit and ZUnit as tools that can help in that process as well.

Although much of the chapter applies to both UNIX and Windows, some of it does not. To provide a consistent set of command-line listings, we have chosen to illustrate with UNIX commands rather than Windows commands. The translation between these two is obvious, and where there might be ambiguity, we explicitly provide both forms.

# Too Many Chefs Can Spoil the Stew!

One of the great strengths of Zope is that it allows many different people at many different locations to work on a single project at the same time. Unfortunately, one of the great weaknesses of Zope is that it allows many different people at many different locations to work on a single project at the same time. In this chapter, we will introduce some techniques that can help maintain control over the process of Zope application development when multiple developers are involved.

## Zope "Versions" Can Help

As you saw in Chapter 1, "The Object of the Web—Optimizing Web Development," Zope already has a "version" system. This system sets cookies in the developer's browser to tell Zope which version is being "worked on." The good news is that using these kinds of versions is easy:

1. Go to a place in the Zope Management Interface (ZMI) where you want to create your version object. This will typically be at the root of the object hierarchy, or in the folder where your application is stored. You should be able to find the Version object listed in the Select Type to Add pop-up menu.
2. Create a Version object in the ZMI at some convenient location. Give the Version object some reasonable ID and name, such as `testVersion` and `testing new nav bar`.
3. When you've created the Version object, click on it in the ZMI and notice the UI that's presented, something like Figure 14.1. In particular, notice that to use a version object, you've got to "join" the version (hence the Join/Leave tab). The verb `join` is used in this case because more than one developer can use a version object simultaneously. It's a little like a group that you can join temporarily and leave later.
4. After you click the "Start Working In..." button, you will be presented with a modified management screen, like Figure 14.2.

At this point you are working in your new version. There is an extra message in the ZMI that tells you that you are working in a version. Any changes that you make to persistent Zope objects will be made only in that version. To see how this works, change the default `<body>` tag in the `standard_html_header` to read `bgcolor="white"`. After the change, you'll see a message in the management UI indicating that you have changed the object, along with the message reminding you that you are working in a version.

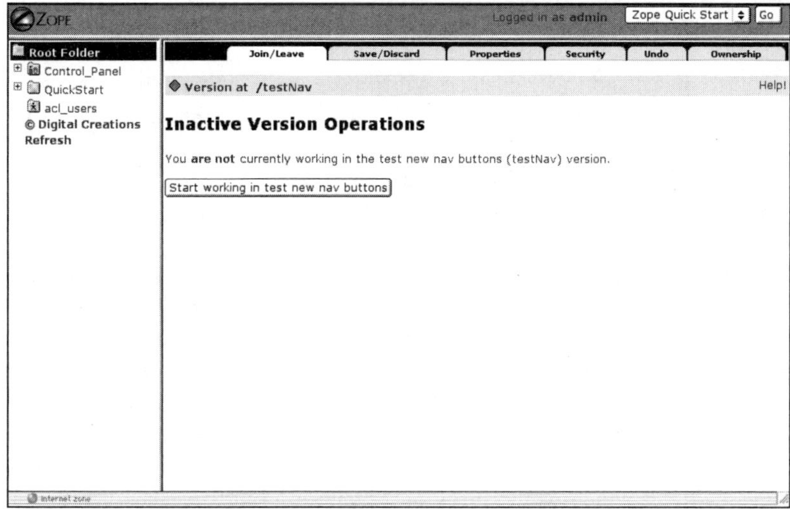


Figure 14.1 Management UI for Zope Version object.

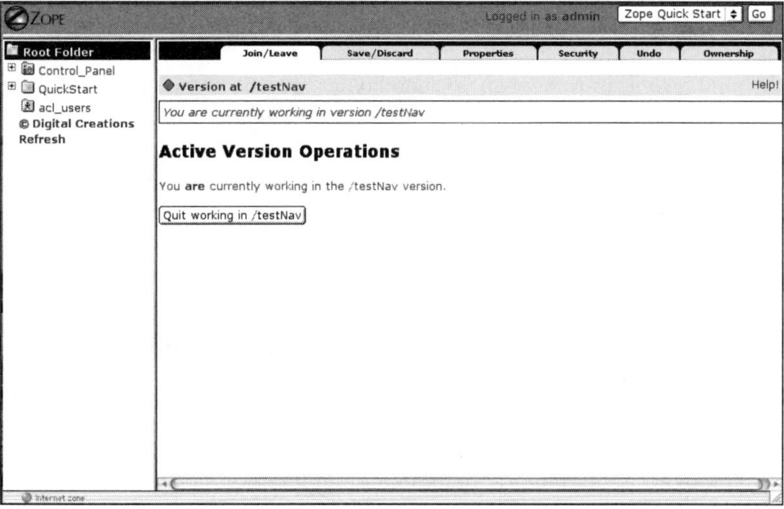


Figure 14.2 Management UI, after joining for Zope Version object.

If you now use the ZMI to browse at the root level, you should see a small red diamond next to the object that you edited—in this case, `standard_html_header`. As you edit other objects, you will see red diamonds appear by each object that you have changed since you started working in your version. You can leave this version whenever you like, and the changes will remain with the version. If you want someone else to work on a version with you, that person can simply go to your version object in the ZMI and "join" it. The person then also can make any changes that his roles have permission to make, and those changes will also be made only to that version. You will notice that most browsers will display "This object has been modified in version…" when you put your mouse cursor over the diamond.

Other developers who have not "joined" your version will not see the changes you have made. However, if they browse the object hierarchy and encounter objects that have been changed by developers working in different versions, they will see not only an indicator showing that the object has been changed, but also a *lock* icon, indicating that the object is *locked* against change outside the version in which it was changed.

When you are finished testing your changes, you can either save the version or discard it. Either way, you are invited to leave a comment about the changes in the version's save/discard management screen. Once saved, all the changes that you made become permanent and "public" in one transaction. The indicators that the objects have been modified, or modified and locked, disappear. This is great for making sets of changes, any one of which would break the application but that taken together are okay. Making all the changes in a version and then saving the version in a single transaction means that there is no site "downtime" during updates.

But what about locking? Doesn't that mean that it's hard to use built-in Zope versions for long-term development? The answer is yes. This is the bad news about Zope's built-in version system. Objects that are changed in a Zope version are "locked" in that version. This means that when you modify any object, such as a DTML Method, a folder, or an SQL query, no developer working outside the version in which the change was made can modify the object in any way. This is especially problematic for folders because merely adding an object to a folder, or modifying one of the folder's properties in a version, locks the folder from being changed (for example, adding or subtracting objects) by developers working outside the version.

So what are versions good for? They are great for fairly quick testing of changes or longer-term testing of changes on a server that is not being used for active development (for example, a `test-only` server.). For active, multideveloper projects, you'll need features that the built-in Zope Version objects don't have.

## CVS for Filesystem Control

Some Zope objects are constructed from source files stored on the local filesystem of the Zope server (such as External Methods, objects provided by LocalFS, custom Zope products, and so on). For these kinds of objects, it makes sense to use a conventional version control system such as Concurrent Version System (CVS). CVS is used by developers all over the world to manage versions of source code for many thousands of software projects. CVS can store essentially any file, in either binary or text form. In fact, the text and figures for this chapter are being stored in a CVS repository!

If you've never used CVS, this section will guide you through the process of creating a CVS repository on a single machine and will suggest some patterns of usage. If you are running Zope on a UNIX-like system, you probably have CVS already installed. If you are running on Windows, you can get a great CVS package at **http://www.wincvs.org**. There is also lots of documentation on the web at **http://www.cvshome.org**. To make full use of CVS with multiple developers, you'll want to use it in network mode.

CVS works by maintaining a centralized repository of all the versions of the source files in a project, as shown in Figure 14.3.

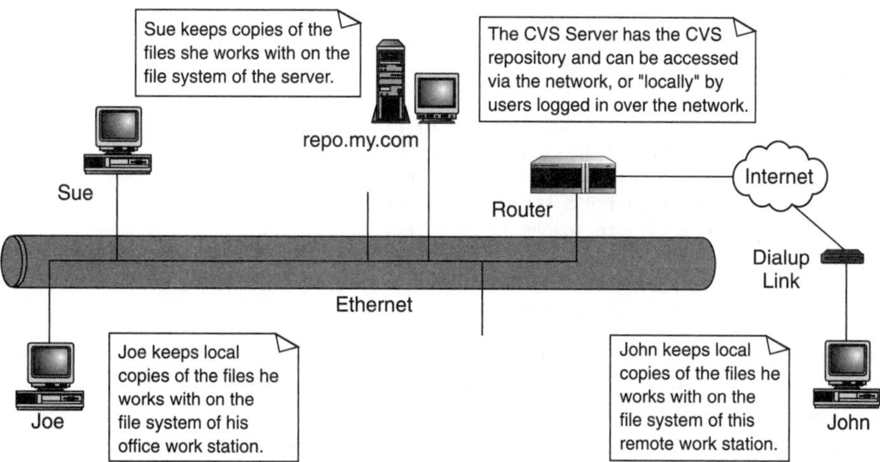


**Figure 14.3** CVS network/repository example.

Developers can work in either a directory that they create on the computer with the repository, or in a directory that they create on a computer that has access to the repository over the network. To work with files stored in a CVS repository for the first time, a developer "checks out" the files onto the filesystem of the computer that he is using as a development platform. If he already has the files checked out from a previous development session but he wants to be sure that they are "in sync" with the other developers, the developer needs to run an "update" that pulls in changes that other developers might have made to the project since they did the checkout or the last update. The developer then modifies the files, adding features, fixing bugs, extending documentation, and so on. After testing that the changes are correct, the developer "commits" the new versions of the files to the CVS repository. CVS automatically adds new versions to files changed, and those changes will be sent to the other developers when they next perform an update. Because CVS can use TCP/IP to communicate with an encrypted data stream, it is generally regarded as safe to use over the Internet.

### Starting a CVS Repository

To create a new CVS repository, log into the computer where the repository will be kept. Decide where you want to store the repository, and issue this command:

```
cvs -d /directory/for/repository init
```

This creates an empty repository, which you can then populate with sources from your own projects. It's helpful to set an environment variable `CVS_ROOT` to point to the directory where your repository exists. This means that you won't have to type the command-line option `-d /directory/for/repository` in all your CVS commands. When the repository exists, you can "import" an existing project into the repository so that it can be brought under version control. For this, you need to use the `import` command. The "help" information for the `import` command is shown here:

```
cvs --help import

Usage: cvs import [-d] [-k subst] [-I ign] [-m msg] [-b branch]
 [-W spec] repository vendor-tag release-tags...
     -d      Use the file's modification time as the time of import.
     -k sub  Set default RCS keyword substitution mode.
     -I ign  More files to ignore (! to reset).
     -b bra  Vendor branch id.
     -m msg  Log message.
     -W spec Wrappers specification line.
```

In most cases, you can just make up a `vendor-tag` that helps you remember who created the project, or who it was for. `repository` is the directory, relative to the root of the repository, where files for this project will be kept. For release tags, you can use anything that tells you that this is the time the project was imported into CVS. For example, suppose that you have a Zope product that you've created to do something totally simple, such as the TotallySimpleProduct example from Chapter 12, "Integrating Applications with ZPatterns." This product has the files listed here:

```
.cvsignore
TotallySimpleProduct.gif
TotallySimpleProduct.py
TotallySimpleProduct.pyc
TotallySimpleProduct.py~
__init__.py
__init__.pyc
addInstance.dtml
refresh.txt

.cvsignore contains only the line:

    *.pyc

And refresh.txt is an empty file.
```

Notice that there is a new file, .cvsignore. This file is used to tell CVS to ignore certain files that are not really part of the project. CVS automatically ignores files that end in ~ because these are usually emacs backup files. We also want CVS to ignore

.pyc files because they are created automatically by python when the source code is byte-compiled. The refresh.txt file is just there to enable the Refresh Product (see Chapter 12) to reload these modules, so it is also not really part of project and should be ignored. So, .cvsignore is just a listing of files to be ignored—in this case, it's refresh.txt and *.pyc. To get this set of files imported into CVS, you would invoke the `import` command as shown here:

```
*cvs import -m "Project Start" zope/lib/python/Products/TotallySimpleProduct
➥sjs start-project*

N zope/lib/python/Products/TotallySimpleProduct/__init__.py
I zope/lib/python/Products/TotallySimpleProduct/__init__.pyc
N zope/lib/python/Products/TotallySimpleProduct/TotallySimpleProduct.py
I zope/lib/python/Products/TotallySimpleProduct/TotallySimpleProduct.pyc
I zope/lib/python/Products/TotallySimpleProduct/refresh.txt
I zope/lib/python/Products/TotallySimpleProduct/TotallySimpleProduct.py~
N zope/lib/python/Products/TotallySimpleProduct/addInstance.dtml
N zope/lib/python/Products/TotallySimpleProduct/TotallySimpleProduct.gif
N zope/lib/python/Products/TotallySimpleProduct/.cvsignore

No conflicts created by this import
```

Notice that CVS tells you that it's ignoring all the .pyc files, and refresh.txt, indicated by an `I` in the output. The `N` in the output indicates a "new" file. It also reports that there were no conflicts with existing files in the repository. This is a good thing! You might be wondering why we used such a long repository path. The reason in this case is that we happen to keep versions of Zope in our CVS repository so that we can make modifications to Zope source, if necessary, to match our needs and so that we can track what those changes were as new releases of Zope are published. You might not have that need, but you will almost surely need to have some hierarchical structure to your CVS repository so that you can keep track of which files belong to which project. Now that you've got your source code imported, you can check it out. Go to another working directory and try the commands listed here:

1. Get to your home directory: `cd`
2. Make a "test" directory there: `mkdir foo`
3. Change to that directory: `cd foo`
4. Check out your project files into that directory:

   ```
   cvs co zope/lib/python/Products/TotallySimpleProduct

   cvs checkout: Updating zope/lib/python/Products/TotallySimpleProduct
   U zope/lib/python/Products/TotallySimpleProduct/.cvsignore
   U zope/lib/python/Products/TotallySimpleProduct/TotallySimpleProduct.gif
   U zope/lib/python/Products/TotallySimpleProduct/TotallySimpleProduct.py
   U zope/lib/python/Products/TotallySimpleProduct/__init__.py
   U zope/lib/python/Products/TotallySimpleProduct/addInstance.dtml
   ```

5. Where are they?

   ```
   find .
   ```

   ```
   ./zope
   ./zope/CVS
   ./zope/CVS/Root
   ./zope/CVS/Repository
   ./zope/CVS/Entries
   .
   . (many lines of output cut to save ink)
   .
   ./zope/lib/python/Products/TotallySimpleProduct
   ./zope/lib/python/Products/TotallySimpleProduct/CVS
   ./zope/lib/python/Products/TotallySimpleProduct/CVS/Root
   ./zope/lib/python/Products/TotallySimpleProduct/CVS/Repository
   ./zope/lib/python/Products/TotallySimpleProduct/CVS/Entries
   ./zope/lib/python/Products/TotallySimpleProduct/.cvsignore
   ./zope/lib/python/Products/TotallySimpleProduct/TotallySimpleProduct.gif
   ./zope/lib/python/Products/TotallySimpleProduct/TotallySimpleProduct.py
   ./zope/lib/python/Products/TotallySimpleProduct/__init__.py
   ./zope/lib/python/Products/TotallySimpleProduct/addInstance.dtml
   ```

   Way down there!

Notice that the five files are there, but they're buried at the bottom of our deep repository path. This is really not great because you need to use modules in the lib/python/Products directory of the Zope server. How can you get them there? Well, if the Zope directory is on the same computer as the CVS repository, you can just move this "checked-out" Product directory TotallySimpleProduct to the lib/python/Products directory of your Zope, carrying along with it the new CVS subdirectory that CVS needs to keep track of the files in that directory. Another, less cumbersome, approach is to define a CVS Module. Here is a step-by-step summary of setting up a CVS module:

1. Go to your home directory: `cd`
2. Create a directory for CVS administrative files:

   ```
   mkdir cvsadmin
   ```

3. Go there: `cd cvsadmin/`
4. Check out the CVS administrative files from the repository: `cvs co CVSROOT`

   ```
   cvs checkout: Updating CVSROOT
   ```

   ```
   U CVSROOT/.cvsignore
   U CVSROOT/checkoutlist
   U CVSROOT/commitinfo
   U CVSROOT/cvswrappers
   U CVSROOT/editinfo
   ```

```
U CVSROOT/loginfo
U CVSROOT/modules
U CVSROOT/notify
U CVSROOT/rcsinfo
U CVSROOT/taginfo
U CVSROOT/verifymsg
```

5. Go into the administrative directory: `cd CVSROOT/`
6. Edit the modules file, and add a line like this:

   ```
   TotallySimpleProduct   zope/lib/python/Products/TotallySimpleProduct
   ```

   The first term is the "Module" name, and the second is the "Module Path," where in the repository the Module is located.
7. When you've finished editing the file, commit this file back to the repository:

   ```
   cvs commit -m "added TotallyStupidProduct to modules"
   cvs commit: Examining .
   Checking in modules;
   /usr/cvsroot/CVSROOT/modules,v  <—  modules
   new revision: 1.31; previous revision: 1.30
   done
   cvs commit: Rebuilding administrative file database
   ```
8. Now test it; go to your Zope lib/python/Products directory:

   ```
   *cd /your/zopedirectory/lib/python/Products/*
   ```
9. You can delete the old TotallySimpleProduct directory:

   ```
   rm -r TotallySimpleProduct/
   ```
10. Check out your CVS version:

    ```
    *cvs co TotallySimpleProduct*

    cvs checkout: Updating TotallySimpleProduct
    U TotallySimpleProduct/.cvsignore
    U TotallySimpleProduct/TotallySimpleProduct.gif
    U TotallySimpleProduct/TotallySimpleProduct.py
    U TotallySimpleProduct/__init__.py
    U TotallySimpleProduct/addInstance.dtml
    ```

    That's it!

### Using CVS After the Repository Is Set Up

The three most important CVS actions are checkout, update, and commit. We've pretty well covered checkout at this point. When you have a checked out a working directory, you'll want to make changes. Let's say that you add a method called `new_method`, following along with these steps:

1. Edit TotallySimpleProduct.py by adding the following method to the TotallySimpleProduct class:

```
    def new_method(self):
        "display a new method"
        return '<html><body>I am a new method of
TotallySimpleProduct</body></html>'
```

2. If you do a "cvs update" now, you should see that CVS knows you've changed something:

```
cvs update

cvs update: Updating .
M TotallySimpleProduct.py
```

3. The `M` means that TotallySimpleProduct.py has been modified by you since you checked out or updated. You can even ask what changed using the `diff` command:

```
cvs diff

cvs diff: Diffing .
Index: TotallySimpleProduct.py
===================================================================
RCS file: TotallySimpleProduct/TotallySimpleProduct.py,v
retrieving revision 1.1.1.1
diff -r1.1.1.1 TotallySimpleProduct.py
33a34,36
>     def new_method(self):
>         "display a new method"
>         return '<html><body>I am a new method of
➥TotallySimpleProduct</body></html>'
```

4. CVS says that three lines were inserted at line 33, which became lines 34 to 36. Then it displays the new lines. If you like the change and it works, you can commit it to CVS:

```
cvs commit -m "added new_method to TotallySimpleProduct"

cvs commit: Examining .
Checking in TotallySimpleProduct.py;
TotallySimpleProduct/TotallySimpleProduct.py,v  <—  TotallySimpleProduct.py
new revision: 1.2; previous revision: 1.1
done
```

5. Other developers will get your change the next time they do an update. It's always a good idea to do an update at the beginning of a session and before you commit a change.

### Using CVS over the Network/Internet

CVS can be used over the network/Internet in a variety of ways. Some are easier to set up than others, and some are more secure than others. We've chosen to describe how you can use `ssh` to connect CVS client to server, but you should read about the other options at **`http://www.cvshome.org`**. The `ssh` option is good because `ssh` encrypts network traffic over the Internet, and it's widely ported to most UNIX-like platforms and Windows. For `ssh` issues, you can refer to **`http://dmoz.org/Computers/Security/Products_and_Tools/Cryptography/SSH/`** for more information.

The basic idea is to let CVS use `ssh` to make a remote shell connection to the computer that has the CVS repository. You can do this by setting the CVS_RSH environment variable. Let's say that your name is John, with a username `john`, and you work at home. The CVS repository is stored on a computer called `repo.my.com`, where the CVS repository is stored in the /cvsroot directory of repo.my.com's filesystem. Figure 14.3 illustrates this setup. You would set the CVS_RSH environment variable and check out your module as shown here:

1. If you're using sh, or one of its derivatives, type this:

   ```
   export CVS_RSH=ssh
   ```

   Or, if you're using csh or one of its derivatives, type this:

   ```
   setenv CVS_RSH ssh
   ```

   On Windows, type this:

   ```
   set CVS_RSH=ssh
   ```

2. Then try this:

   ```
   cvs -z3 \
   -d:ext:john@repo.my.com:/cvsroot/\
   co TotallySimpleProject
   ```

   (Note that the `-z` flag is important. It turns on compression of the CVS networking protocol. Without it, your cvs commands might be very slow!)

3. If you've never used ssh before, you might see this:

   ```
   The authenticity of host 'repo' can't be established.
   RSA key fingerprint is df:34:df:.<lots of codes here>.:.
   Are you sure you want to continue connecting (yes/no)?
   ```

   This is normal if you've never connected with ssh or if you are connecting to a host with a dynamic IP. If you *have* connected with ssh and you see this message, it could be a problem. Contact your administrator!

4. You will probably see this:

   ```
   john@repo.my.com's password:
   ```

Enter your password for the repo computer. After awhile, entering your password might be annoying. You can enter your public key into the .ssh public keys file on the server to avoid having to type it each time. You can copy ssh public keys onto the cvs server to eliminate this step, but the details are outside the scope of this chapter. Visit the ssh site **http://dmoz.org/Computers/Security/Products_and_Tools/Cryptography/SSH/** for more information.

5. Finally, you should get this:

```
cvs server: Updating TotallySimpleProduct
U TotallySimpleProduct/.cvsignore
U TotallySimpleProduct/TotallySimpleProduct.gif
U TotallySimpleProduct/TotallySimpleProduct.py
U TotallySimpleProduct/__init__.py
U TotallySimpleProduct/addInstance.dtml
```

6. When this is done, you can now go to the TotallySimpleProduct directory and use the `cvs` command without the `-d` flag because it is stored in the CVS directory.

There is a lot more to using CVS for filesystem-based objects than we can cover in a short introduction, but this should be enough to get you started with CVS. If you have questions, be sure to see **http://www.cvshome.org** for answers.

Before we move on to Zope objects in CVS, there is one important point left to make. When multiple developers are using CVS, each developer gets a copy of the project source files and runs them on his Zope server while developing and testing. When the files are shown to work, the developer checks them in so that other developers will be able to update their Zope servers with the working sources. When we move to Zope objects, this paradigm shifts just a little, but the basic idea stays the same.

## Using Zope and CVS

CVS works great for filesystem-based objects, but what about objects that are defined purely in Zope? What about ZClasses and editable DTML Methods and Documents? There is a product that can help with that too! It's called ZCVSFolder and can be found at the Zope.org site: **http://www.zope.org/Members/sspickle/ZCVSMixin/**. This URL might look a little weird, but when I started work on ZCVSMixin, it was a class that could be mixed into a ZClass, or Zope product, to give it CVS access. Shane Hathaway contributed patches to make it an object that you instantiated in a container to give its container CVS access, which has proven much more flexible. Other significant contributions have been made by Mikael Berthe, Alcove. At this time, ZCVSFolder is UNIX only; although we have thought about a Windows version, we have no budget to create it at this time. As usual, we will kindly accept patches that enable Windows support.

## Setting Up ZCVSFolder

ZCVSFolder uses Zope's built-in import/export mechanism to save and restore Zope objects to and from the filesystem. It then uses CVS to manage those filesystem representations of the original Zope objects. This part can be confusing the first time you work with it, so we'll describe the situation carefully. ZCVSFolder keeps a filesystem-based representation of all the objects that it manages in a "checked out" directory on the local filesystem of the Zope folder. There is a management tab in the ZCVSFolder object in Zope that lets you tell ZCVSFolder where the filesystem directory for the filesystem copy of the objects is located so that ZCVSFolder can load or store them from or to the filesystem. This means that to use ZCVSFolder, you need to set up a CVS repository just like before. You then need to create a place on the filesystem for your objects. Here is a demonstration of that process:

1. Create an empty directory where your Zope objects will be stored: `mkdir myProject`
2. Go there: `cd myProject`
3. Import the empty directory so that CVS will know about it:
   ```
   cvs import -m "start new module for zopeObjects" \
       zope/zopeObjs/myProject sjs start
   ```
   No conflicts are created by this import.
4. Now remove it and check it back out:
   ```
   cd ..
   rm -r myProject
   cvs co zope/zopeObjs/myProject
   cvs checkout: Updating zope/zopeObjs/myProject
   ```
5. Now you have an empty directory on the filesystem that is under CVS. Now we go to Zope.

Before you restart Zope, make sure that the Zope process has access to the CVS repository as a user. This means that Zope needs to run as a user with rights to the CVS repository if it is on the same computer, or CVS networking needs to be set up for the Zope process so that it can get to the CVS repository over the network. This is done in exactly the same way for Zope as for any other user. For example, you can set the CVS_RSH environment variable in the Zope `start` script. After you install ZCVSFolder in your Zope's Products directory and restart Zope, you should see a new option in the Select Type to Add... pop-up menu in your Zope folders. The new type is CVS Folder. To test your installation, create a Zope folder at the root of your Zope called `testCVS`. In that folder, create a couple DTML Methods, a DTML Document, and a Python script or two. Then add a CVS Folder to the folder. When you select CVS Folder as an object to add, you'll see a Create CVS Folder input form, as shown in Figure 14.4.

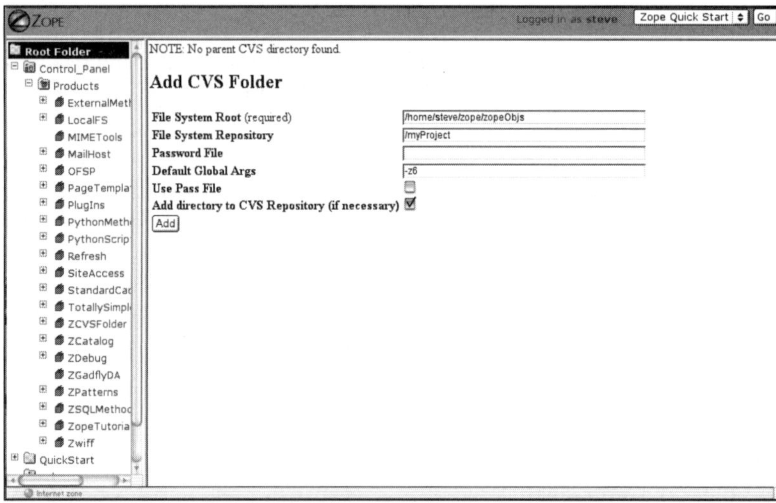


Figure 14.4 Adding a CVS Folder to a container.

When you click on the CVS Folder in the ZMI, you should see a management interface that looks something like Figure 14.5.

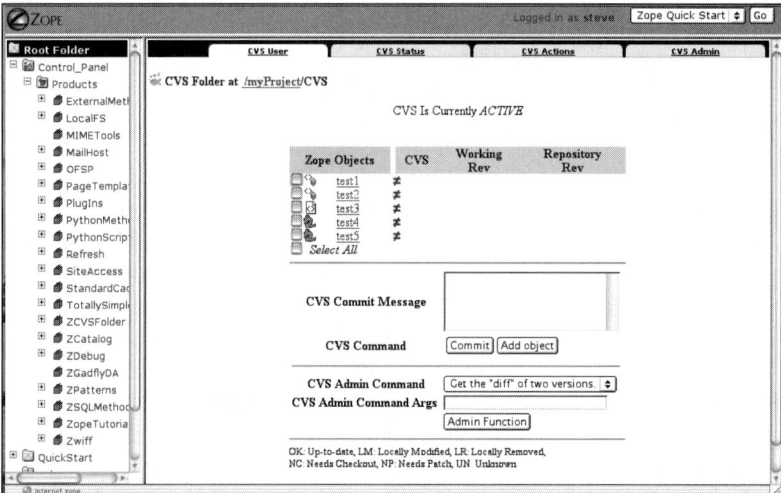


Figure 14.5 Management interface of CVS Folder.

There are several things worth noting in this interface. There are four tabs across the top of the interface called CVS User, CVS Status, CVS Actions, and CVS Admin.

CVS User is the screen that tells you what you want to know 93% of the time. It indicates what files in the current folder are at what version. Notice that, right now, all the objects have a "not-equals" sign because there is no CVS version for them yet. These files have not been added to CVS! To add them all, click the Select All check box, type in a commit message (such as "add all these objects"), and click Add Object. You should get an OK button if everything works. When the objects are added, you'll notice that the "not-equals" signs are replace by equals signs. If you modify one of the objects in the folder and revisit CVS User, it tells you that the version on the filesystem does not match the version in Zope, by changing the equals sign icon back to a "not equals" icon.

CVS Status is a much more informative, but also much more dangerous, display. It has controls to let you check in or check out Zope objects in the current folder, or recursively in all the folders below. Because you modified one of the objects in the folder, you should now see a management interface on the CVS Status tab that looks like Figure 14.6.

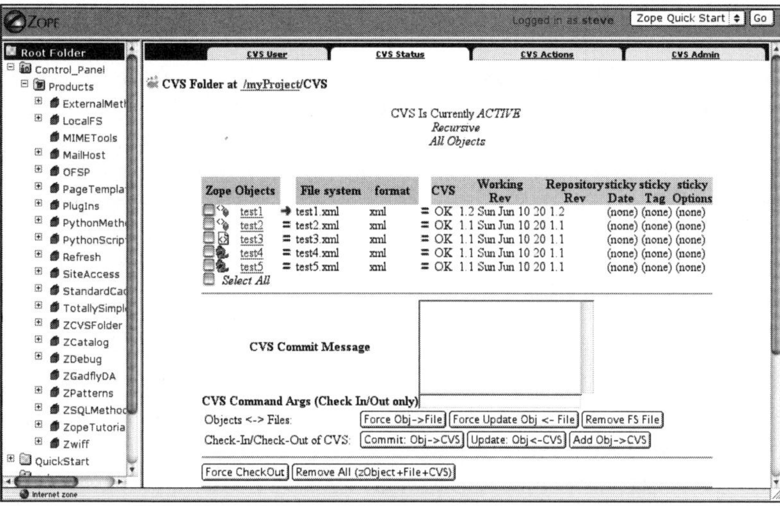


**Figure 14.6** CVS status screen with one object modified.

Notice that there is now an arrow pointing from the Zope side of the window toward the CVS side. This indicates that there has been a change to the Zope object that could be checked into CVS. To perform a check-in, you just type in a commit message, click the check box for the object that changed, and click Commit under the CVS User tab, or Commit: Obj->CVS under the CVS Status page (these both perform the same function).

There are a lot of buttons on the CVS Status page. You should try them out on a test project to make sure that you understand them. Briefly, the top row transfers objects back and forth between Zope and the filesystem, without regard to CVS. This can be useful if your CVS connection is down and you want to restore or back up some objects, or if CVS is confused about an object's date of modification and you want to "force" an update and CVS might complain of a potential conflict. The second row of buttons stores, retrieves, and adds objects to CVS. The third row is the most dangerous. It contains the Force Checkout and Remove All buttons. Force checkout updates the Zope object in Zope with the CVS object without checking first to see if the Zope object might have been modified since it was last checked out. This is dangerous because you might lose changes made to the Zope object. Remove All is dangerous because it removes the object from Zope, the filesystem, and CVS all at the same time. This is difficult to reverse.

There is a lower section of buttons that does CVS administrative tasks. You can get log files for objects, report their detailed status, `diff` from one version to another, and force an update of the filesystem version from CVS.

The CVS Actions tab has only one action at this time, but others might appear here in future versions. This action creates CVS folders recursively throughout the project, if they are not already there. This is great for bringing an existing project into CVS.

Finally, CVS Admin is where the properties of the CVS Folder object itself are kept. This includes the location of the CVS working directory on the local filesystem, the default compression level, and whether and where to keep the .cvspass file, if you are using pserver mode of CVS networking (this is generally not recommended because it is less secure than the ssh mode). There is also a list of metatypes to ignore. This is the Zope equivalent of the .cvsignore file, but it is based on the Zope object's `meta_type`.

## A Typical Scenario

To make it clear how this might be used in a multi-developer setting, we're going to walk through the process of two developers setting up areas on their own Zope server where they work on the same Zope project, coordinated with ZCVSFolder. We already have `john` set up; let's also set up `sue`, who, as you can see from Figure 14.3, is on the company LAN along with the CVS repository. She starts working on `myProject`, so she needs to get a checkout of the myProject zope objects. She does this in the usual way; then she creates a new empty folder in her Zope. She then adds a CVS folder to that new empty folder and points it to the filesystem directory where she checked out the Zope objects.

Her new Zope folder will contain, at this time, only the CVS Folder. If she clicks the CVS Status tab of the CVS Folder, she'll see a screen something like Figure 14.7.

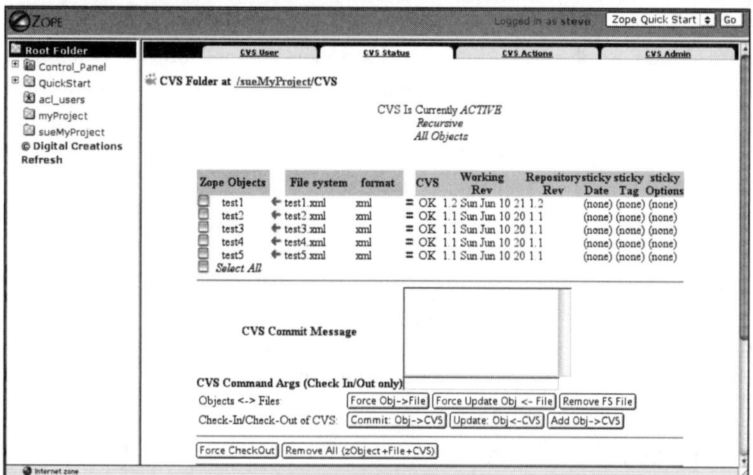


| Zope Objects | File system | format | CVS | Working Rev | Repository Rev | sticky Date | sticky Tag | sticky Options |
|---|---|---|---|---|---|---|---|---|
| test1 | ← test1.xml | xml | = OK | 1.2 Sun Jun 10 21 | 1.2 | (none) | (none) | (none) |
| test2 | ← test2.xml | xml | = OK | 1.1 Sun Jun 10 20 | 1.1 | (none) | (none) | (none) |
| test3 | ← test3.xml | xml | = OK | 1.1 Sun Jun 10 20 | 1.1 | (none) | (none) | (none) |
| test4 | ← test4.xml | xml | = OK | 1.1 Sun Jun 10 20 | 1.1 | (none) | (none) | (none) |
| test5 | ← test5.xml | xml | = OK | 1.1 Sun Jun 10 20 | 1.1 | (none) | (none) | (none) |
| Select All | | | | | | | | |

**Figure 14.7** CVS status screen before objects are checked out.

Notice that CVS Folder knows about the objects that are waiting to be checked out of CVS into Zope. Sue would now simply click the Force Checkout button because there are no Zope objects yet. Now she has all the objects in Zope that were retrieved from CVS.

Now, suppose that Sue makes a change to one of her objects. She tests the change and commits it to CVS with an appropriate message. The next time John visits his CVS User or CVS Status screen, he should notice that his project is no longer up-to-date. His CVS status screen would look like Figure 14.8.

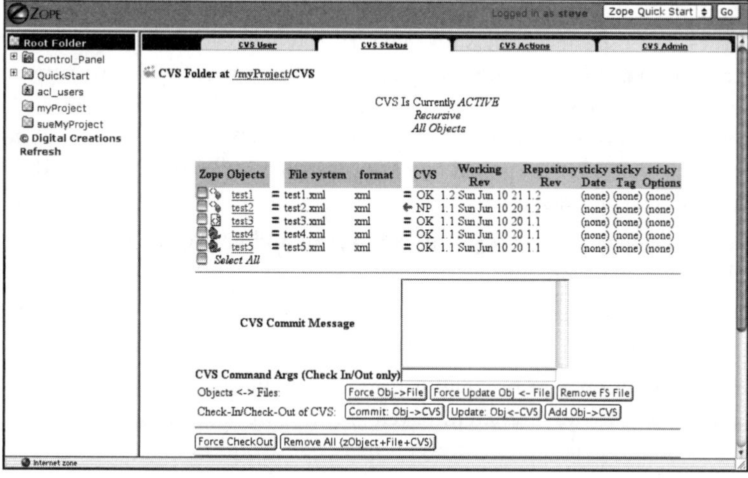


| Zope Objects | File system | format | CVS | Working Rev | Repository Rev | sticky Date | sticky Tag | sticky Options |
|---|---|---|---|---|---|---|---|---|
| test1 | = test1.xml | xml | = OK | 1.2 Sun Jun 10 21 | 1.2 | (none) | (none) | (none) |
| test2 | = test2.xml | xml | ← NP | 1.1 Sun Jun 10 20 | 1.2 | (none) | (none) | (none) |
| test3 | = test3.xml | xml | = OK | 1.1 Sun Jun 10 20 | 1.1 | (none) | (none) | (none) |
| test4 | = test4.xml | xml | = OK | 1.1 Sun Jun 10 20 | 1.1 | (none) | (none) | (none) |
| test5 | = test5.xml | xml | = OK | 1.1 Sun Jun 10 20 | 1.1 | (none) | (none) | (none) |
| Select All | | | | | | | | |

**Figure 14.8** CVS status screen showing object modified by another developer.

On the CVS status screen, there is a left-pointing arrow indicating that another developer has modified an object. Notice that developers can add objects, delete objects, and generally have a lot of freedom to make changes without the problem of locking out other developers. If two developers modify the same object, CVS should catch the conflict when one of the developers tries to update his modified version, another good reason to do an update before a check-in!

You should play with some of the other options for ZCVSFolder. You can check out specific revisions by Date, Tag (you can tag revisions with strings, such as release numbers), or Version number. You can branch and (manually) merge. You can also "update" using ZCVSFolder into a Zope Version for "final testing" before committing the updates objects to a live system. Next, you'll see how you can use CVS to create a systematic staging process for your Zope application.

# Staging with CVS

One of the fundamental realities of application development is that they are never finished. There are inevitable bugs that might manifest themselves only when the application is deployed in the real working environment. There are features that were not implemented in the first version for some reason. There are improvements that are requested after users become familiar with the system and give feedback. It's clear that some changes are going to need to be made. The question is, "How?"

This section suggest a strategy for developing and deploying an application in such a way that it can evolve in a controlled way after initial deployment.

## Each Developer Gets a Zope

First of all, each Zope developer should be using his own instance of Zope. At the very beginning, it might make sense to set up the basic structure of the application, initial classes, ZClasses, and folders on one server, where everybody can work together. However, as soon as the structure "gels," the application should be committed to CVS (filesystem and Zope components). Then the Zope portions can be exported (in .zexp form) and then imported into each developer's Zope. CVS can then be used to keep instances up-to-date after the initial application structure has been imported. This method has several advantages:

- Each developer has free reign to experiment and `break` things without affecting other developers' progress.
- When Zope accesses CVS, it behaves like a `user`. It's nice if Zope simply runs as the developer's uid and acts like that developer as far as CVS is concerned.
- If the application is to be multiplatform, issues of platform dependency can be noticed early because different developers can work on different development platforms and make sure that everyone's code works there.

After each developer is set up, they all can develop their components of the system as described earlier. Tests can be developed, committed to CVS, and propagated to the rest of the development team. It might be necessary to "branch" development at some time. This is complicated with ZCVSFolder because the filesystem representation of objects is "morally" binary, in the sense that XML is not a friendly text representation. When you make a "branch" in CVS, you will almost surely later need to "merge" the branch back to the main code line. With truly binary files (such as images), you just need to pick the one that you want (the branch version or the main version), and you can choose the same options for ZCVSFolder objects. Or, you can fish inside the XML, dig out the part you are interested in, and merge that by hand. Although this can work, it's labor-intensive. There are several efforts underway to improve this situation. Hopefully one of these will succeed.

## Setting Up a Test Server

When it comes time for user testing, it makes sense to set up a "user-test" Zope. This is basically just like a developer machine, except that it generally doesn't run with the most current software. Why not? Running a test server means making "releases" that are well defined. In CVS, you can `tag` code with a release ID. Using ZCVSFolder, you can update the test server, not with the most up-to-date software, but with the software that belongs to a particular release. The beauty of CVS is that you can always reconstruct the system as it existed at the release by `updating` to that release. This is done using the `-r` tag on the command line: `cvs update -r rel-0-1-3b1`.

This updates the current folder, and all folders below it, to the release tagged `rel-0-1-3b1`. You also can do this for objects stored with ZCVSMixin using the command line, or under the CVS Status tab by putting the extra arguments in the CVS Command Args input field.

When the correct release is running on the test server, you can let the users test it, collect bug reports, and start tracking them down. You'll want a bug-tracking system. We have been very pleased with the Zope Tracker (**`http://www.zope.org/Members/klm/TrackerWiki/TrackerCVSInstructions`**). This product is a bug/feature request database that does email notification, collects bug reports, and archives conversations about the bugs, along with many other great features. Thank you, DC, for another great product!

## Going Live with CVS

"Going live" means committing your changes to a production server actively delivering your application. Using CVS, you can update objects from the test server to the live server with the click of a button. However, it sometimes happens that conditions on the live server are not identical to conditions on the test server, so an undiscovered problem can occur. (Virtual host settings are famous for this sort of thing.) This is a situation in which using Zope Versions makes a lot of sense! You can create a Zope version object and start working in that version. Now when you use ZCVSFolder to update the Zope objects in your application, they will be updated *in the version you are working in.* This means that after the update, you can run tests, view various pages, and generally make sure that everything is okay. Then you can save the version, and the live site is instantly updated with the new Zope objects.

# Testing and Versions

As you develop your Zope application, you'll need to break the problem into small sets of objects and methods. How do you verify that these objects work after you create them? You test them, of course! The problem is that an informal, manual test that works today might fail tomorrow due to another change made in the application. So you test again, right? Yes, but what happens on the third day, or the fourth? A complex application can have hundreds of objects and methods. Finding bugs in these methods by manually testing them during development is practically *guaranteed* to fail. Fortunately, you can use much more systematic, thorough, and, therefore, effective testing strategies with Zope. In this chapter, we will use a Zope module called PyUnit to illustrate how "unit testing" can help you systematically test your application components while development proceeds.

> **The Origins of Unit Testing**
>
> Unit testing is a component of a development strategy known as "Extreme Programming." The idea is to make testing so easy that developers test early and test often. A unit test becomes part of the code and is stored in the repository along with the code it that tests. You can find out much more about unit testing and the concepts behind it at **http://www.extremeprogramming.org/rules/unittests.html**. There is a more detailed description of extreme programming in Chapter 3, "Web Event Publishing."

## Unit Testing Means Checking Each Part

The idea of unit testing is that a complex system is made up of many simpler components. It's a lot easier to test the simple components separately than it is to test the entire complex system. If you define what each component does in terms of possible inputs and outputs, verify that each possible input produces the correct output, and connect the components correctly, then the system as a whole should work correctly.

In some of the most disciplined forms of unit testing, software developers spend the time to write programs to test that their components behave correctly *before* they even start writing the software to implement the components themselves!

For Zope, there are two levels of unit testing that we'll consider: unit testing at the Python level, and unit testing in Zope itself. We'll start with standalone Python unit testing, and then we'll describe the Zope product, ZUnit, produced by HiperLogica and contributed to the Zope community.

## Unit Testing in Python

Unit testing is now a built-in part of Python (as of Python 2.1), but it has been shipping with Zope as a standard library since before that. The unittest.py module, called PyUnit, was created by Steve Purcell and modeled after JUnit, by Kent Beck and Erich Gamma, a Java testing module that follows Kent's Smalltalk testing framework. You can find more about PyUnit at **`http://pyunit.sourceforge.net/`**.

The most important class in unittest.py is TestCase. A TestCase is used to test exactly one scenario. You subclass TestCase to create TestCases of your own. The simplest possible useful subclass would override only the `runTest` method. If the `runTest` method of a TestCase returns with no AssertionError exceptions, then the TestCase is considered a success. If it throws an AssertionError exception, the TestCase is a failure. If the TestCase throws some other exception, it is considered a testing framework error. An example will make this more clear. First, suppose that you add a little more flesh to the TotallySimpleProduct example. Listing 14.1 is the definition of a pure Python base class called SimpleBase. We call it "pure" because it doesn't subclass from any of the Zope persistence or acquisition machinery. You can use this as a foundation upon which to add features to your TotallySimpleProduct.

Listing 14.1 **A Very Simple Pure Python Base Class**

```
#
# Base class for a Simple Python Product.
#

class SimpleBase:

    """
    SimpleBase is a pure python class used to
    keep a few simple properties as an example.
    """

    name = ''
    age = -1

    def __init__(self, name=None, age=None):
        """ create a SimpleBase """
        if name is not None:
            self.name = name

        if age is not None:
            self.age = age

    def __repr__(self):
        """ represent yourself to the world """
        displayString = "<SimpleBase instance name=%s, age=%i>"
        return displayString % (self.name, self.age)

```

*continues*

Listing 14.1 **Continued**

```
    def checkAge(self):
        """
        return true if age has been set
        to something intelligent
        """

        return age > -1

```

To test this class, we need to create an instance, execute one of its methods, and then *assert* that the method functioned correctly. It's best to create the TestCase objects in a separate file from the class that it tests. Listing 14.2 illustrates this idea.

Listing 14.2 **Creating a Simple TestCase**

```
# file: testSimpleBase.py
#

from SimpleBase import SimpleBase
import unittest

class testDefaultAge(unittest.TestCase):

    def runTest(self):
        sb=SimpleBase()
        assert sb.age == -1
```

That's not so bad. Notice that runTest creates a clean SimpleBase instance and then *asserts* that the default age is correctly set to `-1`. If this were not true, the assert statement would throw an AssertionError, and the test would fail.

Every test case that needs a SimpleBase object will need to instantiate one and then test it. If SimpleBase performs any resource-consuming functions, those resources need to be freed after the test case is finished (whether it succeeds or fails). You can see that if you create a completely new class for every test case, there will be a lot of duplication. PyUnit defines a more convenient technique called a `fixture`. You can define a method called `setUp` that can be used to create any necessary conditions to perform all the tests. Another method called `tearDown` will take care of housekeeping details that must be completed after the test. Listing 14.3 shows how this can work.

Listing 14.3 **Setting Up a Fixture for Multiple Tests**

```
import unittest

class SBFixture(unittest.TestCase):

    def setUp(self):
        self.sb = SimpleBase()
```

```

    def tearDown(self):
        self.sb = None

class testDefaultAge(SBFixture):

    def runTest(self):
        assert self.sb.age == -1


class testDefaultName(SBFixture):

    def runTest(self):
        assert self.sb.name == ''
```

As you can see, if you run lots of small tests that use the same fixture, you could still end up with lots of duplication. PyUnit allows for a different method of specifying tests in this case: You can pass in the name of the method to run as an argument to the TestCase constructor. In this way, you can combine many tests into the same subclass of TestCase. Listing 14.4 illustrates this idea.

Listing 14.4 **A Single Class with Many Tests**

```
import unittest

class testSimpleBase(unittest.TestCase):

    def setUp(self):
        self.sb = SimpleBase()

    def tearDown(self):
        self.sb = None

    def checkDefaultAge(self):
        assert self.sb.age == -1

    def checkDefaultName(self):
        assert self.sb.name == ''
```

When you instantiate the TestCase objects, you need to specify the name of the test:

```
myAgeCheck = testSimpleBase("checkDefaultAge")
```

Tests start to accumulate quickly once you get the hang of it. You'll need some way to organize them into groups. PyUnit provides the class TestSuite to take care of this for you. You first create an instance of a TestSuite, and then you call `addTest` for each test that you want to include in the suite. It turns out to be convenient to create the suite in a function of the test module that builds the suite and returns it. Listing 14.5 shows how this works.

Listing 14.5 **Creating a Suite of Tests**

```
def suite():

    simpleTestSuite = unittest.TestSuite()
    simpleTestSuite.addTest(testSimpleBase("checkDefaultAge"))
    simpleTestSuite.addTest(testSimpleBase("checkDefaultName"))

    return simpleTestSuite
```

Of course, it's no good if you don't actually *run* the tests! So, you need a way to run them. PyUnit provides TextTestRunner. It is a class that has a method "run" that accepts a TestSuite as its only argument. You can add a function to the end of your testSimpleBase module that creates a runner and calls it, as shown in Listing 14.6.

Listing 14.6 **Creating a TestRunner**

```
def test():
    runner = unittest.TextTestRunner()
    runner.run(suite())

if __name__=="__main__":
    test()
```

The `if` clause at the end of the listing enables you to run the tests from the command line:

```
python testSimpleBase.py
checkDefaultAge (__main__.testSimpleBase) ... ok
checkDefaultName (__main__.testSimpleBase) ... ok
-----------------------------------------------
Ran 2 tests in 0.002s

OK
```

If you have questions or need more documentation about PyUnit, visit the excellent web site for the project at **`http://pyunit.sourceforge.net`**.

## Unit Testing in Zope

Now that you have mastered unit testing in Python, it's fairly easy to do unit testing in Zope. ZUnit is a Python product by Lalo Martins and Leonardo Almeida at Hiperlogica. It is still being developed at the SourceForge site **`http://zunit.sourceforge.net`**, but the last public announcement, and this description, are based on the www.zope.org release at **`http://www.zope.org/Members/lalo/ZUnit`**.

Be careful when you unpack this distribution because it needs to be expanded in the lib/python directory rather than the lib/python/Products directory; it creates a new directory under lib/python/Shared.

ZUnit introduces two new object types: ZUnit External Test Case and ZUnit Test Runner. The ZUnit External Test Case corresponds to a python module on the filesystem that can create a test suite when called. You can test the existing SimpleBase class by creating a ZUnit Test Runner that points to your "suite" method. Create a testing folder in Zope that has the TotallySimpleProduct installed, along with the SimpleBase class module. Create a ZUnit External Test Case with an ID of `testSimpleBase` and a Python path of Products.TotallySimpleProduct.testSimpleBase.suite. This tells the External Test Case where to find the function to call to get the test suite.

To actually run the tests, you need a ZUnit Test Runner. Create a ZUnit Test Runner in the same directory; call it `runTests`. If you inspect the Properties tab of the Test Runner, you'll see a list type property called `test_ids`. This is where you can list the IDs of all the External Test Case objects that you want to run with the Test Runner. Enter `testSimpleBase` into this property. Now, click the Run Tests tab and click Run It. You should see a screen with two periods (`..`) because you defined two tests in the SimpleBase test suite. Each period means that a test passed successfully. If a test fails, you will see an `E`, indicating that an error has occurred.

You can go back later and review old tests by clicking on the contents tab of the TestRunner. It lists there test reports for each execution of the TestRunner.

To test actual Zope objects, you have to create a test suite that works with your Zope object under test. To sew this up a little, let's add the glue to the TotallySimpleProduct to make it a subclass of the pure Python SimpleBase class. For your reference, the complete text of the TotallySimpleProduct.py file is provided in Listing 14.7.

Listing 14.7 **The TotallySimpleProduct Inherits from SimpleBase**

```
#
# TotallySimpleProduct
#

from OFS import SimpleItem
from Globals import HTMLFile

def manage_addTotallySimpleProduct(self, id=None, REQUEST=None):
    "Add a TotallySimpleProduct."
    self._setObject(id, TotallySimpleProduct(id))

    if REQUEST:
        return self.manage_main(self, REQUEST, update_menu=1)

manage_addTotallySimpleProductForm = HTMLFile('addInstance',globals())

__doc__ = "A TotallySimpleProduct"
__version__ = '0.0.1'
```

*continues*

Listing 14.7 **Continued**

```

from SimpleBase import SimpleBase

class TotallySimpleProduct(SimpleItem.Item, SimpleBase):

    "Totally Simple Product"

    meta_type = 'TotallySimpleProduct'

    def __init__(self, id, name=None, age=None):
        "Set the id of the TotallySimpleProduct"
        TotallySimpleProduct.inheritedAttribute('__init__')(self, name, age)
        self.id = id

    def index_html(self):
        "display yourself to the world"
        displayString = '<html><body>I am a TotallySimpleProduct %s
        ➥</body></html>'
        return displayString % `self`

    def new_method(self):
        "display a new method"
        return '<html><body>I am a new method of
        ➥TotallySimpleProduct</body></html>'


def initialize(context):
    context.registerClass(
        TotallySimpleProduct,
        constructors=(manage_addTotallySimpleProductForm,
        ➥manage_addTotallySimpleProduct),
        icon='TotallySimpleProduct.gif',
        )
```

Notice that we had to add to the class declaration, telling TotallySimpleProduct to inherit from both SimpleItem.Item and SimpleBase. We had to modify the constructor to call the `__init__` method of the base class. If you've done Python programming before, you might have expected something more like this:

```
SimpleBase.__init__(self, name, age)
```

However, this doesn't work because SimpleItem.Item inherits from the magical Zope ExtensionClass, which allows Python classes to inherit from C extensions. The `inheritedAttribute` method of ExtensionClass gets a proper unbound method that you can call as you would expect `SimpleBase.__init__` to be called.

You need to create a test suite for your TotallySimpleProduct now. You can't use the plain unittest.TestSuite and unittest.TestCase classes, though, because they know nothing about Zope and especially about the concept of `context` in Zope. Happily, ZUnit provides classes for you to create ZUnit test cases. Listing 14.8 shows the module testTotallySimple.py, which creates a very small `suite` (it's only one test!) callable through the `suite` function.

Listing 14.8 **Test Suite for TotallySimpleProduct**

```
#
# Test the TotallySimpleZope Product
#

from Products import ZUnit
from TotallySimpleProduct import manage_addTotallySimpleProduct

class TotallySimpleTest (ZUnit.Tests.TestCase):

        def testAddSimpleObject (self):
                testFolder = self.ZopeContext
                manage_addTotallySimpleProduct(testFolder, 'foobie')
                assert testFolder.has_key('foobie')

def suite():
    return ZUnit.Tests.makeSuite( TotallySimpleTest )
```

What are you testing? ZUnit creates a new folder for each test. It then sets the `ZopeContext` member of the TestCase to be that folder. You are calling the factory that creates TotallySimpleProducts, using the testFolder as the container and `foobie` as the ID. After the add is finished, you `assert` that testFolder contains such an object.

Go to your test folder in Zope, and create a new External Test Case object, but this time pointing to the path:

```
Products.TotallySimpleProduct.testTotallySimple.suite
```

Call it `testTotallySimple`. Next, go to the `runTests` TestRunner and add `testTotallySimple` to the list of External Test Cases that runTests will perform. Under the Run Tests tab, you'll notice a check box that reads, Keep Data (for Debugging). If you check this box, it will keep the folder created for each test and save it with the results. You can visit this folder after the test is complete and see how things turned out manually. If you don't check the box, the folder is deleted after the test. Now when you click the Run It button under the Run Tests tab, you should see three periods (...). As before, each period represents one test completed successfully.

Accumulating and running unit tests during development is a great way to make sure that your project is still working, in all its parts, as you add features and fix bugs.

## Summary

Starting with version control, through unit testing, and finally touching on staging and deployment, this chapter has presented solutions to many of the problems faced by teams of developers developing complex applications in Zope. There is no panacea! Whenever more than one person is involved, communication and clear areas of responsibility are probably as important as any tool. However, understanding and using the tools will make what would otherwise be an extremely difficult job something that is quite manageable. We hope you find these tools as useful in your work as we've found them in ours.

# V

# Mission-Critical Web Publishing

# 15

# Scaling Up

SO NOW YOU'VE FINISHED YOUR WEB APPLICATION and it is deployed! You've met all the requirements and the bugs are getting squashed. There's only one problem: You've done your job too well. The application is so popular that the chosen server can barely keep up! You're getting so many hits that the server is constantly chugging, and the users are starting to complain of "sluggishness." What to do now? Time to redesign the application? Switch to a RDBMS? Maybe, but not so fast! This chapter is about assessing the performance of Zope, tuning, and, if necessary, scaling Zope to meet the greater demands of a very large community of users.

## Orders of Magnitude

There are no hard-and-fast rules about performance and scaling; however, there are "rules of thumb." A single Zope instance on a modest server with relatively simple documents and scripts can handle several thousands of hits per day with "reasonable" performance. If your application is busier than that, or if your processing is very complex (for example, with time-consuming scripts or templates), then you might need to read this chapter!

## From Class to School to School District

When the attendance application is first deployed, it might be tested in only a few classrooms. This means that in the morning when teachers are recording attendance, there will be a relatively short period of time when each of these teachers might be accessing the system a few times. Let's say that each teacher posts some students to the attendance system five times in 15 minutes. If you have five teachers, this works out to 25 posts in 15 minutes. Next it might be deployed to the whole school, so you get 50 teachers posting in 15 minutes, or 250 posts in 15 minutes. Next, you'll do the whole school district: 500 teachers, or 2500 posts in 15 minutes. How does Zope handle such a rate? How can you find out? It's hard for a single developer with a web browser to test such access rates. One of the first problems that needs to be solved is how to *measure* Zope's capability to handle different kinds of requests at different rates. When you have some ability to tell how a particular application will work under different load conditions, then it's time to decide whether the performance is adequate.

## Estimating and Tool Selection

Luckily, there are a number of tools available to help with this:

- Programmatically "browsing" so that you can write scripts to test your site automatically. Tools such as Client.py in the Zope distribution are invaluable for this sort of thing.
- Benchmarking tools, such as the Apache Benchmarker (ab), to assess how Zope handles various levels of traffic.
- Logging tools, such as STUPID_FILE_LOGGER and the `-M` switch, to determine what is happening when.
- Profiling, built into Zope itself, to identify where bottlenecks are occurring.

To make a complete assessment of how Zope will react when your application is deployed and used by your targeted community, you might need to use some or all of these tools.

### Programmatically Browsing

In the Zope distribution, there is a great script called Client.py. You can find it at YourZope/lib/python/ZPublisher/Client.py. If you type the following:

```
/path/to/python $ZOPEROOT/lib/python/ZPublisher/Client.py
```

on the command line, you should get output like this:

```
Usage: /usr/local/etc/Zope2a/lib/python/ZPublisher/Client.py [-u
username:password] url [name=value ...]
where url is the web resource to call.

The -u option may be used to provide a username and password.
```

```
Optional arguments may be provides as name=value pairs.

In a name value pair, if a name ends in ":file", then the value is
treated as a filename and the file is sent using the file-upload
protocol. If the filename is "-", then data is taken from standard
input.

The body of the response is written to standard output.
The headers of the response are written to standard error.
```

This explains pretty well how this tool can be used. This discussion started with the Attendance application, so let's return to it and try to perform some "actions" on the command line using Client.py. The great news is that Client.py is totally independent of Zope itself, so you can copy the Client.py file to any convenient directory, you can make it executable (`chmod +x Client.py`), and you can call it from anywhere. For the purposes of brevity in the examples, this is done so that you'll see `Client.py -u foo:bar http://somewhere:8080/` rather than the long path used in the first example.

First, make sure that Client.py works by fetching the main Zope page. Type this:

```
Client.py http://localhost:8080/
```

You should see this:

```
server: Zope/(Zope 2.4.0 (source release, python 2.1, linux2), python 2.1.1,
darwin1) ZServer/1.1b1
content-length: 3026
content-type: text/html
connection: close
date: Sat, 04 Aug 2001 20:08:50 GMT

<html><head>
<base href="http://localhost:8080/" />
<title>Zope</title></head><body bgcolor="#FFFFFF">
<!DOCTYPE HTML PUBLIC "-//W3C//DTD HTML 4.0 Transitional//EN"
"http://www.w3.org/TR/REC-html40/loose.dtd">
<html>
<head>
<title>Zope QuickStart</title>
<link rel="stylesheet" type="text/css" href="/manage_page_style.css">

... < a lot more output skipped > ....

</a></p></body></html>
```

Great! This is just the default Zope intro page. Notice that Client.py first prints some information contained in the headers returned by the server and then presents the actual HTML returned. Next, use Client.py to get a listing of students in a classroom. You can do this, assuming that you have the same code from Chapter 12, "Integrating Applications with ZPatterns," still installed, if you type:

```
Client.py http://localhost:8080/attendanceZPatterns/display_app_html
```

You should get output that looks like this:

```
Traceback (most recent call last):
  File "/Users/steve/bin/Client.py", line 635, in ?
    main()
  File "/Users/steve/bin/Client.py", line 628, in main
    headers, body = apply(f,(),kw)
  File "/Users/steve/bin/Client.py", line 226, in __call__
    self.handleError(query, ec, em, headers, response)
  File "/Users/steve/bin/Client.py", line 241, in handleError
    raise t, RemoteException(t,v,f,l,self.url,query,ec,em,response)
bci.ServerError: bobo exception (File:
/Users/steve/Zope/lib/python/DocumentTemplate/DT_Raise.py Line: 128)
500 Internal Server Error for
http://localhost:8080/attendanceZPatterns/Homerooms/index_html
```

What? Hmmm, there is some sort of remote exception. It looks like it is being deliberately raised in DTML (notice the line in the traceback referring to `DocumentTemplate/DT_Raise.py Line: 128`). Because Client.py is designed to be useful not only as a command-line utility but also as a module that can be used for a primitive Remote Procedure Call (RPC) mechanism, when the remote Zope throws an exception, Client.py raises an exception locally to reflect what happened at the "remote" Zope. To sort out what has happened, you can use the most primitive client available: Telnet! (Note that you could do something more sophisticated, such as tcpwatch or webdebug, introduced in Chapter 10, "Survival Gear for Web Masters," to get more detailed clues, but, for purposes of illustration, it's always nice to have something quick and simple handy.) Try the following:

On the system command line, type this:

```
telnet localhost 8080
```

You should see this:

```
Trying 127.0.0.1...
Connected to localhost.spvi.com.
Escape character is '^]'.
```

Now type this:

```
GET /attendanceZPatterns/display_app_html
<enter>
```

You will be rewarded with this:

```
HTTP/1.0 500 Internal Server Error
Server: Zope/(Zope 2.4.0 (source release, python 2.1, linux2), python 2.1.1,
darwin1) ZServer/1.1b1
Date: Sat, 04 Aug 2001 20:42:24 GMT
Bobo-Exception-File: /Users/steve/Zope/lib/python/DocumentTemplate/DT_Raise.py
Content-Type: text/html
Bobo-Exception-Type: LoginRequired
Bobo-Exception-Value: bobo exception
Content-Length: 1884
Bobo-Exception-Line: 128

<... lots of additional output snipped... >
```

Aha! So that's it. Zope wants you to log in! Remember in Chapter 13, "User Management Interfacing with External Systems," that you added a LoginManager-based UserFolder to the Attendance application. Now you see that you can't just fetch the display of the application without authenticating!

From the Zope Management Interface (ZMI), you can query the database in the acl_users folder to see what users are defined. In the acl_users folder, you will recall that there is a UserSource with queries to manage the user database for the attendance application. Remember that the `selectSQL` query is a general-purpose query that can be used to get rows in the database that have any particular values for any of the fields. Because you want to look at the whole users table, click the selectSQL queries Test tab and leave the fields blank (which will translate into an unconditional select of all the data). The Test tab will appear as shown in Figure 15.1.

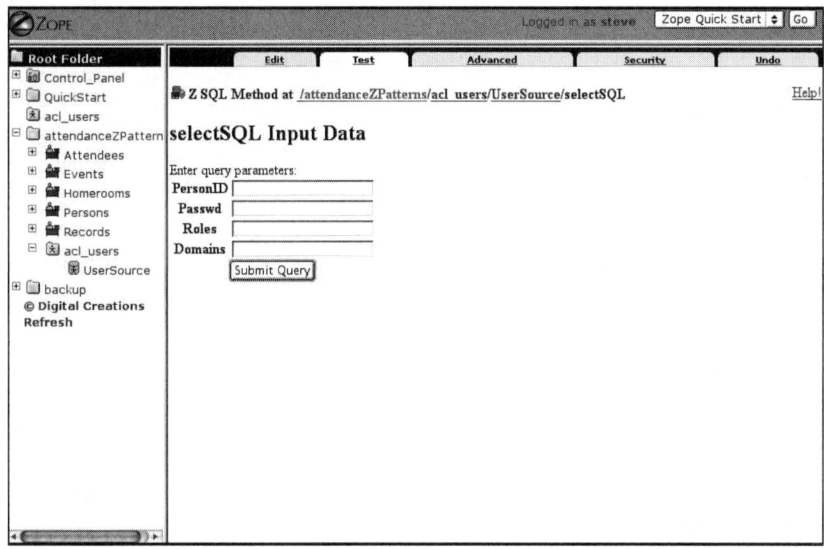


**Figure 15.1** Test tab of selectSQL query for the users table of the Attendance application.

If you now click Submit Query, you'll see the list of usernames, passwords, roles, and domains for the users currently defined in the system. You can use the updateSQL query to change a password or insertSQL to add another user. Click the insertSQL query, click its Test tab, and enter a new username, password, role, and domain. The role should be Teacher or Manager, and the domain should be your current domain or should be blank (which allows all domains in). Supposing that you added a user called testUser with a password of test and a role of Teacher, you should now be able to use Client.py to display the class listing as follows. Type the following line, but this time be sure to include the correct username and password as: `<CODE>Client.py -u testUser:test http://localhost:8080/attendanceZPatterns/display_app_html</CODE>`.

This time you should see this:

```
server: Zope/(Zope 2.4.0 (source release, python 2.1, linux2), python 2.1.1,
darwin1) ZServer/1.1b1
content-length: 1641
content-type: text/html
connection: close
date: Sat, 04 Aug 2001 21:28:04 GMT

<html><head><title>School Attendance Program</title></head><body
bgcolor="#FFFFFF">
<div align="center">
<h2>School Attendance Program</h2>
</div>
<p>
<div align="center">
<table width="75%">
<tr><td>
This is the School Attendance Program. Below you see links for each homeroom. To
enter
attendance for a day, simply click on the homeroom of your choice.
</td></tr></table>

< ... much output snipped ... >
```

So it works! Clearly, there is a lot that you can do here to test your Zope application programmatically. You can "import" Client.py into another Python script as well and use it to contact your Zope application from your test framework.

## Benchmarking

A very useful tool comes with Apache, called ab, or Apache benchmark (**http://www.apache.org/docs-2.0/programs/ab.html**). If you have Apache, you should have ab. If you're already running Apache, you should have it. If you don't have Apache and you want to run ab, you'll need to install Apache. If you run `ab -h` on the command line, you'll get something like this:

```
ab -h
Usage: ab [options] [http://]hostname[:port]/path
Options are:
    -n requests     Number of requests to perform
    -c concurrency  Number of multiple requests to make
    -t timelimit    Seconds to max. wait for responses
    -p postfile    File containing data to POST
    -T content-type Content-type header for POSTing
    -v verbosity    How much troubleshooting info to print
    -w              Print out results in HTML tables
    -i              Use HEAD instead of GET
    -x attributes   String to insert as table attributes
    -y attributes   String to insert as tr attributes
    -z attributes   String to insert as td or th attributes
    -C attribute    Add cookie, eg. 'Apache=1234' (repeatable)
```

```
-H attribute     Add Arbitrary header line, eg. 'Accept-Encoding: zop'
                 Inserted after all normal header lines. (repeatable)
-A attribute     Add Basic WWW Authentication, the attributes
                 are a colon separated username and password.
-p attribute     Add Basic Proxy Authentication, the attributes
                 are a colon separated username and password.
-V               Print version number and exit
-k               Use HTTP KeepAlive feature
-h               Display usage information (this message)
```

Some of the more interesting options include `-n` to set the number of requests to perform, `-c` to set the number of concurrent requests, and `-v` to set the verbosity. You can use ab to test the performance of your Zope application. There are lots of other web benchmarking tools out there, but because most developers are using Apache anyway, it makes sense to work with their tool. Even if you're not using Apache, you can still use ab—and it's free! (For Windows users who don't want to compile ab, there is a binary available at **http://www.remotecommunications.com/apache/ab/**).

To get a baseline for performance, it's good to check the time that Zope requires to render a simple page with very little dynamic text. Create a completely static page: basePage at the root of your Zope. Then run ab a few times to see how Zope does. For these tests, Zope was run on a modest workstation, so don't look at the figures as an absolute measure of the performance that you would expect from Zope running on a "real" server:

```
ab -n 100 http://localhost:8080/basePage

This is ApacheBench, Version 1.3c <$Revision: 1.8 $> apache-1.3
Copyright (c) 1996 Adam Twiss, Zeus Technology Ltd, http://www.zeustech.net/
Copyright (c) 1998-2000 The Apache Group, http://www.apache.org/

Server Software:        Zope/(Zope
Server Hostname:        localhost
Server Port:            8080

Document Path:          /basePage
Document Length:        26 bytes

Concurrency Level:      1
Time taken for tests:   2.973 seconds
Complete requests:      100
Failed requests:        0
Total transferred:      24800 bytes
HTML transferred:       2600 bytes
Requests per second:    33.64
Transfer rate:          8.34 kb/s received

Connnection Times (ms)
              min   avg   max
Connect:        0     0     0
Processing:    26    29    53
Total:         26    29    53
```

You can see that Zope takes about 30 milliseconds (ms) to return a response, on average, even for a small page that is completely static, with an average rate of around 30 requests per second. For the example 15-minute period, 30 requests per second results in around 27,000 requests! This is somewhat encouraging, although remember that this is a best-case rate, with simple static text.

Now let's increase the concurrency (number of simultaneous requests) and see how Zope manages (skipping the output of "ab" that isn't different):

```
ab -c 3 -n 100 http://localhost:8080/basePage

<.. skip ..>

Concurrency Level:      3
Time taken for tests:   2.946 seconds
Complete requests:      100
Requests per second:    33.94
Transfer rate:          8.42 kb/s received

Connnection Times (ms)
              min   avg   max
Connect:        0     0     2
Processing:    27    87   225
Total:         27    87   227

ab -c 12 -n 100 http://localhost:8080/basePage

<.. skip ..>

Concurrency Level:      12
Time taken for tests:   2.997 seconds
Requests per second:    33.37
Transfer rate:          8.36 kb/s received

Connnection Times (ms)
              min   avg   max
Connect:        0     0     1
Processing:   171   341   509
Total:        171   341   510
```

Notice that although each request is taking longer to complete, the total number of requests per second is quite stable, at around 30 rps; that's about the "best case" that you can expect from a modest workstation.

You can also use ab to see what effect traversal and authentication have on Zope. Try running ab with the same form, but now force an authentication by permitting only the Manager role to have the view permission, and create a user testMe with the password test in the root directory. Then type this:

```
ab -n 100 -A testMe:test http://localhost:8080/basePage

Concurrency Level:      1
Time taken for tests:   3.172 seconds
```

```
Requests per second:    31.53
Transfer rate:          7.60 kb/s received

Connnection Times (ms)
             min   avg   max
Connect:       0     0     0
Processing:   28    31    56
Total:        28    31    56
```

Authentication alone apparently takes essentially no time. What about traversal plus authentication? Create a new folder named testTraverse in the root, and then acquire basePage from there, like this:

```
ab -n 100 -A testMe:test http://localhost:8080/testTraversal/basePage

Concurrency Level:      1
Time taken for tests:   3.416 seconds
Requests per second:    29.27
Transfer rate:          7.06 kb/s received

Connnection Times (ms)
             min   avg   max
Connect:       0     0     0
Processing:   30    33    59
Total:        30    33    59
```

As you can see, this shaved off a few milliseconds, but not much. What if you now traverse into the attendanceZPatterns folder and view the same content? Why should it be any different? It's the same content, and you'll use the same authentication! Try it:

```
ab -n 100 -A testMe:test http://localhost:8080/attendanceZPatterns/basePage

Concurrency Level:      1
Time taken for tests:   11.859 seconds
Requests per second:    8.43
Transfer rate:          2.03 kb/s received

Connnection Times (ms)
             min   avg   max
Connect:       0     0     0
Processing:  111   118   206
Total:       111   118   206
```

Whoa! That's more than a factor of three times slower! What could cause such a slowdown? This is where profiling can really help sometimes, but you won't need it for this one. The next attempt clearly illustrates what happens when you use a username/password that LoginManager knows about:

```
ab -n 100 -A sam:teacher1 http://localhost:8080/attendanceZPatterns/basePage

Concurrency Level:      1
Time taken for tests:   4.226 seconds
Requests per second:    23.66
Transfer rate:          5.70 kb/s received
```

```
Connnection Times (ms)
              min   avg   max
Connect:        0     0     0
Processing:    36    41   308
Total:         36    41   308
```

As you can see, when LoginManager is successful at finding a user, the time taken is much less. For the last ab example (for now), look at the effect of displaying some dynamic HTML (with queries). The default display of the application queries several databases to get information about classes and students in them. It's a reasonable example of dynamic DTML including expensive database access:

```
ab -A sam:teacher1 -c 3 -n 100
http://localhost:8080/attendanceZPatterns/display_app_html

Document Path:          /attendanceZPatterns/display_app_html
Document Length:        1596 bytes

Concurrency Level:      3
Time taken for tests:   92.418 seconds
Complete requests:      100
Failed requests:        6
   (Connect: 0, Length: 6, Exceptions: 0)
Non-2xx responses:      6
Total transferred:      202182 bytes
HTML transferred:       178661 bytes
Requests per second:    1.08
Transfer rate:          2.19 kb/s received

Connnection Times (ms)
              min   avg   max
Connect:        0     0    45
Processing:  1417  2730  6289
Total:       1417  2730  6334
```

You can see that this is significantly slower than static content. A rate of one request per second is just about unacceptable for even one user! This is really because you are using Gadfly, which is not at all optimized for multiple simultaneous users such as web browsers.

However, it's clear that ab and tools like it are essential for measuring the performance of web applications. You can learn a lot about your application by building up a known set of performance numbers this way.

## Logging Tools

Zope comes with a couple of different mechanisms to monitor what Zope is doing. Zope usually creates a "standard" web log in zopedir/var/Z2.log. It's a little verbose to include here in full, but a "trimmed" version is helpful (these lines are truncated to fit on the page):

```
tail -f ~/Zope/var/Z2.log

10.0.0.15 - steve [06/Aug/2001:08:05:18 -0500] "GET / HTTP/1.1" 200 3231 ""
➥"Mozilla/4.0
10.0.0.15 - steve [06/Aug/2001:08:05:18 -0500] "GET /manage_page_style.css
➥HTTP/1.1" 200
10.0.0.15 - steve [06/Aug/2001:08:05:18 -0500] "GET /p_/ZopeButton HTTP/1.1" 304
➥186 "htt
10.0.0.15 - steve [06/Aug/2001:08:05:37 -0500] "GET /manage HTTP/1.1" 200 1101
➥"http://lo
10.0.0.15 - steve [06/Aug/2001:08:05:37 -0500] "GET /manage_top_frame HTTP/1.1"
➥200 1403
10.0.0.15 - steve [06/Aug/2001:08:05:37 -0500] "GET /manage_workspace HTTP/1.1"
➥302 419 "
10.0.0.15 - steve [06/Aug/2001:08:05:37 -0500] "GET /manage_page_style.css
➥HTTP/1.1" 200
10.0.0.15 - steve [06/Aug/2001:08:05:38 -0500] "GET /p_/zopelogo_jpg HTTP/1.1" 304
➥186 "h
10.0.0.15 - steve [06/Aug/2001:08:05:39 -0500] "GET /manage_menu HTTP/1.1" 200
➥4052 "" "M
10.0.0.15 - steve [06/Aug/2001:08:05:39 -0500] "GET /manage_page_style.css
➥HTTP/1.1" 200
10.0.0.15 - steve [06/Aug/2001:08:05:39 -0500] "GET
➥/misc_/OFSP/UserFolder_icon.gif HTTP/
10.0.0.15 - steve [06/Aug/2001:08:05:39 -0500] "GET /p_/ControlPanel_icon
➥HTTP/1.1" 304 1
10.0.0.15 - steve [06/Aug/2001:08:05:40 -0500] "GET /manage_main HTTP/1.1" 200
➥21365 "htt
10.0.0.15 - steve [06/Aug/2001:08:05:40 -0500] "GET /manage_page_style.css
➥HTTP/1.1" 200
10.0.0.15 - steve [06/Aug/2001:08:05:41 -0500] "GET
➥/misc_/ExternalMethod/extmethod.gif H
```

Zope recorded the IP address, username, date/time, HTTP command, arguments, and information about the response that Zope sends back to the browser. If you need a more detailed view of each transaction, you can turn on "detailed" logging with the `-M` switch. If you start your Zope process with the `-M filename` flag, Zope will create a highly detailed log file that looks like this:

```
./start -M foo.txt
tail -f var/foo.txt

B 14634460 2001-08-05T22:04:58 GET /testTraversal/manage_main
I 14634460 2001-08-05T22:04:58 0
A 14634460 2001-08-05T22:04:59 200 11952
E 14634460 2001-08-05T22:04:59
B 17009756 2001-08-05T22:04:59 GET /manage_page_style.css
I 17009756 2001-08-05T22:04:59 0
A 17009756 2001-08-05T22:04:59 200 2893
E 17009756 2001-08-05T22:05:00
```

There are several important things to notice here:

- Each line starts with a letter: `B`, `I`, `A`, or `E`.
  - `B`—The start of a request
  - `I`—The start of processing of the request
  - `A`—The start of response output
  - `E`—The end of the request
- Each line has a unique identifying number (such as 14634460), which is basically a "request ID."
- Each line is time-stamped so that you can estimate how long each part of the process takes.
- `B`, `I`, and `A` lines give you some additional details, depending on the details of the services that you are running.
  - `B`—Reports the command and URL for HTTP service
  - `I`—Reports the size of the ContentLength header in the REQUEST
  - `A`—Reports the reply code in the REPSPONSE and the number of bytes returned

Another way to find out which processes are taking a lot of time is to turn on this log file. It's also quite handy if some process gets hung; you can often use this information to track down the guilty party.

> **Process Forking and Zope**
>
> Zope normally runs as at least two processes:
>
> - A monitor process that watches the health of its children and starts new children if they die
> - Children of the monitor that are the "real" processes that serve web, ftp, and other requests
>
> These child processes each run multiple threads, depending on the `-t` option specified in the start file.

Another useful log file is the STUPID_LOG_FILE. Sounds great, eh? Seriously, the only thing "stupid" about the STUPID_LOG_FILE is that it's not very configurable, but it's quite handy! To use it, you'll need to set an the environment variable, STUPID_LOG_FILE, to be the filename of the file that you want to use as a log file:

```
(this example is for UNIX/tcsh)

setenv STUPID_LOG_FILE foo.txt
./start
tail -f foo.txt
------
2001-08-06T13:02:00 INFO(0) zdaemon zdaemon: Mon Aug  6 08:02:00 2001: Houston, we
➥have forked
------
2001-08-06T13:02:00 INFO(0) zdaemon zdaemon: Mon Aug  6 08:02:00 2001: Hi, I just
➥forked off a kid: 590
------
```

```
2001-08-06T13:02:00 INFO(0) zdaemon zdaemon: Mon Aug  6 08:02:00 2001: Houston, we
➥have forked
------
2001-08-06T13:02:08 INFO(0) ZServer HTTP server started at Mon Aug  6 08:02:08
➥2001
        Hostname: localhost.spvi.com
        Port: 8080
------
2001-08-06T13:02:08 INFO(0) ZServer FTP server started at Mon Aug  6 08:02:08 2001
        Hostname: localhost
        Port: 8021
------
2001-08-06T13:02:08 INFO(0) ZServer PCGI Server started at Mon Aug  6 08:02:08
➥2001
        Unix socket: /Users/steve/Zope/var/pcgi.soc
```

The STUPID_LOG_FILE doesn't log every request to the server, like the other two logs. Instead, it records lower-level events that call on the Zope zLOG service to provide. For example, zdaemon.py uses zLOG to produce the "Houston" messages (see Listing 15.1).

Listing 15.1 **The zdaemon.py Program Uses zLOG to Report Its Activity**

```
import zLOG

#this is a bit of a hack so I don't have to change too much code
def pstamp(message, sev):
    zLOG.LOG("zdaemon", sev,
             ("zdaemon: %s: %s" % (time.ctime(time.time()), message)))


# <... skipping lots of lines ... >


def forkit(attempts = FORK_ATTEMPTS):
    while attempts:
        # if at first you don't succeed...
        attempts = attempts - 1
        try:
            pid = os.fork()
        except os.error:
            pstamp('Houston, the fork failed', zLOG.ERROR)
            time.sleep(2)
        else:
            pstamp('Houston, we have forked', zLOG.INFO)
            return pid
```

As you can see, zdaemon.py uses the zLOG module to log its processing. If you create a Python-based product, you can use the zLOG module in exactly the same way. Notice also that zdaemon sent both the log message and an indication of its severity.

It's up to the zLOG module to decide how to handle the message based on its severity. If you define the environment variable STUPID_LOG_FILE, zLOG just saves the information in the file that you name. You can test this by killing zdaemon's child process, and zdaemon will fork off another child. First find out the PID of the child process, kill it, and then see what zLOG recorded:

```
cat var/Z2.pid
589 590

kill 590

tail -25 foo.txt
2001-08-06T13:02:08 INFO(0) ZServer FTP server started at Mon Aug  6 08:02:08 2001
       Hostname: localhost
       Port: 8021
------
2001-08-06T13:02:08 INFO(0) ZServer PCGI Server started at Mon Aug  6 08:02:08
➥2001
       Unix socket: /Users/steve/Zope/var/pcgi.soc
------
2001-08-06T13:32:06 ERROR(200) zdaemon zdaemon: Mon Aug  6 08:32:06 2001: Aiieee!
➥590 exited with error code: 15
------
2001-08-06T13:32:06 INFO(0) zdaemon zdaemon: Mon Aug  6 08:32:06 2001: Houston, we
➥have forked
------
2001-08-06T13:32:06 INFO(0) zdaemon zdaemon: Mon Aug  6 08:32:06 2001: Houston, we
➥have forked
------
2001-08-06T13:32:06 INFO(0) zdaemon zdaemon: Mon Aug  6 08:32:06 2001: Hi, I just
➥forked off a kid: 606
------
2001-08-06T13:32:14 INFO(0) ZServer HTTP server started at Mon Aug  6 08:32:14
➥2001
       Hostname: localhost.spvi.com
       Port: 8080
------
2001-08-06T13:32:14 INFO(0) ZServer FTP server started at Mon Aug  6 08:32:14 2001
       Hostname: localhost
       Port: 8021
------
2001-08-06T13:32:14 INFO(0) ZServer PCGI Server started at Mon Aug  6 08:32:14
➥2001
       Unix socket: /Users/steve/Zope/var/pcgi.soc
```

## Profiling

You can also use Zope's built-in debugging and profiling page to assess what Zope is doing. If you click Control_Panel, Debug, you'll see a page something like Figure 15.2.

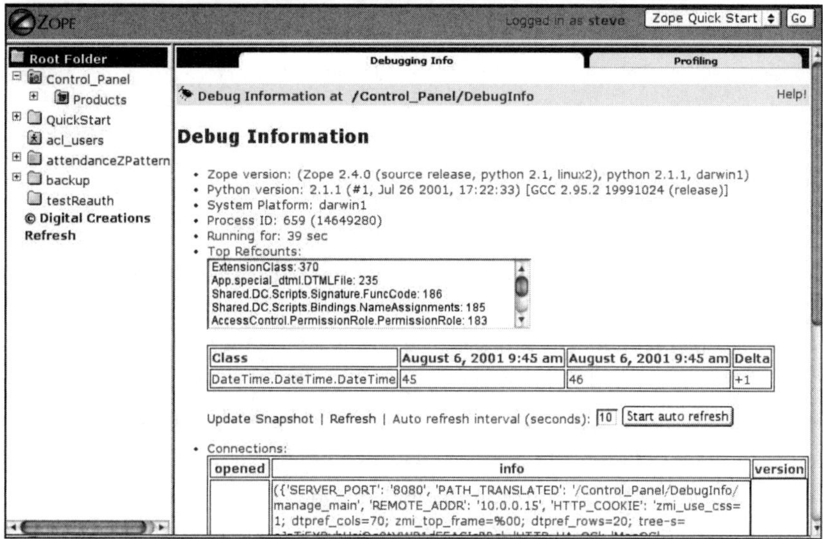


**Figure 15.2** Zope's built-in debugging and profiling page.

You can see that there is a list of active objects in the system and the number of instances in memory by each class. Then there is a list of "deltas" showing how many new instances have been created since the last snapshot. Finally, there is a list of active connections. You can use this list to find any "hung" connections. There are also links to go into "auto" refresh mode and to manually refresh the data on the screen.

Notice that there is also a Profiling tab. If you click this, you'll see a message saying that profiling is not turned on. You can turn it on by defining an environment variable, PROFILE_PUBLISHER, before starting Zope. It needs to be set to the absolute path of a file that will get the profiler's results when Zope is next restarted. So, you'll need to do the following:

- Set the variable.
- Run Zope.
- Do some stuff.
- Inspect the output of the profiler in the Profiling tab.

From the UNIX/tcsh command line, this would look something like this:

```
./stop
setenv PROFILE_PUBLISHER /tmp/foo.txt
./start
ab -n 100 -A sam:teacher1 http://localhost:8080/attendanceZPatterns/index_html
This is ApacheBench, Version 1.3c <$Revision: 1.8 $> apache-1.3

<.. skip ab output which is inaccurate anyway due to profiling .. >
```

```
<.. now view "Profiling" tab of Zope ..>

<.. when you are finished don't forget to turn profiling off! ..>

./stop

unsetenv PROFILE_PUBLISHER

./start
```

If you look at the profiling output, you'll see that it's rather complex. You can sort the output on a number of possible terms, and there are multiple columns:

- `ncalls`, for the number of calls to a function. (If the function is recursive, this is reported as "actual/primitive" so that you can see the effect of recursion.)
- `tottime`, for the total time spent in the given function (but not its subfunctions).
- `percall`, the ratio of `tottime` to `ncalls` (such as time/call).
- `cumtime`, the total time spent in this and all subfunctions.
- `percall`, the ratio of `cumtime` to the number of primitive calls so that recursive calls are not counted in the ratio.

**For More Information**

You can get more details from the Python documentation on the profiler at **http://www.python.org/doc/current/lib/profile.html**.

For this example, the output looks something like this:

```
   ncalls  tottime  percall  cumtime  percall filename:lineno(function)
      102    0.610    0.006   10.410    0.102 BaseRequest.py:231(traverse)
2336/2032    0.550    0.000    3.970    0.002 HTTPRequest.py:813(__getitem__)
      805    0.500    0.001    1.240    0.002
       ➥ZopeGuards.py:105(guarded_getattr)
  300/100    0.450    0.002    4.590    0.046 DTMLMethod.py:168(__call__)
  327/103    0.340    0.001    4.000    0.039 DT_String.py:434(__call__)
      609    0.310    0.001    0.530    0.001
       ➥ZopeSecurityPolicy.py:104(validate)
  800/400    0.270    0.000    2.160    0.005 DTML.py:100(guarded_getattr)
      805    0.270    0.000    0.270    0.000 PermissionRole.py:144(__of__)
      202    0.210    0.001    2.430    0.012 DT_Util.py:204(eval)
      907    0.210    0.000    0.280    0.000 PermissionRole.py:125(__of__)
      102    0.200    0.002   11.060    0.108 Publish.py:122(publish)
      102    0.180    0.002    0.180    0.002
       ➥select_trigger.py:66(pull_trigger)
     1121    0.160    0.000    0.160    0.000
      ➥SecurityManagement.py:113(getSecurityManager)
      100    0.150    0.002    2.440    0.024 UserSources.py:503(retrieveItem)
      102    0.140    0.001    0.310    0.003 HTTPResponse.py:125(__str__)
      912    0.140    0.000    0.300    0.000 HTTPRequest.py:897(get)
```

```
18   302/202    0.130    0.000    0.180    0.001 Traversable.py:125
     ➥(getPhysicalPath)
19       702    0.130    0.000    0.150    0.000 SimpleItem.py:131(getId)
20       102    0.120    0.001    5.570    0.055 mapply.py:104(mapply)
21       102    0.110    0.001    0.330    0.003 __init__.py:31(new_commit)
22       300    0.110    0.000    0.160    0.001 Cache.py:277(ZCacheable_set)
23       603    0.100    0.000    0.100    0.000 Cache.py:201(ZCacheable_getCache)
24     183/1    0.100    0.001    1.340    1.340 kjParser.py:692(DoOneReduction)
25       300    0.100    0.000    0.150    0.000 Cache.py:257(ZCacheable_get)
26       410    0.090    0.000    0.090    0.000
         ➥SecurityManager.py:174(addContext)
27       100    0.090    0.001    3.030    0.030 LoginMethods.py:138(findLogin)
28      1426    0.090    0.000    0.090    0.000 string.py:45(lower)
```

Notice that 100 calls were made, and there were 100 calls to findLogin (line 27); and each took about 30 ms, while the retrieveItem of UserSources (line 15) took 24 ms of that! Clearly, this is a highly detailed account of who is taking what time. It can be a great way to sort out where bottlenecks are occurring.

# Distributing the Load

You can help Zope perform better in several ways. This section discusses two of them:

- Allowing a "traditional" web server to serve static information
- Adding caching to save costly results

## Serving Static Files Externally

Although each web server is different, Apache is used in this example because it's both free and multiplatform. The idea here is that certain content never, or rarely, changes. Why not let Apache take care of serving static content and let Zope handle the dynamic data that it's best at?

This is most easily accomplished with the Rewrite module. An example Apache configuration file follows in Listing 15.2.

Listing 15.2 **Apache Configuration File for Serving Static Content**

```
<VirtualHost 10.0.0.1:80>

ServerName test.spvi.com
ErrorLog /var/log/test-error_log
CustomLog /var/log/test-access_log common

Alias /icons/ "/usr/local/share/apache/icons/"
Alias /pil/   "/usr/local/share/doc/PIL/handbook/"
Alias /post/  "/scratch/docs/"

<Directory /usr/local/etc/Zope2a>
```

*continues*

Listing 15.2 **Continued**

```
AllowOverride All
Options All
</Directory>

<Directory /scratch/docs>
AllowOverride All
Options All
</Directory>

RewriteEngine on

RewriteRule ^/icons - [l]
RewriteRule ^/pil - [l]
RewriteRule ^/post - [l]

RewriteRule ^/(.*) http://mercury.spvi.com:10080/$1 [p]

</VirtualHost>
```

This way, all references to icons in the /icons folder or documents in the /pil folder are served directly by Apache (that's what the `[l]` does). All other requests are proxied out to Zope on port 8080. In this case, there is a SiteRoot object that makes sure that all the links and URLs from Zope are directed correctly back to test.spvi.com. Note that you saw this technique as a convenience in Chapter 10, but it also affects performance, so you see it again here. Notice also that SiteRoot is *easier* to set up in Apache, but it's more cumbersome to deal with in the ZMI, as stated in Chapter 10.

## Caching and Proxies

Another approach to improving performance of Zope is caching. In general, the idea is to save results that are computationally costly to generate and use them repeatedly until they are no longer valid. The problem is usually deciding when they are no longer valid! Specialized programs are available that do nothing but proxying and caching (see **http://www.squid-cache.org/**), but their configuration and use is beyond the scope of this book. However, Zope does include its own built-in cache objects that are worth understanding because they can improve performance significantly, and they affect how external proxy caches interact with Zope.

> **For More Information**
>
> There is a lot of background information on these in the DevSite Wiki at Zope.org: **http://www.zope.org/Wikis/DevSite/Projects/CacheManager/FrontPage**.

### Accelerated HTTP Cache Manager

The Accelerated HTTP Cache Manager is a standard Zope product. It basically allows you to set the headers that get passed back to downstream caches so that they can correctly cache documents. The default setting is to expire cached documents one hour after they have been served. The primary problems are listed here:

- If a page requires authentication, it probably should not be cached downstream.
- If a method is cached that displays only a part of a page, it can affect the headers for the whole page.

In general, you should cache only whole pages, unless you are a real cache expert and understand the consequences!

### RAM Cache Manager

A RAM cache manager is useful for storing fully rendered DTML methods in RAM so that subsequent retrieval doesn't incur the cost of rendering. As an example, install a RAM cache manager in the root of your Zope. Then go to the display_app_html of the attendanceZPatterns folder and click the Cache tab. Associate the document with the RAM cache manager. Now run ab again on the page (remember that ab showed that Zope could return this page at only a rate of about one per second with no cache):

```
> ab -A sam:teacher1 -c 3 -n 100
http://localhost:8080/attendanceZPatterns/display_app_html

Concurrency Level:      3
Time taken for tests:   4.243 seconds
Complete requests:      100
Failed requests:        0

Requests per second:    23.57
Transfer rate:          42.87 kb/s received

Connnection Times (ms)
              min   avg   max
Connect:        0     0     0
Processing:    43   126   263
Total:         43   126   263
```

So, the cache has improved the performance of this page by a factor about 23 or so. Not bad! Of course, it all depends on how often the data used to display this page changes. If the data changes often, a cache might not be a reasonable strategy. Note also that, unlike the Accelerated HTTP Cache Manager, you *can* cache pages that require authentication with this cache manager because it can add AUTHENTICATED _USER (or any other variable) to the cache key. The other possible problem here is lack of RAM. Because each document can be cached multiple times (for example, once per user if each user needs a unique key), it might not be practical or even useful.

# ZEO, Enterprise Objects

By far the most powerful mechanism available to improve performance with Zope is *Zope Enterprise Objects* (*ZEO*). ZEO is a distributed processing system that allows multiple "clients" to use the same object database. This section describes one implementation of a ZEO-based Zope application using Apache and the rewrite module as the front end.

## Distributing and Replicating Objects

The way ZEO works is that a storage server (called *ZEO Storage Server*) runs in a protected part of your network. (ZEO currently does not support authentication or encryption, so you need to take care to protect your ZEO servers from malicious attack by other means.) Multiple ZEO clients can then connect to the server and use it as their primary storage. Users with web browsers can now connect to the ZEO clients and interact with them normally. When a request is received for an object that isn't currently known by a ZEO client, it asks the ZEO server for a copy. If that object is changed and committed, the ZEO server notifies all the other ZEO clients of the change so that they can update their cache (if necessary) with the new version of the object. This layout is illustrated in Figure 15.3.

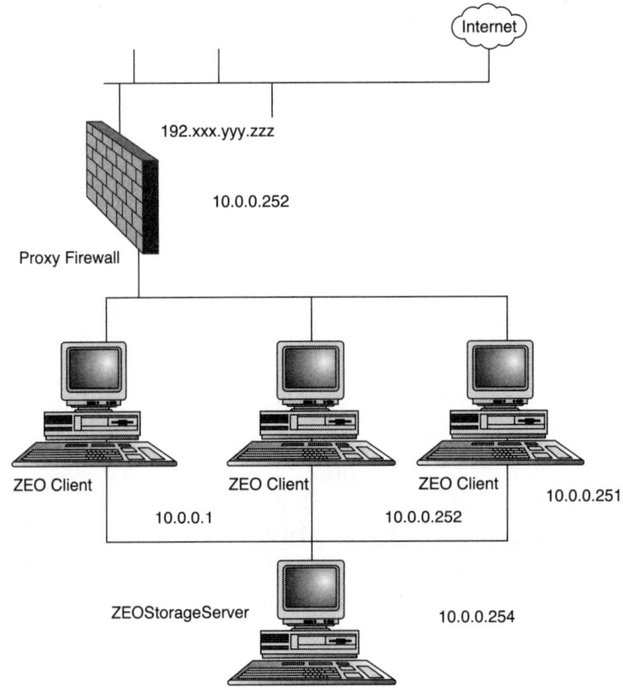


**Figure 15.3** Network layout of example ZEO server and clients.

## ZEO Strategies

You can take advantage of ZEO in different ways. You can run the server and client processes on the same machine or on different machines. You can distribute users using a round-robin DNS approach (in which your DNS server just delivers a rotating set of IP addresses for the same domain name) or a proxy that forwards web requests to different client machines with some algorithm. Each of these has certain advantages under different circumstances.

### Multiple Servers

To get a significant performance boost from Zope, the most powerful and flexible approach is to use multiple client machines. The example setup is pictured in Figure 15.3. An Apache proxy is set up that distributes requests to one of three client systems, each of which refers to a single server system for its object storage.

All ZEO clients and the server should be running the same versions of all Python products and the same version of Zope. For the example setup, you will use the existing Zope that you've been working with (the Attendance application) and clone it to each of the ZEO clients and the ZEO server after you've installed ZEO itself.

ZEO is an "add-on" product that doesn't come with Zope. You can find it at **http://www.zope.org/Products/ZEO**. Download and unpack the tarball. Copy the enclosed ZEO folder to the Zope/lib/python directory. That's it! Now, to start the server, you need to run Zope/lib/python/ZEO/start.py. In this setup, the server is running on 10.0.0.254, so ZEO is started from the Zope directory like this:

```
python lib/python/ZEO/start.py -p 8000 -h 10.0.0.254
```

Notice that this specifies that ZEO runs on port 8000 and attaches only to interface 10.0.0.254. This way, if your ZEO server has public and private interfaces, you can require it to accept connections only on one.

When the server is running, you can start the clients. Installing ZEO the same way, you start a client in the "normal" way after creating a special file in its Zope directory. Create a file called custom_zodb.py. Ours looks like Listing 15.3.

Listing 15.3 **Script custom_zodb.py to Connect to ZEO Server**

```
import ZEO.ClientStorage
Storage=ZEO.ClientStorage.ClientStorage(('10.0.0.254',8000))
```

Notice that this specifies the internal IP address of the ZEO server and the same port number used when the server was started. It makes sense to run all the ZEO clients on the same port number (as long as they are all on different machines) so that it's less likely to get the ports wrong. In this example, we've chosen to run them all on port 14080 (because it was free on all the client systems).

The only thing left is the proxy. This is the trickiest part. You want all the users to connect to the same external IP address (for example, 192.*xxx*.*yyy*.*zzz*), but you want those requests to be forwarded to the ZEO clients in some systematic way. Happily, the Rewrite module is flexible enough for this task. Listing 15.4 shows a possible Apache configuration file for this effect.

Listing 15.4 **Load Balancing Apache Configuration**

```
01 <VirtualHost 192.xxx.yyy.zzz:80>
02     ServerAdmin steve@spvi.com
03     ServerName test_balance.spvi.net
04     ErrorLog /var/log/spvi.net-error_log
05     CustomLog /var/log/spvi.net-access_log common
06
07
08     RewriteEngine on
09     #RewriteLog    /var/log/rewrite.log
10     #RewriteLogLevel  10
11     RewriteMap    balance_load_ext
       ➥prg:/usr/local/share/apache/conf/balance_load_ext.py
12     RewriteRule   ^/(.*)$ ${balance_load_ext:$1}          [P,L]
13
14 </VirtualHost>
```

This is the Apache configuration for the load-balancing proxy for the example ZEO setup. The main magic is in lines 11 and 12. They basically say that whenever Apache gets a request, it should pass the path to the balance_load_ext.py program and then proxy the request to whatever string is returned. This is the ultimate in flexibility! Any program that you can write that takes strings on stdin and writes strings to stdout can be use to proxy web requests. Note that you can also use a "static" map to achieve a similar effect (**http://httpd.apache.org/docs-2.0/mod/mod_rewrite.html#RewriteMap**). We prefer a program map to have more control over how the load is actually balanced. Here is the balance_load_ext.py, in Listing 15.5.

Listing 15.5 **Load Balancing Dynamic Proxy Python Script**

```
#!/usr/bin/env python

count = 0

import sys
import string

def translate(data):
    global count
    count = (count + 1) % 3
    return "http://www%i.spvi.net:14080/VirtualHostBase/http/
    ➥test_balance.spvi.net:80/%s" % (count, data)


if __name__=='__main__':
    while 1:
        data = string.strip(sys.stdin.readline())
        if not data:
            break
        print translate(data)
        sys.stdout.flush()
```

As you can see, the idea is very simple. Increment a counter for every request, and return a proxy path that works with a VirtualHostBase object. You need to set up DNS so that www0, www1, and www2 point to your clients, and you're all set. It would probably be smart to make this algorithm more sophisticated, taking into account load and availability of the client systems, but this is certainly a good start on something simple and effective.

To measure how much speedup you get, it's good to measure each client separately. Each client is a different system, in this case, with different speed, RAM, load, and so on. Running ab three times reveals that the first three lines are the individual clients and the last is the proxy (which delegates to all three clients):

```
Server                           URL                                      RPS

......       ..........................................................  ......
10.0.0.1     http://10.0.0.1:14080/attendanceZPatterns/display_app_html    2.33
10.0.0.250   http://10.0.0.250:14080/attendanceZPatterns/display_app_html  2.98
10.0.0.251   http://10.0.0.251:14080/attendanceZPatterns/display_app_html  2.47

test_balance http://test_balance.spvi.net/atte...s/display_app_html          7.38
```

Notice that you get an almost—but not quite—linear speedup. Naturally, there is overhead in the proxy, but it's not too bad. Also, there is significant variance in these numbers from trial to trial, depending on the number of repetitions and the level of concurrency. You can usually "tune" things up a bit to improve the numbers. (Note that test_balance is not a real hostname.)

### Multiple Processors

Another use of ZEO is to run multiple clients on the same system (on different ports) to make better use of multiple processors, or for debugging. This is simply a matter of starting two client processes on the server. Because they are using remote storage, you don't even need multiple instance of Zope itself. For instance, you could just type this:

```
./start -P8700
./start -P8800
```

Two clients will then happily run on the same computer. Note that Python has a "global interpreter lock," which means that, in certain parts of Python code, only one thread can be "active" at a time. With two processes like this, you can still keep a two-CPU system totally busy. This is also quite handy for debugging. A new client can be started and "stepped through" in the debugger without bringing down the "live" site.

## Move Processing Closer to the Data

For applications that use "real" databases, you can also move some logic into triggers and stored procedures. The details of these technologies are pretty much out of scope here, but it is worth noting that ZC has supplied both a database adaptor and a relational storage technology for Oracle (**http://www.zope.org/Products/DCOracle**) that support these concepts. The basic idea is to move some of the logic into the database itself so that Zope doesn't have to do all the high-level logic. Instead, it can count on some internal consistency in the data due to the existence of automatic "triggers" that fire when certain events occur or procedures that can be executed by the database itself and a part of a query.

## Summary

This chapter discussed many facets of testing and enhancing the performance of Zope. It started with tools that allow a developer to analyze what the performance is and why the performance is what it is. Finally, it presented strategies for improving performance, from caching to involving multiple servers. In general, there is a lot to know about Zope performance and scalability. Hopefully this chapter is useful to Zope developers who need to improve the performance of their Zope applications today.

# 16

# Backup, Disaster Recovery, and Distributed Processing

THE BEST TIME TO THINK ABOUT DISASTER RECOVERY is *not* after the disaster has happened. This sounds obvious. It *is* obvious, when you've been there. Zope is probably a little "scarier" than your average web development system in the sense that the objects are not stored "out in the open" but in a relatively mysterious "storage" that is essentially opaque to the casual observer. In this chapter, we'll suggest strategies that we've found useful in protecting ourselves from disaster, as well as techniques for recovering should some types of disaster occur. Related to that are alternative storage technologies that are beginning to become useful for production Zope sites.

## Object Export Options

The most basic defense against disaster is backup. There are a number of ways to do it, and we'll discuss most of them, but the easiest is to use the Import/Export button. If you click any folder in the ZMI, you'll see a listing of contents, and at the bottom will be a series of buttons that represent actions that you can take on folder whose contents you're viewing. One of the actions is the Import/Export button. If you click the check box next to an object in the folder and then click the Import/Export button, you'll see the a screen like that in Figure 16.1.

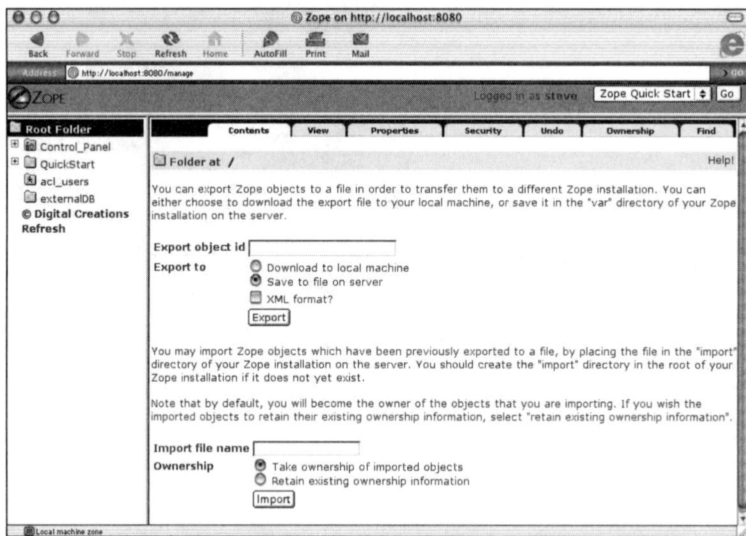


**Figure 16.1** Import/Export screen of the Zope Management Interface.

Naturally, you have some options. The first is *where* you want this export to go. You have two choices. You can have it saved on the filesystem of the Zope server, in the "$ZOPEROOT/var" directory, or you can ask to have it downloaded to your local workstation as a file.

You also have a choice of file format. The most compact format is the Zope Export (zexp) format, which is basically a binary "pickle" of the object that you are exporting. The advantage of this format is that it is smaller and faster. It is essentially the same format as the Data.fs file used for the native storage of Zope objects on the filesystem, so very little translation is required to perform the export. Because the size is smaller, there is also less data to export.

The other available format is xml. This format is text-based so that you can view it with an ordinary text editor. In fact, it is possible to edit objects in their xml form and to use command-line tools, such as diff and grep, to inspect them. However, these also are filled with lots of keys and tags that have to do with containment and interconnection of objects in ZODB that make it cumbersome to do much with these xml files manually.

Both of these formats can be checked into CVS (which is essentially what the ZCVSFolder object does—see Chapter 14, "Multi-developer Projects: Testing and Version Control") or RCS, or they can be saved in any other convenient way to be restored later in the case of an emergency.

## The File System Datastore and Alternatives

To understand how to handle an emergency, it's important to understand how ZODB stores and manages objects using the File Storage system and the Data.fs file.

Zope works by treating each web request as a transaction. ZODB is opened (the transaction is begun). Objects are fetched from ZODB depending on the requirements of the request. If these objects are already in memory, they are quickly available. If they are not in memory, the Data.fs file is consulted to find the objects on disk, and they are "restored" to memory. As a consequence of the request, it's possible that some of these objects are changed. At the end of the request, the transaction is either aborted or committed. If it is aborted, then any changes made to and objects are rolled back to the pretransaction state. If the transaction is committed, then any changes to objects during the transaction need to be saved to the persistent storage (that is, Data.fs). With normal file storage, newly changed objects are added to the *end* of the Data.fs file. This means that in normal operation, Data.fs just grows and grows. Even if "new" content is never added, just making changes to existing content is enough to make Data.fs continue to grow.

This means that if somehow Data.fs gets corrupted, you can usually fix it by truncating the Data.fs file at the point where the corruption occurred. First, it's important to point out that corruption of Data.fs is *extremely* rare. We've been developing Zope applications since 1998, and we've seen only one real case of Data.fs corruption, and it was due to a bug in a third-party product that crashed the Python interpreter at a critical point.

Having said that, we live in a world of manmade software, hardware failures, and other "unforeseeable" events. It's a good idea to know what tools you can bring to the table if you're ever faced with such a problem!

A tool comes with Zope called fsrecover.py. It can be found at Zope/lib/python/ZODB/fsrecover.py. It attempts to automatically detect corruption and recover as much as possible from the file in the presence of various problems. It's easy to use, but if it doesn't see anything wrong, it might not help much. To use fsrecover, follow these steps:

1. Stop Zope.
2. Back up your Data.fs file.
3. `cd` to "$ZOPEROOT/lib/python."
4. Type `python ZODB/fsrecover.py ../../var/Data.fs`

The program either says that there is nothing to recover or prints some diagnostic information about how much was "found" and how long the new Data.fs file is.

Another very useful tool for analyzing Data.fs files is a "simple" little program (about 300 lines of Python) by none other than Ty Sarna (of TinyTable/ZPatterns fame), called tranalyzer.py. (see **http://www.zope.org/Members/tsarna/Tranalyzer**). Tranalyzer produces output that looks something like this:

```
python tranalyzer.py $ZOPEROOT/var/Data.fs

TID: 3292AD04EEDD74D @ 0 obs 2 len 283 (status 'p') By [Zope]
""
        OID: 4 len 123
        OID: 9 len 61

TID: 3292AD00A9073C5 @ 303 obs 41 len 58603 (status 'p') By  amos
"/manage_importHack"
        OID: 13 len 124
        OID: 21 len 770
        OID: 22 len 557
        OID: 23 len 673
        OID: 24 len 495
        OID: 25 len 644
        OID: 1a len 288
        .
        <.. much more output skipped ..>
        .
```

Each transaction is printed along with its absolute position in the file, the number of objects affected, the total size of the transaction in bytes, and the user who committed the transaction.

How can you use this to recover from a corrupted database? It's pretty easy, although it requires some command-line work. The idea is that if there is corruption, it likely relates to one of the most recently made changes. Due to the way transactions are added to Data.fs, the transaction in question should be near the end. If you look at the last transaction printed by tranalyzer.py, it should tell you where to "chop" off the file to remove the last transaction manually:

```
python tranalyzer.py var/Data.fs | tail

TID: 33E93DD73C9DB80 @ 2234865 obs 1 len 240 By  steve
"/foo/manage_editProperties"
        OID: 1dc3 len 151

TID: 33E93FD1460C6E7 @ 2235121 obs 2 len 604 By  steve
"/foo/manage_addFile"
        OID: 1dc3 len 242
        OID: 1dc4 len 238
```

So, this Data.fs file has a final transaction, adding a file, that affected two OIDs (probably the file object and the folder to which it was added). To remove this transaction, open the file in Python and use the `truncate` method of the built-in Python file type to chop off the last transaction, like so:

1. `cd` to your Zope directory:

```
cd $ZOPEROOT
```

2. Stop Zope:

```
./stop
```

3. Make a backup of your Data.fs file:

```
cp var/Data.fs var/Data.fs.mybackup
```

4. Start Python:

```
python
Python 2.1.1 (#1, Jul 26 2001, 17:22:33)
[GCC 2.95.2 19991024 (release)] on darwin1
Type "copyright", "credits" or "license" for more information.
```

5. Open `var/Data.fs` object in "append binary" mode:

```
>>> f = open('var/Data.fs','ab')
```

6. Truncate it to the point of the last transaction reported by tranalyzer.py. Notice that this line

```
TID: 33E93FD1460C6E7 @ 2235121 obs 2 len 604 By  steve
                       ^^^^^^^
```

shows where the last transaction terminated:

```
>>> f.truncate(2235121)
```

7. Close the file:

```
>>> f.close()
```

8. Now, run Tranalyzer to make sure that it worked okay:

```
python tranalyzer.py var/Data.fs | tail

TID: 33E93DC7B3C5E11 @ 2234609 obs 1 len 240 By  steve
"/foo/manage_editProperties"
        OID: 1dc3 len 151

TID: 33E93DD73C9DB80 @ 2234865 obs 1 len 240 By  steve
"/foo/manage_editProperties"
        OID: 1dc3 len 151
```

Notice that you've just clipped off the last transaction manually. If Zope won't start due to a bad transaction, you can still hope to recover using tranalyzer.py.

# Simple Replication and Backup

As easy as exporting (and importing) is, it's not without limitations. It's not easy to export an entire Zope instance (although there are ways to do it—see **http://www.zopelabs.com/cookbook/991076140**). Another approach is to use the rsync program that is available for most platforms that does a "sync" of two files (possibly across the network). It's nice because it uses a protocol (using checksums, file sizes, and so on) to copy only *differences* from source to target. This can make a huge difference in time when the Data.fs file starts to grow very large.

Listing 16.1 is part of a nightly *sh* script that we use on our UNIX systems, inspired by the HowTo at Zope.org (see **http://www.zope.org/Members/jrush/howto_rsync_zope**) to back up and pack several of our Zope sites nightly. Although *sh* scripting is out the scope of this book, it's worth a few brief comments.

Listing 16.1 **A Nightly sh Script to Back Up and Pack FileStorage Databases**

```
#!/bin/sh
##########################################
# File: /etc/cron.daily/zbackup.cron
#
# Backup Zope Database Daily
##########################################
#
# rsync arguments:
# -q        ::= Quiet operation, for cron logs
# -u        ::= Update only, don't overwrite newer files
# -t        ::= Preserve file timestamps
# -p        ::= Preserve file permissions
# -o        ::= Preserve file owner
# -g        ::= Preserve file group
# -z        ::= Compress during transfer
# -e ssh    ::= Use the ssh utility to secure the link
#
ARCHTOP="/home/steve/archive/zope/"
CRONDIR="/home/steve/crons"
DOW=`date +%A`
ARCHDIR="${ARCHTOP}${DOW}"
RSYNC="/usr/local/bin/rsync"
ZCLIENT="/usr/local/bin/python
/usr/local/etc/Zope2/lib/python/ZPublisher/Client.py"
. ${CRONDIR}/auth.conf

#
# Insure Our Day-of-Week Directory Exists
[ -d ${ARCHDIR} ] || mkdir ${ARCHDIR} || {
    echo "Could Not Create Day-of-Week Directory: ${ARCHDIR}" ; exit 1
}


THISZOPE="Zope2"
THISZOPEDIR="/usr/local/etc/${THISZOPE}"
THISARCHDIR="${ARCHDIR}/${THISZOPE}"

[ -d ${THISARCHDIR} ] || mkdir ${THISARCHDIR} || {
    echo "Could Not Create Zope Directory: ${THISARCHDIR}" ; exit 1
}

. ${THISZOPEDIR}/zope.conf
```

```
43 THISZPORT=$(($ZPORT + 80))
44
45 #
46 ${RSYNC}  -q -u -t -p -o -g ${THISZOPEDIR}/var/Data.fs ${THISARCHDIR}
47 #
48 #
49 # pack database...
50 #
51 #
52 ${ZCLIENT} -u ${ZAUTH} http://localhost:${THISZPORT}/Control_Panel/manage_pack
days:float=0
53 #
```

Lines 37–39 are there to create a target directory for the backup to be stored. Client.py is one of the utilities that you used in Chapter 15, "Scaling Up," to test the function of Zope from the command line. In this case, you are using it to "click the pack button" from a script that is invoked from the cron daemon. The cron daemon is set up to execute every night at 3:03 using crontab, as shown by the command `crontab -l`:

```
SHELL=/bin/sh
MAILTO=steve

3 3 * * * /bin/sh -v $HOME/crons/zopeCron.sh
```

You can change the time of the job using `crontab -e`. See `man crontab` for more details.

> **Packing ZODB**
>
> It's a good idea to periodically "pack" your Zope database. If you are using the default storage (FileStorage), as time goes on your Data.fs file will grow very large. This makes Zope start more slowly, and it wastes disk space (unless you really *need* every revision of every object in your Zope!). Packing automatically makes one backup and destroys any old backup of Data.fs before attempting to pack. You do not need to shut down Zope to pack your database.

For this to work, you also need to start Zope a little differently than the default Zope start script. Listing 16-2 shows the start script for the Zope instance that is backed up by the script in Listing 16.1.

Listing 16.2 **Zope start Script That Works with Listing 16.1**

```
#! /bin/sh
reldir=`dirname $0`
PYTHONHOME=`cd $reldir; pwd`
export PYTHONHOME
. zope.conf
exec /usr/local/bin/python \
     $PYTHONHOME/z2.py \
     -P $ZPORT "$@"
```

There are several things to notice about these scripts:

- The file zope.conf contains a command to set the environment variable `$ZPORT` to the port used by the Zope server in question. This is important so that the backup script can pack the database. zope.conf consists of a single line: `ZPORT=8000`. This sets a particular Zope instance to run Web Services at port 8080. If you have several Zope instances being packed with this script, you can have each running on a different port, and the zope.conf file will maintain consistency between the Zope instances and the packing script.
- The file auth.conf contains a command to set the environment variable `$ZAUTH` so that the `pack` command in the rsync script can authenticate with Zope to perform the pack. auth.conf consists of a single line: `ZAUTH=username:password`, where, naturally, you put the username and password of a user with permission to pack the database. For security purposes, it's a good idea to allow only administrative users to read this file (that is, `chmod 600 auth.conf`).
- The `rsync` command is run *first*, and then the database is packed. In this way, if there is a problem with the pack (there almost never is), the copy in the backup will be before the problem.

When this is set up, your archive directory will fill up with copies of your Data.fs files (one per day of the week) until one week has passed. At that point, the Data.fs files will be updated each night with the changes that have occurred in the intervening week.

This scheme has worked well for us. We essentially have a one-week undo period, in case of emergency, but the database is packed each night, keeping down "change bloat."

# Storage Options

You're already familiar with FileStorage and ClientStorage (see Chapter 15, "Scaling Up"), but there are a few other storage types in which you might be interested.

## ExternalMount

The ExternalMount product is used by **www.zope.org** to keep the Wiki pages in separate storage so that they never have to be packed. The product is available at **http://www.zope.org/Members/hathawsh/ExternalMount**. There is little documentation, but the following explanation should help. The first thing to do is to create the external method that will set up the mounted database. In this example you'll use FileStorage (although you can use any storage that you like, including ZEO.ClientStorage from Chapter 15). Listing 16.3 is a Python script that you'll use to create an ExternalMount. You'll need to set the path to the actual path where you want to keep the database file.

Listing 16.3 **ExternalMount Method Used to Create an Externally Mounted Database**

```
import ZODB
def externalDB():
    Storage = ZODB.FileStorage.FileStorage('/Users/steve/Zope/var/external.fs')
    return ZODB.DB(Storage)
```

With this created, you need to actually create the database file and add some support objects to it so that it can be used by Zope. Listing 16.4 shows a Python script that does exactly that. It creates an Application object in the empty storage, and then it creates a folder that will be used as an anchor to patch into Zope's main storage.

Listing 16.4 **Python Script to Create an Application Object in an Empty Storage**

```
#
# Python script to create an Application Object in our new Storage.
#
import Zope
from App.Extensions import getObject
#
# first, use the external method 'externalDB' to get the database object
#
database = getObject('externalDB', 'externalDB', 0)()
connection = database.open()
dbroot = connection.root()
#
# Next create an Application object, and save it in the database.
#
from OFS.Application import Application
dbroot['Application'] = Application()
get_transaction().commit()
#
# Now create a folder in which to store the new objects.
#
from OFS.Folder import Folder
externalFolder = Folder()
externalFolder.id = 'externalDB'
externalFolder.title = "The External Database"
dbroot['Application']._setObject('externalDB', externalFolder)
get_transaction().commit()
connection.close()
```

When this is done, you're ready to attach your storage to Zope. Go to a point in Zope where you want to attach this external storage, and select Mount via External Method from the Select Type to Add pop-up menu (you need to install the ExternalMount product before you'll see this option). You should see a screen like that shown in Figure 16.2.

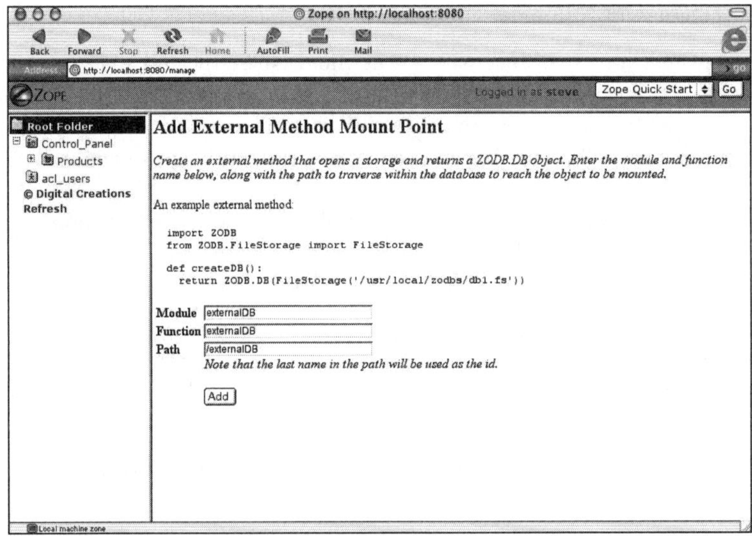


**Figure 16.2** Creating an external mount to secondary storage.

Now if you pack the main database, you'll notice that the historical revisions have not been removed from changes made in externalDB. You have a completely separate storage mounted seamlessly in your Zope. This is not a panacea, however, because you can't do everything with a mounted storage that you might want to (for example, packing and undo are problematic), but you can isolate one branch of a Zope site from another in this way.

## Berkeley Storage

Berkeley Storage uses SleepyCat Software's BSDDB (see **http://www.sleepycat.com**) for storage. It's fairly easy to set up and use, but its performance is not (yet) as good as that of FileStorage. It is fully transactional, and in some ways it might be more robust. The BSDDB database is a "key:value" database, so the only query that you can perform is "give me the value for this key." However, it has essentially unlimited key and value sizes, and the value can be in any format because the database doesn't *care* what you have for a value (why should it?). You can store data of any type or format equally well. To install BerkeleyStorage, you'll need the following:

- BSDDB version 3.2.9 (**http://www.sleepycat.com/update/3.2.9/db-3.2.9.tar.gz**)
- Robin Dunn's bsddb Python module (**http://pybsddb.sourceforge.net/**)
- The BerkleyStorage release itself (**http://www.zope.org/Products/bsddb3Storage**)

To build BerkeleyStorage for UNIX, unpack the distribution and then do this:

```
cd db-3.2.9/build_unix/

make

<.. become root, or use sudo.. > make install
```

To build Robin Dunn's package, do this:

```
cd bsddb3-3.0.1

python setup.py build

<.. become root, or use sudo ..> python setup.py install
```

After you build and install the first two of these products, download and unpack BerkeleyStorage and run its setup.py script as `path/to/your/python setup.py install`. It will be installed in your Python (which could be in your Zope installation).

You can use the custom_zodb.py file from the "doc" directory of the Berkeley distribution, which works just like the custom_zodb.py that you used with ZEO in Chapter 15, except that it connects to BerkeleyStorage rather than ZEO.ClientStorage. Listing 16.5 is the custom_zodb.py that shipped with BerkeleyStorage.py when you installed it last.

Listing 16.5 **The custom_zodb.py Script for BerkeleyStorage**

```
# Uncomment the line corresponding to the storage you want to use
# This syntax requires Python 2.x
#
#from bsddb3Storage.Packless import Packless as ConcreteStorage
#from bsddb3Storage.Minimal  import Minimal  as ConcreteStorage
from bsddb3Storage.Full     import Full     as ConcreteStorage

import os
env = os.path.join('var', 'bsddb3Storage')

Storage = ConcreteStorage(name='BerkeleyStorage', env=env)
```

When this is in place, restart Zope, and you'll find yourself using a pristine BerkeleyStorage, as shown in Figure 16.3.

You might notice that the performance when loading new objects is slower than in FileStorage, but it is a "real" database, with transactional integrity and more third-party support than Zope's FileStorage. Some folks really like that.

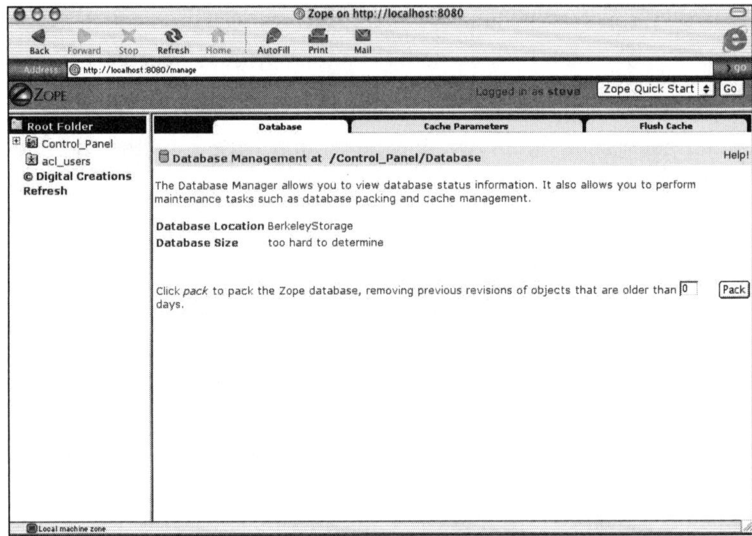


**Figure 16.3** Manage Database screen for BerkeleyStorage database.

> **For More Information**
>
> You probably noticed that three types of storage are defined in custom_zodb.py. You used "full" storage here, which is transactional and undoable. Packless is a non-undoable storage that doesn't keep historical revisions of objects. Minimal is the beginning of a new, potentially more robust form of Packless, but it currently still requires you to periodically "pack" it. All the details can be found at Zope.org (**`http://www.zope.org/Products/bsddb3Storage/README`**).

## Oracle Storage

There is also a relational storage for Oracle databases. It is similar to BerkeleyStorage in the sense that it replaces the Data.fs file with a "real" database. It also doesn't perform quite as well as FileStorage, but it has other advantages. The biggest is that some users have invested heavily in Oracle infrastructure and expertise along with Oracle's replication technology. All this can make Zope more robust in those environments with access to those kinds of resources.

Although it was not possible to provide a complete walk-through of OracleStorage for this chapter, there is a lot of support material on the OracleStorage area at Zope.org (go to **`http://www.zope.org/Products/OracleStorage/`**).

# Distributed Processing Today

Distributed processing is a way of letting multiple computers share the work of producing some output. You used a form of distributed processing in Chapter 15 when you built a ZEO "cluster" of Zope servers. A few other technologies are available today that permit Zope to share work with other Zopes, and this section provides at least a brief overview of those technologies.

## Zope as Web client

First of all, you can use Client.py (see Chapter 15) to gather content from other sites and inject it into your application. This can be done using a Python product that imports Client.py or an external method. Listing 16.6 shows a simple external method that gets some HTML from another Zope.

Listing 16.6 **Using Client.py to Pull Content from Another Zope**

```
from ZPublisher import Client


def grabURL(self, url, user, passwd, **kw):
    f = Client.Function(url, username = user, password = passwd)
    return apply(f,(),kw)[1]
```

## XML RPC

XMLRPC is a protocol that is being more widely adopted (see **http://www.xml-rpc.com/**). Zope also has XMLRPC built in (see **http://www.zope.org/Members/Amos/XML-RPC**). Basically, this allows you to call on other (non-Zope) servers for processing using a standard XML protocol for selecting functions and passing arguments. There are several examples of XMLRPC usage at **http://www.zope.org**. Although we don't have room for many details, using xmlrpc is as simple as this:

```
>>> server = xmlrpclib.Server('http://10.0.0.1:8080')
>>> print server
<Server proxy for 10.0.0.1:8080/RPC2>
>>> print server.index_html()
<html><head><title>Zope</title></head><body bgcolor="#FFFFFF">
<!DOCTYPE HTML PUBLIC "-//W3C//DTD HTML 4.0 Transitional//EN"
"http://www.w3.org/TR/REC-html40/loose.dtd">
<html>
<head>
<title>Zope QuickStart</title>
<link rel="stylesheet" type="text/css" href="/manage_page_style.css">
</head>
<body bgcolor="#ffffff" link="#000099" alink="#000099" vlink="#000099">

<... much html output snipped ... >
```

As you can see, we got the QuickStart page from a Zope instance in two lines of Python using xmlrpclib. The nice thing is that xmlrpc automatically marshals arguments to functions and results that are returned. It's also related to the emerging concept of Web Services, which is evolving right now at Zope Corporation (**`http://www.zope.org//Wikis/DevSite/Proposals/WebServicesForZope`**).

## XML Non-RPC

Lots of other programs out there also can speak XML, but in a less than standard way (that is, *not* with XMLRPC). An example is Flash, or Director from Macromedia. You can still use Zope to talk with these programs, but it takes a little extra work. Here are a couple of external methods that can work with XML from Flash. First, Flash doesn't send its XML in a normal QUERY_STRING format so that Zope can parse it. To get at the raw XML, you need to seek on the StringIO object that Zope creates and read it back in again, as shown in Listing 16.7.

Listing 16.7 `getRawInput` **Retrieves Raw Data from an HTTP** `POST`

```
def getRawInput(self, REQUEST):

    meth = REQUEST.environ.get('REQUEST_METHOD','GET')

    if 1:  # meth != 'GET':  # leave this here in case Flash is fixed someday.
                             # See comment below
        #
        # Flash has a broken .sendAndLoad() method on Windows.. so we need to
        # force a "POST" response rather than handle "GET" differently.
        #

        REQUEST.stdin.seek(0)
        result = REQUEST.stdin.read()
    else:
        result = REQUEST.environ.get('QUERY_STRING','')

    return result
```

As you can see, getRawInput retrieves whatever Flash sent in the body of a post as a string. This turns out to be pure XML data from Flash, so you can pass it to the `handleXML` method for processing. The external method `handleXML` uses the ParsedXML module to convert the XML from Flash into a dictionary, as shown in Listing 16.8.

Listing 16.8 **Convert Flash XML POST to a Dictionary**

```
#
# Handle XML input from Flash.
# Needs ParsedXML product installed.
#

if __name__=="__main__":
```

```
    """ For in 'IDE' testing.. """
    import sys
    sys.path.append('/usr/local/etc/Zope2b/lib/python')
    import ZODB

from Products.ParsedXML.DOM import ExpatBuilder

try:
    from cStringIO import StringIO
except ImportError:
    from StringIO import StringIO

def handleXML(xmlString, debug=0):
    return toDict(DOMParseString( None, xmlString), debug=debug)

def DOMParseString(self, xml):
    file = StringIO(xml)
    return ExpatBuilder.parse(file)

def toDict( xmlThing, currDict=None, debug=0 ):

    if currDict is None:
        currDict = {}

    if hasattr(xmlThing,'data'):
        currDict['data'] = xmlThing.data

    if hasattr(xmlThing, '_attributes'):
        if debug:
            print "checking attributes:",  xmlThing._attributes

        for attr in xmlThing._attributes:
            if currDict.has_key(attr[1]):
                oldVal = currDict[attr[1]]
                if type(oldVal)==type(''):
                    currDict[attr[1]]=[oldVal, attr[4]]
                else:
                    oldVal.append(attr[4])
            else:
                currDict[attr[1]] = attr[4]

    if hasattr(xmlThing, '_children'):
        for subThing in xmlThing._children:
            newDict = toDict(subThing)

            if hasattr(subThing, 'data'):
                currDict['data'] = subThing.data

            elif hasattr(subThing, 'nodeName'):
                if currDict.has_key(subThing.nodeName):
```

*continues*

Listing 16.8 **Continued**

```
57                     oldVal=currDict[subThing.nodeName]
58                     if type(oldVal)==type({}):
59                         currDict[subThing.nodeName]=[oldVal, newDict]
60                     else:
61                         oldVal.append(newDict)
62                 else:
63                     currDict[subThing.nodeName] = newDict
64
65     return currDict
66
67 theXML = """<?xml version = "1.0"?>
68 <CD title="2 Against Nature">
69 <track title = "gaslighting abbie"/>
70 <track title = "what a shame about me"/>
71 <track title = "two against nature"/>
72 <track title = "janie runaway"/>
73 <track title = "almost gothic"/>
74 <track title = "jack of speed"/>
75 <track title = "cousin dupree"/>
76 <track title = "negative girl"/>
77 <track title = "west of hollywood"/>
78 <relatedItems artist = "Steely Dan"/>
79 <relatedItems artist = "Walter Becker"/>
80 <relatedItems artist = "Donald Fagen"/>
81 </CD>
82 """
83
84 if __name__=="__main__":
85
86     #print handleXML('<querySources level="/my/favorite/place"/>')
87     print handleXML(theXML, debug=1)
```

The handleXML external method shows another development trick that is worth pointing out. Even if you don't need full-blown unit testing, as described in Chapter 14, it's still worthwhile to build tests into your source code. Because external methods are *imported* into Zope, you can test to see whether the module is being imported or run (tested) from the command line, or Python IDE. If the built-in variable `name` is set to the string `main`, it means that the program is being run outside of Zope. Line 06 of Listing 16.8 checks for this condition; if it tests true, the "lib/python" directory is added to the current lookup path (as it would be already if the file were being imported into Zope). The same test is done at the end of the file (line 84) to decide whether to run a test using the hard-coded XML string at the end of the file. It's not unit testing, but it's nice to find bugs *before* testing in Zope, where things are a bit more complex.

Finally, you need a way to glue these together. Listing 16.9 is a Python script that does just that.

Listing 16.9 **Python Script That Glues getRawInput and handleXML Together**

```
## Script (Python) "setupRequest"
##bind container=container
##bind context=context
##bind namespace=_
##bind script=script
##bind subpath=traverse_subpath
##parameters=
##title=
##
import string

REQUEST=context.REQUEST

rawInput = context.getRawInput(REQUEST)

if len(rawInput):
 try:
     xmlDict = context.handleXML(rawInput)
 except:
     xmlDict = {}
else:
 xmlDict = {}

sfParams = xmlDict.get('SortFilterParams',{})
print sfParams

start = sfParams.get('start','')

if len(start) == 0:
 start = 1
else:
 start = int(start)

# ... more code that inspects xmlDict, and REQUEST for values
```

As you can see, setupRequest gets the XML from Flash, passes it to handleXML, and then checks the resulting dictionary for data. On the other side, sending XML back to Flash is easy because DTML methods can be constructed that create XML based on objects in Zope. For example, in one system we developed all our simple classes defined index_xml methods that rendered their attributes in XML, and collection classes (such as Specialists) had index_xml methods that iterated over their members and called the index_xml method of each instance. It worked out quite well! We ended up with a great Zope application that didn't even use web browsers, but that used Flash or Director Applications (projectors) as its clients.

## CORBA and Zope

An effort worth mentioning here is called the Zope CORBA Connection (see **`http://www.zope.org/Members/jheintz/ZODB_CORBA_Connection`**). Common Object Request Broker Architecture (CORBA) is an OMG-standard mechanism for objects to interact remotely. Although this effort is only beginning as this book is being written, it looks very promising and is certainly worth watching. On one hand, it's very much like the XMLRPC feature, but it brings a much larger possible audience to Zope's object infrastructure and doesn't suffer as much from the overhead of converting everything from and to XML.

> **For More Information**
> There's another, somewhat simpler way to handle external web pages as well. You might want to look at KebasData (**`http://www.zope.org/Members/kedai/KebasData`**) as an alternative to some of these more complex approaches.

## Summary

This chapter discussed how to explore and back up Zope applications so that, in case a problem occurs, you can restore or move your application to a working environment. The chapter gave concrete examples of backup scripts that we use in our production environments to ensure that our Zope instances are safely saved each night. The chapter also presented other Zope storage mechanisms, including mounted storages and the newly released Berkeley Storage. Finally, the chapter explained some of the distributed processing technologies available to Zope, including XMLRPC and Client.py.

# VI
# Appendix

# Glossary

**access control list (ACL)** A list of users and the roles that they have.

**ACL** *See* access control list.

**acl_users folder** A special type of folders in which Zope user accounts are created and maintained. "ACL" stands for "access control list."

**acquisition** The capability of objects to derive characteristics (properties) from their surroundings, such as containers and URL-based acquisition parents. See the "Why Acquisition Works" section of Chapter 8, "Getting Content Under Control."

**AttributeProvider** A type of DataManager PlugIn that has the job of getting the attributes of a DataSkin. An attribute provider can use any Zope object or method to retrieve the data associated with attributes of a DataSkin. This is a component of the ZPatterns Framework (`http://www.eby-sarna.com`). See also Chapters 11, "Design for Integration the ZPatterns Way"; Chapter 12, "Integrating Applications with ZPatterns"; and Chapter 13, "User Management: Interfacing with External Systems."

**Calendar tag** A Zope product that produces a display calendar using HTML table tags. The calendar works in such a way as to allow date-specific information to be associated with the display. (See `http://www.zope.org/Members/jdavid/Calendar`.)

**channel** A listed source of Resource Description Framework (RDF) or Rich Site Summary (RSS) information.

**CMF** *See* Content Management Framework.

**Concurrent Versions System (CVS)** An open source version-control system used by many open source developers. (See `http://www.cvshome.org`.)

**container** An object that serves as a holder of other objects. Within a Python script "container" represents the object in which a Python script is contained, its immediate parent.

**containment** For Zope, "containment" is the concept that describes the location of an object in the folder-like hierarchy of objects. Objects are "contained" by other folder-like objects and can acquire methods and attributes from other objects that contain them.

**content** The text or graphical information contained on a web page.

**Content Management Framework (CMF)** A framework of objects and interfaces designed to create applications that specialize in managing content of various kinds. (See `http://cmf.zope.org`.)

**context** With respect to Zope, "context" means the relationship that an object is placed into by use of a URL. Objects in Zope are accessed via the web through their address or URL. Other objects can be placed in the URL of an object to give that object access, through acquisition, to the other object's methods and attributes. Within a Python script, "context" specifies the "environment" in which the script is running, even if it is acquired.

**Coordinated Universal Time (UTC)** Sometimes called Greenwich Mean Time (GMT). This is the time at the prime meridian and longitude 0 degrees, Greenwich, England. It is the universal reference point for dates and times.

**.cvsignore** File that CVS uses to tell which files in a directory to ignore for the purposes of version control.

**.cvspass** File that CVS uses to store a password on the filesystem for CVS to send to the repository server when using pserver mode.

**CVS** *See* Concurrent Versions System.

**DataManger** An object that gets attributes and handles data-related transactions for a DataSkin. This is a component of the ZPatterns Framework (see `http://www.eby-sarna.com`). See also Chapters 11–13.

**DataSkin** A Python class that allows instances of DataSkin to get their attributes' data from a DataManager. The classes that you use to build a ZPatterns-based application will inherit from ZPatterns::DataSkin. This is a component of the ZPatterns Framework (see `http://www.eby-sarna.com`). See also Chapters 11–13.

**decomposing** Identifying and isolating the component parts of a web page into reusable objects.

**dtml** *See* Document Template Markup Language.

**dtml-sendmail** A built-in Zope tag that facilitates the creation and delivery of email programmatically.

**Document Template Markup Language (DTML)** One of Zope's ways of inserting dynamic objects into HTML documents (template).

**empty** A logically "false" value, such as 0, an empty string '', an empty list [], an empty tuple (), or the null object "None."

**Encapsulation** The process of compartmentalizing the elements of an abstraction that constitute its structure and behavior; encapsulation serves to separate the contractual interface of an abstraction and its implementation. [1]

**epoch** An arbitrary starting point in time used as a zero reference point. Although an epoch is arbitrary, the one used by Zope is the one used by the UNIX system, which is January 1, 1970.

**Extensible Markup Language (XML)** A subset of the Standard Generalized Markup Language (SGML). A markup language, like HTML, is used to embed commands or controls into a standard text document. XML is a dynamic markup language that allows the easy creation of new codes (tags) for communication among various applications.

**ExternalMount** Product that allows externally mounted Zope Object Database (ZODB) storage to be used inside a Zope instance.

**Extreme Programming (XP)** A new paradigm for programming that revolves around the concepts of simplicity and communication. It was designed for small teams of programmers who need to produce products quickly when the specifications are constantly changing.

**`GET` Method** A form of HTTP data request. In a `GET` request, all the information sent to the web server is encoded in a `QUERY_STRING` at the end of the URL.

**GMT** *See* Coordinated Universal Time (UTC).

1. Booch, Grady. Object-Oriented Analysis and Design with Applications, Second Edition. Reading, MA: Addison-Wesley Publishing, 1994.

**IMAP** *See* Internet Message Access Protocol.

**initialize** To assign a value to a variable at the time that it is created, even if it is an "empty" value.

**International Organization for Standards (ISO) date and time notation** A universally accepted, human-readable, and easily parseable format for displaying dates and times. The format is YYYY:MM:DDThh: mm:ssTZD, where YYYY = a four-digit year, MM = a two-digit month (01 = January, and so on), DD = a two-digit day of the month (01 through 31), hh = two digits of an hour (00 through 23) (am/pm are *not* allowed), mm = two digits of a minute (00 through 59), ss = two digits of a second (00 through 59), s = one or more digits representing a decimal fraction of a second, and TZD = time zone designator (Z or +hh:mm or -hh:mm). (See **`http://www.iso.ch`**.)

**Internet Message Access Protocol (IMAP)** Similar to the popular POP protocol, but it allows the user to remotely manage multiple mailboxes and directories in much the same way as local mailboxes and directories would be maintained. As with the POP protocol, IMAP provides no support for outgoing email.

**ISO date and time notation** *See* International Organization for Standards date and time notation.

**LoginManager** A Specialist that acts as a UserFolder substitute that allows user data to come from a set of essentially arbitrary data sources.

**LoginMethod** A data plug-in that collects authentication information from a REQUEST and hands it off to a User object for authentication.

**Mail Host** A Zope object that acts as a proxy for outgoing mail created by a `dtml-sendmail` tag.

**mail transfer agent (MTA)** Manages the routing of emails. The most popular MTA on UNIX systems is a program called sendmail.

**MTA** *See* mail transfer agent.

**namespace** The context for determining what a variable or object name refers to. When a Python script is called from DTML, this is the caller's DTML namespace; otherwise, it is an empty namespace. It gives a Python script access to all the variables and objects that were available to its calling object.

**object publishing** The process of distributing collections of objects, which are dynamically composed into pages, via the web.

**permissions** The right to perform some action within Zope.

**PlugIn** A configurable DataManager used to handle some aspect of the data sources for DataSkins. (For example, a SkinScript PlugIn can provide attributes to a DataSkin or can provide events related to a DataSkin's data.) This is a component of the ZPatterns Framework (see **`http://www.eby-sarna.com`**). See also Chapters 11–13.

**POP3** *See* Post Office Protocol version 3.

**POPMail object** POPMail is a Zope product that reads and organizes mail from a standard POP3 mail server. (See **`http://www.zope.org/Members/dshaw/POPMailProduct`**.)

**portal** Roughly described as a user-centered or member-based, customizable view of a web site with readily searchable content.

**`POST` Method** A form of HTTP data request. In a `POST` request, all of the data sent to the browser is sent as a `QUERY_STRING` after all the other headers have been sent.

**Post Office Protocol version 3 (POP3)** A set of rules for allowing computers to retrieve email from a server via a temporary connection. This protocol is especially useful for portable machines that are not connected permanently to the Internet and, therefore, require a mail holding server ("post office"). POP provides for only receiving mail and does not support sending email.

**PrincipiaSearchSource** A built-in Zope property, and the name of one of the default ZCatalog indexes that is created on the contents of some Zope objects stored in a ZCatalog. This is also a historical reference to the predecessor of Zope, Principia.

**procmail** Another means of routing emails. Unlike mail transfer agent (MTA), procmail is a mail delivery agent and does not require root access by the user to be configured.

**property sheet** A grouping of ZClass properties. Properties can be gathered into logical groups and stored in separate property sheets, or they can all be contained on a single property sheet. They are generally managed through the Properties tab of the Zope Management Interface (ZMI).

**`QUERY_STRING`** A string used to supply values to elements in a web form. It is a standard element of the Hypertext Transport Protocol (HTTP) and the Common Gateway Interface (CGI).

**Rack** An object that manages DataSkins. It acts as their DataManager and a keeper of data PlugIns that are used to provide PlugIns for objects of a particular class. This is a component of the ZPatterns Framework (see **http://www.eby-sarna.com**). See also Chapters 11–13.

**RDF** *See* Resource Description Framework.

**request** A message sent from a browser to a web site to initiate the download of a web page. There is also a Zope REQUEST object, which is an object that encapsulates all the information in the actual request.

**Resource Description Framework (RDF)** An XML format that is used to provided syndicated web content.

**Rich Site Summary (RSS)** A specific implementation of RDF developed by Netscape.

**role** In Zope, a named set of permissions that can be assigned to a user.

**RSS** *See* Rich Site Summary.

**RuleAgent** Acts as an event-based trigger that fires when certain conditions are satisfied. These can be used to carry out specific tasks when data needs to be stored, created, or deleted. This is a component of the ZPatterns Framework (see **http://www.eby-sarna.com**). See also Chapters 11–13.

**script (Python)** A Zope object wherein Python, the primary language of Zope, can be accessed directly. From within a Python script, `script` references the actual script itself.

**Secure Socket Layer (SSL)** A popular protocol used to encrypt data.

**sequence-index** A built-in Zope variable name that returns the sequence position of the sequence-item.

**sequence-item** A built-in Zope variable name that refers to the object currently being processed in a loop.

**Simple Mail Transfer Protocol (SMTP)** A set of rules governing the electronic transfer of mail between computers.

**SkinScript** A simple language used to implement several important classes of data management. It is "documented" on the ZPatterns Wiki (**http://www.zope.org/Members/pje/Wikis/ZPatterns**).

**SMTP** *See* Simple Mail Transfer Protocol.

**Specialist** Handles the interaction between the rest of the system in objects of a particular kind. When a Specialist is created, there is normally a Rack with the ID `defaultRack` created at the same time that is owned by the Specialist. Because a Specialist can have multiple Racks, the data associated with these objects can be highly diverse. This is a component of the ZPatterns Framework (see **http://www.eby-sarna.com**). See also Chapters 11–13.

**SQL** *See* Structured Query Language.

**SSL** *See* Secure Socket Layer.

**Structured Query Language (SQL)** A standard language used to formulate database queries.

**structured text** A simplified markup system. Zope comes with objects and methods that use structured text markup as input and can generate various formats of output including HTML.

**subpath** When a Python script is invoked from a URL, the subpath represents the portion of the string *after* the name of the script. In other words, if a Python script is named myScript and it is invoked using the URL **http://www.domain.com/myScript/folder1/object1**, then the subpath = folder1/object1.

**syndication** Making dynamic web content available in a way that is uniform and easily available for use by numerous web sites.

**thread** The term given to a bulletin board issue or news item and all related messages.

**TinyTablePlus** A Zope product that can contain data in a tabular form for easy reference and use. (See **http://www.zope.org/Members/hathawsh/TinyTablePlus**.)

**Tkinter** A GUI development framework often used by Python programs that require a standalone GUI.

**tree** A type of containment hierarchy, such as a disk file system with directories, subdirectories, and the files therein.

**unit test** A test that checks for the correct behavior of a single unit of component of a system.

**user** Concept that Zope uses to know what activities a visitor to the Zope site is allowed to participate in.

**UserSource** A Rack that supplies user data to a LoginManager.

**UTC** *See* Coordinated Universal Time.

**Version object** Zope has a built in concept of a Version object. These can be created in the ZMI with the Select Type to Add pop-up menu.

**virtual host** The appearance that a web site (such as **http://www.xyz.com**) is served exclusively by a single web server, whereas in reality, many sites might be served by a single instance of Apache or Zope.

**Wiki** A web page that can be edited by any user through his web browser.

**wrapper** An object that has internal references to other objects but is not a container object. Wrappers are used to pull together content in a uniform format.

**XML** *See* Extensible Markup Language.

**XP** *See* Extreme Programming.

**XRON** A Zope product that performs periodic tasks. It is similar to the cron feature found on most UNIX systems. (See **http://www.zope.org/Members/lstaffor/Xron**.)

**ZCatalog** A Zope object that is used to index objects and perform rapid searches on those indexed objects. ZCatalog is a built-in Zope object.

**ZClass** A Zope object that can be created and modified entirely through the web. ZClass is a built-in Zope object.

**ZEO** *See* Zope Enterprise Objects.

**ZEXP** *See* Zope binary import/export format.

**Zope binary import/export format (ZEXP)** Zope can import and export objects in text or binary format. ZEXP is the name of the binary format.

**Zope Enterprise Objects (ZEO)** Zope technology that allows a single Zope database to be shared by many Zope clients/web servers to improve application performance.

**Zope Management Interface (ZMI)** The web-based interface used to manipulate Zope objects through the web.

**ZMI** *See* Zope Management Interface.

**ZPatterns** A system that allows for easier object reuse by separating attribute from object behavior. (See **http://www.eby-sarna.com**. See also Chapters 11–13.)

**ZSearch Interface** A Zope object that facilitates creation of search forms for retrieving and reporting information from any "searchable" Zope database.

**ZWiki** A Zope-based version of a Wiki with the added features provided by Zope's built-in security.

# Index

## Symbols



## A

## B

## C

## D

# E

## F

## G



## H

## M

## P

## Q-R

## T

## U

## V

## W

## X-Y



## Z

# RELATED NEW RIDERS TITLES

ISBN: 073570921I
800 pages
US$49.99

## MySQL

Paul DuBois

*MySQL* teaches you how to use the tools provided by the MySQL distribution, by covering installation, setup, daily use, security, optimization, maintenance, and trouble-shooting. It also discusses important third-party tools, such as the Perl DBI and Apache/PHP interfaces that provide access to MySQL.

ISBN: 073570970X
768 pages
US$49.99

## PHP Functions Essential Reference

Graeme Merrall,
Landon Bradshaw, et al.

Co-authored by some of the leading developers in the PHP community, *PHP Functions Essential Reference* is guaranteed to help you write effective code that makes full use of the rich variety of functions available in PHP 4.

ISBN: 0735710643
664 pages
US$49.99

## Berkeley DB

Sleepycat Software

Sleepycat Software has partnered with New Riders to make the Berkeley DB documentation available in printed form. The first section is a tutorial on using Berkeley DB, covering methods, architectures, data applications, memory, client-server, debugging issues, configuring the APIs in Perl, Java, and Tcl, and much more. The second part of the book is reference section on the various Berkeley DB APIs.

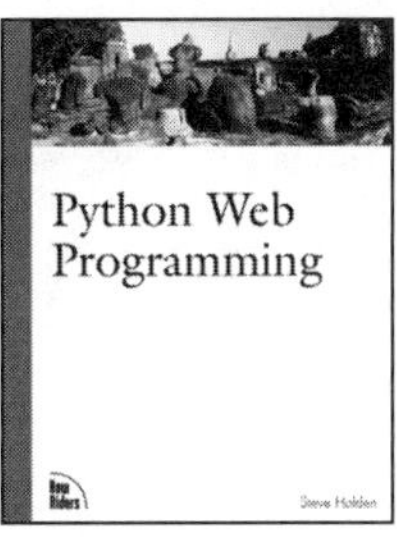


ISBN: 0735710902
720 pages
US$49.99

## Python Web Programming

Steve Holden

If you want to skip the introductory details and dive right into using Python within web-enabled applications, this is the perfect book for you! From page one, you'll begin learning how to harness the power of the Python libraries to build systems with less programming effort.

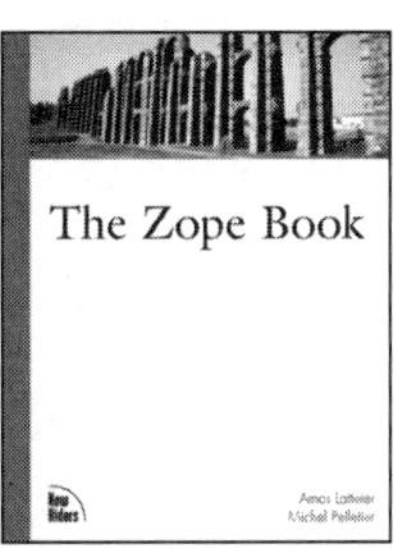


ISBN: 0735711372
400 pages
US$39.99

## The Zope Book

Amos Latteier, Michel Pellatier

The much-anticipated first book on Zope from the creators themselves! This book teaches you to efficiently create and manage websites using the leading Open Source web application server.

ISBN: 0735710910
416 pages
US$34.99

## Python Essential Reference, Second Edition

David Beazley

*"This excellent reference concisely covers the Python 2.1 language and libraries. It is a model of what a reference should be: well-produced, tightly written, comprehensive without covering the obsolete or arcane."*

—An online reviewer

# Colophon

The photo on the cover of this book is of the ancient ruin Paquime, or Casas Grandes, located in the northwest corner of the Mexican state of Chihuahua. Paquime emerged from shadowy origins early in the 13th century. Many mysteries remain regarding the people who lived there and how it came to its eventual collapse. To date, it is the largest and most culturally complex settlement in northern Mexico and the southwestern United States; during its time, it bore the imprints of both the puebloan cultures of the Southwest and the great Mesoamerican cultures of southern Mexico and central America. It served as a cultural beacon for prehistoric people within a 30,000-square-mile area, which encompassed far-west Texas, southern New Mexico, southeastern Arizona, northeastern Sonora, and northern Chihuahua. It collapsed in the mid-15th century, perhaps a century before the arrival of the Spanish, who first spoke of the ruin in 1560.

This book was written, technically edited, and developed in structured text. It was then converted to Microsoft Word to be copyedited and indexed, and it was laid out in QuarkXPress. The fonts used for the body text are Bembo and MCPdigital. It was printed on 50# Husky Offset Smooth paper at R.R. Donnelley & Sons in Crawfordsville, Indiana. Prepress consisted of PostScript computer-to-plate technology (filmless process). The cover was printed at Moore Langen Printing in Terre Haute, Indiana, on 12pt, coated on one side.